SPIRITS OF THE CIVIL WAR
A GUIDE TO THE GHOSTS & HAUNTED PLACES

by TROY TAYLOR

REVIEWS FOR OTHER BOOKS ABOUT GHOSTS & HAUNTINGS BY TROY TAYLOR

HAUNTED ILLINOIS is a generous introduction to the resident wraiths of one of the nation's most haunted states... from its most prolific ghost writer. This book is a must for natives, ghost hunters, and aficionados of Americana and will hold captive anyone with an interest in the wonderful experiences so often omitted from the "proper" historical record.
URSULA BIELSKI, author of CHICAGO HAUNTS

Troy Taylor has done it yet again. In HAUNTED ILLINOIS, the author has hit that rare (and delightful) middle ground between fascinating paranormal research and compelling storytelling. His stories will put you on the edge of your seat and his knowledgeable insights into the supernatural will keep you there. A rare and delightful find and an absolute must-read from one of the best ghost authors writing today.
MARK MARIMEN, author of HAUNTED INDIANA & SCHOOL SPIRITS

SPIRITS OF THE CIVIL WAR

A GUIDE TO THE GHOSTS & HAUNTED PLACES

by TROY TAYLOR

Previous Books by Troy Taylor

HAUNTED ILLINOIS (1999)

DARK HARVEST (1997)
THE COMPLEAT HAUNTED DECATUR

HAUNTED DECATUR (1995)
MORE HAUNTED DECATUR (1996)
GHOSTS OF MILLIKIN (1996)
WHERE THE DEAD WALK (1997)

GHOSTS OF SPRINGFIELD (1997)
THE HAUNTED HISTORY OF ABRAHAM LINCOLN & THE SPIRITS OF THE PRAIRIE CAPITAL

GHOSTS OF LITTLE EGYPT (1998)
GHOSTS AND HAUNTINGS OF SOUTHERN ILLINOIS

THE GHOST HUNTER'S HANDBOOK (1998)
THE ESSENTIAL GUIDE FOR INVESTIGATING GHOSTS & HAUNTINGS

This book goes out with much thanks to many friends in the
ghostly field, without whom this book could not have been written.
I owe a heartfelt thanks to my friends Dennis William Hauck, Helen Sievers, Fiona Jackson, Nancy
Napier, Glen Elam, of course, the Barrett Clan and others too numerous to mention.
But without question, this book is again dedicated with much love, devotion and
admiration to my wife, Amy. She is the reason that my strange little world continues to exist.
Thank you.

Interior Art Design and Graphic Layout
TROY TAYLOR

Original Photography
TROY & AMY TAYLOR
All other photographs credited to owner in text
Back Cover photo by Michael Barrett

Original Cover Designed by
GOSS GRAPHIC DESIGN
Decatur, Illinois

This Book is Published by
WHITECHAPEL PRODUCTIONS PRESS
515 East Third Street
Alton, Illinois 62002
(618) 465-1086

First Printing
June 1999
ISBN: 1-892523-02-7

Printed in the United States of America

There is no hesitation to my reply when I have been asked to name some of the most haunted places in America.... without a doubt, I can list Gettysburg and several other places which are related to the Civil War. More Americans died in that conflict than in our other wars behind.
Such an event has undoubtedly left its mark behind.....
From THE HAUNTING OF AMERICA

If the dead can come back to this earth and flit unseen around those they loved, I shall always be near you; in the gladdest days in the darkest nights....always, always, and if there be a soft breeze upon your cheek, it shall be my breath, as the cool air fans your throbbing temple, it shall be my spirit passing by. Sarah do not mourn me dead; think I am gone and wait for thee,
for we shall meet again.....
A letter to Sarah Ballou from her husband, Major Sullivan Ballou
of the 2nd Rhode Island, in July 1861.
He was killed one week later at the first battle of Bull Run.

When I think of the death of our president, it seems as it if was
my own flesh and blood called away
A Union soldier's wife

"'Who is dead in the White House"' I asked one of the soldiers.
'The President,' was the answer, 'he was killed by an assassin.'"
Abraham Lincoln recalling a dream that he remembered a few days
before he was killed

The dead were all around us; their eyeless skulls seemed to stare steadily at us..... the trees swayed and sighed gently in the soft wind.
As we sat smoking, an infantry soldier... suddenly rolled a skull on the ground before us and said in a deep low voice: 'That is what you are all coming to, and some of you will start toward it tomorrow.'
A Union soldier recalling a night camped on the
old Chancellorsville battlefield

- TABLE OF CONTENTS -

- INTRODUCTION: PAGE 8 -

- CHAPTER ONE -
SPIRITS OF THE CIVIL WAR : PAGE 10

- CHAPTER TWO -
THE WAR BETWEEN THE STATES : PAGE 14
The Common Man's Timeline to the American Civil War

-CHAPTER THREE -
THE GHOSTS OF SLAVERY & THE UNDERGROUND
RAILROAD : PAGE 19
Slavery in America and the Road to the Civil War - The Underground Railroad - Spirits of Slavery - The Old Slave House - The LaLaurie Mansion - Phantoms of Abolition - Elijah Lovejoy - The Events at Harper's Ferry - Ghosts of the Underground Railroad - Woodburn - Halcyon House - Octagon House - Hannah House - Darkish Knob

- CHAPTER FOUR -
HAUNTED PLACES OF THE CIVIL WAR : PAGE 48
Carlisle Hall - The Choctawhatchee Bridge - Burleson-McEntire House - General Sickle's Ghost - Kalorama - Kennesaw House - Piedmont Hotel - Old Governor's Mansion - Old State Capitol Building - Hay House - Tift College - Panola Hall - Fort McAllister - Ebenezer Swamp - Greenwood Cemetery - Curse of Anne Mitchell - Beauregard House - Griffon House - Cottage Plantation - Port Hudson - Cocky's Tavern - Frederick County - McRaven House - Longwood - Deason House - Lochinvar Plantation - James Family Farm - Stephens College - Fort Fisher - Phantom Rider of the Confederacy - Lucas Bay Light - Morgan House - Hagley Landing - The Gray Man - Carter House - Carnton Mansion - Shy House - Harper's Ferry Ghosts - Spirits of the Shenandoah Valley - Waverly Farm - Black Walnut Plantation - Hauntings of Jefferson Davis

- CHAPTER FIVE -
HAUNTED PRISONS OF THE CIVIL WAR : PAGE 137

Prisons and Prison Camps of the Civil War - Old Brick Capitol - Alton Confederate Prison - Point Lookout - Johnson's Island - Andersonville

- CHAPTER SIX -
THE HAUNTED PRESIDENT - THE SPIRIT-FILLED LIFE AND DEATH OF ABRAHAM LINCOLN : PAGE 156

The Early Life of Abraham Lincoln - An Eerie Vision in Springfield - The War and the Supernatural - The Death of Willie Lincoln - Lincoln and the Spiritualists - Dreams of Death - The Return to Illinois - The Secrets of the Grave - The Lincoln Home - The Haunted White House

- CHAPTER SEVEN -
SPIRITS OF THE ASSASSINATION
THE EVENTS SURROUNDING THE DEATH OF LINCOLN AND THE GHOST TALES WHICH FOLLOWED : PAGE 184

The Assassination of President Lincoln - The Mystery of John Wilkes Booth - The Curse of Mary Lincoln - The Robert Lincoln Curse - The Tragedy of Major Rathbone - The Hauntings of Mary Surratt - The Ghost of Dr. Mudd - The Judge's Ghost

- CHAPTER EIGHT -
HAUNTED BATTLEFIELD OF THE CIVIL WAR : PAGE 197

Spirits of Antietam - Bloody Lane - The Pry House - Burnside Bridge - The Piper House - The Hell-Hole of Georgia - Stones River Battlefield - The Slaughter Pen - Chickamauga... The River of Death - Old Green Eyes - Wilder Tower - Shiloh Battlefield - Petersburg - Fredericksburg - Bentonville

THE SPIRITS OF GETTYSBURG

The Guns of Gettysburg - Gettysburg Days One to Three - The Cashtown Inn - Gettysburg Haunts - The Farnsworth House - Pennsylvania Hall - The Thompson Barn... or Buried Alive - Battlefield Hauntings - Weikert House - Hummelbaugh House & General Barksdale's Dog - Rose Farm - The Triangular Field - The Devil's Den... Gettysburg's Most Haunted

INTRODUCTION

There are two things in which I have always maintained an interest throughout my entire life. One of these things has always been the study of ghost stories and the paranormal. The other has been the history of America... and thanks to a high-school teacher who presented the subject as anything but boring, that thirst for historical knowledge has always centered around the years of the Civil War.

As a ghost hunter, I have found that one of the best ways to discover why a location might be haunted is to research its history. Lucky for me, the Civil War is one of the most historically documented events in our history. Nearly every Civil War battlefield, prison or former hospital also seems to have at least one ghost story to go along with it.... thus making my interest a natural one.

But I know what you're thinking.....

There are two types of people who may have picked up this book. One type is that of the Civil War scholar, who thinks that all this talk of ghosts and supernatural events around the old battlefields is nothing but lunacy and that this book could be nothing but a collection of campfire stories or even outright lies.

Then there are the die-hard ghost hunters, or at least the ghost story collectors, who have picked up this book and are dismayed to think that it might be nothing other than a dry, rehash of the Civil War.

But here's the story..... This book is neither one of those things. I have tried to present both sides of the issue, from the events behind the battles and the history of the locations to the complete recollections of the ghost stories which revolve around these places.

I am certainly no historical expert and no Civil War scholar. I did not spend hours in libraries sifting through dusty battle plans to put this book together. You will not find serious discussions here of battle analysis or the whys and hows of who lost or won a battle.

What you will find is (I feel) one the most complete book ever written about the ghosts and haunted places of the Civil War. Of course, I could not have collected every single ghost story that the Civil War has to offer... there are far too many for that. I have managed to, however, collect stories that are both familiar and unfamiliar, have been lost and forgotten by time or have never appeared in print before.

Whether you are an expert or an amateur, in ghosts or the Civil War, I don't think you will be disappointed by this book.

What I have managed to collect are stories of all kinds of hauntings and strange events, all associated in some way with the war. Many of the tales are of the actual battlefields, some are of homes or locations connected to the battles, some are ghostly stories of Civil War prisons and others may not be true ghost stories at all.... but were so strange and unusual that they had to be included.

Can I tell you that every one of the stories in this book is true? I can't tell you that, although every one of them was documented, or told to me, as being the truth. I will leave the truth of each tale for you to decide upon.

As mentioned before, I am sure there are many tales of ghosts and the war which have eluded me. There are haunted places in America which have gone unreported since 1865 and remain hidden, or forgotten, today. I do not claim to have uncovered every ghost story of the Civil War, but I will reveal both the war's haunted history and many of the its restless spirits in hopefully a way that has not already been done many times before.

There are many who will ask if these historical places are really haunted as the stories say....

You might finish this book but may still be unable to accept the fact that ghosts might exist. If you are that person, I can only hope to entertain you with the history, and what you will consider the folklore, of the Civil War.

But don't be so sure that you have all of the answers...

Can you say for sure that ghosts aren't real and that the spirits of lost soldiers do not still walk the battlefields of yesterday? Those are the questions that you really have to ask yourself.... and I dare you to do it some night while standing among the rocks of the Devil's Den at Gettysburg. The answers may not seem so simple, nor so clear cut then.....

Is that moaning sound that you hear really the wind.... or the voice of some slain soldier still crying out in the darkness? Is that merely a patch of fog drifting among the scattered boulders.... or could it be the form of a lost Union soldier, wandering through eternity? Is that sound that you hear in the distance really just thunder or traffic on a distant roadway... or do the guns of Gettysburg still echo in the night? Is that rustling in the leaves really just the passing breeze... or are those footsteps coming up behind you?

If you turn to look, then you may not be totally convinced that ghosts are the elements of our imaginations. You may have to consider that we don't have all of the answers, that the unknown is still out there, beckoning to us......

So sit back, turn down the lights and throw an extra log on the fire and return with me to places that you have never really been....

Come with me to glory years of the passion and pain of the Civil War and then take one more step.... to the other side of the unknown.

Troy Taylor
June 1999

CHAPTER ONE
The Spirits of the Civil War

Before we begin our exploration of the haunted places of the Civil War, we should take a short journey into the shadowy world of the unknown and discuss briefly just what types of "ghosts" are most commonly found haunting battlefields and places related to the war.

There are many theories and ideas out there as to what, or who, ghosts actually are and why they choose to haunt the places they do. I can't tell you that I know everything about ghosts... I won't have that kind of knowledge until I am one myself, but I can provide you with some of my own experiences about what ghosts are. I have been active in paranormal research for a number of years and have investigated and visited several hundred allegedly haunted locations, including a number of Civil War locations and battlefields.

People often ask me if I have seen a ghost? I guess that I would say that I'm not for sure. I have certainly seen and experienced a lot of things that I cannot explain, but seeing a ghost isn't always the only way to experience them.

This was something that I learned on a trip to Gettysburg....

The strange incident occurred while I was on one of the "ghost tours" of the city. It was a rainy evening and we were walking along Baltimore Street in a small group and we stopped along the street for the guide to recount another of his ghostly tales.

I didn't think much about it at the time, but as I stood there, I caught the overpowering smell of peppermint. As I said, I thought nothing of it, believing that perhaps someone close by was eating a piece of candy.

Our guide began his talk, telling of how people have experienced the images of soldiers running past them on this street in the wee hours of the morning.... then he mentioned the other strange phenomena connected to Baltimore Street.

He told of how people walking along the street would often be struck by the scent of vanilla or peppermint, for no apparent reason. According to the legends, in the days following the Gettysburg battle, the bodies of the men who lay in the town started to smell quite bad. Ladies who would leave their homes would soak handkerchiefs in vanilla or peppermint and press them to their faces to combat the odor of decomposing flesh.

It is said that people still encounter these "phantom smells" today.... and they do, because I certainly smelled the scent of peppermint. My imagination? I don't think so, because I smelled it before I even learned that I was supposed to!

But was it a ghost? And there you have me.... because I can't tell you that it was. But could I explain it? No, I couldn't, and that's what makes this all so fascinating. It may not have been a ghost, at least what we think of as a ghost, but it is a haunting and that's what we need to discuss in the chapter which follows.

What are ghosts? And what is a haunting? And how do these things relate to the locations of the Civil War?

The two different types of paranormal phenomena that seem to be most commonly connected to the Civil War are the "intelligent spirit" and the "residual haunting".

The intelligent spirit is everyone's traditional idea of a ghost. It is a lost personality or spirit that for some reason did not pass over to the other side at the moment of death. It shows an intelligence and a consciousness and often interacts with people. It is the most widely accepted kind of paranormal activity because it is the easiest to understand. It is there because of a connection to the site or to the people at the location.

This ghost is the personality of a once living person who stayed behind in our world instead of crossing over. This sometimes happens in the case of a murder, a traumatic event, because of some unfinished business which was left undone in a person's life.... or because a person's life ended violently and suddenly, as in the case of thousands of soldiers during the war.

At the time of death, this spirit refused to cross over to the other side because of these events. There is also a good chance that this spirit does not even realize that it has died, which could happen if the death was sudden or unexpected.

If this sounds too much for you to believe, look at this way. This spirit is simply the personality, or soul, of someone who once lived. If you can accept the idea that each person is made up of a personality, making us who we are, then it is not too much of a stretch to consider the idea that this personality lives on. There is no scientific proof that says that the personality even exists... yet most people believe that it does. So who is to say that this personality, which again, science cannot say even exists, will not exist outside of the body at the time of our physical death?

If you are a religious person, you probably believe that your soul goes on to heaven, or some better place, when you die.... but what if some of them don't? What if some of these spirits still walk the earth?

It makes you think, doesn't it?

In the pages that follow, you will see many examples of these types of ghosts and you will begin to understand how these spirits can still exist in our world. The years of the Civil War were some of the most violent and bloody times in American history and were filled with events that led to the deaths of thousands.

Could some of them have stayed behind after their physical bodies were destroyed?

I'll leave that up to you to decide.

The most common type of haunting that will appear in this book has nothing to do with intelligent, or conscious, spirits at all. It is much more common than people think and is often confused with an intelligent spirit. It is unexplainable and fascinating..... and can be more than a little spooky too!

This type of haunting is called a "residual haunting" and the easiest way to explain it is to compare it to an old film loop, meaning that it is a scene which is replayed over and over again through the years. These hauntings are really just a piece of time that is stuck in place. Many haunted places, like former war hospitals or battlefields, experience events which may imprint themselves on the atmosphere of a place in a way that we don't yet understand. This event suddenly discharges and plays itself at various times... thus resulting in a place being labeled as haunted.

The "phantom" events are not necessarily just visual either. They are often replayed as sounds and noises that cannot be explained, like footsteps that go up and down the stairs of the Pry House at Antietam when no one is there or the fabled phantom guns of Gettysburg. They can also sometimes appear as smells or other sensory events, such as the case of the "phantom" peppermint that I experienced on Baltimore Street in Gettysburg.

Often the sounds and images "recorded" are related to traumatic events which took place at the location and caused what might be called a "psychic disturbance". In other situations, they have been events or actions repeated over and over again to cause the impression. Researchers have suggested that there exist so many haunted staircases because of the number of times that people go up and down them and the amount of energy expended in doing so.

These locations act as giant storage batteries, saving up the impressions of sights and sounds from the past. Then, as the years go by, these impressions appear again as though a film projector has started to run. Eventually, many of these hauntings wear down and eventually fade away, while others continue for eternity.

In the following pages and chapters, this type of haunting will be seen over and over again. Admittedly, this is not the usual idea of a ghost but no one can deny that these hauntings belong in the realm of the unexplained. Ghosts? Perhaps not.... but ghostly, nonetheless!

So how do we know that ghosts are real?

Remember that just because you have never seen a ghost does not mean that they don't exist. Belief has little or nothing to do with being able to see them. When ghosts are seen, it is usually because they are "all in the head" of the person who sees them.

That doesn't mean that ghosts are a hallucination though. We must remember that one part of our perception uses our five senses and the other part is the processing of those senses, which is done by our brain. The brain only allows us to see what it thinks we can handle and will add and subtract information depending on what it is processing.

Some people may not have this same kind of screening process and we think of them as "psychic" or at least on a different "wave-length" than the rest of us. They have the ability to sense things that others cannot....and some people gain this ability quite by accident and sometimes just for a few moments. This results in an ordinary person seeing a ghost.

Here's another way to explain it..... Just imagine for a moment that all around you are millions of radio waves, passing by you without a sound. If you turn on a radio, and tune it to the right station, you will suddenly be able to hear one of the radio waves that moments before was silent. Seeing a ghost for the ordinary person is much the same thing. Just for a moment, you might be somehow "tuned to the right station" and see something that may have existed already, although was inexplicably unseen.

So what evidence exists which says that ghosts are real?

We have already discussed how they are only seen by accident, or only by certain people, so how will we ever prove that ghosts are real? Perhaps the best way to prove that these disembodied personalities exist is by gathering witness testimony and details about the spirits and what they do, then researching that information and matching it to those persons when they were alive.

If you are a skeptical reader, you are probably already thinking that we will never be able to prove that ghosts are real... at least to your satisfaction. And perhaps you're right! But perhaps that is part of the allure and mystery of the unknown.... the idea that ghosts are unexplained. Perhaps if we knew how everything worked, the spirit world would not hold such a fascination for us.

Because what is it all really about but a chance for we humans to have a little faith in something? Is death the end for us? Do we continue on after the life spark has left our body? Perhaps we do.....

In our souls, we carry with us the moments of our life. Our spirits recall every breath we have taken and every moment that we have lived.

Do the spirits of heroes and soldiers of the Civil War still walk the abandoned houses, the forgotten sites and the now silent battlefields of the war?

If they do, then for them, the battle for freedom and union still continues on... the cause is not yet lost, the house remains divided.

Is the Civil War still being fought in a world beyond our own? I guess you will have to be the judge of that for yourself.

CHAPTER TWO
The War Between the States

In the introduction to this book, I promised that it would not be a dry history lesson or an attempt to shed light on the cause and effect of the Civil War. I freely admit that I am no historian, although the history of the war has always fascinated me. There is much "hidden history" to the war... stuff that you never learned in history class.

We forget that the soldiers and the leaders of the war were merely people.... both great and small. Into this history fits the ghost stories and the strange events of the war, because what are ghost stories but tales of people?

Before we begin our trip to the haunted places of the war, let us take another trip through the history of the Civil War itself. To truly understand our ghosts, we must first understand our history.

Don't worry though.... as I have said already, I am no historian, so you can think of this as the "Common Man's Timeline to the Civil War". I want to just provide the reader with an overview of the events before and during the war... events that have left a lasting impact on America today.

We will begin our timeline, as we will our sections of ghost stories, with the impact that slavery made on America. I know that many people will argue and say that the Civil War was not about slavery. These critics will say that soldiers on both sides were fighting neither in defense of or to destroy slavery. The Civil War may not have been about slavery... but it was fought because of it. All of the other reasons for the war were merely political differences, and reasons that could have been settled if not for the passionate convictions on both sides about the slavery question.

Regardless of how you feel, there is no way to divide the issue of slavery from the war itself and we will begin our timeline there, when the first slaves came to America.

THE COMMON MAN'S TIMELINE OF THE CIVIL WAR

1619 In August of that year, a Dutch slave ship arrives in Jamestown, Virginia bearing the first cargo of black slaves from Africa to ever be brought to the New World. They were intended to be sold as indentured servants rather than as slaves, although the difference meant little to them.

In time, as the United States formed and grew, the southern states would become slave states, basing their entire economy on the labor of the slaves.

In the chapter that follows, we will discuss more about the history of slavery in America, the Abolitionist movement to free the slaves, the famed Underground Railroad..... and the ghost stories that were spawned because of them.

August 1821 Missouri is admitted to the United States as a slave state under the terms of the Missouri Compromise, which prohibits slavery elsewhere in the territory of the Louisiana Purchase, north of the southern boundary of the state.

August 1850 Debate begins which leads to the Compromise of 1850 and the Fugitive Slave Act. The compromise admits California to the Union as a free state, creates New Mexico and Utah and gives them the option for slavery, abolishes the slave trade in the District of Columbia and creates severe penalties against individuals who interfere with the capture and return of escaped slaves.

May 1854 The Kansas-Nebraska Act become law and authorizes the creation of the two states. It also voids the earlier Missouri Compromise by placing the decision to be a slave state or a free state in the hands of the state governments. Many believe this act may have been the initial beginning to the Civil War, as debate over slavery began to escalate to frightening and violent levels.

October 1859 A radical abolitionist named John Brown leads a raid on a federal arsenal in Harper's Ferry, Virginia. His plan is to free the slaves and help them to rise up against their white, southern masters. He is captured and hanged on December 2.

November 1860 Abraham Lincoln, a lawyer from Illinois, is elected as the 16th president of the United States.

December 1860 South Carolina votes to secede from the Union and by February, it is followed by Mississippi, Florida, Alabama, Georgia, Louisiana and Texas.

February 1861 The Confederate States of America are formed at a convention in Montgomery, Alabama.

April 12, 1861 South Carolina troops bomb Fort Sumter, a Union fort located in the Charleston harbor and it is surrendered the following day by Union Major Robert Anderson.

April 15, 1861 President Lincoln calls for 75,000 volunteers to join the Union army for a period of only three months. No one believes that the war will last any longer than that.

April 17, 1861 The state of Virginia also secedes from the Union and one month later, the city of Richmond will become the capital of the Confederacy.

July 21, 1861 The Union army begins a blockade of the Confederate coastline and events escalate which lead to the first Battle of Bull Run. Confederates under General Pierre Beauregard rout the Union troops at Manassas Junction and the poorly prepared and disorganized Union soldiers flee back to Washington.

The battle was observed by citizens of Washington who came out to the site in carriages, bringing basket lunches, and expecting the war to be over in one day. They were in for quite a surprise.

October 21, 1861 The Union commanders lick their wounds over the summer months and Federal troops again engage the Confederates at the Battle of Ball's Bluff. The Union troops are once again soundly defeated. Lincoln is dismayed as he fires one ineffectual commander after another.

November 1, 1861 The command of all Union troops falls under General George McClellan, who fancies himself the next Napoleon.

February 1862 The Union army takes Nashville without a struggle, establishing a foothold in the western part of the Confederacy.

March 1862 Lincoln finds yet another disappointment in McClellan and demotes him. He is placed in charge of a troop advance toward Richmond and McClellan draws short on the outskirts of the city to await reinforcements. This is a common method of operation for McClellan, who spends most of the war believing that he is outnumbered and fails to act.

In June of 1862, Robert E. Lee is named as the Commander in chief of the Army of Northern Virginia. McClellan finds himself no match for his new adversary and during the Seven Days Battle (from June 26 - July 2) the Confederates under Lee force McClellan to retreat, ending the Union threat to the capital.

April 1862 The Confederate Army begins conscripting soldiers for their ranks. This is the first military draft ever to take place in America.

April 6-7, 1862 The Battle of Shiloh takes place in Tennessee and advancing Union troops under an Illinois farmer turned General named Ulysses S. Grant turn back southern troops. By June, the city of Memphis would also fall, leaving most of Tennessee in the hands of the Union.

May 1862 The city of New Orleans falls to Union forces led by Admiral ("Damn the Torpedoes") Farragut and General Butler. It would be the first major southern port to fall and it would effectively cut off the use of the Mississippi River for the Confederacy.

August 28-30, 1862 Confederate forces once again clash with Union troops under General Pope at the Second Battle of Bull Run. The Union once again leaves Manassas as the loser.

September 17, 1862 The Battle of Antietam marks Lee's first attempt to take the war onto northern soil. His troops and the Union army under McClellan meet in Maryland and the battle becomes the single most bloody day of the entire war with 23,110 dead, wounded and missing.

October 8, 1862 Confederate troops invade Kentucky but fail to gain any local support. They are met by General Buell at the Battle of Perrysville and are forced to retreat south.

November 5, 1862 President Lincoln finally tires (again) of McClellan's failure to fight and replaces him with General Burnside, who would also soon be replaced.

McClellan would show up again to plague Lincoln in 1864 when he would make an unsuccessful run against him as a presidential candidate.

December 13, 1862 Burnside shows his own leadership skills at the Battle of Fredericksburg when he is routed by the Confederates. Burnside would also fade away and is best remembered today for his decorative facial hair.

December 31, 1862 The Battle of Stones River, near Murfreesboro, Tennessee, is fought and while inconclusive, has a very heavy casualty rate.

January 1, 1863 President Lincoln signs the Emancipation Proclamation, theoretically freeing the slaves. There is a mixed reaction to this as Lincoln really has no right to free the southern slaves and many oppose the idea of the war becoming a battle to end slavery.

March 1863 Lincoln signs the north's first conscription act, which means that men who are drafted, but do not want to serve can hire substitutes to take their place for $300.

In mid-July, riots would erupt over what many feel to be an unfair draft law. Mobs react violently in many cities across the northeast as the poor are forced to fight what they feel is a "rich man's war".

May 1863 The Bureau of Colored Troops is established by the War Department to recruit black soldiers for the Union Army.

In July, the first black regiment, the 54th Massachusetts Volunteers, would assault Fort Wagner in the Charleston harbor, inspiring a book and the film *Glory*.

May 2-4, 1863 Lee's forces defeat General Hooker's Army of the Potomac at the Battle of Chancellorsville. It is a major victory for the Confederacy, although General Stonewall Jackson is accidentally killed by his own troops. Jackson had been Lee's strongest general and it is no coincidence that the tide soon began to turn against the Confederacy.

May 22- July 4, 1863 Union troops lay siege to the city of Vicksburg and thanks to a clever flanking movement by General Grant, the Confederates are eventually starved into surrendering.

This became a high point in the war as the Union began taking control of the west.

July 1-3, 1863 Confederate troops under General Lee invade southern Pennsylvania and at Gettysburg, engage a much large Union force under General Meade. Despite three days of battle, the Confederates fail to dislodge the Union troops and are forced to retreat to the south.

It will become the most studied and written about battle of the war and will also become known as the turning point to an eventual northern victory.

September 19-20, 1863 The Confederates force the retreat of the Union army at the Battle of Chickamauga. It gains recognition (albeit dubious) as the bloodiest battle of the war.

It is followed a short time later by the Battle of Chattanooga, which lies directly north of Chickamauga Creek. This time, the Union troops take control and force open Georgia to the Union army in Tennessee.

March 9, 1864 Ulysses S. Grant becomes the head of all Union armies.

April 12, 1864 Confederate General Nathan Bedford Forrest captures Fort Pillow in Tennessee and many believe that he ordered a massacre of the captured Union troops. Over 300 black and 53 white soldiers are murdered in the aftermath.

May 1864 The Union commanders begin the first move to end the war, driving south into the Confederacy. Grant begins the advance toward Richmond while General Sherman begins the March across north Georgia to Atlanta.

The Battle of the Wilderness takes place in early May and while it is a horribly bloody two days, it ends in a draw.

It would be followed by the Battle of Spotsylvania, which took place as Grant was attempting to maneuver around Lee in his race toward Richmond. The two armies clashed in this Virginia town for five days but it ended in a stalemate.

Two weeks later, they would meet again in Cold Harbor with Grant launching an assault on Lee's forces. There would be heavy casualties on both sides.

This would lead to the Battle of Petersburg on June 15. Lee would be able to halt Grant's invasion of the town, but Grant would then lay siege to the Confederate troops.

September 2, 1864 Sherman finally arrives in Atlanta and proceeds to capture and burn the entire city. By November, he would begin his March to the Sea, devastating the countryside from Atlanta to Savannah.

November 8, 1864 Despite the growing unpopularity for the war in the north, Lincoln handily wins reelection as president of the United States. The strongest turn-out in support comes from the Union army, despite the fact that their former commander is running against Lincoln.

January 31, 1865 Congress passes the Thirteenth Amendment to the Constitution, which will abolish slavery in America. The first state to ratify the amendment is Illinois on February 1. It will be ratified completely by December 31.

February 17-18, 1865 The war is beginning to come to a crashing halt for the Confederacy as Union troops under Sherman capture and burn Columbia, South Carolina.

The following day, the Union fleet would capture Charleston and Fort Sumter would once again be in Union hands.

March 13, 1865 Ruin is in the air for the Confederacy and weakened by desertions from the army, the government approves the arming of slaves to fight for the south. Any slave who does so will be freed at the end of the war.

April 1, 1865 The Battle of Five Forks marks one of the final battles of the war as General Sheridan routs a Confederate force that attacks the Union siege of Petersburg.

April 3, 1865 Union forces finally enter Petersburg and Richmond. Confederate president Jefferson Davis flees the city, moving the government further south.

On April 5, President Lincoln arrives in Richmond and is cheered by the city's former slaves. He feels that his journey is complete when he sits in the chair that once belonged to Jefferson Davis.

April 9, 1865 The remaining Confederate troops, pursued by Grant, move west across Virginia. Finally, General Lee formally surrenders to Grant at Appomattox Court House, Virginia on April 9. Grant's terms of surrender are generous and the two men part on good terms.

The war is at long last over.

April 14, 1865 Black Easter An actor and southern sympathizer named John Wilkes Booth assassinates President Lincoln at Ford's Theater in Washington.

Booth is killed two days later.

April 18, 1865 Confederate General Joseph Johnston formally surrenders to Sherman nine days after Lee's surrender, marking the formal end to the Confederate resistance.

May 10, 1865 Confederate President Jefferson Davis is captured in Georgia and imprisoned.

May 24-25, 1865 Over 150,000 Union troops participate in the Grand Review in Washington, marking the end of the war. The soldiers are mustered out of the service and many of them return home for the first time in over four years.

I hope that you have enjoyed this brief overview of the war. Believe me, we have only scratched the surface and I have barely been able to resist adding more detail about some of the little-known stories and incidents of the war. For that, I encourage you to pick up a general history of the Civil War.

As for our task at hand, I can promise that you will read much more detail in the pages that follow about many of the battles and places mentioned in the previous chapter. There are thousands of stories to be told about the Civil War. My job is to pass along the haunted history of it..... and of that, there is much to come.

SOURCES

The Civil War: An Illustrated History by Geoffrey C. Ward with Ric Burns & Ken Burns (1990)
A House Divided edited by Edward L. Ayers (1997)
Don't Know Much about the Civil War by Kenneth C. Davis (1996)
Historical Times Illustrated Encyclopedia of the Civil War edited by Patricia L. Faust (1986)
Complete Idiot's Guide to the Civil War by Alan Axelrod (1998)

CHAPTER THREE
The Ghosts of Slavery and the Underground Railroad

Slavery has within itself the seeds of its own destruction. Keep it within its limits, let it remain where it is now, and in time it will wear itself out.
David Wilmoth, U.S. Representative from Pennsylvania

Here, before God, in the presence of these witnesses, I consecrate my life to the destruction of slavery.
John Brown

A house divided against itself cannot stand. I believe this government cannot endure, permanently half slave and half free.... it will become all one thing or all the other.
Abraham Lincoln

When did the Civil War actually begin? Was it in 1859 when the radical abolitionist named John Brown took over the federal arsenal in Harper's Ferry, Virginia? Was it when the first blood was spilled in Missouri and Kansas?

Or was it much earlier, on a dark night in November of 1837?

It was November 7 in Alton, Illinois and on that shadowy night, a mob of nearly two hundred men carrying torches surrounded a brick warehouse on the eastern side of the Mississippi River. The warehouse held the offices of an abolitionist newspaper called the *Observer* and the editor's name was Reverend Elijah P. Lovejoy. The outspoken denouncer of slavery had already been driven out of St. Charles, Missouri for his abolitionist views. In August, Lovejoy had been warned to stop publishing his abolitionist newspaper, but he refused. On three different occasions, angry mobs had hurled the newspaper's printing presses into the river.

On the afternoon of the final attack, a boat arrived in Alton carrying Lovejoy's fourth printing press and it was taken to a warehouse by the river. Lovejoy and a number of his friends gathered at the warehouse with guns to defend it but the day passed without incident. It would not be until that evening before trouble would come. At some point in the evening, a mob gathered outside of the warehouse. Most of them were intoxicated and called loudly for the press to be surrendered to them.

When that demand was refused, they tried a different approach and began throwing rocks, which shattered the windows of the warehouse. Several members of the mob waved guns and Lovejoy, or someone inside the building, fired their own weapon through a broken window. One of the men outside crumpled to the ground and the mob was enraged. They stormed the warehouse, intent on revenge.

Someone placed a ladder against the building and climbed to the roof, a burning torch in his hands. Lovejoy ran outside with a pistol in his hands and ordered the man to come down. Before he could fire his own weapon, several men in the crowd opened fire on the editor and he was hit five times. He fell to the ground, crying out "My God, I am shot!", and died in just moments. After he fell, the defenders inside of the warehouse surrendered. The mob pushed their way inside, broke the printing press into pieces and then threw them into the muddy waters of the river.

The next day, a grave was hastily dug on a high bluff and the body of Elijah Lovejoy, without ceremony, was thrown into it and haphazardly covered. Some years later, this spot was chosen as a place for a cemetery and when the main road was set to cross over Lovejoy's grave, his body was exhumed and moved to another spot. Today, a fine monument stands in tribute to the fallen abolitionist and while he is highly regarded in these less troubled times, his death was never avenged. No one would ever really be punished for his murder, although legend has it that one of the leaders of the mob was later killed in a brawl in New Orleans, another died in an Ohio prison and many others ended their lives in violence and disgrace.

In the end however, the results were the same. The actions of the mob certainly did not settle the issue of slavery, they merely fanned the flames. The news spread quickly in abolitionist circles..... Elijah P. Lovejoy was dead on the streets of Alton. The first white man had been killed in the fight over slavery.

A storm was coming to America.

There may have been many causes for the Civil War, from political ones to questions of economics, but slavery was what essayist John Jay Chapman called "the sleeping serpent". He wrote that it was on everyone's mind, though not always on their tongues.

In 1619, a Dutch frigate sailed into the port of Jamestown, Virginia and sold twenty black African slaves to the colonists there. Within a few years, there would be hundreds of thousands of slaves in the American colonies, where they worked on the farms and plantations growing tobacco, indigo and rice.

Historians have pointed out the irony of the American Revolution, which began in 1775, being fought over the idea that "all men are created equal" and yet slavery was legal in all of the thirteen colonies at the time.

By the time our forefathers crafted the Constitution in 1787, slavery had been banned in the northern states, but fifteen of the creators of our country were slave owners. Despite the freedoms assured for every man with this document, not one of the delegates considered the idea of ending slavery.

For years after, discussions of unrelated concerns like interstate commerce and protection of private property all allowed the question of slavery to creep into the debates. It was a question to be avoided, if possible, but as time passed political adversaries in both the north and the south began to take more stubborn stands concerning it continuation or its end. It could not be avoided for much longer. Finally, a decision was reached that international slave trading would be ended after 1808.

While this may have seemed like a milestone, it did nothing to stop the flourishing domestic trade in slaves. Slavery was a different sort of business than manufacturing.... with slaves you could make an initial investment and then wait while the investment reproduced into a larger one. Thousands of children were born into slavery every year and there was simply no need to continue buying slaves from outside the country.

Despite this, many believe that slavery was dying out by the end of the 1700's. The factories and the mills of the north were dominating American exports and the southern plantations were slowly dying with no real products to sell to the north nor to the lucrative markets overseas. If things had continued as they were going, slavery, for the most part, would have been gone and forgotten within a few decades.

But in 1792, something happened which changed all that. A young Yale graduate named Eli Whitney traveled south to Savannah, Georgia, where he planned to work as a tutor. Instead, he came up with an idea that would revolutionize the cotton business in the south. He talked with a group of planters who complained that there needed to be a better way to separate the cotton seeds from the fiber. Working all day, a slave could clean about one pound of cotton. This time-consuming process kept cotton from being a major cash crop. The mills in New England were demanding more of it, but there was just no quick way to provide it for them.

Whitney devised a machine called the "cotton engine" (later shortened to "cotton gin") that used toothed cylinders to snag the cotton lint and leave the seeds behind. This meant that instead of one pound of cotton lint being produced per day, the cotton gin could produce from 300 to 1000 pounds each day.

Within two years, the cotton states were exporting 1,600,000 pounds of cotton to the mills of New England and Europe and by 1850, the figure has risen to more than a million tons.

Cotton could only be grown in the deep south. It needs about two-hundred days without frost and at least twenty-four inches of rain to grow. The cotton gin had changed the production of cotton lint forever, but the planting and picking of the cotton was still tedious and hard work..... in other words, the perfect work for a slave.

While a short time before, slavery was on its way out, it was now saved by the invention of the cotton gin. It would continue on for more than six decades.

While the south tended the fields and tied itself to slavery, the northern states continued to grow. By 1850, only a third of America's population lived in the south. Northerners invented the steamboat, the telegraph, the mechanical harvester, the typewriter, the lead pencil and even the straw hat. While the northern states grew wealthier, the south grew poorer. It was suggested that perhaps if the southern states were allowed to expand, they would prosper.

In 1820, Missouri was admitted to the Union as a slave state, but a line was also marked through the rest of the old Louisiana Territory that would create a border and ban slavery to the north of it. This border would hold for 25 years and then would be shattered by blood.

In 1831, the abolitionist movement began to grow in strength. There were now enough people in the north who dared to speak out openly on what they considered to be the injustice of slavery. It was in this year that publisher William Lloyd Garrison began the militant anti-slavery newspaper, the *Liberator*. The movement was still small at this point, but Garrison became their chief spokesman. He worked hard with a small band of allies, both white and black.

Chief among them was a former slave, the son of a black woman and white man, named Frederick Douglass. Douglass became an eloquent anti-slavery speaker who purchased his freedom from slavery with $600 that was given to him by English admirers.

The same year that Garrison began the newspaper, a slave named Nat Turner led an uprising in Virginia, which ended with 57 whites killed and the entire south in a state of panic. Southerners blamed the northern abolitionists for the uprising and after Turner and his followers were hunted down and killed, the legislature of South Carolina offered $5000 for the arrest of Garrison.

Slavery had now become a strong and frightening issue. Laws were passed and stiffened about teaching blacks to read. A gag rule was passed in Congress that banned delegates from discussing slavery on the floor... but still the discussion would not stop.

In 1846, a young lawyer from Illinois named Abraham Lincoln was elected to Congress. He was opposed to slavery, if for no other reason than it was morally wrong, but he was opposed to trying to put an end to it. The wrongs of slavery would be righted in time, Lincoln believed. It was a "minor question" and one "on the way to extinction."

That same year, the United States went to war with Mexico and in the aftermath added over 1 million square miles of territory to its borders. Almost half of this land was south of the line that had been drawn to separate the free and slave states in 1820.

The south was elated. They saw the expansion of slavery to the western territories as essential to their survival. They began to talk of secession from the Union if their demands were not met for more land.

The idea of secession was not a new one in America. There had even been talk of it by the states in New England during the War of 1812. The states believed they had created the Federal government and had the right to withdraw from it if they believed they were being injured by such a union. The idea that the Federal government would attempt to stop such a secession by force was unthinkable at that time and believed to be unconstitutional.

In 1850, a new compromise, presented by Senator Henry Clay of Kentucky, permitted California to enter the Union as a free state, while at the same time it strengthened the fugitive slave laws. Federal agents were now ordered to assist in the capture of runaway slaves and anyone who helped a slave to escape was subject to a hefty fine and six months in jail.

There was an uproar on both sides concerning the tightening of the laws and the unsteady compromise that had been reached. But as Abraham Lincoln said, "I hate to see the poor creatures hunted down... but I bite my lip and keep quiet."

But others refused to keep quiet. The city council of Chicago passed a resolution which declared the Fugitive Slave Act to be in violation of the Constitution and the laws of God. In Ohio, a band of students burst into the Wellington jail and freed a captured slave and in Boston, it took Federal troops to return a runaway slave to his master.

Then, the next nail was hammered into the coffin of slavery.

It was in 1850 that a woman named Harriet Beecher Stowe published a book called *Uncle Tom's Cabin, or Life Among the Lowly*. The book was poorly written and factually inaccurate (the author had spent precisely one weekend in a slave state before penning the book in Brunswick, Maine) but no one cared. The readers were stunned by the author's portrayal of slavery as cruel and brutal. More than 300,000 copies of the book were sold that same year and a million and a half copies were sold worldwide. The novel spawned songs, plays and even a card game and it was said that Queen Victoria wept over it.

Years later, when President Lincoln met Harriet Beecher Stowe for the first time, he was introduced to her and said, "So, you're the little lady who started the war."

The 1850's would be remembered as a decade of broken promises and bloodshed in regards to the institution of slavery. It would also be remembered as the strongest years for the peculiar escape route for slaves known as the "Underground Railroad".

In his autobiography, former slave Frederick Douglass spoke of his escape route from Baltimore in 1838, but deliberately left out the details so that those who helped him would not be in danger.

Douglass was not the only slave to flee from bondage in the south using the dangerous escape route. The Underground Railroad, or the "Liberty Line" as it was sometimes called, was a loose national network of abolitionists who illegally aided fugitive slaves in reaching the northern free states or Canada.

The Underground Railroad was started in the 1780's under the auspices of the Quakers and other church groups. The network gradually grew into a widespread trail of safe houses into the free states. There was, of course, never an actual railroad but the system inexplicably gained this name and the safe houses became known as "stations" or "depots". Along the route, the slaves were often guided, at great risk, by "conductors".

Although routes ran from the north to the deep south, most of the successful escapes were made from the upper south. They traveled by night and relied on rumors of safe houses and isolated farms where someone might shelter them. During the daylight hours, the fugitives were concealed in barns and caves and watched over and fed by the conductors.

Perhaps the most famous conductor was the legendary Harriet Tubman, called "Moses" by her people. She was born in Maryland and worked as a field hand and a house servant on a Dorchester County plantation. She was still a slave when she married a free black man named John Tubman and after learning that she and her children might be sold, she decided to escape. She walked by night to Philadelphia, where she was taken in by William Still, a central figure in the Underground Railroad.

Tubman soon became known as the Railroad's most famous conductor. She made at least 19 trips back into slave territory and carried with her laudanum, a drug used to quiet crying babies, and a gun to deal with slavecatchers. She personally helped more than 300 runaways escape to freedom, including her own parents and six of her ten brothers and sisters. Her notoriety grew to the point that $40,000 was offered for her capture.

The tales of the Underground Railroad escalated and it gained legendary status. Nearly as important as the system itself was the publicity given to the freed slaves and their accounts of the inhumanity of slavery. By the mid-1850's, there was such an antipathy toward slavery that it transformed public opinion and produced dramatic confrontations over the return of captured fugitives.

However, this publicity was double-sided. The open defiance of the north for the Federal fugitive laws infuriated the southern slaveowners. This continued to fan the flames of hatred and mistrust between the north and the south.... making any compromises over slavery nearly impossible.

There would be one compromise however which may have been directly responsible for the war itself. In 1854, one of the leading figures in the Senate was Stephen Douglas of Illinois, the man who sparred with Lincoln in the famous series of debates. Douglas proposed a new compromise for the western states of Kansas and Nebraska, which would allow them to choose to be slave or free states for themselves.

The northern states felt betrayed by this new compromise and it seemed as though slavery's "progress toward extinction" had suddenly stopped. Thousands of northern Democrats deserted their party and the old Whig party disappeared. A new party was formed, mostly on the basis of stopping slavery from further spread. They were called the Republican party and would soon be headed by Abraham Lincoln.

The events that soon followed in the state of Kansas were perhaps the bloodiest events leading up to the Civil War.

Five Thousand pro-slavery Missourians crossed into Kansas and illegally seized polling places and installed a legislature that made even speaking against slavery a crime. The antislavery settlers quickly set up their own government and were backed by abolitionists who sent in reinforcements and Sharps rifles (nicknamed "Beecher's Bibles" after Henry Ward Beecher, the Brooklyn clergyman who purchased them with the help of his congregation).

The political fighting soon turned into the real thing. There were shootings and stabbings and then when a pro-slavery sheriff was killed at Lawrence, Kansas, 800 southerners raided the town in search of his killer.

The violence in Kansas reached as far as the floor of the United States Senate when a South Carolina congressman named Preston S. Brooks caned abolitionist Senator Charles Sumner into unconsciousness. Sumner had spent two days denouncing the actions of pro-slavery Missourians when Brooks hit him over the head a reported 30 times with his gold-headed cane.

In the next three months, more than 200 men would be killed in "Bleeding Kansas". The killing along the Missouri border would continue for another 10 years.

Worse news for the anti-slavery forces was still to come. In 1857, the United States Supreme Court handed down a decision that disenfranchised blacks in the territories of the country. At this time, they were already non-citizens in the states themselves. A decade earlier, a slave named Dred Scott had sued for his freedom on the grounds that he lived on the free soil of the Missouri Territory for several years. The Supreme Court now turned him down. Scott was still considered a slave and, according to the court, always would be.

Abraham Lincoln, who was about to return to politics and challenge Stephen Douglas, denounced the Dred Scott decision as a southern plot, politically motivated to prepare the way for another court decision which might make it unconstitutional to bar slavery in any state.

The north and south continued to move apart and talk of secession reached a fevered pitch. By the time of the presidential election in 1860, the Democratic Party, which had been in the White House for more than forty years, had splintered into factions over the issue of slavery. Stephen Douglas was the nominee of the northern faction while John C. Breckinridge represented the south. To further confuse matters, the remnants of the Whig Party had nominated John Bell of Tennessee (a descendant of the John Bell of the "Bell Witch" fame).

The Republicans saw their chance to take the election and nominated a former congressman of moderate anti-slavery views named Abraham Lincoln. He was the compromise candidate, who while he believed he could do nothing to abolish slavery, at least pledged to stop its further spread.

South Carolina warned that it would secede from the Union if a president who planned to stop the spread was slavery was elected. By the time of the election, Lincoln was cheered in northern cities and burned in effigy across the south.

The South Carolina legislature called for a convention to consider leaving the Union.

And the first step was taken toward all-out war.

Spirits of Slavery

The haunted sites related to the "peculiar institution" of slavery are nearly as varied and as numerous as the slaves themselves.

There is no question that slavery was a brutal and spirit-breaking position in life. For every slave who was cruelly treated by their master, there were a dozen more who were treated with care. The investment involved in owning slaves was not a small one and we have to question just what sort of business person would destroy what they considered to be property. This leads many modern historians to believe that the horrible conditions that we often hear of were not the normal life of a slave.... but regardless, is there anything that you can think of that would be worse than being owned by another person? To be treated as something even lower than an animal?

A slave usually entered the world in a one room, dirt-floored shack. The cabins were cold in the winter, hot in the summer and infested with all sorts of disease and vermin. Fewer than 4 out of 100 slaves ever lived to the age of 60. They worked from dawn until dark in the plantation fields, except for the few who were brought in to be house servants. The female slaves didn't fare well here either, often being ill-used for the sexual satisfaction of their masters.

The slaves were no more than animals, sold on the auction block like a good race horse. They were directed to jump about and dance to show their good disposition and were often stripped to show how strong they were and how little they needed to be whipped.

Today, we can only imagine what it must have been like to be born and raised as a slave.... but as horrible as all of this sounds, sometimes it was worse.

If hauntings are sometimes caused by great distress, trauma and death, then the following locations are certain prime candidates for ghosts.

THE OLD SLAVE HOUSE

High on a windswept rise in southern Illinois is a place called Hickory Hill. It has been known as many things over the years from plantation house, to tourist attraction, to chamber of horrors to the men and women brought here in chains. But for those who grew up in rural and southern Illinois, it was the Old Slave House.

For nearly seventy years, tourists have come from all over the country to see this mysterious and forbidding place. The secrets of Illinois slavery hidden here were given up decades ago, but there are other dark secrets here.... secrets which will not allow the dead to rest in peace.

Hickory Hill was built by a man named John Hart Crenshaw. He was born on November 19, 1797 in a house along the North and South Carolina borders. His parents moved west and settled in Saline County, Illinois after their home in New Madrid, Missouri was destroyed by the great earthquake of 1811. The Crenshaw family settled into a farm on the east side of Eagle Mountain and was located near a salt well called Half Moon Lick.

William Crenshaw died shortly after arriving in Illinois, leaving his eldest son, John, to provide for his mother and six brothers and sisters. By the time that he was 18, he was already toiling in the salt refineries.

Today, it is hard for us to understand the demand which existed for salt in the early 1800's and before. In those days, salt was even sometimes used as money and a man could purchase goods in Illinois using salt, as well as gold. The salt reservation in southern Illinois had been created in February of 1812 to address the demand for the salt located there. The product was of great need to the growing country, as it was most often used as a preservative for meat.

The work in the mines was brutal and laborers were needed for the operations. Many blacks immigrated north from Kentucky and Tennessee to work in the mines. Some of them were free blacks and others had escaped from slavery on the southern plantations. Housing and controlling the blacks soon became a problem, so the mine operators gave them a small piece of land and erected a number of cabins on it. The overseers resided nearby and the complex was called U.S. Salines. The post office here was established in 1812. The village would eventually be renamed "Equality" in July of 1827.

The salt mines belonged to the state of Illinois and were leased by their individual operators. Soon, the government learned that the salt mines were only profitable to the salt manufacturers and they authorized the sale of more than 30,000 acres of salt lands. The land was sold off, with half of the profit going toward the construction of the first state penitentiary in Alton and other improvements in the eastern part of the state.

On July 8, 1829, a land office opened in the village of Equality for the sale of the salt lands. Two days later, the 16th sale of land was made to John Crenshaw. This was the first of a series of purchases that he made over the years, ending with his owning several thousand acres of salt land.

Crenshaw was on his way to becoming an important man in southern Illinois. In 1817, he had married Sinia Taylor and after living for a time at Half Moon Lick, he soon began developing business interests which would allow him to amass a large fortune. In fact, he made so much money that at one point it was said that he paid one-seventh of all of the taxes collected in the state.

Crenshaw would go on to be a salt operator, toll bridge owner, farmer, land speculator, railroad builder, land commissioner, state bank director for a bank in Shawneetown, would hold various positions in the Gallatin County Democratic party, and would be a supporter of the Equality Methodist Church. Despite all of this, he would be best remembered for Hickory Hill and his ties to Illinois slavery, kidnapping and illegal trafficking in slaves.

How was this possible in Illinois, a state where slavery was not allowed?

In its first years, Illinois was hardly a northern state. Cairo is further south than Richmond, Virginia and many of the settlers of southern Illinois came from the southern states. They brought with them their southern customs and traditions, including the institution of slavery.

Illinois was technically a free state, although it did recognize three types of slavery. The slaves and descendants of the early French settlers were protected under the Treaty of 1783; indentured servants were allowed for a contracted length of time and provisions were made for leased slaves working on one-year contracts in the salt lands of Gallatin, Hardin and Saline counties.

There was a great demand for the blacks in the salt mines, as noted earlier. They worked the salt wells, cutting trees and hauling wood to heat the salt water as it moved along a row of 20 to 30 cast-iron kettles. At the end of the line, the slaves scooped salt into wooden barrels, which were also made on the site. The salt was then hauled by oxen to Shawneetown and then loaded into keelboats.

The work was back-breaking and hot and few men could be hired to labor there. Because of this, slavery became essential to the operations of the salt lands. Provisions for the slaves had been written into the Illinois constitution of 1818 and soon, many of the operators learned that more money could be made from the slaves themselves than from even the profitable salt mines.

There were a number of laws covering slavery in Illinois. Slavery was discouraged in southern Illinois, but stopped short of being illegal. In 1819, Illinois enacted a slave code that made life uncertain for and gave only minimum protection to free blacks in Illinois. A certificate of freedom and a description of every member of a family had to be recorded at the county seat to insure that they were not harassed as slaves. Freedom, of course, did not bring these blacks equality before the law because a black man's word meant nothing in the legal system. It also allowed that runaway slaves and any blacks deemed as "lazy or disobedient" could be whipped. Whites were also regulated by this law. A fine was levied against anyone who hired a black man without a certificate of freedom and to harbor an escaped slave was punishable by a fine and a lashing of 35 strokes. The law also forbid bringing slaves into Illinois for the purpose of allowing them freedom.

But little in the law discouraged the common practice of kidnapping free blacks. It allowed only civil prosecution and officials seldom interfered with the gangs of men who seized blacks in the river towns and carried them down south for sale at auction, whether it was illegal or not.

From 1831 to the mid-1840's, the bands of men called the Regulators enforced the laws in some of Illinois' southeastern counties. The men usually operated at night and both outnumbered and were better equipped than local law officers. They made the laws and enforced them to their own satisfaction and local people were glad to have them until they found that the Regulators had a number of off-shoot riders who were not exactly on the side of law and order. The Regulators, and their adversaries, were accused of everything from murder to arson until finally the state militia came to restore order in late 1846.

It was at this time that many learned the Regulators, and the other night riders, had been involved in other crimes, namely the kidnapping of free blacks and selling them into slavery. The night riders had been on the look-out for escaped slaves, who could be ransomed back to their masters or returned for a reward. They also kidnapped free blacks, and their children, and took them to the south. Here, the blacks, with no rights under the law, were sold as property. The night riders had created a reverse "underground railroad" where slaves where spirited away to the southern states instead of being brought north to freedom.

Local tradition in southeastern Illinois says that Crenshaw captured runaway slaves as a profitable sideline to his business interests. By law, Crenshaw's men could capture these runaway slaves and turn them over to the local law officer. He could then bill the county for the expenses involved in capturing the slave and then claim whatever reward had been offered for the slave. If there was no reward, the county would pay him a flat fee of $10. In addition to Crenshaw making money from the runaway, the county could then lease out the labor of the runaway for one year. After that, if the slave was not claimed, he would be given a certificate of freedom and released.

No one knows how closely this procedure was actually followed because tales of southern Illinois claim that Crenshaw found more profit in working the slaves himself and in selling them directly into the southern slave market. While there exists no direct evidence that Crenshaw was involved in this illegal slave marketing, it has long been believed that he was.

No one had any idea that Crenshaw, who was a respected businessman and pillar of the church and community, was involved in kidnapping blacks and keeping many of them as his captives. The slaves were held in the barred chambers of the third floor at Hickory Hill. Here, they found horrible cruelty and the women found the breeding chambers. It was here that females met one of Crenshaw's slaves named "Uncle Bob" Wilson. He was a giant of a man who had been chosen as a "stud" slave because of his intelligence and physical size. He had been selected to breed better and stronger slaves and to make more money for Crenshaw. On the southern slave market, a pregnant black woman was worth much more than a female without a child. Crenshaw was said to have sold as slaves any workers that were in excess of what he needed on the farms and in the salt mines. The practice turned a nice profit and kept Crenshaw supplied with workers.

According to Uncle Bob Wilson, he sired no less than 300 children in a span of ten years at Hickory Hill. Researchers and historians have over 40 affidavits from people who met and talked with Uncle Bob concerning his life in service to Crenshaw. Wilson would go on to serve in the Confederate Army during the Civil War. He lived to be 112 years old and died in the Elgin, Illinois Veteran's Hospital in 1949.

The classic Greek plantation house that Crenshaw built still stands today. It is located near the town of Equality and is a short distance from Harrisburg. The border of Kentucky lies just a short ride away by horseback and it was here that Crenshaw would station his "slave-catchers" to kidnap runaway blacks who crossed the Ohio River at night.

Hickory Hill, as the mansion was called, stands on a high hill overlooking the waters of the Saline River. The structure was built in the Classic Greek style of the period and stands three stories tall. There are huge columns spanning the front of the house which support wide verandahs. Each of the columns was cut from the heart of single pine tree. The house was equipped with a main door and another door just above it on the upper verandah, allowing the Crenshaw's to look out over the countryside for some distance. The interior was furnished with original artwork and designs imported from Europe and each room was individually heated with its own fireplace. There were 13 rooms on the first and second floors.

The most unusual additions to the house cannot easily be seen. Legend has it that there was once an underground tunnel that exited the house and led to the Saline River, where slaves could be off-loaded at night. While there remains some question as to whether or not this tunnel actually existed, the stories state that it was real.

Perhaps the most interesting portions of the house were the strange additions on the third floor and the inclusion of a driveway into the house with large doors which could hide a carriage or wagon from view. This carriage drive would allow wagons loaded with slaves to be brought into the house and then unloaded on the first floor. The back of the house is still marked with the carriage entrance today. It is apparent that Crenshaw had something out of the ordinary in mind when he designed Hickory Hill.

Located on the third floor of the house are the infamous confines of the attic. It is reached today by a flight of well-worn stairs that exit into a wide hallway. There are about a dozen cell-like rooms with small barred windows facing the hall. These cells are very small and probably only afforded the captives the space to turn around and lie down on the flat, wooden bunks that are built into the walls. The only cell bigger than the others is the one marked as "Uncle Bob's Room", which measures about nine by twelve feet.

Between the row of cells is a corridor that opens to wide windows at either end. These windows are the only source of ventilation in the attic and during the summer months, with dozens of slaves in the room, it must have been unbearable. The windows also provided the only source of light for the captives.

The prisoners here were secured to heavy metal rings which hung on the walls, or were attached to the floor, of each cell. There are still scars on the wood where the rings were mounted and weighty iron balls and shackles are kept on display. There are also two "whipping posts" located in the attic where slaves were flogged for their indiscretions. It was said that the whipping posts were "built of heavy timber pegged together. A man of average height could be strung up by his wrists and his toes would barely touch the lower cross-piece."

There have been many stories told about the cruelties that Crenshaw inflicted on the slaves, from frequent beatings to disfigurement. Many of these stories were told by owners of the Old Slave House but even worse tales have come from the relatives and descendants of Crenshaw himself. One descendant recalled stories told by her grandmother about racism and abuse in the family and according to her, Crenshaw forced his family to watch when he whipped the slaves. Other family members say that Crenshaw was unjustly accused of his crimes of kidnapping and abuse of the slaves..... while others say that he was guilty of actions which bordered on being totally inhumane and beyond the ordinary mistreatment of slaves.

A Gallatin County grand jury charged Crenshaw with kidnapping a free black family in the 1820's after rumors spread about his unsavory business dealings. He was indicted but a trial jury acquitted him. Because of the laws at that time, the crime of kidnapping was hard to prove in court. The state first had to prove the forced abduction of the victims and according to the newspaper accounts of the trial, they succeeded. Then, the prosecutor had to prove that the victims were taken out of the state. On this count, the state failed. They knew that Crenshaw had taken the victims out of Illinois but no one knew where. Later, after the trial was over, it was discovered that the victims had been sold to a plantation owner in Texas. Crenshaw could not be tried again for the same crime.

Crenshaw was indicted again for kidnapping in the late 1820's, along with two other men, but the cases were never proven before a jury. Despite being indicted several times, and the fact that several letters remain today implicating him in other kidnappings, Crenshaw was able to maintain his standing in the community.

Ironically, in September of 1840, the Crenshaw house had a guest who would someday achieve fame as not only the president, but as the man who emancipated the southern slaves. His name was Abraham Lincoln and, according to tradition, he spent the night in the southeast bedroom of the house. At that time, Lincoln was in Gallatin County participating in a series of political debates in Equality and Shawneetown. Several members of the Crenshaw family recalled the visit and apparently Lincoln attended a party hosted at Hickory Hill in honor of the politicians. Following the customs of the time, Lincoln spent the night in the house, along with several other guests. As a single man, Lincoln would have shared the room with other male guests, possibly even with his Democratic debate opponents.

Whether or not Lincoln ever learned of the heinous secrets in the attic of the house is unknown.

In early 1842, Crenshaw was indicted again on criminal charges, this time for the kidnapping of a woman named Maria Adams and her children. According to the *Illinois Republican* newspaper in Shawneetown, Crenshaw took the woman and her children from her home and then kept them hidden for several days until an accomplice arrived in the middle of the night. The family was then tied up, placed in a wagon, and driven out of state. Unfortunately, the prosecutor knew more than he could prove and Crenshaw, and his accomplice, were once again acquitted.

By this time, public opinion about Crenshaw was starting to turn. Newspaper accounts of his business activities started to hint that just because he was a member of the church, he might not be considered much of a saint. The children of one of his brothers also publicly claimed that he had cheated them out of their share of their father's estate. The rumblings combined with the indictment in the Adams case and many local people were outraged. On Friday, March 25, 1842 Crenshaw's steam mill at Cypressville was burned to the ground.

The mill was burned just two days before Crenshaw's trial began in the Adams case and although no one was killed, two workers were badly burned. It is unknown how the fire got started although tradition holds that it was set by a group of free blacks who wanted to revenge themselves against Crenshaw for the kidnappings.

Crenshaw's profitable business holdings eventually began to fail in 1846. There were court actions against him and salt deposits were discovered in Virginia and Ohio that proved to be more profitable than the mines in Illinois. He also had problems with the slaves, the worst of which involved him losing one of his legs. Although some of the Crenshaw descendants would claim the leg was lost in a sawmill accident, tradition says that it was chopped off by an angry slave. One day, Crenshaw was beating a black woman in the fields when another slave picked up a large ax and severed Crenshaw's leg with it.

During the Civil War, Crenshaw sold Hickory Hill and moved to a new farmhouse closer to Equality. Kidnappings continued in southern Illinois until after the war but it is unknown if Crenshaw was involved. After moving away from Hickory Hill, he became more interested in farming the thousands of acres of land that he owned and diversified into other businesses like lumber, railroads and banks. Many believe that as he grew older, he gave up his life of crime.

Crenshaw died on December 4, 1871 and was buried in nearby Hickory Hill Cemetery, where his grave can still be seen today. The cemetery is located just northeast of Hickory Hill on a lonely piece of ground.

Whether John Crenshaw spends his eternity in peace is unknown... but according to the tales of the area, many of his victims most certainly do not. According to the old stories... "mysterious voices can be heard in that attic, sometimes moaning, sometimes singing the spirituals that comfort heavy hearts."

And as you are about to learn.... those stories are just the beginning.

In past years, I have visited the Old Slave House more than a dozen times. The attic of the house is still disturbing today. I can always feel my heart clench a little as I start up that narrow stairway. The remains of the slave quarters are often hot and claustrophobic... and then at other times filled with mysterious chills that I am unable to explain away. The whipping posts are still there and the scars remain on the floor where the metal holding rings were once bolted to the wood.

I have never encountered one of the ghosts at Hickory Hill.... but I believe something lingers there. I think it is very possible that the lonely, tormented souls of the slaves remain a presence in the attic.... and the haunted history of the house just may confirm it.

I have spoken to the owner of the house, Mr. George Sisk, on several visits and once I asked him if he believes in ghosts. "The house is haunted," he told me, "I don't believe in ghosts, but I respect them." He also told me that he never goes into the attic unless he has to and when he does, he doesn't stay there for long.... and he always keeps the door to the attic locked when no one is up there.

But the Sisk family hardly created the stories of ghosts in the house. That distinction belongs to the scores of tourists who have come to the house over the years and who have had encounters with something beyond the ordinary at Hickory Hill. The house has been in the Sisk family since 1906, when George Sisk's grandfather purchased it from a descendant of John Crenshaw. It was at about this same time when the house began to achieve a notoriety unlike any place else in southern Illinois.

Fifty years had passed since the death of John Crenshaw before residents of the region started calling the mansion the "Old Slave House", because of the stories and legends which surrounded the place. In 1926, tourists began visiting the place and asking for tours. This time period was the dawning of the automobile vacation in America as motor cars began to become available to the everyday person and families began to travel, especially in the summer months. The Old Slave House became a destination point for many Midwestern travelers and soon the tourists became so numerous that, in 1930, the owners began charging an admission of ten cents for adults and a nickel for children.

And soon, it would gain a reputation for being haunted.

Shortly after the house began to be visited on a regular basis, tourists began reporting that strange things were happening in the house. The visitors complained of odd noises in the attic.... noises that sounded like cries and whimpers and even the rattling of chains. A number of people also mentioned feeling very uncomfortable in the slave quarters, claiming feelings of intense fear and the sensation of being watched.

Soon, the stories stated that the Old Slave House was haunted by the ghosts of the slaves who had once been imprisoned there. No official records exist to say that anyone ever died in the house, but then no records could be found stating John Crenshaw kidnapped free blacks either, until recent years. Regardless, it is possible that the spirits of the slaves who experienced great trauma and horrible events there could return to the place after death. These types of locations, where terrifying things take place, seem to act as a magnet to the wandering spirits of the dead. It is also possible that Hickory Hill is "residually" haunted by events from the past which have imprinted themselves on the atmosphere of the house. These events may be replaying themselves over and over again like an old film loop.

The legend began to spread that no one had ever spent the night in the attic of the house since the slaves had been imprisoned there and soon people began taking up the challenge.... only to leave long before sunrise.

In the late 1920's, according to the Benton, Illinois newspaper, the *Post-Dispatch*, a "ghost chaser" named Hickman Whittington visited Hickory Hill one night. The story read:

> *"Whether ghost chaser Hickman Whittington expects to see a white or black ghost remains to be seen. He said he had recently learned that cries have been heard coming from the post where slaves were whipped for disobedience, and he intends to do something about it".*

George Sisk told ghost writers Richard Winer and Nancy Osborn Ishmael in an interview that whatever happened to Whittington after coming to the house that night scared the life right out of him. "When he visited the place, he was in fine health," Sisk told them, "but just after he left here, he took sick, and he died in a small town nearby just hours after his visit..... you might say that something scared him to death."

Winer then asked him what he thought that 'something' might have been and he had no answer. "I wouldn't want to be the one to say," he told them, "but it could have been the same thing that scared those two Marines that tried to stay in the attic overnight in 1966. They had the good sense to leave before anything disastrous happened.... they came flying down those stairs about one-thirty in the morning. Said they saw forms coming at them. They were in a state of shock. I really didn't get to talk to them very long. They tore out of here in a hurry.... didn't even bother to go back upstairs to get their belongings".

In a longer account of the incident, the two Marines, who had seen combat in Vietnam, volunteered to spend the night in the house. They scoffed when they were told that others had tried to spend the night in the attic and had fled in terror. After several hours, they started to grow bored. The only light in the attic came from a kerosene lantern and just as they started to go to sleep, the lantern began to flicker. There were no drafts or air movement, but yet the lantern began to grow dimmer. Then, an agonized moan filled the air, seeming to come from everywhere at once. The moaning was followed by the sounds of other voices and then, just before the lantern went out, the Marines claimed to see swirling forms appear out of the darkness. Terrified, they fled the attic in a panic and never returned.

It wasn't long after that before Mr. Sisk stopped letting thrill-seekers into the attic after dark. He explained to me that a small fire had accidentally been started by an overturned lantern.

In 1978 however, he relented and a reporter from Harrisburg named David Rodgers was allowed to spend the night in the attic as a Halloween stunt for a local television station. The reporter managed to beat out nearly 150 previous challengers to become the first person to spend the night in the slave quarters in more than a century.

Sisk didn't believe that he would make it through the night and announced that he probably wouldn't last beyond one o'clock in the morning. "Other reporters before Rodgers had tried to stay the night, but none of them made it. " They all said they heard shuffling feet and whimpering cries in the slave quarters at night," Mr. Sisk explained.

Rodgers admitted that he had felt "queasy" before going into the house and that his experience was anything but mundane. "I heard a lot of strange noises," he said, minutes after leaving the place. "I was actually shaking. The place is so spooky. The tape recorder was picking up sounds that I wasn't hearing."

Rodgers admitted also that while he felt pretty good about himself, he "didn't want to make the venture an annual event". He had gone into the house at 8:00 P.M. on Halloween night and emerged the next morning. To occupy his time, he had taken along a couple of books but managed to make it through just one chapter of the first one. It isn't hard to imagine why his concentration may have been otherwise occupied.

Besides the stories and encounters by ghost hunters and curiosity seekers, the tales from the tourists have also continued over the years. One incident was even witnessed by the Sisk family. A woman came downstairs from the attic and asked about the peculiar things that were going on up there. They followed the woman upstairs and she showed them how, in certain locations, all of the hair on her arms would stand on end. She demanded to know why it was happening but, of course, no one could tell her.

I have talked to others who also claim to have experienced some of the cold and eerie chills that I previously described. Others complain of strange sounds and whispers, while still others have had more frightening experiences.

For most visitors, the trip to Hickory Hill is not so bizarre. Most of them just relate feelings of being uncomfortable, and even frightened in the attic. Many of their emotions become very strong and grown men report being reduced to tears. Proof of the supernatural? Perhaps not, but the attic is certainly a very odd place.

The Sisk family has seen their own share of strange events over the years too. Mr. Sisk says that he has never encountered a ghost in the house, but his wife has not been so lucky.

"The sounds here bother me a lot," she said in an interview. "I can make excuses for some of them.... I tell myself it's the wind but one night when we were lying in bed, I heard a loud crashing sound like glass breaking. Thinking that a window had broken, we got up to investigate. There was nothing broken... Another sound that shook me up tremendously happened one night when I was lying here in bed. There was a loud sound like something, or someone, banging from under the floor with a hammer. I clearly heard it three times, but what it was, I don't know."

Mrs. Sisk said that she eventually stopped trying to find out the source of some of the strange sounds. "I know now that there is something here," she explained.

She also said that she never takes baths in the evening anymore. "Just in the morning," she said, "or when my husband is home. Our bathroom is located in the back part of the house, right off the dining room. When I take a bath in the evenings, I hear someone call my name. No one's there.... no one's ever there."

If you should ever get the chance, mark the Old Slave House as a historical, and haunted, place to visit. If you climb those stairs to the attic, you will probably feel just like I do... your stomach will clench a little and you may even be overwhelmed by a feeling of sadness. Is it your imagination or perhaps the tragedy of the place still lingering in the attic?

Who knows? But I can guarantee that you will find yourself speaking softly in the gloomy corridor, your voice lowered in deference to the nameless people who once suffered in the place. We must remember this part of our past, no matter how difficult that it may be, because he who does not remember the past is doomed to repeat it.

THE LALAURIE MANSION

The haunted history of the LaLaurie Mansion in New Orleans is perhaps one of the best known stories of haunted houses in the city. It tragically recounts the brutal excess of slavery in a horrifying and gruesome manner because for more than 150 years, and through several generations, the Lalaurie house has been considered the most haunted location in the French Quarter.

Let's just say this story is not for the faint of heart.... and not for the weak of stomach either.

The origin of the ghostly tale dates back to 1832 when Dr. Louis Lalaurie and his wife, Delphine, moved into their Creole mansion in the French Quarter. They became renowned for their social affairs and were respected for their wealth and prominence. Madame Lalaurie became known as the most influential French-Creole woman in the city, handling the family's business affairs and carrying herself with great style. Her daughters were among the finest dressed girls in New Orleans.

For those lucky enough to attend social functions at 1140 Royal Street, they were amazed by what they found there. The three-story mansion, although rather plain on the exterior, was graced with delicate iron work but the interior was lavish by anyone's standards. The house had been made for grand events and occasions. Mahogany doors that were hand-carved with flowers and human faces opened into a bright parlors, illuminated by the glow of hundreds of candles in gigantic chandeliers. Guests dined from European china and danced and rested on Oriental fabrics which had been imported at great expense.

Madame Lalaurie was considered one of the most intelligent and beautiful women in the city. Those who received her attentions at the wonderful gatherings could not stop talking about her. Guests in her home were pampered as their hostess bustled about the house, seeing to their every need.

But this was the side of Madame Lalaurie the friends and admirers were allowed to see. There was another side. Beneath the delicate and refined exterior was a cruel, cold-blooded and possibly insane woman that some only suspected.... but others knew as fact.

The finery of the Lalaurie house was attended to by dozens of slaves and Madame Lalaurie was brutally cruel to them. She kept her cook chained to the fireplace in the kitchen where the sumptuous dinners were prepared and many of the others were treated much worse. We have to remember that, in those days, the slaves were not even regarded as being human. They were simply property and many slave owners thought of them as being lower than animals. Of course, this does not excuse the treatment of the slaves, or the institution of slavery itself, but merely serves as a reminder of just how insane Madame Lalaurie may have been.... because her mistreatment of the slaves went far beyond cruelty.

It was the neighbors on Royal Street who first began to suspect something was not quite right in the Lalaurie house. There were whispered conversations about how the Lalaurie slaves seemed to come and go quite often. Parlor maids would be replaced with no explanation or the stable boy was suddenly just disappear... never to be seen again.

Then, one day a neighbor was climbing her own stairs when she heard a scream and saw Madame Lalaurie chasing a little girl, the Madame's personal servant, with a whip. She pursued the girl onto the roof of the house, where the child jumped to her death. The neighbor later saw the small slave girl buried in a shallow grave beneath the cypress trees in the yard.

A law that prohibited the cruel treatment of slaves was in effect in New Orleans and the authorities who investigated the neighbor's claims impounded the Lalaurie slaves and sold them at auction. Unfortunately for them, Madame Lalaurie coaxed some relatives into buying them and then selling them back to her in secret.

The stories continued about the mistreatment of the Lalaurie slaves and uneasy whispering spread among her former friends. A few party invitations were declined, dinner invitations were ignored and the family was soon politely avoided by other members of the Creole society.

Finally, in April of 1834, all of the doubts about Madame Lalaurie were realized.....

A terrible fire broke out in the Lalaurie kitchen. Legend has it that it was set by the cook, who could endure no more of the Madame's tortures. Regardless of how it started, the fire swept through the house.

After the blaze was put out, the fire fighters discovered a horrible sight behind a secret, barred door in the attic. They found more than a dozen slaves here, chained to the wall in a horrible state. They were both male and female.... some were strapped to makeshift operating tables... some were confined in cages made for dogs.... human body parts were scattered around and heads and human organs were placed haphazardly in buckets.... grisly souvenirs were stacked on shelves and next to them a collection of whips and paddles.

It was more horrible that anything created in man's imagination.

According to the newspaper, the New Orleans Bee, all of the victims were naked and the ones not on tables were chained to the wall. Some of the women had their stomachs sliced open and their insides wrapped about their waists. One woman had her mouth stuffed with animal excrement and then her lips were sewn shut.

The men were in even more horrible states. Fingernails had been ripped off, eyes poked out, and private parts sliced away. One man hung in shackles with a stick protruding from a hole that had been drilled in the top of his head. It had been used to "stir" his brains.

The tortures had been administered so as to not bring quick death. Mouths had been pinned shut and hands had been sewn to various parts of the body. Regardless, many of them had been dead for quite some time. Others were unconscious and some cried in pain, begging to be killed and put out of their misery.

The fire fighters fled the scene in disgust and doctors were summoned from a nearby hospital. It is uncertain just how many slaves were found in Madame Lalaurie's "torture chamber" but most of them were dead. There were a few who still clung to life.... like a woman whose arms and legs had been removed and another who had been forced into a tiny cage with all of her limbs broken than set again at odd angles.

Needless to say, the horrifying reports from the Lalaurie house were the most hideous things to ever occur in the city and word soon spread about the atrocities. It was believed that Madame Lalaurie alone was responsible for the horror and that her husband turned a blind, but knowing, eye to her activities.

Passionate words swept through New Orleans and a mob gathered outside the house, calling for vengeance and carrying hanging ropes. Suddenly, a carriage roared out of the gates and into the milling crowd. It soon disappeared out of sight.

Madame Lalaurie and her family were never seen again. Rumors circulated as to what became of them.... some said that ran away to France and others claimed they lived in the forest along the north shore of Lake Ponchatrain. Whatever became of the Lalaurie family, there is no record that any legal action was ever taken against her and no mention that she was ever seen in New Orleans, or her fine home, again.

Of course, the same thing cannot be said for her victims.....

The stories of ghosts and a haunting at 1140 Royal Street began almost as soon as the Lalaurie carriage fled the house in the darkness.

After the mutilated slaves were removed from the house, it was sacked and vandalized by the mob. After a brief occupancy, the house remained vacant for many years after, falling into a state of ruin and decay. Many people claimed to hear screams of agony coming from the empty house at night and saw the apparitions of slaves walking about on the balconies and in the yards. Some stories even claimed that vagrants who had gone into the house seeking shelter were never heard from again.

The house had been placed on the market in 1837 and was purchased by a man who only kept it for three months. He was plagued by strange noises, cries and groans in the night and soon abandoned the place. He tried leasing the rooms for a short time, but the tenants only stayed for a few days at most. Finally, he gave up and the house was abandoned.

Following the Civil War, Reconstruction turned the empty Lalaurie mansion into an integrated high school for "girls of the Lower District" but in 1874, the White League forced the black children to leave the school. A short time later though, a segregationist school board changed things completely and made the school for black children only. This lasted for one year.

In 1882, the mansion once again became a center for New Orleans society when an English teacher turned it into a "conservatory of music and a fashionable dancing school". All went well for some time as the teacher was well-known and attracted students from the finest of the local families.... but then things came to a terrible conclusion.

A local newspaper apparently printed an accusation against the teacher, claiming some improprieties with female students, just before a grand social event was to take place at the school. Students and guests shunned the place and the school closed the following day.

A few years later, more strange events plagued the house and it became the center for rumors regarding the death of Jules Vignie, the eccentric member of a wealthy New Orleans family. Vignie lived secretly in the house from the later 1880's until his death in 1892. He was found dead on a tattered cot in the mansion, apparently living in filth, while hidden away in the surrounding rooms was a collection of antiques and treasure. A bag containing several hundred dollars was found near his body and another search found several thousand dollars hidden in his mattress.

For some time after, rumors of a lost treasure circulated about the mansion.... but few dared to go in search of it.

The house was abandoned again until the late 1890's. In this time of great immigration to America, many Italians came to live in New Orleans. Landlords quickly bought up old and abandoned buildings to convert into cheap housing for this new wave of renters. The Lalaurie mansion became just such a house.... and for many of the tenants even the low rent was not enough to keep them there.

During the time when the mansion was an apartment house, a number of strange events were recorded. Among them was an encounter between a occupant and a naked black man in chains who attacked him. The black man abruptly vanished. Others claimed to have animals butchered in the house; children were attacked by a phantom with a whip; strange figures appeared wrapped in shrouds; a young mother was terrified to find a woman in elegant evening clothes bending over her sleeping infant; and of course, the ever-present sounds of screams, groans and cries that would reverberate through the house at night.

It was never easy to keep tenants in the house and finally, after word spread of the strange goings-on there, the mansion was deserted once again.

The house would later become a bar and then a furniture store. The saloon, taking advantage of the building's ghastly history was called the "Haunted Saloon". The owner knew many of the building's ghost stories and kept a record of the strange things experienced by patrons.

The furniture store did not fare as well in the former Lalaurie house. The owner first suspected vandals when all of his merchandise was found ruined on several occasions, covered in some sort of dark, stinking liquid. He finally waited one night with a shotgun, hoping the vandals would return. When dawn came, the furniture was all ruined again even though no one, human anyway, had entered the building. The owner closed the place down.

Today, the house has been renovated and restored and serves as luxury apartments for those who can afford them. Apparently, tenants are a little easier to keep today than they were one hundred years ago.

Is the Lalaurie house still haunted? I really don't know for sure, but one has to wonder if the spirits born from this type of tragedy can ever really rest?

A few years ago, the owners of the house were in the midst of remodeling when they found a hasty graveyard hidden in the back of the house beneath the wooden floor. The skeletal remains had been dumped unceremoniously into the ground and when officials investigated, they found the remains to be of fairly recent origins.

They believed that it was Madame Lalaurie's own private graveyard. She had removed sections of the floor in the house and had hastily buried them to avoid being seen and detected. The discovery of the remains answered one question and unfortunately created another. The mystery of why some of the Lalaurie slaves seemed to just simply disappear was solved at last..... but it does make you wonder just how many victims Madame Lalaurie may have claimed?

And how many of them may still be lingering behind in our world?

Phantoms of Abolition

As discussed earlier in the chapter, the abolitionist movement began to grow in strength in the early 1830's. There had always been those opposed to slavery and in the northern states the institution had been totally banned. The southern states maintained that they needed the slaves for their economy to survive but the abolitionists demanded that slavery be stopped, no matter what the reason.

By the 1830's, there were those who finally dared to speak out against slavery and some did more than speak.

In 1831, a Virginia slave named Nat Turner led a rebellion against some of the white slave owners in the area. On the night of August 21, Turner and seven fellow slaves used hatchets to murder the family who owned him. They raided the house and slaughtered the family as they slept and then set out across Virginia countryside, traveling from one plantation to the next and picking up sixty more slaves to join the rebellion.

For the next 48 hours, Turner and his followers rampaged toward the Southhampton county seat of Jerusalem, where they planned to capture the armory. Finally, the disorganized rebellion fell apart after meeting a well-armed militia. The slaves were killed and captured although Turner managed to escape with twenty of his followers. After another battle, he and four of his men escaped again and hid out for six weeks before being captured. Nat Turner was hanged on November 11, 1831.

The rebellion spawned a wave of terror throughout the south for whites and blacks alike. The white slave owners feared uprisings by their own slaves and at the same time, state and federal troops swept through Virginia, killing as many as 200 blacks in reprisal for Turner's actions.

The south pointed to the radical northern abolitionists and the problems they were causing among the slaves. In the wake of the Turner rebellion, strict new laws were passed which forbid slaves to read and write and eliminated what few rights they enjoyed at the time.

While most abolitionists contented themselves to writing about slavery and speaking out against it, a few took things ever further, resorting to violence and bloodshed. Many believed that slavery would never fade away on its own. They believed that it had to be rooted out like a cancer.... by any means possible.

Violent retribution was coming to America.... and in its wake would come fear, loathing and the restless spirits of those who would fall in its path.

THE LINGERING SPIRIT OF ELIJAH LOVEJOY

In the opening section to this chapter, we discovered the strange legacy of Reverend Elijah Lovejoy as the first white man to be killed in the name of slavery abolition.

Along the banks of the Mississippi River in Alton, Illinois is the place where the old warehouse once stood that held the printing presses of Lovejoy's abolitionist newspaper. On a cold night in November of 1837, an angry mob took the life of Reverend Lovejoy after shots rang out from the warehouse. The mob had marched on the place, intent on destroying the third of Lovejoy's printing presses.

As the years have passed, the warehouse was replaced by grain mills and all trace of it has vanished.... or has it? According to those who live on the nearby bluffs and those who are natives of the area, the martyred Lovejoy may not rest in peace. The legends say that his spirit may still roam the waterfront in despair. Others claim that the spirits of that night in November do not walk, but the terror experienced there has left an impression on the area that still reverberates today. Many who have visited the location claim to be able to fear the madness of the crowd, the desperation of Lovejoy and his friends and the energy pulsing through the entire incident.

But Alton is not the only location associated with the Lovejoy family, or at least their lingering spirits. The other location is a place on the other side of the river in St. Charles, Missouri. It is called Lindenwood College and it was founded in 1853 as the first college for women west of the Mississippi River.

There are several ghost stories associated with the school, including the spirit of a girl who committed suicide in a tower room. It is also said to be haunted by the co-founder of the school, Mary Sibley, who is said to still play the organ there. She is also said to be responsible for instances of good luck because before her death, she assured the girls that she would always watch over Lindenwood. Her body also remains there as she is buried with her family in a small cemetery on the campus grounds.

The Sibley home was the school's first residence hall and it is also the source for the school's most famous ghost story. One summer when the school was empty, Sibley Hall was being renovated.

There was no one in the building but workmen and all of the doors were kept locked. The men were busy one day on the lower floor when they heard the sound of girl's voices upstairs, loud sounds like drawers being opened and closed and sounds like trunks being dragged across the floor.

At quitting time, several of the men went upstairs to make sure the ladies could get out and to make sure they locked the doors on their way out. They had no idea what they were going to find, assuming that several young ladies were upstairs doing some work of their own.

They found no one there. The upper floors were completely vacant.

But this is not the only ghostly tale to plague Lindenwood. Residents, students and faculty members report unexplained sounds of horses galloping and the sobbing sounds of a woman which seems to come from nowhere. It is believed that these sobbing sounds belong to the ghost of Elijah Lovejoy's widow. The Sibleys were close friends of the Lovejoy family and had offered the Reverend refuge on many occasions when his enemies plotted to kill him. After his death, Mrs. Lovejoy came to stay with the Sibleys for short time at Lindenwood. They helped the expectant widow return to her parents there in St. Charles.

It is believed the impression left by her grief and outrage, both of which she undoubtedly suffered during her visit, may "echo" today and may be the eerie source for the sobbing sounds.

THE EVENTS AT HARPERS FERRY

Anyone who has ever visited the scenic town of Harper's Ferry, West Virginia has undoubtedly been taken with the beauty of the area overlooking the Potomac River and has been thrilled with the wonderful preservation efforts done in the old town area. Even Thomas Jefferson expounded on the glory of the area. "The passage of the Potomac through the Blue Ridge is, perhaps, one of the stupendous scenes in nature," he wrote.

It is ironic with all of the scenic splendor and the rich history of the area, that Harper's Ferry is best remembered as the place where the radical abolitionist John Brown took over the federal arsenal and perhaps caused the events that set the nation in motion toward Civil War. It may have been the violence and bloodshed here in 1859 that finally pushed the south on to secession and to war.

And it would be this the same violence and bloodshed that would leave ghostly presence behind.

John Brown was a zealot and possibly a madman, with a hatred so strong against slavery that he would do anything to stop it, even kill. He was a hero to many of the northern abolitionists, was hated by the south and feared by everyone who knew him. Frederick Douglass would say of Brown, "His zeal in the cause of freedom was infinitely superior to mine.... I could live for the slave but John Brown could die for him".

He created chaos everywhere that he went, all in the name of destroying slavery. He was a deeply religious man who used violence to impose his views on others, dating back to many years before the events at Harper's Ferry. Brown's original convictions were strengthened in 1837, when he first heard about the death of Elijah Lovejoy, a man that he considered to be a martyr in the war against slavery.

In 1856, Brown had been one of the fighters in "Bloody Kansas". The raid on Lawrence, which resulted in a pro-slavery mob virtually destroying the town, enraged Brown, who was considered a fanatic even by hardened abolitionists. Two days following the raid on Lawrence, Brown set out with his four sons and three other men to Pottawatomie Creek, where a pro-slavery settlement was located. They vowed revenge for the Lawrence raid and killed five men in cold blood. This wholesale slaughter started a running battle in the territory that would lead to more than 200 deaths.

Three years later, Brown devised a plan which he believed would free the slaves of the south. He would lead a band of his followers into the town of Harper's Ferry, Virginia and capture the small federal arsenal that was located there. Once he had done this, using the weapons they would take, he and his men would arm slaves from all over the region. He believed they would flee from the plantations of the Shenandoah Valley and come to Harper's Ferry, where Brown would organize his army and begin a rebellion against slavery.

This was his plan on October 16, 1859. Brown, with 15 recruits, including his sons and four black men, loaded a wagon at a small farm south of Sharpsburg, Maryland. The wagon was loaded with weapons which included 400 rifles and pistols and 950 iron-tipped pikes. They set out for Harper's Ferry under the cover of darkness and managed to surprise the handful of defenders at the arsenal.

Brown and his men quickly took charge. They took over several buildings and captured a number of hostages, trading gun shots with some of the townspeople along the way. One of the hostages was great-grand-nephew of George Washington, who was forced to give Brown a sword that had been a gift to Washington from Frederick the Great of Prussia. Brown strapped it on for the battle ahead. The raiders set up their headquarters in a brick fire engine house and waited for the slaves to come to them.

After that, everything went wrong. The first man that was killed by Brown's men was the town baggage master, a free black man. Instead of his army of slaves, Brown was instead met by angry townspeople who surrounded the engine house. The first of Brown's men to be killed by the locals was Dangerfield Newby, a former slave who hoped to liberate his wife and children from slavery in Virginia. Someone cut off his ears for souvenirs.

Before everything was said and done, nine more of Brown's followers would die, including two of his sons.

On Tuesday morning, a militia force commanded by Colonel Robert E. Lee arrived in Harper's Ferry. Brown refused to surrender and the troops stormed the building. They quickly overpowered Brown's men but Brown himself held out in the firehouse with the hostages.

They did not hold the troops off for long and soon Brown was wounded and captured. He was turned over to the Virginia authorities and tried for treason against the state and for conspiracy to incite insurrection.... offenses which were punishable by death.

The southerners were not surprised by what the north had to say when word of the raid got out. Many abolitionists praised the courage and zeal of John Brown, overlooking his fanaticism and men like Herman Melville called Brown "a meteor of war". He would go on to become the new martyr in the war against slavery.

Needless to say, Brown was convicted of his crimes and was sentenced to hang on December 2, 1859 at Charles Town. He rode to the site on a wagon, seated atop his coffin and climbed the 13 steps of the gallows. There were 1500 troops guarding the hanging and among them were cadets from the Virginia Military Institute, led by Thomas J. Jackson, an eccentric instructor in military tactics who would later earn the nickname "Stonewall". Also present was a cadet named John Wilkes Booth.

Brown disappointed the crowd by not having any last words before the hangman's noose took his life, but he did hand one of his guards a note. " I, John Brown," the note read, "am now quite certain that the crimes of this guilty land will never be purged away but with blood."

According to the legends, Brown's body was removed from the gallows and those present were said to be horrified by his eyes. They were said to shine brightly as if they were still alive. The doctor who was present examined him three times before finally certifying that he was dead and yet the eyes still continued to glow. Finally, candle wax was poured over them.

In the years that have followed, there have been few reports of John Brown's ghost returning to the scene of the raid on Harper's Ferry although some claim that he has been back.... at least once.

A few years ago, a mysterious man showed up in the old town area of Harper's Ferry. He only stayed for a few days, but he created quite a sensation. The man was seen walking the streets of town and those who noticed him said that he bore a remarkable resemblance to John Brown. In fact, he was so striking that tourists assumed that he was an actor who had been hired to portray the man and add atmosphere to the town. Visitors to the area of the old town, which is now a national park, asked the man to pose for photographs and curiously, the man did so without complaint.

When the film was developed later, the family members in the photos were clear, but the John Brown look-alike was nowhere to be seen. This was not an isolated incident either. It happened to several people and created a tantalizing mystery about the lingering ghost of John Brown.

There is one other story associated with John Brown's raid on Harper's Ferry and it involves the first of Brown's men to die in the fighting, Dangerfield Newby. He was a black man and former slave who had joined up with Brown in an attempt to retrieve his wife and children from a farm near Warrenton, Virginia. Newby had originally raised the money to buy his family out of slavery but had been turned down by their owner. Angry and bitter, he joined up with John Brown, planning to take use violence to free his family.

At some point during the fighting, Newby, who was wearing baggy pants and an old slouch hat, was killed at the arsenal gate. There has been some confusion as to how he was killed, some saying that he was shot through the neck and some saying that he was slain with a metal spike. Regardless, his throat was badly damaged and he bled to death. According to reports, someone cut off Newby's ears as souvenirs but his body was left lying on the street for more than 24 hours after he was killed. After that, his body was dumped into a nearby alley where hogs were kept.

What followed was a gruesome sight as the hogs descended on the body of the black man and almost completely devoured it. Several of the townspeople saw this happen but did nothing to stop it and, according to author Joseph Barry, did not appear to "be at all squeamish about the quality or flavor of their pork that winter."

Ever since that night, the alley between High and Potomac Streets has been known as Hog Alley. It is here that many people, according to eyewitness accounts and newspaper reports, have seen the apparition of a man wearing a slouch hat and baggy trousers walking along the alleyway. The man has been reported to have an open and bloody throat although he only appears for a few seconds.... and then abruptly vanishes.

Ghosts of the Underground Railroad

It was a dark and rainy night in the years before the Civil War and a small contingent of escaped slaves from the south slipped into the town of Emmons, New York. These fugitives were led to a stable where they could rest for the night but were turned away for fear of being captured. The slave laws prohibited anyone from helping them to escape to freedom.

For several years, there were many stops in Emmons where escaped slaves could hide and find food. They were stops on the legendary Underground Railroad, providing safe shelter for travelers from the deep south to Canada.

Finally, the six slaves were led to a small house near the river. They were taken into the basement and given some food and drink. They would be able to rest for a short time before moving on. A boat would meet them at the river and continue them on their journey. To avoid being seen, a tunnel had been dug from the basement to the river side.

After a short time, the men were given dry clothing and they entered the underground tunnel to meet the boat that would taken them to freedom. The passageway was damp and close and only a small lantern gave them light to see. The sound of the rain overhead pounded into the earth and water dripped onto the fugitives as they edged along the passageway.

After a few minutes, a light appeared ahead of them. It was the men from the boat, signaling the way toward the mouth of the tunnel. Then, the unspeakable happened! Weakened by days of rain, the tunnel collapsed in on itself, burying the slaves beneath thousands of pounds of dirt and rock! Despite the best efforts of the conductors, they could not save the trapped men and they died there, beneath the free soil of the north.

As the years have passed, people who pass by the area today report hearing cries of agony and terror from beneath the streets of Emmons... the same place where the escape tunnel was located so many years ago. The phenomena is most common during the spring time, when the rain has been especially heavy.

Is it the strange effect of rain water echoing in the remains of the tunnel below? Or the lingering spirits of the slaves who died there years ago? No one knows for sure, but it is just one of the eerie stories connected to tragic events of the Underground Railroad.

As mentioned in the early part of the chapter, the Underground Railroad was an unorganized network of abolitionists who illegally aided fugitive slaves in reaching the northern free states or Canada.

It was started in the 1780's by the Quakers, other church groups and a number of free blacks. The network gradually grew into a widespread trail of safe houses into the free states. The safe houses, where fugitives could find food or rest, became known as "stations" or "depots". Along the route, the slaves were often guided by "conductors". The routes ran from the north to the deep south and escaped slaves traveled by night and relied on rumors of safe houses and isolated farms where someone might shelter them. During the daylight hours, the fugitives were concealed in barns and caves and watched over and fed by the conductors.

There were a number of tragedies which took place over the years where slaves were killed... sometimes just before reaching freedom. The Underground Railroad was filled with peril and death and many slaves never reached the north. Because of the danger and death, a number of places associated with the Railroad have been considered haunted over the years. Many are places of great history... where lingering spirits still seek the release of the other side.

WOODBURN

Located in Dover, Delaware is one of the Underground Railroad's most famous haunts. Even though this is not the only ghost said to be present at the house, and it is not the ghost of an unfortunate, escaped slave, it has been connected to the Railroad for many years.

The mansion, Woodburn, was built around 1790 and has been the official residence for the governors of Delaware since 1966. The house was built by Charles Hillyard on land that was deeded to him by William Penn in 1683. The mansion was designed as an elegant home with seven bedrooms, a music room and spacious fireplaces but apparently, Hillyard was not as refined as his new home.

He was well-known in the area for his fiery temper and many believe the unhappy man is one of the many ghosts who inhabit this house. There have been a number of strange encounters over the years with ghosts and apparitions. Hillyard himself has even been seen in front of the old fireplace in the former master bedroom... seemingly warming his feet.

There is also said to be a wine-drinking ghost who resides in the house. Former Delaware governor Charles Terry, Jr. was quoted as saying the house was haunted during the time he lived there. According to Terry, one of the legends of the house concerned a couple who lived at Woodburn and each evening after a meal, they would fill the wine decanter and leave in on the dining room table. The following morning, the decanter would always be empty!

But most interesting to our purposes here is the ghost who actually inhabits an area outside of the house. There is a large tree, a gnarled old poplar, located in the yard of Woodburn that has been dubbed the "Dead Man's Tree".

In the years before the Civil War, Woodburn served as a station on the Underground Railroad. Slaves were hidden in the house until it was safe for them to slip through a tunnel to the nearby river.

Rumors circulated in the area about Woodburn and the activities going on there and eventually some Southern sympathizers learned of the hiding place. Several of them got together one night and went to the house. They believed they could capture the slaves and ransom them back to their masters and also put an end to the abolitionist activities of Woodburn's owner.

The owner at that time was a man named Daniel Cowgill. He had opened his home to the escaped slaves and on that night, managed to stand off the raiders single-handedly while the slaves ran away to freedom. After a short time, the slavers retreated... although one lone sympathizer remained behind. He climbed into the large poplar tree in the yard and hid himself among the branches.

Apparently, he planned to break into the house and rob, or even kill, Cowgill later on that night. But before he could follow through with his plan, he slipped and fell to his death. Before he hit the ground, his hair tangled in the tree branches and he was hanged.... dangling from the tree until his breathed was sucked out him.

As the years have passed, legends have sprung up around the tree as neighbors and passers-by have claimed to see the apparition of the slave-catcher still dangling from the branches.

HALCYON HOUSE

Although the ghosts of the Underground Railroad are far from the only restless spirits to roam this house, the reported encounters with them here are among the most disturbing.

The house was built in the District of Columbia when the idea of such a district was still in the planning stages. It was built by Benjamin Stoddert, a former Revolutionary War Cavalry officer and the man whom President George Washington had commissioned to design the District of Columbia. He built his own home on a Georgetown bluff and while it still stands today on Prospect Avenue, Northwest, it bears little resemblance to the original cottage that Stoddert built.

Perhaps this is why the rappings and sounds of a haunting seem to center around the oldest parts of the renovated and enlarged structure.... perhaps Stoddert himself is expressing his displeasure.

Halcyon House was named for the mythical bird whose presence was said to calm the sea... but Stoddert spent few calm times of his own in the house. Personally, he was well-liked and was friends with many of our country's early leaders, but professionally, his career was in shambles. Besides serving as the Secretary of the Navy for a time, he also ran a shipping business, which was nearly bankrupt by the end of John Adam's presidency. Within a year, Stoddert, depressed and destitute, passed away.

Several families lived in Halcyon House in the years that followed and just before the Civil War, the house became an important link on the Underground Railway.

The stories said that runaway slaves would swim the Potomac River at night and then enter a tunnel that led into the basement of Halcyon House. Here, they were sheltered and fed before continuing on with their journey to the north. Unfortunately, gaining access to this below water tunnel was not as easy as it sounds. Many of the slaves drowned trying to make it inside and those who survived were often weak from effort or became sick from their exposure to the cold water. There were said to have been a number of escaped slaves who died in the basement from exhaustion, fever and disease.

Those who have lived in the house claim to have heard the cries of these slaves coming from the basement. In the early 1900's, a family who lived in the house decided to brick up the tunnel entrance to prevent rats from coming inside. The carpenter who did this work got much more than he bargained for from the experience.

He first thought that the sound he heard was just the wind blowing through the entrance to the passage... then he realized it was a moan. This moaning was joined by the sound of sobbing, then plaintive cries and weeping.

He worked as quickly as he could, trying to convince himself that the sounds has a plausible explanation. He plastered over the new wall and just as he did, he heard a startling scream from the tunnel on the other side.

The carpenter fled the cellar and never came back to pick up his tools.

In the years that followed, others would report those strange cries and moans coming from the old tunnel. If you combine these disconcerting sounds with the other hauntings of the house, you end up with a very strange and mysterious places.

Among the other haunts at Halcyon House are encounters with a ghostly woman; phantom footsteps; strange shapes; the bizarre eccentricities of a former owner which may have led to his own ghost hanging around; levitations; odd legends and more....

All of which make Halcyon House a noted destination on the haunted highways of America!

THE OCTAGON HOUSE

Another of Washington's famous haunted spots is the Octagon House, although it was rumored to be home to otherworldly guests long before the spirits of the Railroad were left behind.

The Octagon is located at the corner of New York Avenue and 18th Street, Northwest. The house is perhaps most famous for the fact that it was used by President and Mrs. James Madison while the White House was being rebuilt after the fire of 1814. Dolley Madison's ghost has been spotted there from time to time, along with a number of other haunts.

There have been ghost stories recorded about this house for many decades, some involving the great spiral staircase, the subterranean kitchen and of course, the dark cellar.

The house was built for Colonel John Tayloe, a close friend of George Washington, by Dr. William Thornton, who also designed the Capitol building. The lot the house was to sit on was odd-shaped, so the building was designed with six sides (although the Tayloe family called it the "Octagon") which made for some rather interesting architecture. Some of the rooms are positioned at angles that make for weird corners and closets which open into other closets.

In addition to the ghosts of the Underground Railroad and Dolley Madison, the house is also said to be haunted by two of the Tayloe daughters.

The Tayloe family occupied the house from the early 1800's to the death of Mrs. Tayloe in 1855. The Colonel and his wife had fifteen children, seven sons and eight daughters. According to period accounts, the Tayloe daughters were known for their grace and beauty... and their turbulent love affairs.

Just before the War of 1812, one of the Tayloe girls fell in love with a British officer, which was a relationship that her father would not allow. His refusal to allow the officer into the house began a heated argument and the girl stomped off up the grand staircase. Seconds later, there was a scream and the girl plunged off the staircase and to her death. Whether she fell or committed suicide is unknown, but her ghost is said to haunt the staircase today in the form of the flickering candle that she carried that night as she ascended the stairway.

After the war, Tayloe offered the use of the house to President Madison while the White House was being rebuilt, after being sacked and burned by the British during the fighting. The house was the scene of a number of lavish parties and gala events to celebrate the end of the war and then after the White House was completed, the Tayloe family returned... to meet with more tragedy.

Apparently, one of the daughters had eloped and then had returned home to ask her father for forgiveness. The father and daughter clashed on the same stairway. The Colonel brushed the girl aside as he passed her and she managed to lose her balance and fall, breaking her neck. It is hard to imagine how the death of another daughter on the same staircase must have affected Colonel Tayloe but many believe that it contributed to his premature death a short time later.

Many believe that this second daughter also returns to the scene of her death. People who have never heard this tale tend to walk around the spot at the bottom of the stairs where the girl died. It is said that one can feel a strange sensation, or a cold spot, in this area.

And there are other stories too.....

For more than 100 years, occupants of the house were plagued by thumping sounds from within the walls. No one was ever able to find the source of the noises until one day when workmen were repairing a damaged wall. Behind the stone, they found the skeleton of a young girl. The fingers of the corpse were clenched tightly, as if she had died while knocking on the wall. The body was removed and given a proper burial and the sounds were never heard again.

How the body had gotten there was unknown, but there was a tale of a soldier and a slave girl which dated back to the early 1800's. Apparently, the two had been lovers but in a jealous rage, the soldier had killed her and somehow managed to seal her body in the hollow wall.

After the death of Mrs. Tayloe in 1855, the Octagon changed hands several times and was allowed to deteriorate. There were many tales of ghosts and haunts in the house and this was enough to keep many people away. According to reports of the time, people often heard screams of agony and sobs of despair in the house.

Another legend of the house concerns the closed-off tunnels that are supposed to have led to the White House and to the Potomac River.

There are legends concerning the tunnels which say that enemies of President Lincoln once planned to kidnap him and take him out of the White House via the tunnel system of the then deserted Octagon.

The tunnels were also the source of some of the house's other ghostly tales. According to period reports, the river tunnel had been used as a link on the Underground Railroad. During the Civil War, the Union Army also used the house as a temporary war records office and as a hospital for wounded and dying men. Because of this, there are conflicting stories that claim the moans, screams and sobs heard in the house are either the spectral voices of escaped slaves or those of wounded soldiers.

Regardless of where the sounds came from, the Sisters of Charity moved into the house in 1891, determined to put an end to the ghost talk once and for all. They "purified" the house from top to bottom with holy water but it did no good and soon, the Sisters were telling ghost stories of their own. They decided that it was time for something to be done and they recruited a dozen men to spend the night in the house and investigate.

Shortly after midnight, a number of terrifying sounds ripped through the dark house. They heard "female shrieks, the clanking of sabers, and thumping sounds in the walls".... and soon, the dozen intrepid investigators had abandoned the house in a hurry.

In 1902, the house was purchased by the American Institute of Architecture who renovated it and still inhabit the place. Over the years, they would have their own ghost stories to relate, of phantom soldiers and disembodied footsteps and as far as I know... the Octagon House remains haunted today.

THE HANNAH HOUSE

Far removed from the slave-holding plantations of the south is a historic home in Indianapolis, Indiana called the Hannah House. But even here, in the northern states, the specter of slavery, and of the Underground Railroad, still manages to make itself known.

The house was built in 1858 by Alexander Moore Hannah, a prominent figure in Indiana history. Originally, the house had been constructed to house Hannah and his staff but at age 51, he married Elizabeth Jackson and another wing was added on for the servants.

Hannah was well-known in Indiana for his stand against slavery. It was a time of coming change in America where political opponents fiercely debated the question of slavery and President James Buchanan openly supported it. Hannah was a firm abolitionist and this is the reason his former home has such a reputation for being haunted.

The source of the haunting remained a mystery for some time. The stately mansion had seen few owners over the years and unlike most haunted houses, had seen little in the way of trauma or death... or so most people believed.

Hannah himself had owned the home until 1899, when his heirs sold the place to another family. Since that time, there have been reports of many strange things in the house, moving objects, phantom sounds... and the unexplainable smell of death. Apparently, the Hannah House held a dark secret and one that would not be easily explained away by saying that one of the Hannah's had returned to haunt the house. This secret was much darker... and much more terrible.

Prior to the outbreak of the Civil War, Hannah's staunch abolitionist views had led him to allow the house to be used as a station on the Underground Railroad. Escaped slaves were brought into the house at night and given shelter until the following nightfall. Then, the Hannah's would load the slaves into a wagon and they would be transported to the next station. We have to remember how dangerous this was, especially to a person of Hannah's standing. This was a time when even assisting an injured runaway slave could be punishable by law.

One night, a lantern was overturned in the basement of the house and a number of slaves were trapped by the flames. Several of them burned to death. The fire did extensive damage to the basement and the lower floors of the house. While the fire was being put out, the source of the blaze had to be kept hidden and the fact that the house was an Underground Railroad station had to be covered up. This is the reason that no one knew the source of the haunting for so long.

One of the upstairs rooms of the house sometimes smells like gangrene and decay and this odor has been attributed to the death of the slaves in the house. Those who have been in the room report, besides the occasional smell, the sounds of moaning and whining. It has also been said that doors in the house suddenly open and close by themselves and that cold drafts are felt when no windows are open to cause them.

The secrets that remain at Hannah House are certainly dark ones, and be the haunting a conscious or a residual one, it still continues to plague the curators of this historic mansion today.

DARKISH KNOB

Our final entry in the relating of ghosts of the Underground Railroad may be little more than a folk legend... but who really knows for sure? In chasing down ghost stories over the years, always looking for true encounters, I have discovered that the legends and folk stories make an excellent place to begin the search. Many of the "legends" may have a root in genuine phenomena. I have learned to not ignore the stories which seem too good to be true... there may be more to them than meets the eye.

Near the town of Parsons in West Virginia is a tall and treacherous hill that is covered in loose rock and gravel. There is one narrow path that leads over this hill and most consider it to be impassable. The hill itself is called Darkish Knob.

In the years before the Civil War, a line of the Underground Railroad passed close to Parsons. One of the best routes out of the south led through the mountainous terrain of West Virginia. There were plenty of places to hide during the daylight hours, although sometimes the travel at night could be hazardous. The few trails that the escaped slaves dared to use were so dangerous that few people would even attempt them during the daylight.

One of the best-known stations in the region was located in a small valley at the foot of Darkish Knob. It was so well hidden that guides had to be posted along the paths to direct the slaves to the house for food and shelter.

And there begins out story.....

One dark night, a young black girl was attempting to find the Railroad station. None of the guides knew she was coming and soon she was lost. Frantic in her efforts to find the place, she didn't realize that she had taken a wrong turn. She was riding on a horse that she had stolen from her owner's plantation and in the darkness, she missed the valley where the station was located and started up the narrow path over Darkish Knob.

Her horse was exhausted, but she pushed him harder. The top of the hill drops straight down into the Cheat River and near the rise, the horse lost its footing and rolled down the hill toward the water below. As the girl plunged to her death, her scream was heard for miles.

Since that night, the girl's ghost is said to return to the top of Darkish Knob each year on the anniversary of her death. At the instant of her fatal plunge, the ghost is said to let out the same blood-curdling scream.

Does it sound too good to be true? Perhaps it is... but then again, who can really say for sure?

SOURCES

Don't Know Much about the Civil War by Kenneth C. Davis (1996)
The Civil War: An Illustrated History by Geoffrey Ward with Ric Burns & Ken Burns (1990)
A Short History of the Civil War by James L. Stokesbury (1995)
Haunted Illinois by Troy Taylor (1999)
Haunted Houses by Richard Winer and Nancy Osborn Ishmael (1979)
More Haunted Houses by Richard Winer and Nancy Osborn Ishmael (1981)
Haunted Heartland by Beth Scott and Michael Norman (1985)
Illinois: A History of the Prairie State by Robert P. Howard (1972)
Old Illinois Houses by John Drury (1948)
Ghosts of Little Egypt by Troy Taylor (1998)
Haunted Places: The National Directory by Dennis William Hauck (1996)
New Orleans Ghosts by Victor C. Klein (1993)
Haunted America by Michael Norman and Beth Scott (1994)
Jeffrey Introduces 13 More Southern Ghosts by Kathryn Tucker Windham (1971)
Civil War Ghosts of Virginia by LB Taylor (1995)
A Ghostly Tour of Harper's Ferry by Shirley Doughtery (1982)
Haunted Houses USA by Dolores Riccio and Joan Bingham (1989)
The Ghostly Register by Arthur Myers (1986)
Ghosts! Washington's Most Famous Ghost Stories by John Alexander (1975 - revised 1998)
Encyclopedia of Ghosts and Spirits by Rosemary Ellen Guiley (1992)
Coffin Hollow by Ruth Ann Musick (1977)

Personal Interviews and Correspondence

CHAPTER FOUR
HAUNTED PLACES OF THE CIVIL WAR

It is well that war is so terrible, or we should grow too fond of it.
General Robert E. Lee on the Union retreat at Fredericksburg, December 1862

War is at best barbarism... Its glory is all moonshine. It is only those who have neither fired a shot, nor heard the shrieks and groans of the wounded who cry aloud for blood, more vengeance, more desolation. War is hell.
General William T. Sherman

Before the sunlight faded, I walked over the narrow field. All around lay the Confederate dead, clad in butternut. As I looked down on the poor pinched faces all enmity died out. There was no "secession" in those rigid forms nor in those fixed eyes staring at the sky. Clearly, it was not *their* war.
Private David L. Thompson, 9th New York

In the glades they meet skull after skull
Where pine cones lay - the rusted gun, green shoes full of bones., the moldering coat and cuddled-up skeleton; And scores of such.
Some start as in dreams, and comrades lost bemoan;
Herman Melville

In previous chapters of this book, we described both the events that led up to the bloodiest conflict in our nation's history and the events of the Civil War itself. As stated in our introduction, this book was not designed to be a history book, but a look at the haunted history of the Civil War.

In this pursuit, we learned that ghosts and history will be forever connected, especially when it comes to the events of the Civil War.

As we begin this next, and perhaps lengthiest, chapter of the book, we will not begin with another look at the war nor biographies of the men and women who lived and died for and from the events of 1861-1865. Instead, we will introduce you to these histories as we present each place where the spirits of the past are still said to linger.....

This section of the book has been designed to feature the haunted places connected to the war itself. We have reserved special chapters for some of the most important haunted places of the war, like the prisons and the actual battlefields, in later chapters. In this chapter, we will focus on the private homes, the churches, the universities, the cemeteries and other places connected to the war..... places where strange events of the war still replay themselves and where the specters of dead soldiers still lurk.

We will begin our ghostly journey in the state of Alabama and end it in Virginia, a place which I believe may be the most haunted state in America. There was more fighting in Virginia during the war than any other state and perhaps this is why the place is still so haunted today.

So sit back and relax, stoke up the fire, and prepare to journey into the most haunted and mysterious corners of America.... places where the cannons of the Civil War still continue to thunder.

ALABAMA

Alabama has a lot of ghost stories.

You can stop in just about any small town in the state and ask about the local haunted spots and undoubtedly, someone will direct you to one. These places run the gamut from the local graveyard to the dilapidated remains of a former plantation... but there is no question that many of these haunted spots will have some connection to the Civil War.

CARLISLE HALL
Located in Perry County, just west of the town of Newton stands an old house that is definitely an unusual sight in the deep south. This odd house is a strange combination of architectural styles from Romanesque arches, to Japanese roof lines to Moorish balconies and general Gothic design.

Built by Edwin Kenworthy Carlisle in 1827, the house has had a wide variety of owners and even stood abandoned for many years. During the 1930's, the house was renovated and modernized by A.S. Hill, a naval officer and teacher who left for World War II and sold the house to W.E. Belcher, who rarely occupied the place.

During the time the home was owned by Belcher, vandals ransacked Carlisle Hall and destroyed all 56 windows, tore apart the staircase banister, broke the marble fireplace mantles and even dug up trees and plantings in the yard.

The house was later restored again and remains in beautiful condition today..... but this did not stop the tales of ghosts and haunts at the old mansion. The stories began shortly after the death of Edwin Carlisle and concerned a ghostly blue lantern light that could be seen from the window of his old bedroom. There was also the story of young woman who is said to appear on the staircase of the house.... and it is here where our attentions should focus.

The ghostly occupant of the house is said to be that of Anne Carlisle, the daughter of the home's owner. Anne grew up in Carlisle Hall and in her teenage years, fell in love with a young man who lived nearby. The two planned to be married, only to have those plans interrupted by the outbreak of war.

Anne's lover joined a group of men from Perry County who enlisted in the Confederate Army and he soon departed for war, promising her that he would marry her on his return. He then promised that he would send his personal servant back to her with news after the first battle that he engaged in. Anne believed that if he survived the initial fighting that he would return to her after the war. It should probably be mentioned that, at that time, no one really believed the war would last for more than a few months.... with of course their own side, north or south, emerging victorious.

Anne asked her lover to send the slave back with news, carrying a white flag if the young man survived and a red flag should he have perished. Anne promised to be watching from the tower on the house.

And so began Anne's vigil. She climbed to the window every morning to watch the road in front of the house. Servants brought her meals up to her, family members visited to help her pass the time, but Anne never wavered from her post. Only when darkness fell, and it became too shadowed to see the road any longer would Anne come down from the tower window.

One day, after several more weeks passed, the sound of a horse could be heard pounding up the roadway. Anne was having her dinner and she threw the tray aside and hurried to the window. What she saw on the road below chilled her heart.... it was her lover's servant riding toward Carlisle Hall.

Above the man's head fluttered a dark red flag.

A scream tore from Anne's throat and without hesitating, she flung herself over the stairwell from the tower and plunged to the stone floor three floors below. When her father, who heard the scream, reached her bloodied and broken body, she was already dead.

For years after, the sound of Anne's scream and her spectral form, were both seen and heard on the staircase as she went to join her lover in death.

THE CHOCTAWHATCHEE BRIDGE

Although the ghost of William Sketoe has never actually be seen, there is little doubt to the folks near Newton that his spirit exists. They can take you to a place near where the old bridge crossed the Choctawhatchee River and show you proof that his ghost has been there. The evidence is a hole, just below where Sketoe was hanged, that is always as clean and fresh as when it first appeared.

Even if that very hole had been filled with dirt the day before, the dirt will always disappear during the night, uncovering the hole again in the morning.

William Sketoe was born in Spain and came to Alabama with his parents in the early 1800's. He was a hard-working boy and gained the respect of his neighbors. When he grew up, he became a minister and traveled the area, preaching in various churches, and eventually gained a church of his own in a log cabin Methodist church near Newton. He eventually married and settled down to raise a family.

When the Civil War broke out in 1861, Sketoe was quick to enlist in the Confederate Army. He fought bravely for three years, until late in 1864, when he received word from home that his wife was very sick. Sketoe decided to hire a substitute to take his place in the military so that he could go home and be with his wife.

This was not an unusual thing at the time as many affluent southerners either hired a man to take his place in case of an emergency or even to avoid military service altogether.

As soon as the substitute reported for duty, Sketoe headed back to Newton. There, he found his wife seriously ill and he was forced to stay with her until she recovered.

By 1864, the threat of defeat hung like a black cloud over the Confederacy. The war had turned badly against the South and now every man who was able was needed in service. Under these circumstances, Sketoe's extended stay at home was starting to arouse resentment and suspicion among the neighbors. Many of them, who knew that Sketoe had come to Alabama from Spain, realized that he was a foreigner and now were starting to wonder if he might be a traitor too.

There was a group of men in Newton who had organized themselves to round up and punish deserters from the Army. They called themselves Captain Brear's Home Guard. There were those who wondered why these men were safely at home while others were off fighting, but the Guard defended themselves by saying they were too old or infirm to fight. This was obviously a pretty flimsy excuse and the Guard tended to attract men who were ducking service themselves or who were just slightly on the wrong side of the law.

Regardless of their reasoning, the members of the Home Guard heard about Sketoe's return from the Army and branded him a deserter. They made plans to ambush him.

On the night of December 3, 1864, members of the Home Guard hid near the Choctawhatchee River bridge and stopped Sketoe when he passed by. They questioned him about where he was going and he showed them the medicine that he had just purchased for his wife.

While he was talking, several of the men came up behind him and wrapped a noose about his neck. Surprised, Sketoe was soon overpowered and the men tied his hands behind his back and took turns kicking him as he lay on the ground. Then, they looped the end of the rope over a stout tree limb and pulled Sketoe to his feet.

They asked him if he had any last words and the minister asked them if he could pray. But instead of praying for himself, Sketoe prayed for his attackers. "Forgive them, dear Lord," he prayed. "Forgive them."

The prayer so angered the Home Guard that before Sketoe even finished, they lashed a horse, which was tied to the end of the rope, and the minister was jerked off the ground. Sketoe's neck refused to break and he slowly started strangled to death in the noose. The tree limb he was strung over started to bend before Sketoe lost consciousness and his toes brushed the ground.

Quickly, one of the men, a cripple, grabbed his crutch and used it to dig a hole in the sandy soil under Sketoe's dangling body. This way, his feet would not be able to touch the ground. The noose tightened and Sketoe died.

News of what happened at the bridge reached Sketoe's friends too late but several of them went to the place and removed his body. He was later buried in the cemetery at the Mount Carmel Church, where his tombstone can be seen today.

But this is not the end of the story....

The six men who actually hanged Sketoe were said to have never passed a peaceful day afterwards. Every one of the men ended up meeting a violent death, killed by thrown horses and drowning and one was even struck by lightning.

The hole that had been dug beneath Sketoe's feet had been filled in by his friends, but curiosity-seekers who visited the spot claimed that the dirt had been removed. Efforts were made to fill the hole, but the dirt always vanished. The legends said that William Sketoe's ghost was returning to the scene and removing the dirt from the hole to remind everyone that he had been an innocent victim who had punished unjustly.

The story was told for many years, and is still told today. A few years back, a tale was told by two men who were part of the crew building the new bridge across the river. They decided to camp out for the night on the spot where Sketoe was hanged and prove that his ghost did not haunt the place. They filled the dirt into hole and then pitched their tent right on top of it.

The next morning, the two men amazingly discovered that the dirt was gone! They had slept on top of it and were never disturbed... yet the hole had reappeared!

The hanging oak where William Sketoe met his demise no longer stands but the hole is still there. According to newspaper accounts, it is about thirty inches wide at the top and slopes to a depth of about eight inches.

Perhaps someday it will be filled again.... when the innocent man who died here finally finds his rest in the next world.

THE BURLESON/ MCENTIRE HOUSE

The historic Burleson/ McEntire Mansion in Decatur is a showplace of the old south but regardless of this, it still bears the scars of its involvement in the war. The house was occupied at various times by both Union and Confederate troops and damage can still be seen by the fighting that took place there in the bullet-marked columns on the front of the structure.

The house was built by slave labor in 1824 and changed hands several times until it was purchased by A.A. Burleson near the time of the Civil War. The war brought death and terror to the mansion as it was used as both a command center and a hospital by both armies. It was around the dining room of the house that General Albert Sidney Johnston planned the battle of Shiloh in April of 1862. Later, after the fall of Vicksburg, Union Generals Grant, Sherman and Blair used the house to hold meetings and in 1864, it was used as a headquarters for General Grenville M. Dodge.

A horrible event that took place here during the war is said to be responsible for at least one of the hauntings.

Union troops who crossed the nearby Tennessee River were often fired upon by Rebel sharpshooters hiding in the First National Bank building in town. One Union soldier was wounded by this gunfire and taken to the hospital, then quartered at the Burleson house, where he died. Attacking Confederate forces made it impossible for his friends to bury him, so they ripped up the floor boards in the front parlor and placed the soldier in a shallow grave below. A few days later, the Union troops captured the city again and were able to move the corpse for a proper burial.

But many believe the damage had already been done....

Shortly after the turn-of-the-century, residents of the house began spotting a man inside of the house and many believe that he could be this young soldier whose body was hidden beneath the floor. But there are other candidates.... and other ghosts.

Thanks to its use as a hospital and a headquarters, the Burleson house was one of only five buildings left standing in the wake of fires and battles that nearly destroyed Decatur during the war.

Because of this, it became a political center and a makeshift headquarters for northern speculators, called "carpetbaggers", after the war ended. One such man was Judge Carlton, a northerner who occupied the house for a short time.

Because of his northern ties, the Judge was fervently against the Ku Klux Klan, the white supremacy group that was originally organized to stop northern interference in the south's recovery after the war. He spoke out against the Klan and death threats were commonly made against him. Finally, he had heard enough and he planned his escape from Decatur to Mexico. He made a quick trip to the bank in Nashville and was assumed to be returning home when his body was discovered between the railroad depot and the Burleson House. His murderers were never discovered, although it was suspected that the Klan had a hand in it.

It is believed that the Judge may also be lingering behind in the house, still wondering how his life came to such and abrupt and murderous end.

The third ghost is said to be an army paymaster. Little is known about him, but legends say he was killed near the front gate while on his way to pay the troops who were quartered in the house. The money was found to be missing when his body was discovered and some feel that he may still be looking for it from beyond the grave.

WASHINGTON, DISTRICT OF COLUMBIA

As you will soon discover, and in chapters to follow later in this book, our nation's capital is a very haunted place. Washington is rather unique in that it is a place where past and present are intertwined... where history replays itself on a daily basis and where the very roots of America are planted.

Perhaps that is why the city, and the district, seems to hold so many haunted spots.

This will not be out last visit to Washington in this book. This is merely a stop along our journey... a journey which will bring us back to Washington again to explore the mysterious man who was Abraham Lincoln and the lingering spirits of his assassination.

GENERAL SICKLE'S GHOST

This will not be the last time in this book that you will read of Lafayette Square in Washington. The area is a haunted place in its own right, but one story of the city does begin here in 1859. It was in this year that a high-profile murder took place... which still reverberates today.

In 1859, Washington society was stunned by the shocking scandal involving Daniel Sickles and Phillip Barton Key, the son of national anthem composer Francis Scott Key.

Sickles was a well-known former congressman from New York who was married to the beautiful daughter of an Italian music teacher. Theresa Sickles was described as being charming and well-educated, along with being very attractive. After his marriage, Sickles worked in London for the foreign service for a short time and then was involved in the election campaign of President James Buchanan. He and his wife moved into their home on Lafayette Square and became a major part of

Washington's elite society. Twice weekly they entertained the influential of Washington and the house became the center of both social and political circles.

Sickles later succeeded in winning back his congressional seat in New York and this caused him to start spending a lot of time away from home, leaving his wife, who had been just 17 when they married to fend for herself. While Sickles was away, Theresa began being spotted in the company of handsome widower Phillip Barton Key.

Tongues began to wag about the illicit couple, especially when Key took an apartment just a block away from the Sickles home.

The affair turned out to be short-lived as someone slipped the congressman an anonymous note telling him about the "guilty intrigue" between his wife and Key.

Sickles was enraged and distraught about the affair. He confronted Theresa and she admitted the whole thing. She implored her husband to "spare her", which Sickles did.... after she signed a complete confession in front of two witnesses. "I am a dishonored and ruined man", Sickles told a friend that same day.

The next morning, Key walked past the Sickles' house and allegedly signaled to Theresa as he walked past. That was the last straw! Later, when Key was leaving the Washington Club, Sickles confronted him. "Key, you scoundrel!", he shouted at him. "You have dishonored my house- you must die!"

At that, Sickles fired at him with a pistol. Key grabbed at his own vest and lunged at Sickles, trying to keep him from reloading. Sickles dodged away and pulled out another gun, which caused Key to start running back toward the Washington Club. Sickles followed and was 10 feet away when he fired again, killing the other man in the street.

The lifeless body of Key was removed and buried and some say that his ghost has never left Lafayette Square. Witnesses claim they have seen his apparition strolling along the street, off to meet with Theresa Sickles, or lying on the sidewalk where his body finally fell.

As for Sickles, he was of course, arrested for murder and his trial was a spectacular one. He hired the best lawyers that money could buy and was acquitted on the grounds of "temporary aberration of the mind", which was the first time that temporary insanity was ever used as a criminal defense in America.

Despite the murder of Key, and the fact that his marriage ended, Sickles career never faltered. Within a few years, Theresa died but Sickles continued with his congressional duties and his social obligations as though nothing had happened.

When the Civil War began, he raised a contingent of men from New York and organized them for battle. His patriotism so impressed President Lincoln that he assured Sickles a position after the war.

Sickles political sway had earned him a brigadier general's star and he rose to the rank of major general. At Gettysburg, Sickles continued his controversial career by deciding to move his corps forward from its assigned position in General Meade's "fish-hook" line. This jeopardized the entire Union line at the same time that Longstreet's Confederates were moving to attack the very place that Sickles had been ordered to hold.

In the battle, General Sickles' right leg was hit and horribly mangled by a cannonball. On his way to the field hospital, where the leg would be amputated, Sickles calmly sipped wine. The wound ended his active service but he displayed the stump of his leg as a sign of his valor and heroism. In fact, he was so proud of his wound that he donated the shattered leg to the Army's National Medical Museum.

Legend has it that Sickles would often drop by the museum where his leg was "enshrined" and bring friends with him to see it. And after his death, his spirit has been reported to be still dropping by to admire the leg.

A number of years ago, a custodian claimed that he had seen a fat apparition with one leg that seemed to float in the hallway near the display. The man threatened to quit his job the following morning unless he was moved to the day shift.

THE KALORAMA

There was a time many years ago when a large amount of Northwest Washington was occupied by the Kalorama estate, which was owned by Joel Barlow. The mansion was constructed in 1807 and stood on what is now the 2300 block of S Street, Northwest.

In the early 1800's, Kalorama was the home of General John Bomford, a close friend of Commodore Stephen Decatur and his wife, Susan. When Decatur was killed in a duel in 1820, Susan Decatur became a guest on the Kalorama estate for quite some time. Bomford even allowed Decatur's body to be buried in a tomb on the estate.

There is a legend about Decatur, besides the one that has his apparition haunting his former home, which says his ghost was unhappy at Kalorama and that blood from his wound would sometimes appear on the outside of the tomb. Some say that this is why Susan Decatur finally had the body removed to Philadelphia, where his parents were buried. They say this removal finally stopped the bloody stains from appearing on the stone walls of the crypt.

During the Civil War, Kalorama became a hospital for wounded soldiers. There were hundreds of them who were treated and cared for in the mansion and on the grounds of the estate. It is believed that the first tales of ghosts come from the time when the house was used as a hospital.

On Christmas Eve of 1865, the soldiers at the Kalorama Hospital decided to throw a party. Unfortunately, a defective stovepipe caused a fire to break out, which swept through the building. The flames spread through the entire east wing of the house before it was brought under control. The building was badly damaged but most of it was saved.

Soon, however, stories started to be told about the ruins of the east wing and about the tree-shaded grounds of the estate. It was said that screams and moans could be heard there, coming from the darkness.

Some of the visitors to the hospital ruins told of hearing sounds and voices from the "house's past" and of seeing strange lights appearing among the rubble of the damaged wing. The reports became more prominent as the years passed and a newspaper account in 1905 reported that "the few people who lived in the vicinity were seized with cold tremors when they heard the howls and screeches that came from within the walls".

Occasionally, visitors would report cold spots in the house and unexplained odors which seemed to be the smells of blood, morphine, sweat and gunpowder.

Eventually, the growing population of Washington took over the Kalorama estate and what was left of the house was replaced with a newer home in the early 1900's. There are those who still say that even though the estate has vanished, the cold spots and the sickly smells still remain.... and that a few former patients of the Kalorama hospital are still lingering behind.

GEORGIA

Of all of the regions of the south, the state of Georgia has perhaps the richest and most varied history. It also has perhaps the most dramatic landscape of the southern states, from coastal islands to northern mountains. It is no surprise that the state is virtually overflowing with ghost stories.... including a number associated with the war.

There is no doubt that some of the most dramatic and memorable events of the last days of the Civil War occurred in Georgia, from the sacking and burning of Atlanta to Sherman's March to the Sea.

By 1864, the Union Army, now under the command of General Grant, was determined to end the war once and for all. Grant decided to strike at the Confederacy with four coordinated, simultaneous blows. Benjamin Butler was to lead an army up from the James River. Franz Sigel would advance up the Shenandoah Valley. George Gordon Meade was to advance south against Lee.

And William Tecumseh Sherman was to strike hard from Chattanooga to Atlanta. Sherman was to seize the city, the "Gate City of the South" and the second most important manufacturing city in the Confederacy, and to smash the combined army of Joseph E. Johnston, who was sure to try and stop him.

On May 6, 1864, Sherman pushed south from Chattanooga with over 98,000 men under his command.

Outgunned, outnumbered two to one and short on supplies, Johnston's southern army could only hope to slow Sherman's advance. They did not count on Sherman's meticulous planning and brilliance however. In a matter of hours, engineers rebuilt the bridges that the Confederates burned in his path and replaced the destroyed rail lines.

Sherman and his men forced Johnston out of Dalton, Resaca, Cassville, Allatoona and New Hope Church. He made steady and slow progress, battling both the Confederate Army, the heat and the insects. "The men's bodies are alive with creeping things," wrote a private from Illinois. "They will crawl through any cloth and bite worse than fleas."

By mid-June, Johnston's men were dug in across the face of Kennesaw Mountain, just 20 miles from Atlanta. Sherman decided to attack them and destroy the southern resistance in one grand battle. On June 27, 13,000 Union men stormed the Confederates on Kennesaw Mountain and failed against the superior positions of the southerners. The Federal soldiers were mowed down like standing targets. One Confederate soldier said that "all that was necessary was to load and shoot."

Three days after the battle, an armistice was granted for burying the dead, as they had become quite ripe under the hot Georgia sun. Confederate and Yankee burial details worked together to try to bury the fallen men.

Soon, Sherman was on the move again. He turned back to his familiar flanking methods against Johnston and was soon within sight of Atlanta itself. This would prove the undoing of Johnston's career. On July 17, he was relieved of command by Jefferson Davis, the Confederate leader believing that Johnston lacked the desire to win.

Johnston was replaced by General John Bell Hood, who had lost a leg at Chickamauga and whose arm had been mangled at Gettysburg. On July 20, Hood attacked Sherman at Peachtree Creek, north of Atlanta. The attack, which started late in the day, was driven back while at the same time, Sherman's most trusted aide, James B. McPherson marched on Atlanta from the east.

Hood rushed to move men against McPherson and on July 22, the Battle of Atlanta began. It raged all afternoon, the lines forming, attacking and then falling back. McPherson himself went to inspect a threatened Union position and rode right into a band of Rebel soldiers. He was ordered to surrender but McPherson raised his hat, turned his horse and rode off. The Confederates shot him in the back.

Sherman, stunned with grief, covered his friend with an American flag and wept.... but his shock didn't last for long. He replaced McPherson with a southern Illinois General named John

"Black Jack" Logan, who reformed the men and launched a massive counterassault. He rode hard up and down the lines crying "McPherson and revenge, boys!"

Hood's army was driven from the field in less than 30 minutes. In a little more than a week, he had retreated back into Atlanta. The Confederates waited for Sherman to attack but Sherman saw no need to hurry. He sealed off the city's supply lines and waited. Federal guns began shelling Atlanta and the siege continued for a month.

Finally on August 31, Sherman charged against the Macon Western Railroad south of Atlanta in a final attempt to break Hood. It worked and the next day, the Confederates fled from Atlanta. The Union Army set to work burning, sacking and destroying the city.

Once Atlanta was in his grasp, Sherman now proposed a new plan. He would lead his army through Atlanta to the coastal city of Savannah. His army would live off the land during the march and destroy everything in its path. He promised to "make Georgia howl".

He began his March to the Sea on November 16, 1864. Sherman himself recalled his last look at Atlanta. "Behind us lay Atlanta, smoldering and in ruins, the black smoke rising in the air and hanging like a pall..."

The great parade of men, over 62,000 thousand strong, moved out in two columns of 218 regiments with a supply train that stretched back 25 miles. Sherman believed that he could defeat the enemy's army by crushing the will of the civilians who sustained it. The troops looted homes and mansions, burning, raiding and stealing until nothing was left behind. " We cannot change the hearts of the people of the south", Sherman stated, "but we can make war so terrible and make them so sick of war that generations will pass away before they again appeal to it."

The Union Army marched west. At Milledgeville, the Georgia capital, Sherman's men boiled coffee over bonfires of Confederate currency and then they ransacked the state library.

Before it was all over, Sherman and his army would cross 425 miles of hostile territory and do over $100 million worth of damage.

On December 22, 1864, Sherman sent a telegram to President Lincoln. "I beg to present you, as a Christmas gift, the city of Savannah, with 150 heavy guns and plenty of ammunition. Also, about 25,000 bales of cotton."

The feats of William Tecumseh Sherman have never been equaled in the history of American warfare. Never before, or since, has one man's army been able to bring an entire state to its knees. Because of this, Sherman is hated more than any other Union leader by the people of Georgia and the south, even today. This was a fact that he was well aware of in the years following the war. "I doubt if history provides a parallel to the deep and bitter enmity of the women of the south," he later admitted. "No one sees them or hears them, but must feel the intensity of their hate."

KENNESAW HOUSE

The Kennesaw House, located in Marietta, was once the finest hotel in the area around the time of the Civil War. It has not been used as a hotel for a number of years however and today, a restaurant is on the ground floor of the building while above is the Marietta Museum of history. The museum boasts exhibits from the Civil War, displays from the days of the Creek Indians and, if the curators and staff member are to be believed, a number of ghosts.

The building was originally constructed from red brick on the site of an old stagecoach station. Before the war, the three-story hotel was a luxury resort and one of the most popular in the state. During the Battle of Kennesaw Mountain, the hotel was turned into a hospital and morgue, first for Confederate troops and then for the Union. The restaurant and museum are today located on the edge of the Kennesaw Mountain National Battlefield Park.

It is believed that the battles which raged nearby are the source of the hauntings in the old hotel.

Over the years, especially since the place was turned into the history museum, staff members have described a number of strange occurrences which have been attributed to the ghosts, including strange sounds and apparitions.

The old elevator in the building is said to be haunted too. According to reports, the elevator rises by itself, the doors open and close on the top floor and then it comes back down again. This only occurs when the building is empty of visitors and only a staff member or two is around to witness it.

They have also seen the apparition of a man inside of the building....a man who suddenly vanishes when approached. The gentleman spirit always wears a black, felt hat and a long, cream-colored coat. He has been seen standing in the hallway and walking about the place. The curators believe the man may be a former visitor to the hotel, who came here during the battle.

The building was owned at that time by a man named Dix Fletcher, who had moved south from Massachusetts and was sympathetic to the Union. Fletcher had a nephew who was an officer and a doctor in the Federal Army named Wilder. Once the Union troops occupied the city, Wilder found the Fletcher family and his connections kept the house from being burned. He managed to get it used as a hospital and headquarters instead. Many believe the ghost seen in the old hotel is Dr. Wilder.

GENERAL LONGSTREET AND THE PIEDMONT HOTEL

General James Longstreet was known by various nicknames, most of which have endured through time. To his friends, he was "Old Pete" and to Robert E. Lee, he was " My Old War Horse". Longstreet was from South Carolina by birth, was raised in Georgia, was appointed to the United States Military Academy from Alabama. He would also become the only General who was not from Virginia to head an infantry corps in Lee's Army of Northern Virginia, at least until the final days of the war.

Like so many other leaders on both sides of the war, Longstreet participated in the Mexican War. He served under General Zachary Taylor at the battle of Monterey and then joined the forces under General Winfield Scott for the expedition to Mexico City. He was wounded at Chapultepec and promoted to the rank of major, a rank which he maintained until June of 1861, when he resigned and joined the Confederate Army.

He was commissioned as a brigadier general, in spite of his desire to assume an administrative rather than a military role in the war. He was in command of troops at the first Battle of Bull Run and because of his skillful leadership was promoted to a major general and given command of a division under General Johnston.

Longstreet would make a number of decisions that are regarded as errors today like his failure to follow through with orders at Seven Pines in 1862 and his slowness to act on the return to Bull Run later that year. In the years that followed, Longstreet would be regarded to have one major flaw and that would be that he was slow to act on orders if he did not fully agree with his superior's plans. This would be a constant sore point between he and General Lee and although they usually did not see eye-to-eye, their never lost their personal fondness for one another.

In spite of all of the criticism of Longstreet, it can be said that whenever a full scale attack was launched by the Army of Northern Virginia and Longstreet was present, he was placed in charge. Although he normally favored a defensive position, he would never waver in an attack. At Gettysburg, Longstreet argued against the offensive on the second day but once committed, gave it everything. He was the man who gave General George Pickett a tearful nod on the third day at Gettysburg... even though he felt the charge was a mistake.

Because of this, and because of the fact that he was considered quarrelsome by some, many southerners blamed Longstreet for the loss at Gettysburg.

After the war, Longstreet was considered even more controversial when he became a Republican and accepted posts in the administration of his old friend, President Ulysses S. Grant.

When Democrat Grover Cleveland became president, after having Republicans in the White House for more than 25 years, Longstreet returned to his former home in Gainesville, Georgia. Here, he took up farming and operated a 40-room establishment called the Piedmont Hotel. He played host to a number of famous guests, including his Gettysburg adversary, General Daniel Sickles, General Joe Johnston and *Uncle Remus* author Joel Chandler Harris.

In his later years, Longstreet became a colorful and eccentric, although well-liked, figure about town. On the hills surrounding the hotel, he constructed terraces which looked to the locals as though he was digging in for a siege. They began calling the place "Little Gettysburg". He took to wearing a long, white linen duster and a broad-brimmed hat and passed time at the Gainesville railroad depot, greeting travelers and drumming up business for his hotel.

The year 1889 saw the death of Longstreet's wife of more than 40 years and a few years later, when he was 76, he married a 34-year old woman named Helen Dorcth. Longstreet also took another position with a Republican president and was named Commissioner of Railroads under William McKinley. During this time. the General was able to travel extensively with his young wife, although old age was starting to catch up with him.

Around the turn-of-the-century, Longstreet began to deteriorate badly. Rheumatism caused him severe pain and he could only walk in a shuffle. His deafness made it necessary for him to use an earhorn and his weight dropped from around 200 pounds to just 135. Finally, cancer even afflicted one of his eyes.

On January 2, 1904, he and Helen were visiting at a daughter's home in Gainesville when he was felled by pneumonia. He began coughing up blood and sinking fast. He died later that afternoon. The "Old War Horse" was gone.

He was buried in an elaborate ceremony in the local Alta Vista Cemetery.... but the people of Gainesville had not seen the last of General Longstreet.

In the years that followed the death of the general, stories began to circulate among the towns people, and in the local newspapers, about a mysterious figure in a hat and a white, linen duster who had been seen lurking about the railroad depot platform. He had almost always been seen standing in the steam of the locomotives and when the steam cleared, the man would be gone. The local residents believed that man was General Longstreet.

The Piedmont Hotel would not be without its share of strange stories either. After the place closed down, it was used by cadets from the Georgia Military Institute for housing and some time later, descendants of Longstreet turned the place into their residence. It was later turned into private apartments.

In recent years, the place has undergone extensive renovations and carpenters who were working there over the last several years have had some odd stories to tell. One afternoon, two of them were working and one man was inside of a room. He heard his friend walk past the room and go down the hallway. He called out to him but heard no reply. He started for the doorway to see what his partner was doing and just then noticed that the man was actually outside.... and had not been inside the house at all.

The two of them stayed out on the porch for awhile, but saw no one else come out of the building. Finally, they searched the building and discovered that no one else was there.

Over the next few months, they would complain of tools and other items disappearing and then turning up again in other parts of the house and they also noticed that doors in the building had an uncanny habit of opening and closing on their own.

And they weren't the only ones to feel uncomfortable in the place as many visitors have complained of uneasy sensations, strange sounds and even the feeling of someone standing close behind them.

Perhaps General Longstreet never really left Gainesville after all!

THE OLD GOVERNOR'S MANSION

The Governor's Mansion in Milledgeville stands at the corner of Clark and Hancock Streets and was home to the governors of Georgia from 1838 to 1868. In 1864, during his March to the Sea, General William T. Sherman commandeered the mansion for his headquarters. According to local legend, all of the brass fixtures in the house were hurriedly painted black by the displaced residents because they knew of the Union's need for the metal to make armaments. Despite the rampant looting by the northern soldiers... all of the brass in the mansion remained behind after Sherman vacated the place.

The days when Sherman's army was in Milledgeville was horrible on both sides. There were times when the Union troops seemed out of control. They came into town and destroyed fences, homes and barns in search of fuel and food; blew up a powder magazine and an arsenal, damaging two churches in Capitol Square, and committed at least one unspeakable crime.

Mrs. Kate Latimer Nichols, the wife of a Confederate Army Captain, was in bed with an illness at her farm outside of Milledgeville when the Union Army arrived. She was alone in the house, except for her servants and one Negro guard, who stood duty at the door. Two Federal soldiers broke into the house, entered the bedroom and raped Mrs. Nichols.

She would later die in a mental institution.

But the brutality witnessed there was not committed by the Union Army alone. Word of Confederate atrocities reached the Federals in Milledgeville as well. It was said that Confederates had cut the throats of men captured near Macon and if this was not bad enough, the Union soldiers were able to witness evidence of southern cruelty with their own eyes.

Lincoln's day of Thanksgiving was celebrated while the Union troops were occupying Milledgeville. During the noisy celebrations around campfires, a few ragged and corpse-like men appeared in the street. Silence fell around the fires. These men were Federal veterans who had escaped from the terrible prison camp at Andersonville, far away to the southwest. They had come almost 100 miles through enemy territory, searching for Sherman's troops. The men wept at the sight of the blue-coated soldiers, the roasting food and even the American flag itself.

Colonel C.D. Kerr wrote that his troops were "sickened and infuriated" when they saw the condition of the escaped prisoners.

During Reconstruction, the capital of Georgia was moved to Atlanta and the old governor's mansion was abandoned. It was turned into a boarding house until 1879 and then it was used as a dormitory for the Georgia Military and Agricultural College. In 1890, the house was converted into a private residence for the president of the college and remained in that capacity for a number of years. Today, the mansion is a historical showplace and is open to the public for tours.

It is also home to a number of ghosts.

One of the most intriguing ghosts, at least to anyone who loves a good home-cooked meal, makes herself known in the form of cooking smells. On some mornings, it is reported that the odor of baked blueberry muffins wafts through the house, tantalizing the appetites of the staff members who are present. Upon investigation, they always find that the fireplace and the stoves are both cold and empty. On other occasions, the smell of wood smoke is noticed on the lower level of the building although no fire has burned in the place for years.

There are those who believe that this ghost is "Molly", a legendary cook who spent her entire life in the governor's mansion, cooking for the former politicians who resided there, the Georgia College presidents and possibly, even General Sherman himself. Many believe that Molly is still at work.... just on the other side of this world.

Besides the smell of the muffins in the morning, some staff members claim that the smell of pork and black-eyed peas can be noticed in the late afternoons.

Besides the "cooking ghost", some have also reported the smells of cigar smoke in the library, even though no one (living, that is) has smoked in there for many, many years.

And not all of the ghostly tales of the mansion are new ones. A number of years ago, when guests still stayed at the house, a servant went upstairs to change the linen in a room that had been occupied the night before. A little while later, the occupants returned to the room to find the bed unmade again and the linens in a heap on the floor. Puzzled, the servant returned to the room and made the bed up again. This happened over and over again, with the bed unmaking itself. The servant was so frightened by the experience that he began avoiding the room whenever possible.

There have also been documented instances of lights turning on and off by their own power, locked doors opening and closing by themselves, phantom footsteps going up and down the corridors and even full-bodied apparitions of spirits in period clothing.

In 1994, a Georgia College student, who helped to cater an elegant dinner held at the mansion, was working alone in the ballroom. She nearly dropped what she was doing when a woman suddenly appeared in the room with her. She spoke to the woman and the lady smiled and nodded her head in response. The woman appeared to be wearing some sort of costume to the college student, dressed in a long, dark dress and with her hair pulled back into a bun. She stood there for several seconds and then as silently as she came, simply vanished.

THE OLD STATE CAPITOL BUILDING

The old state capitol building in Milledgeville was constructed in 1807 and is the oldest public structure of Gothic design in America. Although parts of the building have burned down and have been rebuilt (three times on the same site), it served as Georgia's seat of government from 1807 to 1868. It was here that the state of Georgia voted to secede from the Union in January of 1861. The men who signed the secession document had no idea that in less than four years, the state of Georgia would be in flames or that the city of Milledgeville would be in ruins.

When Sherman marched to the sea from Atlanta, he cut a path west through Milledgeville. The city was looted and burned while Sherman himself was headquartered in the governor's mansion. Union troops pillaged the town, starting a bonfire with Confederate currency in the old Capitol Building and watching it burn. They also destroyed the state's government records, dated prior to 1864, and then sacked and burned the large state library. Some of the northern soldiers balked at destroying the leather bound volumes of the library. "I don't object to stealing horses, mules, niggers and all such little things", wrote one private from New England, "but I will not engage in plundering and destroying public libraries!"

The Capitol Building itself saw a large amount of damage during the occupation as northern troops camped out there and held mock sessions of government in the representative chambers.

After the removal of the state government to Atlanta during Reconstruction, the building stood empty until 1871, when it was converted into the Baldwin County Courthouse. In 1880, it was changed over again into the Middle Georgia Military and Agricultural College. Today, the building is used by the Georgia Military College as administrative offices.

The location does seem to have some ghostly ambience also. Over the years, people have reported the sounds of infantry soldiers marching across the green of the old capitol. Some believe that it may be the sound of Sherman's troops as they marched up Greene Street and seized control of the town.

There is also the ghost of a lone Confederate sentry who has been reported marching near the gate in front of the capitol building. He has been seen pacing back and forth down Greene Street, to the old governor's mansion and back again. No one knows for sure who he is or why he still guards the place, but he has been seen many times over the span of several decades.

The interior of the building is not without its own tales. According to those who have been in the building at night, it is not uncommon to hear the sounds of footsteps in the former legislative chambers when no one else is present. Visitors often claim to have heard the footsteps following behind them but when they look... they find they are in the room alone.

Or are they?

THE HAY HOUSE

The elaborate residence on Georgia Avenue in Macon, which has served as home to the Johnston, Felton and Hay families, is one of those places which often turn up in books of haunted history as a location that is decidedly *not* haunted. At least that is what the curator and the staff members would like you to believe......

Like so many other places across America, the officials of the Hay House will tell you that the house is definitely not haunted. They are under the mistaken impression that the ghost stories and tales of restless spirits in the house somehow detract from the atmosphere of the place. We know, of course, that this is wrong but there are simply people who feel the need to destroy the stories of the past because of some misguided ideas about propriety and preservation.

But, in keeping with the wishes of the curator, we must say here that the official word is that the Hay House is not haunted..... although for a house that is not haunted, it certainly seems to have a lot of ghosts!

William Butler Johnston was a retired railroad magnate when he came to Macon in 1855 and began building a 24 room Italian Renaissance villa for his wife, Ann Tracy. The Johnston had discovered the architectural style while on their honeymoon in Italy and they imported a variety of furnishings and decorations to be installed in their completed home. The house took 5 years to build and when finished was regarded as one of the most beautiful in the state. It was the one of the first in America to boast indoor plumbing with hot and cold running water in three bathrooms and to have a ventilation system that carried cool air throughout the house.

The house also had a large assortment of art displayed throughout and a picture gallery with thirty-foot ceilings and over 1200 feet of display space.

Despite the wonderful house, the Johnston's personal life was destined to be tragic. Their first child was born in 1852 in Paris, while the couple was still on their grand tour. The baby died shortly after and the shock of this began a decline in Ann Tracy's health. She was so weakened that they stayed in Europe for 2 years longer than they had planned. They returned to Macon in 1854 and within a year, were expecting another child. She was born in August and died the following Spring from the croup. The same fate befell their third child just two months after his birthday. In 1860, their fourth child was born and also died of the croup two months later.

The Johnston's were so shattered by tragedy after tragedy that they delayed in completing the upper floors of the house and spent two years living in rooms on the basement level. Ann Tracy was confined to her bed with grief and when she finally did start to make appearances again, she was always dressed in black.

In 1862, their fifth child was born, a daughter named Caroline. Fate allowed this daughter to live to old age, along with the Johnston's sixth child, Mary Ellen. In addition to her own children, Ann Tracy also raised her sister's orphaned son and her deceased brother's two children, completing the family that she never thought she would have.

During the Civil War, the Johnston home was the center of what little social scene still existed in Macon. Many famous and important people visited the house in those years, including Jefferson Davis.

William Johnston was named as the receiver for the general depository in Macon, which protected the largest portion of the Confederacy's gold, held outside of Richmond. There were times when Johnston had well over $1 million in gold in his safe-keeping. No one knows where the treasure was hidden, but some have speculated that it may have been in a secret room on the third floor of the house. Others argue that the wooden floors of the upper floor of the house could not have held the weight of the gold and that it must have been kept in a hidden vault in the basement.

No matter where the gold was hidden, Johnston was able to produce a portion of it when it was needed during the war. When the destitute men of the Macon Militia came to Johnston for food and medicine, he immediately gave them $125,000 in gold for supplies. No one has been able to learn where the gold actually came from.

During the closing days of the war, Sherman bypassed Macon on his March to the Sea, sparing the city and the grand homes like the Johnston house from destruction.

The war officially ended on April 9, 1865, but Union General James H. Wilson attacked Macon three weeks later when Georgia troops refused to surrender. The Federal artillery guns were aimed at the cupola of the Johnston house but the shot fell short and cannonballs raked huge furrows into the lawn. These holes remained unfilled until just a few years ago. Finally, on May 3, Governor Brown surrendered the Georgia troops and the war was over.

After the war, the mansion remained at the center of Macon society for many years. The house was inherited by the Johnston's daughter, Ellen Tracy Felton, and then by her son, William, who sold it to the Hay family in 1926.

By the 1950's, a period of neglect took its toll on the house and upkeep and repairs became too expensive to keep up with. Upon his death, Hay endowed a foundation to take over the care of the home and extensive restorations were undertaken. Today, the mansion, now known as the Hay House, is part of the National Historic Trust and is open to the public.

Restoration began on the house in 1980. Despite recent claims to the contrary, not all of the former caretakers of the house have been opposed to the idea that spirits of the dead may reside there. One former director, Fran La Farge, was convinced that supernatural activity occurred there and that it was stirred up by the renovations.

Many of the former workmen and staff reported strange sounds and apparitions on an almost daily basis. Mrs. La Farge reported that a staff member once saw the ghost of a woman in the hallway who closely resembled Ann Tracy Johnston. The staff member was so frightened that she left the upper floor and refused to ever return there alone.

Mrs. La Farge, and others, also reported the sounds of disembodied footsteps in the house. On one occasion, the curator was alone in the house and heard the sound of someone climbing the stairs to the second floor. She got up to check and saw no one. An instant later, the security sensor began making a clicking noise, as if someone actually were going up the staircase.

That was when she started to believe in ghosts.

Many curators, staff members and directors have come and gone from the Hay House since Fran La Farge allowed the belief in the ghosts of the house to exist. But take my advice and don't worry what others think... judge for yourself when visiting the Hay House.

You might be surprised at what you find there.

HOSPITAL HAUNTS AT TIFT COLLEGE

As we discussed in the initial chapters of this book, ghosts tend to linger behind in places of great terror, pain and tragedy. This would explain why there are a number of ghost stories, some mentioned already and some still to come, connected to the field hospitals of the Civil War.

One such location is in Forsyth, near Atlanta, where the Forsyth Collegiate Institute once stood. This institute served as a field hospital in 1864 and 1865. Wounded soldiers were transported to Forsyth by rail car and they were tended to by the college students, who acted as nurses.

The campus became known as such a place of tragedy, pain and death that dozens of ghost stories began to be told of the numerous spirits who still reside there today. The Institute reopened after the war, becoming the Monroe Female college in 1871. Eight years later, a fire would destroy all of the buildings on campus but apparently the spirits who lingered here were not connected to the buildings at all.... but the location itself.

In 1883, a new college was built directly on the site of the old one and the school was renamed Tift College in honor of Bessie Willingham Tift, whose husband was a major benefactor to the new school. A new dormitory called Tift Hall was opened in 1903 and in time, became known as the most haunted building on campus.

From this location, and from others, came reports of spectral soldiers, strange sounds, smells and other unusual encounters. Tift Hall itself was known for more than 70 years as the home of a female ghost. She was called "Bessie", in honor of the school's namesake, but it is believed that her origins lay elsewhere. The ghost was known for walking up and down the corridors of the building at night, her heels tapping on the floor as she moved past, reportedly stopping long enough to rap on doors and rattle the doorknobs. If the door was opened at her summons, the student always found the corridor to be empty. When the door was closed, the tapping heels would be heard again as they moved off down the passage.

"Bessie" was also said to traipse up and down the stairs, open and close doors and windows, turn water faucets on and off and create the sounds of harsh breathing in empty rooms.

Legend had it the ghost might actually be that of a tragic Civil War nurse who worked at the old field hospital. Surprisingly, there happened to be a story of a heroic nurse who could be imagined to have lingered behind.

Located near the campus is a cemetery that holds the graves of 299 Confederate soldiers and one young woman, named Honora Sweney. According to the legend, she was one of the Forsyth Collegiate Institute students who stayed to nurse the fallen soldiers brought to the hospital. She contracted typhoid fever and when she realized that she could no longer assist the wounded men, she asked to be buried anonymously with the soldiers that she had been taking care of. They say she was buried, following her request, in a grave that is simply marked "Confederate".

They also claim that her ghost stayed behind with the men she so diligently cared for.... becoming lost and never passing on to the next world.

In 1972, Tift Hall was torn down and replaced with a more modern building. Campus legend says that someone from the history department photographed the building as it was being torn down, just minutes before the wrecking ball began to swing. Although the building was vacant and locked, the faces of two young men appeared in different windows in one of the photographs. No one could explain how this could have happened, or who the two men could be.

The photo was so impressive that it was enlarged and displayed in the lobby of Lies Hall until the college closed in 1987. Strangely, the photo has vanished today and although a number of people recall seeing it, no one is aware of what became of it.

Those who remember the photo say that the faces appeared to belong to young men. They recall that their features were not clear, but slightly filmy and transparent.

Could they have been the spirits of men who died in the building more than 100 years before?

After Tift Hall was torn down, many wondered what would happen to the ghosts who haunted the building. The ghosts had originated on the campus long before Tift Hall was even built so it came as no surprise to learn, a short time later, that strange phenomena was occurring West Dorm as well.

Another ghost was also reported in Lies Hall, a relatively new building, in 1973. They called him Jefferson and he appeared to be a young soldier. Perhaps another who had perished at the field hospital and who had never found his way to the other side?

One thing is clear about the campus in regard to its ghosts.... you can tear down the old buildings, but the hauntings remain. The stories and events of the campus are still told today, even though the college is no longer there. Today, it is used by the Ebon Academy as a private boarding school for exceptional children.

I wouldn't be surprised, however, if the current residents might have stories of their own to tell.

PANOLA HALL

Located in Eatonton is a magnificent mansion called Panola Hall, which means "cotton" in the language of the Choctaw Indians. The house is a southern antebellum mansion with the squared-off appearance and white columns that are typical of the plantation houses. The mansion has been home to a number of families over the years... all who share the residence with a resident ghost. The beautiful and elusive phantom seems so real on appearance that one former occupant of the house, Louise Hunt, named her "Sylvia", after a popular song of the late 1800's, and was inspired to write a poem about her. Louise also tried to prevent a visitor, a frequent houseguest of the family, from falling in love with the ghost.

Believe it or not, she was unsuccessful at this and this strange turn of events ended in tragedy.

Panola Hall was built in 1854 by a successful plantation owner named Henry Trippe. At the time of the construction, Trippe was happily married with a son and two young daughters. Six years later, in the 1860 census, only Trippe, his wife, and the boy remained in the house. Whatever became of the two girls remains a mystery that has never been solved.....

It is possible that the girls may have married and moved away, although some believe that the spectral Sylvia may be one of the Trippe's young daughters. There is also speculation that the ghost may have been a friend of the Trippe family, who was visiting the plantation during Sherman's march through Georgia.

Regardless, it is believed that Sylvia fell in love with a Confederate soldiers who escaped capture and who hid at the plantation while Sherman's men were in the area. There is a long-standing legend of the house which says that ten or twelve soldiers were hidden away in two tunnels that are located beneath the house. One of the tunnels was said to lead into a well in the front yard and the other to a chamber beneath the courthouse in downtown Eatonton.

According to the story, Sylvia later learned that her young lover had been killed and in her grief, committed suicide by leaping from the second floor balcony of the house.

As romantic as the story sounded, there was no proof that Confederate soldiers were ever hidden at Panola Hall.... until 1979. At that time, a resident discovered a secret chamber in a remote location of the attic. Here, he discovered a musket, a shotgun, a saber and several loose musket balls. This gave credence to the legends of the soldiers hiding out there and the story was further enhanced a short time later when a concrete chamber with a vaulted ceiling was discovered beneath the mansion.

If the stories of the soldiers were true.... then many believed this went a long way in authenticating the legend of the ghost herself!

After the deaths of Henry and Elizabeth Trippe, the family rented the mansion to Dr. Benjamin Weeks Hunt of New York. He married a local girl named Louise Reid Purdon and they settled into Panola Hall.

Dr. Hunt was interested in farming and he brought with him 50 registered Jersey cows to Eatonton. He used his expertise to help other area farmers and they turned Putnam County into the dairy capital of Georgia. He also introduced Bermuda grass as a forage crop and was responsible for establishing the first rabies treatment facility in the state. This foray into medicine occurred after Hunt believed that he had been exposed to the disease. There was no local treatment available, so he had to travel all the way to Paris for treatment. In 1922, he was awarded an honorary Doctor of Science degree by the University of Georgia.

Apparently, while the Hunts were living in Panola Hall, they often saw Sylvia, although they rarely talked about her. Louise wrote a poem about the girl and after she passed away, Dr. Hunt allowed it to be published.

The ghost was apparently seen quite frequently in the house, always leaving the mysterious scent of roses behind her. Louise first saw her while she was sitting in the library. She looked up and saw a young girl leaning over the balcony of the staircase laughing at her. "Who are you and how dare you laugh at me in my own house?", Louis demanded. The girl laughed again and then came gliding into the library. She disappeared into thin air.

Louise didn't tell her husband about the ghost until someone else saw it. He was a friend from Ohio who often visited the family. No one knows for sure, but he is believed to have been a wealthy man named Nelson. He met Sylvia on his way downstairs to dinner one evening. He looked up and saw a beautiful girl in a white dress with long, dark hair. He stood back to let her pass him and she smiled at him shyly as she passed. She left the sweet scent of roses behind as she vanished into another room..... or so he thought.

Nelson was surprised to see the young lady was not at dinner and when he saw the table was only set for three, he asked the Hunt's the identity of the girl. They explained to him that she was their resident ghost and Nelson thought they were playing a trick on him.

As time passed, he reluctantly accepted the story, but Sylvia remained quite real to him. He often wrote love letters to the ghost and he asked that Louise open the letters and leave them in rooms where hopefully Sylvia might read them.

According to the story, Nelson eventually died, penniless and alone, and disowned by his family for some unknown reason. All that he had left to cling to were his memories of Sylvia. His final wish had been to be buried with a copy of Louise's poem about the girl in his hand and placed just above his heart. He loved her until the very end.... and one has to wonder if they might be together now.

The stories of Panola Hall continued on throughout the years, tales of more sighting of Sylvia in the house and on the grounds were common and frequent. The house is still believed to be haunted today although is it closed to the public.

FORT MCALLISTER

The garrison at Fort McAllister, located just below Savannah, was a Confederate earthen fort that only boasted nine guns. Located on the Ogeechee River, it proved to be a major defense against the Union Navy. The fort protected the best passage for blockade runners to reach Savannah and because of this, it was a target for Union gunners.

The fort managed to withstand every attack aimed against it from the sea, including several attacks by iron clad ships. It was constructed by John McGrady, the engineer who designed the defenses of Savannah. The massive, earthen walls of the fort were built primarily by hand, using shovels and wheelbarrows. After the site had been cleared of trees, a wooden frame work was built and it was then filled with earth and allowed to settle. Last, the frame was removed and sod was staked in place to stabilize the walls.

To guard against an assault by land, mines were placed along all of the approaches and sharpened stakes were placed around the perimeter. The fort also had a moat, although it was never filled with water.

An example of how well-built the fort was really was is evidenced by an attack launched from the Federal ironclad, the *Montauk*, in January 1863. The vessel, accompanied by a number of wooden craft, approached the fort and began a bombardment that would last for 5 hours.

The fort stayed firm because the sand and earth walls absorbed the impact of the incoming projectiles. The damage that was done was repaired during the night.

The 2,000 defenders of the fort were finally overrun by 4,000 Union troops on December 13, 1864, ending General Sherman's March to the Sea.

After the war, the fortifications were neglected until they received the attention of inventor and industrialist Henry Ford in the 1930's. He had some business interests and a home in nearby Richmond Hill. Fort McAllister is considered to be the best preserved earthwork fortification remaining in the south today and is now a state park. During the renovations, workmen refused to stay in the fort at night because of strange sounds and reports of apparitions.

What ghostly events are still haunting the fort today?

In February of 1863, the *Montauk* once again attacked Fort McAllister with heavy artillery, laying siege to the earthwork for seven days. According to the reports, the ironclad opened fire on the fort and damaged an area of the earthworks commanded by Major John B. Gallie. He was first wounded in the face by a fragment of a shell, but refused to be relieved. He continued his duties in spite of his pain but was hit again. This time, an enemy shell hit him in the head. The official report reads that the wound exposed his brains although some claim he was scalped by the projectile. Regardless, he died from a massive head wound.

In the 1960's, some of the groundskeepers at the fort told of a strange event. One February morning, near the anniversary of the Major's death, the men were working around the area where he had been killed when an icy chill surrounded them. Then, they saw the headless figure of a man hovering nearby. The macabre apparition was turned toward the sea as if looking for something and then it disappeared....

And ghosts of slain Confederate soldiers are not the only things rumored to be haunting the old fort.... they are joined by the earthwork's former mascot. The animal was a coal, black cat named "Tom Cat", who was fed and admired by all of the men.

According to the reports, Tom Cat would run back and forth along the grassy wall, dodging the cannon and musket balls during assaults on the fort. He was finally killed in an attack on March 3, 1863. Three ironclads, three mortar schooners and two wooden gunboats shelled the fort for seven hours but Tom Cat was the only casualty.

The death of the cat was greatly regretted by the men to the point that his death was mentioned in the official reports to General Pierre Gustave Toutant Beauregard.

Now that the fort is open to the public, a plaque has been erected to Tom Cat's memory.... but it is not apparently just a memory which lingers here. Many visitors and Civil War re-eneactors, camping out at the site, have reported seeing a black cat running through the fort, even though no earthly creature resides there. They have reported him running over the tops of the earthen mounds, looking around corners and some have even felt his warm fur rubbing against their leg.

The staff of the fort deny that a living cat is anywhere on the premises, leading many to believe that the spirit of old Tom Cat is still around, perhaps wondering what ever happened to all of his friends from long ago.

EBENEZER SWAMP

The stories of ghosts in Ebenezer Swamp, located in southeast Georgia and just north of Savannah, date back to the years just after the Civil War. The tales of ghostly cries and voices began at that time and continue today, especially on dark nights when the river is flooded by rain. It is said that mournful screams and pleadings for help can be heard echoing in the night time mist of the swamp.

Whose voices are they and what tragic event occurred here to mark the place with such a terrible, and terrifying, replay of the past?

By December of 1864, Sherman's army was well to the east of Macon and Augusta. There were no signs of serious rebel opposition and yet the pace of the march had slowed considerably. The roads of the Georgia swamp country were narrow and soft, and with stream crossings being more frequent, the troops found only flimsy wooden bridges to march over. Often these bridges had to be reinforced, or even rebuilt, to make the crossings possible.

Even more trying to the Federal officers were not the roads and bridges, but the bands of black camp followers at the rear of each unit, hindering the progress of the army. Newly liberated slaves and black refugees followed the army, slowing them down. Over 25,000 slaves had flocked to Sherman's army, jubilant that they had been liberated. They were also fearful of straying too far away from the safety of the columns, in case they were captured by Confederate guerillas and killed or returned to slavery.

Sherman was annoyed by this civilian army, which ate up his supplies and got in his way. Never the diplomat when it came to the blacks, Sherman wrote: "Damn the niggers. I wish they could be kept at work."

While Sherman fumed over the situation, Union General Jefferson C. Davis, a pro-slavery man from Indiana, had his own solution to the problem. On December 3, the corps under Davis' command was crossing Ebenezer Creek, on the northern flank of the advance. Davis ordered the blacks with his column to halt at the roadside and allow the troops to pass forward, ready to meet the Confederate resistance that had been reported ahead. The blacks ignored the order and pushed ahead. Davis then moved his men ahead at double-time and left the blacks to the rear.

The creek, which ran through the muddy swamp, was about 100 feet wide and was swollen with recent rains. The Confederates had burned the bridge over the creek to slow the Federal march but Colonel George Buell's 58th Indiana Regiment had worked all night to lay a pontoon bridge. The troops began crossing as soon as the sun came up.

Davis watched the bridge as his men crossed to the other side. He then ordered the blacks to be halted on the other side. The officers held them under guard as the wagons and guns crossed the creek and then told the blacks that there was fighting ahead and they were being held back for their safety. Soon afterward, the soldiers suddenly cut loose the pontoon bridge and pulled it to the opposite bank, abandoning the blacks on the far side.

A cry then went up from the side of the river where the former slaves stood, someone shouting "Rebels!". The blacks made a mad rush for the river, men, women and children plunging into the river.

Sympathetic soldiers on the far bank tossed logs and pieces of wood into the stream and several men turned them into makeshift rafts. The men used blankets to tie the logs together and they began ferrying women and children across the creek. Those who could not wait for the raft tried to swim across. Some were washed away in the surging current and others drowned. Federal soldiers cut down trees on their side of the water and some of the blacks were able to get across clinging to trunks and branches. Men, women and children screamed in despair and agony.

A few minutes later, Confederate riders came into sight and opened fire on the blacks, but they soon turned away.

The last of the Federal soldiers had disappeared from sight by the time the Confederate cavalry arrived. A company of riders herded together the blacks who had not escaped, or drowned, and most of them were returned to the owners from whom they had escaped.

The army's reaction to the heartless abandonment of the blacks by Davis was mild. Few soldiers mentioned the incident in their letters and diaries but criticism by some would later cause problems for Sherman and Davis. A private from Minnesota was disgusted by the entire affair. "Where can you find in all the annals of plantation cruelty anything more completely inhuman and fiendish than this?" he wrote.

And fiendish it may have been.... because of the reports and stories are true, then there is a small patch of river, near the town of Springfield, Georgia, where the spirits of those abandoned former slaves still do not find peace today.

ILLINOIS

Removed from the battlefield and the fighting of the war, Illinois has little to offer in the way of Civil War haunts, although it has numerous haunts of other kinds. The reader will find a few places here and there and scattered throughout the book which are related to the war, from the Old Slave House to the haunted prison site in Alton.

There is one place, which fits well into this section, were the dead are definitely still believed to walk.

GREENWOOD CEMETERY
Greenwood Cemetery is undoubtedly the most haunted place in Decatur, Illinois. The cemetery has been graced with literally hundreds of ghosts stories and individual haunted sites

throughout the years from spook lights to premature burials, to spectral brides, phantom mourners and more. The spookiest section, however, is without a doubt the old Civil War section..... because besides the ghosts, it has a macabre history all it's own.

Located on a high, desolate hill in the far southwest corner of Greenwood Cemetery is a collection of identical stone markers, inscribed with the names of the local men who served, and some who died, during the brutal days of the Civil War. The silence of this area is deafening. Visitors stand over the remains of some of the city of Decatur's greatest heroes and the bloody victors of the war. But not all of the men buried here served under the stars and stripes of the Union Army....

There are dark secrets hidden here.....

During the years of the Civil War, a great many trains passed through the city of Decatur. It was on a direct line of the Illinois Central Railroad, which ran deep into the south. The line continued north to Chicago and ran near the prison camp that was located there, Camp Douglas. Many trains came north carrying Union troops bound for Decatur and beyond. Soldiers aboard these trains were often wounded, sick and dying. Occasionally, deceased soldiers were taken from the trains and buried in Greenwood Cemetery, which was very close to the train tracks. These men were buried in the cemetery and their graves were marked with honor by the citizens of Decatur.

But that wasn't always the case....

On many occasions, trains came north bearing Confederate prisoners who were on their way to the camp near Chicago. These soldiers were not treated so honorably. Often, Confederates who died were unloaded from the train and buried in shallow, unmarked graves in forgotten locations. Most of these soldiers were unknown victims of gunshot and disease and many were past the point of revealing their identity. These men will never be known and their families will never have discovered what became of them after they departed for the battlefields of war. Those men are now silent corpses scattered about the confines of Greenwood Cemetery.

Why was there such a hatred for the Confederacy in Decatur? Besides being the home of the 116th Illinois Regiment, it seemed that nearly everyone in the city had a friend or relative in the Union army. A number of places in Decatur were also used as stations on the "Underground Railroad", which means that the abolitionists also had a stronghold here.

This was the reason, in 1863, when a prison train holding southern prisoners pulled into Decatur, it was given the kind of reception that it was. The stories say the train was filled with more than 100 prisoners and that many of them had contracted yellow fever in the diseased swamps of the south. The Union officers in charge of the train had attempted to separate the Confederates who had died in transit, but to no avail. Many of the other men were close to death from the infectious disease and it was hard to tell which men were alive and which were not. They called for wagons to come to a point near the cemetery.... but no one would answer the summons.

Several soldiers were dispatched and a group of men and wagons were commandeered in the city. The bodies were removed from the train and taken to Greenwood Cemetery. They were unloaded here and their bodies stacked in piles at the base of a hill in the southwest corner of the graveyard. This location was possibly the least desirable spot in the cemetery. The hill was so steep that many of the grave diggers had trouble keeping their balance. It was the last place that anyone would want to be buried and for this reason, the enemies of the Union were placed there.

Ironically, years later, the top of this same hill would be fashioned into a memorial for Union soldiers who died in battle and for those who perished unknown.

The men from the city hastily dug shallow graves and tossed the bodies of the Confederates inside. It has been said that without a doctor present, no one could have known just how many of the soldiers had actually died from yellow fever.... were all of those buried here actually dead?

Many say they were not, some of them accidentally buried alive, and this is why the area is the most haunted section of Greenwood.

To make matters worse, many years later, Spring rains and flooding would cause the side of the hill itself to collapse in a mudslide and further disturb the bodies of these men. Not only did the Confederate remains lie scattered about in the mud, but the disaster also took with it the bodies of Union men who had been laid to rest in the memorial section at the top of the hill. This further complicated matters, as now, no had any idea how to identify the bodies. In the end, the remains were buried again and the hill was constructed into terraces to prevent another mudslide in the future. The bodies were placed in the Civil War Memorial section and the graves were marked with stones bearing the legend of "Unknown US Soldier"..... and it will never be known just who these men may be.

But what causes this section of the cemetery to be considered as haunted? Psychic impressions from the past or angry spirits? Some people believe that it may be both as investigations, and reports from eight decades, have revealed unexplainable tales, and strange energy, lingering around this hill. Visitors here have told of hearing voices; strange sounds; footsteps; whispers; and some even claim to have been touched and pushed by unseen hands.

There are also the reports of the soldiers themselves returning from the other side of the grave. Accounts have been revealed over the years that tell of visitors to the cemetery actually seeing men in uniform walking among the tombstones.... men that are strangely transparent.

The most stunning tale was reported a few years ago and was told to me first-hand. It happened that a young man was walking along the road in the back corner of the cemetery. He saw a man standing on the top of the hill, who beckoned to him. The boy walked up to him and was surprised to see that he was wearing tattered gray clothing which was very dirty and spotted with what looked like blood. The man looked at the boy oddly and he wore an expression of confusion on his face.

"Can you help me?", the man asked softly of the boy. "I don't know where I am..... and I want to go home."

Before the boy could answer, the man simply vanished.

KENTUCKY

Never before in the history of American warfare was the adage of "brother against brother" as true as during the years of the Civil War. In many cases, northern and southern family members actually came face to face with each other on the field of battle. Journals and letters would often speak of encountering cousins, uncles, and even brothers who fought for the other side.

And it would be the men from Kentucky for whom the adage would prove to be the most tragically accurate.

The border state of Kentucky, which was the native state of both Abraham Lincoln and Jefferson Davis, was always considered to be strongly in favor of the Union, although its economy was dependent on the slave-holding ways of the south. For a generation before the war, the state had managed to straddle the fence when it came to conflict but things began to change in the early days of the conflict. Kentucky leaders attempted to remain neutral, refusing to secede with the other southern states but also ignoring Lincoln's call for men after the attack on Fort Sumter.

Lincoln assured the Kentuckians that no Federal troops would be sent into the state, as long as they remained peaceful. The state was certainly divided in its loyalties to north and south, but seemed determined to remain neutral in the fighting to come.

Many of the state's residents volunteered for service in both armies and a home guard was also created, with of course, 2 factions... one loyal to the Union and one to the Confederacy.

But Kentucky's precarious position would not last. On September 3, 1861, Confederate General Leonidas Polk led his forces into Kentucky from Tennessee, seizing Hickman and Columbus on the Mississippi River. On the northern edge of the state, General US Grant countered Polk's advance by invading Paducah. The two factions of the state militia rushed in to aid the armies which claimed their respective loyalties and the entire state reeled with confusion.

To make matters worse, Kentucky soldiers of the Confederacy held a convention at Russellville in November of that same year and adopted an ordinance of secession. It would have went through too.... if not for the fact that the pro-south governor was handicapped by a pro-Union legislature.

The question would eventually be decided, not by politicians, but by soldiers. In February 1862, after the falls of Fort Henry and Fort Donelson in Tennessee, the Confederate defenses in Kentucky were lost and the border state fell under Union control. In October, a major offensive would be launched into Kentucky by Confederate Major Generals E. Kirby Smith and Braxton Bragg, but after being outnumbered and after sustaining heavy casualties, the southerners retreated back into Tennessee. After that, Kentucky was secured for the Union for the remainder of the war.

There is no question that Kentucky was a place of great tragedy during the war, but not all of the ironic and heart-breaking tales of the state were the result of battle. The following is a tale of lost love, war and of one of the famed generals of the Confederacy.

THE CURSE OF ANNE MITCHELL

Near Mount Sterling, Kentucky, there once lived a young woman named Anne Mitchell. She was a dark-haired girl of great beauty who many people called "the belle of Central Kentucky". Anne was known throughout the region as a gentle and sweet girl and as she grew older, she had her choice of suitors from around the area. However, in her late teens, she fell in love with just one of her gentleman callers, a tall, blond youth named John Bell Hood.

Hood was the son of Dr. John W. Hood, who lived near the Mitchell home and who operated a small farm and a medical school for aspiring doctors. The younger Hood went to West Point in 1849 and when he returned home on furlough, he began courting Anne Mitchell. The two of them fell passionately in love. They often met for walks in the evening and their favorite trysting place was in the garden of the Hood home.... a place where Anne's ghost is still said to walk today.

According to the legends, another young man came on the scene as a rival for Anne's affections. He is remembered today as only "Mr. Anderson", and although Anne did not care for him, her family took to him immediately. Unlike Hood, Anderson was very wealthy and promised Anne's parents that he would build her a home on property which adjoined their own.

Anne's family began to pressure her incessantly and finally, she agreed to marry Anderson on the condition that she be able to write a letter to John Hood at West Point... a letter that would be read only by him. In her letter, Anne poured out her heart to the young cadet and promised him that she "would love him forever" and "whether in this world or the next, she would only walk the garden path with him".

Not surprisingly, when Hood received the letter, he immediately left school and rode for Kentucky. He managed to get Anne a message and promised to meet her a few nights later near her home. He promised to have an extra horse saddled for her and together, they would ride off and be married.

One of the Mitchell slaves discovered Anne's absence only minutes after she left for her rendezvous with Hood and raised the alarm. Anne's father and brothers went in pursuit of her and discovered the young lovers just as Hood was putting Anne on her horse. She was quickly returned home and was locked in her room and not allowed to leave until the day that she married Anderson.

I imagine that Anne's family, and her new husband, must have sighed with relief when the couple finally exchanged their marriage vows.... although their troubles were just beginning. Despite the affection and wealth that was heaped upon her, Anne refused to forgive the fact that she had been forced to marry a man she did not love. She refused to leave her room in the old Mitchell house and remained moody and depressed. When she learned that she was pregnant, she stopped speaking altogether and even Anderson himself was banned from entering her rooms.

When she finally spoke again, it was after the birth of her son, Corwin, and what she uttered made everyone's heart stand still. Her words were a curse.... "upon all who had any part in making her marry Anderson when her heart would always belong to John Bell Hood." A few hours later, the curse began to have a dire effect on the family... or so it would seem.

Late that afternoon, the sky overhead began to darken and a strangely localized thunderstorm swept through the area. A lightning bolt struck the corner of the Mitchell house and a portion of the brick home collapsed. Although nothing else in the area was damaged, three people at the Mitchell house were killed... including Anne herself. Also dead were one of Anne's brothers, who had been involved in stopping Anne and Hood from eloping, and the slave girl whose warning had sent the Mitchell men in pursuit of Anne when she ran away.

After three persons died within hours of Anne uttering a curse on the family, the story of the curse soon began to spread. In the years that followed, it began to be taken quite seriously too....

Anne's son, Corwin Anderson, died from the shock of witnessing a fatal assault on his youngest son by his oldest. This man, named English Anderson, was already known for his brutal murder of a black cook and in this instance, knocked his brother from a horse with a brick. Corwin staggered to his bedroom and died of a heart attack and the youngest son perished from his injuries a short time later.

English Anderson did not fare well either. Soon after the deaths of his father and brother, he killed a man in a knife fight, then beat to death a young boy who was working on his farm. In revenge, a group of his slaves actually stoned him to death.

The family continued to be plagued with strange and violent deaths as the years passed and descendants believed them to be the results of the curse. As recently as the 1940's, Anne's great-grandson, Judson Anderson, inexplicably walked into a pond on his farm, drew a gun and shot himself in the head.

The various residents of the Hood house, who moved in after the family left, had little luck either. One owner committed suicide and another attempted to after an unhappy love affair. In the local area, both events were attributed to Anne's influence.

Although her curse was definitely a malevolent one.... her ghost is considered to be a better reflection of her truly gentle soul. Many persons spoke of seeing her wandering the gardens of the old Hood home and she was never believed to have frightened anyone, despite some reported encounters with shaken residents of the property. Her haunting has always been a quiet one and if the stories are to be believed, it remains so today.

With all of the victims of Anne's fatal curse, one has to wonder what became of John Bell Hood after their separation. Some believe that her restless spirit may have inadvertently passed the effects of the curse on to him, despite how much she loved him, because Hood's career was forever shadowed by failure and tragedy.

After his departure from Kentucky, Hood did his best to forget about Anne Mitchell, although he remained a bachelor for many years afterward. He became a young military officer on the Texas frontier under the command of Lieutenant Colonel Robert E. Lee. After the outbreak of the war, Hood followed Lee into service for the Confederacy, becoming a commander in the Texas Brigade, an outfit considered to be one of the toughest in the southern army. Hood's career began to flourish and he earned a sterling reputation as a leader, always pushing his troops forward in person. At Gettysburg, he lost the use of one arm and later had a leg amputated after leading his corps into battle at Chickamauga.

At the age of 33, with only half his limbs, Hood rose to the rank of full general and was placed in command of the western army. He was now at the peak of his career... and his decline began soon after.

He had taken over the defense of Atlanta, with Sherman was approaching, but was driven out after a series of intense battles. In the Winter campaign of 1864, his Army of Tennessee was virtually annihilated at the battle of Nashville... and it became known as the worst defeat suffered by a Confederate general. From that point until the end of the war, he was in disgrace, a general with no command.

After the war, Hood settled in New Orleans, became a cotton broker, married a local woman and fathered 10 children over the next 12 years, including three sets of twins. It was not long before his commission business went bankrupt and he lost everything. Then, during the yellow fever epidemic of 1879, he and his wife both died, leaving his children as orphans who were scattered from Mississippi to New York.

And finally, whatever happened to Anderson, Hood's rival for the hand of Anne Mitchell?

At the outbreak of the war, with his wife dead, he enlisted in a Texas regiment. A few months later, that brigade was placed in command of .... General John Bell Hood.

What happened to him next is anyone's guess. So far as any records go, Anderson simply appeared to vanish from the earth.

LOUISIANA

There is no question that Louisiana is one of the most haunted states in America and that her shining jewel, New Orleans, is undoubtedly the city with the most ghosts.

The war in New Orleans came early and the city spent the greatest amount of the war under Union control, despite being located so far into the enemy territory of the Confederacy.

In April of 1862, a fleet of 24 ships, under command of David G. Farragut, was ordered to sail up river and seize New Orleans. The Confederate defenders did everything they could to stop him. To reach the city, Farragut's ships had to get past Fort Jackson and Fort St. Phillip. Commander David Dixon Porter, Farragut's younger foster brother, came up with a reckless plan. They would send a collection of small sailing vessels, each bearing a huge mortar, into the harbor and anchor them below the forts so that they could pound the defenses in advance of the fleet. They tried this but after six days of battering, the forts remained standing. Farragut decided on an even more daring scheme..... under the cover of night, they would run past the forts, smash the barricades and steam into New Orleans.

At two o'clock in the morning, Farragut's warships started past the forts. The forts opened fire and the lead ship was hit 42 times. It caught fire but they managed to quench the flames and start forward again. It was a test of sheer will, but the four flagships somehow made it past the forts.

As they approached New Orleans, a makeshift Confederate squadron of 8 ships sailed out to meet them. Farragut sank all but 2 of them and the city surrendered without a shot.

After the surrender, Lincoln named Benjamin F. Butler the military governor of occupied New Orleans. Butler saw no need to be gentle in his position and his methods earned him both admiration and scorn on both sides. He hanged a man suspected of desecrating the American flag, closed a secessionist newspaper and confiscated the property of anyone who would not swear allegiance to the Union.

The women of New Orleans insulted Butler's men in the streets, calling them names and screeching at them. When a woman in the French Quarter opened her window and emptied the contents of a chamber pot over Admiral David Farragut's head, Butler issued General Order Number 28. It simply stated that any woman who insulted a member of the United States Army would be treated from that point as a prostitute, in the midst of plying her trade.

Needless to say, the men and women of the south were outraged and called Butler everything from "unchivalrous" to "Beast". Butler refused to back down and the harassment of his men stopped and no woman was ever arrested.

Butler also tore apart two other old New Orleans institutions... a historical landmark and the institution of slavery.

The statue of Andrew Jackson had been standing in the city's Jackson Square for six years when the Union troops arrived, honoring the fact that Old Hickory had saved the city from the British in 1815. Butler order these words carved into the pedestal, calculated to enrage the citizens of New Orleans: "The Union must and shall be preserved."

Butler also quickly turned the friction between masters and slaves to the Union's advantage. He declared the plantation owners to be disloyal to the Union and he confiscated their property, in this case, their slaves, and set them free. The freed blacks left the plantations and fled behind Union lines. "I was always a friend of southern rights, " Butler said, "but an enemy of southern wrongs".

New Orleans has several haunted places connected to the Civil War and even to actions and orders that came from Benjamin Butler himself. Outside of the city, Louisiana also has a number of haunted places to interest us here, including some of her better-known locations.

For many years, we have heard stories of the many ghosts at the Myrtles Plantation, which vies for the position of "most haunted house in America". The most famous ghost of the Myrtles is that of Chloe, a vengeful slave who accidentally poisoned the children of her master, but there is also the ghost of a Confederate soldier who appears here each May and June.

There are also many readers who will be familiar with the famous "lady in black" of the Oak Alley Plantation. What some readers may not know is that there is another ghost here also... that of a hapless Civil War soldier who fell in love with the daughter of a former owner of the mansion, only to be killed by her protective father and brother. The young man was said to have been murdered in the famed alley of oak trees in front of the house and he has been seen here on many occasions since his death.

Besides these famous haunted places, with only a touch of the Civil War, there are a number of other spots, whose connections to the war go much deeper.

THE BEAUREGARD- KEYES HOUSE
During the daylight hours, the Beauregard-Keyes House in New Orleans plays host to visitors and tourists from across the country, all stopping in to see its rooms with antiques and artifacts of the

past. But some say at night, after the tourists and guides have left for the day, other visitors come to this house... spectral travelers from a time long past. The sounds of gunshots and cannon fire fill the air... the sounds of screaming and men and horses howling in agony as the battlefields of the Civil War are recreated inside the walls of this house!

General Pierre Gustave Toutant Beauregard was one of the leading generals of the Confederate Army. He was the man who gave the order to fire upon Fort Sumpter in April of 1861, he was responsible for the stunning southern victory at Bull Run and will always be remembered as for both his successes and his failures...like the terrible defeat at Shiloh. After the war, the general returned to New Orleans and settled into the house at 1113 Chartres Street in the French Quarter. He took a position as a chief engineer for a railroad, became involved with a streetcar company, became the supervisor for drawings of the Louisiana State Lottery and wrote three books about the Civil War.

There is no record that the house was haunted before the general's death in 1893, or for many years afterward... but it did become the scene of death and tragedy a short time later.

In 1909, the house was purchased by the Giacona family, a well-to-do Italian clan who were known for their dinner parties and gala affairs. One night, neighbors reported hearing the sounds of gunshots and angry shouting at the house. When the police arrived, they found three men dead and a fourth man wounded. The victims were identified as members of the Mafia and it was learned the Giacona's had been victims of an attempted extortion plot. When the family wouldn't pay off, mobsters came after them but the family was ready and killed the would-be assassins.

The attempt to wipe out the family was repeated several times in the years that followed and the Giacona's maintained the house like a fortress. Finally, in the early 1920's, they moved on to more peaceful territory.

In 1925, the new owners of the house decided to convert it into a macaroni factory. A number of concerned residents in the area became worried about the loss of this historic site and an association was formed to buy the house and turn it into a museum to General Beauregard and the Civil War. It later became a National Historic Site.

In the years following World War II, rumors began to surface about the sounds of men in battle coming from the house and from the garden behind it. The sounds were not those of modern arms either... but the sounds of Civil War period pistols, muskets and cannons.

What was going on at the house? Could the residual energies of the Giacona family have been left behind at the house, leaving an imprint on the atmosphere because of the violence that took place? Or could the Civil War itself have left behind an impression... even though no battles had ever taken place at, or even near, the house? Or stranger still... could the books written by General Beauregard have left an impression behind? Perhaps the general's vivid recollections of bloody battles like Shiloh had, in some strange way actually created their own "ghosts"? Could this be possible?

No one knows for sure and the people who manage the house aren't talking. Like many other historic sites in America, the staff members deny that anything strange takes place at the house. The director of the house in 1977, Alma H. Neal, denied all of the stories in an interview. "We do not know of anything supernatural taking place here," she said. Recent tour guides claim the stories are "old wives tales". But are they really?

Do the ghosts of Italian mobsters and Civil War soldiers really haunt the Beauregard house? Try walking down Chartres Street sometime late at night..... and make sure that you listen closely to the sounds of the night!

THE GRIFFON HOUSE

Outside of the French Quarter in New Orleans, stands a house at 1447 Constance Street which has been haunted for as long as anyone in the neighborhood can remember. Whether it is still haunted or not, remains a question, but the stories that have been told about the place over the years can still manage to chill your blood.

The house on Constance Street was built in 1852 by Adam Griffon, who lived there for only a few years, abandoning the house when the Civil War came to New Orleans. When General Benjamin Butler's Union troops occupied the city in the early years of the war, they began selecting homes and buildings in which to house men and supplies. The house on Constance Street was one of the buildings selected for occupation.

The first soldiers who entered the house heard a chilling sound... that of rattling chains and groaning coming from upstairs. In the third floor attic, they found several slaves shackled to the wall and in a state of advanced starvation. They were removed to a field hospital where they could be better taken care of and the house was turned into a barracks for soldiers.... and prisoners.

When Butler occupied New Orleans, he passed an order that anyone caught looting would be shot and this included his own Union troops. Two Union officers were arrested for this offense and were confined to the house on Constance Street. They spent much of their time drinking and singing over and over again the northern song "John Brown's Body".

Actually, this repetitive singing was really a ruse to hide the fact that they were actually Confederate deserters who had stolen the Union uniforms. They were wearing them when they were caught. They knew if they were discovered to be southerners, they would be killed, so they attempted to hide this fact by singing "John Brown's Body".

When they learned that even Union soldiers caught looting would be shot, they bribed a guard to bring them a pair of pistols. They lay down beside each other on the bed, pointed the guns to one another's hearts and pulled the triggers at the same time.

After the war, the building was used for commercial purposes as a lamp factory, a mattress factory and a perfume bottling plant. In the 1920's, it was a union hiring hall and one owner was a old man who rebuilt air conditioners... until he disappeared one day without a trace.

Over the years, the stories of a haunting in the house were many. One occupant claimed to discover blood dripping from the ceiling one day and when she checked the upper floor, she found nothing. Another man was in the building one night alone when he heard the sound of marching boots and the voices of drunken men singing "John Brown's Body".

On another occasion, two owners arrived to open their factory one morning when a huge chunk of concrete came flying down the stairs at them. They charged upstairs to find who was there and discovered the place to be empty... and the floors had been freshly painted the day before, yet they found no footprints.

In August of 1951, New Orleans was hit by a hurricane that took 275 lives. Damage was done all over the city, including on Constance Street. The old slave quarters behind the house was destroyed and when the debris was cleaned out, a tunnel was found running beneath the house and to the street. An old chest was found in the mysterious passage, along with some chains, some old trash and a few uniforms.

In the late 1970's, a family bought the house with the intention of restoring it. In an interview, that said they had experienced nothing strange at the old place.... but for some reason, they never occupied the house. Residents of the decaying neighborhood weren't speaking much after the 1970's, but one anonymous witness told an interesting story. He said that the rundown area (near a housing project) had deteriorated to the point that any abandoned house in the neighborhood had become fair game for drug addicts. The house at 1447 became one of these, but within a month, it had been deserted, even by the addicts. They claimed they saw two white men there in "police uniforms" who walked through walls and sang! The house today belongs to a local sculptor and his family and while they are aware of the haunted history of the house, they have never witnessed anything supernatural. Perhaps the two soldiers have finally found rest.....

COTTAGE PLANTATION
Although it was destroyed nearly 40 years ago, the Cottage Plantation still lingers in the memories of many who live in the area of St. Francisville, Louisiana. The place is remembered for what it used to be, what it became.... and for the ghosts who are said to still walk here.

The Cottage was built in 1824 by Colonel Abner Duncan as a wedding gift for his daughter and her husband, Frederick Daniel Conrad. The house had 22 rooms and was considered one of the finest in the Baton Rouge area. Visitors to the house included such notables as Jefferson Davis, Henry Clay, Zachary Taylor, and the Marquis de Lafayette. The Conrad family itself had esteemed beginnings, tracing its ancestry to George and Martha Washington. In the years before the Civil War, life was very good at the Cottage. They imported furniture, collected a fortune in jewelry and amassed great wealth.

In the 1850's, another man came to live at the Cottage, a traveling teacher named Holt, who would become the private tutor to the Conrad children and Frederick Conrad's personal secretary. Holt became a part of the Conrad family and lived in the house happily until war came.

Life, after the beginning of the Civil War, changed forever. The Union Army took over the Cottage and removed everything that could be found of value, from horses to furniture and jewelry to even the clothing of the children. The troops occupied the plantation and held the family prisoner, being especially brutal with Frederick Conrad and his secretary, Mr. Holt.

After the troops left, the family abandoned the house and it was taken over and used as a hospital for Union soldiers with yellow fever. In the years that followed, this is probably what saved it from being destroyed by vandals. Many had died from the disease in the house and were buried on the grounds.... the fear that the sickness lingered kept many people away.

A few years later, Frederick Conrad died in New Orleans and Holt returned to the abandoned Cottage. He was changed from the light-hearted man who most remembered, becoming a recluse, spending all of his time trying to repair the old house for what remained of the Conrad family, most of whom had been his students. He stopped shaving and was seen wandering the grounds of the Cottage with a long, white beard. Many local people avoided him, but they could never forget the wonderful man that he had once been and made frequent gifts of food to sustain him while he stayed on at the house.

When Holt finally died, friends went through his many trunks and found huge quantities of books and clothing, along with moldy half-eaten biscuits and portions of meals. Holt had taken to walking about the house at night, reliving the happier times in the place, and as he walked, he would munch on biscuits and meat and then throw the uneaten portion into one of his trunks.

Holt's body was taken away and lovingly buried in a local cemetery. The Conrad children would never forget what the man had meant to them....

But many would wonder if her really ever left the Cottage?

As the years passed, the mansion again stood empty. People who lived nearby said it was haunted. No one would go near the house after dark, fearing that Holt's ghost was still there. There were reports of doors opening and slamming by themselves and sightings of apparitions on the grounds. These shadowy figures were often seen, but when investigated, the place was found to be empty.

In the 1920's, the Conrad family began a restoration of the house. Luckily, thanks to the rumors of ghosts and yellow fever, the house had managed to survive fairly intact throughout the years. In the 1950's, it was opened to the public and served as a museum to the memory of the Old South. It attracted a great deal of interest and artists came from all over the world to capture the flair of the south before the Civil War. It was also used at the set for several movies, including *Cinerama Holiday* and *Band of Angels*, starring Clark Gable.

During these days, the rumors of ghosts still persisted. Some visitors would report the sounds of singing and strange music in the house and on the grounds. It seems that in the heyday of the house, before the war, the Conrads would often entertain their guests by having their slaves sing for them and play music. Now, nearly a century later, the sounds of that music could still be heard at the house, a residual and ghostly echo from another time.

Other visitors had their own encounters... with Mr. Holt. He was said to be seen walking through the house, pulling at his long beard and mumbling to himself. One reporter for the *Elks Magazine* even photographed the ghost by accident. He was doing a story about the Cottage and after having his film developed, he noticed the image of an old man looking out the window. He was sure that no one had been there at the time and after showing it the staff members at the house.... they identified the man as Mr. Holt!

On a February morning in 1960, the Cottage burned to the ground. The firemen who were on the scene would later report a very strange incident. It seemed that while they were directing water on the house from the side garden, a man appeared in the upper window of the house. The fire fighters directed him to jump, but he never seemed to notice them or the fire that was all around him. The roof suddenly collapsed and the man was gone. After the fire was put out, they sifted the debris, searching the man's remains.... but they found nothing!

There are nothing but ruins now where the Cottage once stood but there are people who still venture out onto the land and claim to hear the sounds of music and singing there. They also claim to encounter the ghost of Mr. Holt as he wanders about the property.... perhaps still imagining life the way that it was many years ago.

PORT HUDSON

Port Hudson, which is located near Zachary, Louisiana, is one of the almost forgotten footnotes of the war. The events which took place here are barely remembered today and yet to the men who experienced them in 1863, they were so vivid that some of these men, or at least their ghosts, have never left.

By the Spring of 1863, the Union Navy had all but closed the Mississippi River to southern traffic. Only two ports remained open and they were Vicksburg in Mississippi and Port Hudson in Louisiana. Vicksburg was the more important of the two and yet both ports were needed to keep open the stretch of river that ran between them.

The Federal troops needed to secure the river to prevent the Confederates from sending supplies further west so General Ulysses S. Grant moved on Vicksburg, beginning his long siege of the city, and General Nathaniel P. Banks marched toward Port Hudson.

Banks was considered an inept commander, something that was quite common in the Union Army, and had earned his rank as general because of the number of men and supplies he provided to the war effort and not because of his leadership skills. He had lost so many supplies to Stonewall Jackson in the Shenandoah Valley the year before that the Confederates had nicknamed him "Commissary" Banks.

On May 23, Banks moved his army of 30,000 men into a position north of the city. They surrounded the 7,000 Confederates of Major General Franklin Gardner and Banks believed that a decisive push would force Gardner to surrender or be forced back over the 100-foot bluffs that made Port Hudson such a stronghold in the first place.

Banks made his first direct assault on May 27 and was pushed back. The Confederate earthen works around the city seemed impregnable and Banks lost 2,000 men to the Rebel's 200.

At the same time, General William Emory, the commander of the Federal garrison at New Orleans, requested troops from Banks for defense of the city. Banks refused, obsessed with taking Port Hudson.

The siege continued. The Federal troops were sapped of all energy by the terrible heat of southern Louisiana and men began dropping from malaria and other diseases that breed in the swamps. Morale began to wane on the Confederate side too and deserters began slipping over to the Union lines. To make matters worse, a number of the troops on the Federal side had enlistment's that had run out and many of the men were grumbling about going home.

Banks made another attack on Port Hudson on June 13. He ordered a heavy, day-long artillery bombardment but when it was over, Banks' demand for surrender was refused. Convinced that Gardner could not withstand another attack, Banks ordered another frontal assault the following day.

Wave after wave of Federals threw themselves against the Confederate position and were cut down. By the time that it was over, Banks had lost 1800 men to Gardner's 47. It was the most one-sided defeat of the entire war.

Banks knew that he would face a mutiny if he ordered another attack, so the siege continued. By June 29, the Confederate deserters who were still coming in reported that the only meat left inside the garrison were the mules.

Then, on July 4, the fate of Port Hudson was sealed. Vicksburg finally fell to Grant and on July 8, General Gardner received news of the loss. He realized that the defeat of the garrison was eminent and Gardner surrendered Port Hudson on July 9. The siege of Port Hudson, 48 days, was the longest continuous siege, without outside aid, during the war. The Mississippi River now belonged solely to the Union and together with Lee's defeat earlier in the week at Gettysburg, the Confederacy had suffered several blows from which it would never recover.

Today, Port Hudson is a state park which covers more than 600 acres of the original battlefield. There have been a number of curious incidents that have taken place here over the years that lead many to believe that the place is haunted.

One such incident took place in the mid-1980's when a relic hunter and a friend were searching the park late one night. They were hunting in an area that had been inside of the Confederate lines when something caught the attention of one of the men. He looked up and saw the distinct form of a Confederate soldier, standing there and slowly shaking his head. The man called out to his friend but when the other man looked, the soldier vanished. The two men went straight to the ranger's office and reported the event the following morning.

There was another story of a man walking along the railroad tracks close to the northwestern corner of the Confederate lines. Little fighting had taken place there, although one man had been killed there on May 27. The tracks had actually been built in the 1890's and ran near the Confederate earthworks. The incident here occurred on a rainy summer afternoon in the 1970's. It was his habit to walk along the tracks after the rain and pick up small relics that washed up.

His attention was focused downward as he walked and as he stepped from one railroad tie to another, he happened to glance up and see that he was standing directly in front of a Confederate soldier. Startled, the man stumbled and reached out to the soldier to steady himself. He felt right through the apparition. "There was nothing to grab onto but a blast of icy air," he said later.

When he stood back upright again, the soldier had disappeared.

Another encounter involved a park ranger who spent the night in the ranger station at Fort Desperate in the early 1990's. The station is built near the site of the camp of the 15th Arkansas Regiment. The ranger reported that he did not get much sleep that night as he was awakened several times by the voices and sounds of men outside. When he got up to go and see who it was, he found no one.... and no tracks in the wet grass.

Many other visitors have also had their own strange encounters at Port Hudson, especially on the trails that weave throughout the park. It is said that even on the hottest and most humid days, cold spots will mysteriously appear. They report that if they return to the same spot a few minutes later, the cold spot will have disappeared.

This story is similar to encounters that have been related to me by some paranormal investigators who visited Port Hudson in 1997. They walked the trails of the park using devices to measure both temperature changes and anomalous electro-magnetic fields, both of which can signal the presence of ghosts. They discovered that both moving cold spots and strange energy fields that would come and go were literally all over the place. Could the park really be as haunted as the stories claimed?

It would appear that it is.

MARYLAND

The state of Maryland has a unique place in the history of the Civil War. Located to the north of Washington, it was essential to the Union that the state remain loyal to the north. There were many in the state who had sympathies to the south, but ironically, the Confederate forces were usually met with apathy by the people of Maryland and even dislike after they held two of Maryland's cities hostage.

Preferring compromise and neutrality, Maryland remained indecisive during the war. The eastern portion of the state had strong social and economic ties with the south, while the west was loyal to the north. Despite some early question, Maryland would remain loyal to the Union.

The war's first bloodshed occurred here on April 19, 1861 on President Street in Baltimore. The 6th Massachusetts Militia, marching through Baltimore en route to Washington, was pelted with stones by an angry crowd. Shots were exchanged and 4 soldiers and 12 civilians were killed. The crowd was mostly made up of anti-abolitionists who believed the war was about the question of slavery.

To President Lincoln, Maryland was a vital border state that had to kept, forced if necessary, from seceding to the Confederacy. For an entire month, Governor Thomas H. Hicks delayed in calling the Maryland legislature into session. His "masterly inactivity" stalling the disunionists from pressuring the legislature into secession. The city of Baltimore was then placed under martial law and General Benjamin Butler was moved in to occupy Federal Hill, which overlooked downtown Baltimore. The Federal government supervised state affairs, elections were manipulated, Unionists were installed in key government posts, the writ of *Habeas Corpus* was suspended and even persons deemed subversive were arrested. These persons included the mayor of Baltimore and 19 members of the legislature. Maryland has the unique honor of being the only state which was literally forced into remaining in the Union.

Maryland would become a key place of battle during the war. Thanks to the nearby Shenandoah Valley offering such an inviting avenue for invasion, a number of battles and skirmishes took place in central Maryland. General Robert E. Lee, anticipating recruits for the Confederate Army, invaded the state in 1862 but was met with coolness by the residents of the western part of the state. Brutal fighting took place in the South Mountain passes before the battle of Antietam near Sharpsburg. Union General George B. McClellan attacked Lee on September 17 and the battle became the bloodiest single day of the war. Lee held his position but heavy odds eventually forced his retreat into Virginia.

The Confederates returned to Maryland in 1864 during General Jubal Early's raid on Washington. Early levied a ransom from the city of Frederick in the amount of $200,000, while Brigadier General John McCausland levied $20,000 from Hagerstown. On July 9, the Battle of Monocacy took place near Frederick and forced Major General Lew Wallace to fall back toward Baltimore. Early advanced to Silver Spring but after fighting near Fort Stevens forced him back, he decided against his Washington assault and retreated to the south.

All of this, combined with political infighting, deceit and bloodshed, has created a perfect setting for the ghost stories of the state.

COCKY'S TAVERN

The tales of ghosts and haunted houses in Westminster, in Carroll County, are widespread and varied. There are a number of stories around town and one of them is the story of the ghost at Cocky's Tavern on East Main Street.

The tavern was built in the early 1800's and continues to operate today as a place for fine food and spirits.... both the alcoholic and the ethereal kind. The ghost here, or ghosts perhaps, are very active residents and are known for their boot-stomping, phantom footsteps, glass-rattling and picture-moving.

One of the otherworldly residents of the tavern is suspected to be the spirit of a soldier who lost his life nearby during the Civil War. His heavy boots are often heard tramping up and down the tavern's center stairway. He is also said to be fond of other spirits... namely, the liquor that can be found in the establishment's bar. According to what was witnessed by one of the tavern's former owners, the soldier is said to help himself to a drink from the bar, as evidenced by the sound of rattling glasses, vanishing liquor, and reports by tavern customers of an apparitional being who has been seen near the end of the bar itself.

The ghost also seems to be fond of moving things about in the bar. There have been a number of items that have vanished from the bar, only to turn up again in other places in the building. The phantom also amuses himself by moving around the pictures that hang on the walls. The staff members and owners believe this is the way the ghost chooses to express himself.

The story has it that a tired waitress, who was standing near the stairway, complained of the lateness of the evening and of how loud a particular party was in the tavern. As if to express agreement with the waitress, one of the four pictures hanging in the stairway promptly sailed off its hook and landed at the feet of the startled woman.

A second incident occurred when a discussion among some of the guests about the tavern's unexplained activities revealed a skeptic of ghosts. Supposedly, one of the women in the discussion loudly voiced the opinion that there were no such things as ghosts and that she most assuredly did not believe in them. As if on cue, a picture that had been hanging on the wall above the woman's head fell off and struck her.

Needless to say, that was the last time that she expressed such sentiments in Cocky's Tavern.

On one other occasion, the ghost seemed to display a rather sentimental feeling toward one of the tavern's regular patrons. A waitress who was cleaning tables in the dining room noticed that a photograph of General Grant, which usually hung on the nearby wall, had been moved and turned facedown on a table that was regularly frequented by a local lawyer and his wife. Later, the staff learned that the lawyer had passed away on that very night.....

FREDERICK COUNTY

There is no doubt about the fact that Frederick County in Maryland played an important part in the state's history of the war. In October of 1859, when word was received that John Brown had raided the arsenal in Harper's Ferry, the first offer of assistance accepted by President James Buchanan was from Frederick's militia.

In July of 1864, the city of Frederick was forced to pay a ransom to Confederate General Jubal Early. Lee had sent Early to the north to take some of the pressure off the poorly supplied southern troops by harassing northern towns, exacting tribute from those who could pay and to even threaten Washington itself.

Early burned the Maryland home of Union Postmaster General, Montgomery Blair, in retaliation for a Union General razing the Virginia Military Institute. To avenge this fire, General Benjamin Butler sent troops to Fredericksburg to burn down the country home of James Seddon, the Confederate Secretary of War.

During this series of events, Early was ransacking and terrorizing northern cities with demands of payment to keep his men from burning the cities to the ground. Besides Frederick and Hagerstown, Early also threatened Chambersburg, Pennsylvania. When the residents refuse to cough up the money, he burned the business district.

While the people of Frederick eventually paid up, they purposely delayed the negotiations with the Confederates so that Union forces could form a line of defense and prepare for the Battle of Monocacy. While Early was tied up with this, reinforcements were sent by General Grant and after fighting at Fort Daniels, the Confederates were sent back to the south.

Throughout the war, troops of both armies crossed through the state. At one point, Frederick County alone had as many as 17 hospitals for wounded Union and Confederate soldiers. Many area homes and buildings were also commandeered as headquarters for both armies.

There remained a sympathy toward the Confederacy among some Frederick County families. One family welcomed a wounded Rebel soldier into their home and when a company of Union troops appeared, they hid him in their cellar. The Union soldiers were expected to take whatever supplies they could from the house and leave, but unfortunately, they did not. The company commandeered the house as a headquarters and set up a field camp on the front lawn.

They stayed for weeks and the family was unable to get to the cellar and free the wounded Confederate.

Finally, after more than 2 months had gone by, the cellar was opened.... only to find the decayed and rotting corpse of the young southern soldier.

After the discovery of the body, moaning and scratching sounds were often heard in the cellar and below the floor of the kitchen. It was also said that occupants of the house and visitors were often startled to see a young man in a Confederate uniform stomping through the house.

On September 10, 1862 the armies of the south under Generals Lee, Jackson and Longstreet began to march west across Frederick County toward Antietam Creek and Sharpsburg. On September 14, those same armies would be forced to retreat from South Mountain after a costly battle.

There were other places in Frederick County where the fighting extracted a deadly toll from the Confederacy. One such place was on the outskirts of Burkittsville, just below a spot that is now a memorial to Civil War correspondents.

The town of Burkittsville was built in 1807 around a tannery complex, complete with blacksmith shop, which employed about 50 men. General Lee had two wheels of an ambulance repaired there and at another point, Lincoln and McClellan ate a meal in the house next door.

It was here that both armies decided to attack each other by surprise, both at sunrise. The Confederate troops were poorly prepared and while spending several hours positioning cannons on the hill, were attacked by Union troops, armed only with rifles. The southerners retreated, taking heavy losses.

In 1862, the wounded were attended in the tannery and in every other sizable place in town. Many of those buildings are still standing, but the tannery, which was abandoned for years, finally fell into ruin. It was said that strange sounds and voices haunted the area for many years and later, a more unique phenomena began to be reported. It was said that anyone who left their car in the vicinity of where the old tannery once stood would discover that footprints had appeared on it during the night.

Some believe that the soldiers who were killed here have returned to haunt the place. Many of the troops who were killed had to be left behind by their comrades, so the people of Burkittsville buried the men in shallow graves, believing that once the fighting subsided, the armies would come back and bury the men properly. They never did.

The area around the town is also believed to be haunted by soldiers from the past. For many years, there have been accounts of sightings and odd occurrences in the area. Occasionally, eerie campfires can be seen in the mountains and open fields. Phantom soldiers have been seen to be warming themselves near the fires.... only to vanish.

One of the strangest places, located on the edge of town and near the Civil War Correspondent's Memorial Arch, is a place known as Spook Hill. It is said that if you stop your car here, and shift it into neutral, your car will move by itself and pull you back up the hill. Many believe this strange movement is caused by the spirits of the fallen soldiers..... possibly believing that they are still pulling their cannons up that same hill.

MISSISSIPPI

Mississippi became the second state to secede from the Union in 1861 and became the "Republic of Mississippi" under the Confederate States of America. The fact that Confederate president Jefferson Davis hailed from Mississippi gave the state a particular closeness to the new government and then it would go on to have a pivotal role in the Confederacy throughout the war.

Beginning in the spring of 1862, Mississippi became a battleground and there were few sections of the state which did not see destruction and devastation. When the war was over, nearly the entire state lay in ruins.

The city of Vicksburg is perhaps the most historical city in the state, and the one that is perhaps more steeped in history, legend and lore than any other. The siege of the city during the Civil War is perhaps one of the most memorable events of the conflict.

By the autumn of 1862, President Abraham Lincoln had become disgusted with yet another of the generals that he had placed in command of his army. By this time, he had appointed and had dismissed Winfield Scott; Irvin McDowell; George McClellan; John Pope; McClellan again; Ambrose Burnside; and Joseph Hooker.... he knew that he had the men to win the war and end the Confederacy, he just could not find the right man to lead them.

By that fall, he had found the right man, although no one realized quite yet that the man was a hard-drinking farmer from Illinois named US Grant. In early December, Lincoln gave Grant the task of capturing the Mississippi River port of Vicksburg, a city that was of vital importance to the Confederacy. As far as Lincoln was concerned, once Vicksburg fell, the Mississippi would belong to the Union. Naval forces had already tried to seize Vicksburg and had failed. The only option that remained was to try and take it by land.

Under Grant's command, the Army of Tennessee left Memphis for Vicksburg. The drive was spearheaded by a force under General William Tecumseh Sherman, but they were stopped cold in their tracks by Confederate forces at a place called Chickasaw Bluffs.

Grant pushed on and at the end of January 1863, his 45,000 men had reached Young's Point, which lays 20 miles above Vicksburg, on the opposite side of the river. Here, he was met by a Union naval force under Admiral David Dixon Porter, who attempted to attack Vicksburg, only to be repelled. The city, located on a high river bluff, seemed to be impregnable... but Grant would not give up. He knew that the river could not be controlled until they could hold Vicksburg.

For the next two and a half months, Grant tried in vain to dig, cut or float his army through the thick bayous and seize the bluffs on the north and south sides of the city. He even tried digging a canal that would connect one part of the Mississippi to another, allowing Porter's fleet to bypass Vicksburg. They dug for several weeks before abandoning the plan. Nothing seemed to be working and the press began accusing Grant of everything from stupidity to laziness, they also claimed that he was drinking again and began to call for his dismissal.

Finally, in late March, Grant devised his most daring plan... one so foolhardy that even Sherman, never known for his lack of reckless valor, advised against it. Grant decided that he would march down the river, cross below Vicksburg and with no hope of re-supply or reinforcements, come up from behind and take the city. To confuse the Confederate defenders, Sherman was ordered to make an attack north of Vicksburg, while 1700 calvary were directed to go inland and destroy the railroad lines into the city.

The attack was on. For the next three weeks, Grant's army marched more than 180 miles, cut off from all communication with the outside world. They fought and won five major battles between their former position and Vicksburg, out-maneuvered Confederate commander Joseph E. Johnston and finally surrounded Vicksburg itself, trapping a force of 31,000 men under General John C. Pemberton.

The Union forces barreled ahead with an all-out attack on the city, but were beaten back. They tried twice more before Grant settled in for a siege, aided by a constant artillery barrage. The shelling had little effect as the soldiers and civilians vowed to ignore it. It was simple enough for them to burrow into the hills of the city and, so they believed, wait for Grant to leave.

The siege would continue until July... just after the defeat of the southern forces at Gettysburg. Over the course of several months, Grant had been slowly "tightening the noose" around the city. Day by day, his forces had moved closer to the Rebel defenses, while gunboats on the river had pounded Vicksburg without mercy.

Inside the city's borders, civilians had dug more than 500 caves into the hillside, shelters which were dirty and infested with snakes, although effective. Fewer than a dozen of the locals were killed in the shelling and only 30 were injured. Food ran low in the city and soldiers and civilians alike were reduced to eating mules, horses, dogs and a horrible bread made from corn and dried peas. Rats were even sold in the butcher shops and were described as tasting like "squirrels". By late June, almost half of the Confederates were on the sick list or in the hospital.

"The houses were in ruins", wrote one Confederate sergeant, "rent and torn by shot and shell... fences torn down and houses pulled to pieces for firewood... Lice and filth covered the bodies of the soldiers. Delicate women and little children.... peered at the passer-by with wistful eyes from the caves in the hillsides."

Regardless, the city continued to hold out. When there was no more newsprint, the local newspaper was even printed on old wallpaper. The editorials remained defiant.

Finally, General Pemberton decided to surrender, feeling that the toll that had been taken on his men and the civilians of Vicksburg was what he called "a useless waste of life and blood." He surrendered the city on July 4, 1863... the 48th day of the siege. The Union men did not cheer in victory, nor did they jeer their captives. "They knew that we had surrendered to famine, not to them," wrote one Confederate chaplain.

In continued defiance, July 4 would not be celebrated as a holiday in Vicksburg for 81 years.

THE MCRAVEN HOUSE

Perhaps the most famous haunted house in Vicksburg is McRaven, a now beautifully preserved example of southern architecture which somehow survived the devastation of the war and the Federal occupation that followed. The house today is owned Leyland French, who painstakingly maintains the house and keeps it open for tour groups and visitors. The mansion was built during three different time periods and according to the stories, is home to a number of resident spirits... from the era of the Civil War and before.

The most active ghost in the house is said to be that of Mary Elizabeth Howard, who is believed to have died in childbirth here prior to the war. Her husband, Sheriff Stephen Howard, constructed a portion of the house in 1836. Mary's ghost is said to move objects about the house and generally try to make herself known to the visitors to McRaven. She has also been spotted in various forms of attire, from a brown morning dress to a formal gown.... which she was seen wearing during a wedding that was held at the house.

And Mary Howard does not haunt this house alone.

During the siege of Vicksburg, records say that the front yard of the house was the scene of a skirmish known as the Railroad Redoubt. The bodies of the dead and wounded were scattered all about the property and the house itself still bears marks from the battle.

Afterward, the grounds of McRaven were used as a Confederate field hospital and many of the men who did not survive the primitive medical techniques of the time were buried on the property. Many researchers believe that it may be the ghosts of these men who are still seen lingering near the house.

Despite the house being used a battleground, perhaps the most tragic death connected to the place was that of a former owner, who was murdered by Union soldiers during the war. In 1864, more than ten months after the surrender of Vicksburg to General Grant, the owner of McRaven, John H. Bobb and his nephew, Austin D. Mattingly were walking up the road to the house when they noticed a group of Union occupation soldiers on the front lawn. The men were from a nearby encampment and were picking flowers from the yard.

Irritated, Bobb ordered the men to get off his property. Tempers flared and Bobb got into a fight with a sergeant, which resulted in McRaven's owner knocking the other man to the ground with a brick. The angry soldiers retreated, but promised to return and burn the house to the ground.

Bobb went immediately to the headquarters of General Henry W. Slocum, the Union commander in Vicksburg. He assured Bobb that he would restrain the soldiers and make sure that no harm came to him, his family or his home..... but Slocum never got the chance to make good on his promise. Bobb and Mattingly were heading home when they were seized by the same group of soldiers. They were marched down Stout's Bayou and behind the railroad machine shop, Bobb was shot twice and left to die. Somehow, Mattingly managed to escape.

Selina Bobb had followed her husband to Federal headquarters, but not finding him there, started back towards home. When she heard shots ring out near the machine shop, she instinctively turned in that direction. As she grew closer, she heard the shouts of the soldiers and saw her husband crumpled on the ground. She was found, streaked with blood and cradling her slain husband, by a Union Major named Gwinder a short time later. He had been dispatched from headquarters to see what the disturbance was about. He ordered the arrest of the soldiers, but the sergeant was the only man ever charged. What became of the others is unknown....

Selina sold the mansion five years later and then disappeared without a trace.

In 1882, McRaven was purchased by a man named William Murray, whose family would reside there for the next 80 years. Murray was a Yankee who had been wounded at the Battle of Shiloh in 1862. He remained in the military for the next several years and was working as a blacksmith for the occupation army when he met Ellen Flynn in Vicksburg in 1865. They married and went on to raise seven children. He died in the house in 1911.... but some say that he has never left.

The first ghost that current owner Leyland French encountered in the house was the spirit of William Murray. He was coming up the great flying wing staircase when he turned and noticed a solid-looking man coming up behind him. He recognized the former owner from some old photographs that he had seen and admitted being frightened at first. He ran upstairs to the Bobb bedroom, then slammed and locked the door. Since that initial experience, he has come to believe that "all of the spirits in his home are harmless."

Ellen Murray passed away ten years after her husband, followed by two other children who died in the house in the years that followed. Eventually, only two daughters, Annie and Ella, remained alone in the place.

During their solitary years of residence, the house earned a reputation as the local haunted house, mostly thanks to the run-down condition of the place. The two women allowed few visitors and their only regular caller was their doctor, Walter Johnston. When Ella became ill in 1960, Dr. Johnston was called to McRaven to attend to her. He later wrote that Ella's death "was the eeriest thing that I ever experienced in my life"..... although what actually occurred remains a mystery to this day. Annie was sent to a nursing home, where she passed on in 1972.

Not surprisingly though, with this house of spirits, the two sisters are also rumored to have lingered behind. It is said that the two ladies are sometimes seen in the house and in the gardens and that sometimes a favorite piano will plink out a few notes on its own.

The mysteries of McRaven are many, leading no one to claim that they have all of the answers about this beautiful, yet spirited, mansion.

LONGWOOD

Founded by the French in 1700, Natchez is the oldest city on the Mississippi River. Thanks to its location, on the high bluffs over the river, the city fared better than most other southern cities during the war. Many of the large homes in Natchez were used as hospitals and command buildings, saving them from destruction. After the war, most of the local residents found their finances so drained that they were unable to modernize their homes as the years passed. Because of this, many of the buildings in Natchez still have the antebellum look of yesterday.

One of the most legendary of Natchez's old homes is Longwood. The history of this great house is filled with sadness and tragedy and represents the unfinished dream of a broken man whose future was destroyed by the government that he cherished and supported.

The house was started in 1859 by Dr. Haller Nutt and it is said to be his ghost, and the ghost of his wife, who haunts the place.

The design of the house was created by a Philadelphia architect named Samuel Sloan and it resembled an eight-sided castle. It also has a sixteen-sided cupola on the top with an onion-shaped dome. It was designed to be six stories tall and made of brick, marble and plaster with eight rooms on each floor, surrounding a rotunda. Orders were placed which would allow the house to be furnished with expensive European designs, although most of these costly goods would be seized by Federal blockades at the start of the Civil War.

It would be the war that would signal an end to Nutt's dream of his grand and unusual home. The construction on the house continued through 1860 but came to a halt the following Spring when war broke out. The Pennsylvania architect and his workers returned home to fight for the Union, leaving Nutt's home far from complete.... which is exactly how it still stands today.

The Union forces would not reach Natchez until 1863, which gave a few remaining local workers the time to close in the basement of the house and make it into an apartment where the Nutts could live throughout the war. Upstairs, the window openings and doorways were simply boarded up.

The war not only took away Nutt's home, but his wealth as well. Nutt settled his family into the house and watched as the South burned around him. Although he was a Union loyalist, he saw over $1 million of his rich cotton land either burned or confiscated by the Union soldiers. The northern troops also took everything of value from Longwood, including lumber, building supplies, cattle, horses and thousands of bales of cotton. Dr. Nutt withdrew into his own little world, spending his days walking about in the empty corridors of the upper floors of the house. Here, the dust had settled over the abandoned tools and cobwebs stretched between the door frames in silent surrender to the elements. Completely broken and without the will to live, Nutt slowly wasted away from pneumonia and died in 1864. He was only 48 years old.

Before he died, Dr. Nutt filed a claim against the Union forces for damage done to Longwood. It would take many years, but his wife Julia would later receive money from the government, but only enough to allow her to stay on in the unfinished home.

In time, the Nutt children grew up and moved away. Julia remained at Longwood with an unmarried daughter until 1890, when she passed away at the age of 75. A grandson, James Ward, then moved into the house. He became a recluse, rarely leaving the place, and he allowed the house to deteriorate badly. Although the mansion remained sound, the paint began to fade and the wooded grounds became overgrown and tangled with weeds and brush.

Not surprisingly, stories of ghosts and strange happenings began to circulate.

It was said that phantom footsteps were often heard coming from the upper floors of the house, as though Dr. Nutt was still roaming about the dilapidated mansion in despair. At times, the footsteps were reported pacing back and forth for hours on end.... with no rational explanation.

Locals dubbed the house "Nutt's Folly" and the Nutt family descendants remained in the house for a number of years before finally donating it to the Pilgrimage Garden Club of Natchez, who maintains it today and who conducts tours of the premises. After taking over ownership of the house, the local group had it restored back to the condition that it was in when Dr. Nutt was still living there. All of the remaining tools and building materials were left exactly as they were when the northern workers fled the coming war. The upper floors remain unfinished today, but have been reinforced for visitors to explore the place in safety.

Author Richard Winer spoke to the caretakers of the house in the late 1970's and they reported that visitors to Longwood often reported strange noises there and, among other things, the spectral smell of jasmine which permeated the air at various times. Some researchers have connected this smell to perfumes used in the late 1800's.

Perhaps a favorite of Julia Nutt?

The caretakers also spoke of an occasion when some documentary filming was being done at the site and a local, off-duty fireman volunteered to watch over the equipment during the night time hours. Before the night was over, the fireman was so frightened that the caretakers (who lived on the premises) had to stay with him until daylight.

Longwood remains one of the most unusual sites in the south.... and if the stories are to be believed, the spirits who reside within it are still making their presence known.

THE DEASON HOUSE

The Civil War left an indelible mark on the state of Mississippi but the old home of Amos Deason is a place where the Civil War does not seem to have completely ended.....

The house was built in 1845 by Amos Deason, one of the wealthiest men in the region. While you wouldn't know it by visiting the house today, there are many dark secrets here which remain hidden... from a blood stain that will not fade to a door that opens by itself on the anniversary of a terrible event.

At the time of the Civil War, the people of Jones County in Mississippi were mostly poor farmers who owned few slaves. When the question of secession from the Union began to be addressed, the Jones County people refused to get involved. They instructed their delegate to the secession convention in Jackson to vote against withdrawing from the Union. But when he arrived in Jackson, he was caught up in the excitement and voted with the secessionists. His angry neighbors hanged him in effigy.

Reluctantly, Jones County prepared for war. It was said that Amos Deason prepared for the coming war in his own way by burying his gold on his property for safe-keeping.

During the war, the old men, women and children were left behind while the younger men went off to fight. The property was left nearly defenseless and the people struggled to survive. To make matters worse, the Confederate cavalry, whose job it was to find food and supplies for the army, descended on Jones County, raiding farms and taking food and farm animals that the people could not afford to give.

At the beginning of the war, some Jones County men joined the Confederacy but others refused until the draft was instituted in 1862. One of those was a farmer named Newt Knight. He refused to fight for a cause he did not believe in, although when he was drafted, he did serve as a hospital orderly.

Knight reached his breaking point when he learned that if a man owned 20 or more slaves, he could avoid military service. Knight, and the other poor farmers from Jones County, felt they were right then they suspected the conflict was a "rich man's war and a poor man's fight." At this point, Knight deserted and went home.

He banded together with other deserters and formed a renegade army which was based in the Leaf River Swamp. Their hideout, known as the Devil's Den, was called home for over 100 Confederate deserters. They came out of the swamp to visit their families, work their farms and according to the stories, conduct raids on trains headed to and from Mobile. The men devised elaborate methods of communication and signals to alert them to impending danger.

And that danger was very real...... Despite a large number of Jones County deserters, most of the people in the area remained loyal to the south. To these people, Newt Knight and his men were criminals and they refused to offer them safe harbor in Jones County. In addition, Confederate troops were determined to capture Knight and his men. They raided the woods and the swamps, looking for the renegades, but with no success. Finally, the Confederacy sent Major Amos McLemore, a native of Jones County, to capture Knight.

McLemore knew the swamps nearly as well as Knight and was determined to bring him in. He and his men ransacked the woods, getting dangerously close to Knight's hideout. Knight realized that something had to be done.... McLemore had to be killed.

The Major had made his headquarters in the home of Amos Deason, a loyal Confederate man, so Knight decided to go to the Deason home to kill McLemore. One wet, rainy afternoon in September, after McLemore had returned to the house, Knight threw open the door. He found McLemore standing in front of the fireplace and he shot him point-blank. McLemore gasped "I'm killed!" as he fell to the floor in a pool of spreading blood. McLemore's men chased after Knight, but he managed to escape back into the swamp.

The legends say that McLemore's blood seeped into the pine flooring of the Deason house and no matter how much scrubbing was done, it would never disappear. After many years of seeing the blood, descendants of the Deason's finally covered the wooden floor with new flooring. This may have hidden the blood stain, but it did not stop the front door of the house from bursting open on the anniversary of the murder each year.... only to reveal an empty, silent porch.

Simply an echo from the past? Or the restless spirits of the participants from this deadly event of long ago? We may never know these answers for sure....

LOCHINVAR PLANTATION

Lochinvar Plantation is a true part of the old south, steeped in the lore of the southern states and drenched in the traditions of long ago. Built in the late 1830's, the mansion was home to the Gordon family for many years and watched over by an old caretaker. The Gordon family is long gone now.... but the legends say that the old caretaker still watches over the place.

Lochinvar was built by Robert Gordon, a Scottish adventurer, in the late 1830's as a gift for his wife. At the time, Gordon owned a strip of land which stretched all of the way from Pontotoc to Aberdeen, sixty miles away. Aberdeen was Gordon's own town. He had founded a trading post there in the early 1830's and named the place Dundee in honor of a town in Scotland. He later changed to the name to Aberdeen. It was near Pontotoc where Gordon found the land where he wanted to build his home. The location that he chose had been the land of the Choctaw Indian chief, Chinubi and once the Indians were gone from the area, he began building the new house.

After moving into the grand mansion, the Gordons would have one child, a son named James. His earliest memories of Lochinvar included magnificent parties and his personal servant, named Ebenezer. He could not remember a time when Ebenezer had not been a part of his life. He taught James to hunt and fish, told him stories, supervised his manners and when he was old enough, packed his trunks and watched him leave for the University of Mississippi at Oxford in 1851.

As the years passed, the beloved slave grew older and became known by the respectful name of "Uncle Eb". He remained particularly close to James Gordon and their relationship went far beyond that of just master and servant.

In February of 1856, James married Virginia Wiley and in December of that year, their daughter Annie was born. From that time that she could walk, Annie was attached to Uncle Eb. She followed him everywhere and begged him to push her on the swings and to tell her stories. Delighted, Uncle Eb took under his wing a new generation of Gordons.

Then came the Civil War. Robert Gordon, now too old to be involved, gave his support and advice to James and they raised a company of Confederate cavalry, the first from northern Mississippi. Before James Gordon left for service, he called Uncle Eb to see him. "Take care of my family and the plantation," he told his mentor, "My father needs your help and I need to know that you are here with my family. Don't let anything happen to them and I'll be back home soon." He embraced the older man and told him goodbye.

This began Uncle Eb's role as the caretaker and guardian of Lochinvar. Every afternoon, he would begin his rounds of the property, making sure the gates were closed, the doors to the house were locked and that there were no strangers lurking around the plantation. He moved his bed to the hallway outside of Annie's door, where he slept from that night on. He took to roaming the grounds at various times throughout the night, carrying an oil lantern and making sure that everything was secure.

As time passed, he learned other skills and began making repairs on the house and the farming equipment. He learned to cook and prepare the meals and even to darn socks and make repairs on clothing.

Night after night, the light from Uncle Eb's lantern circled the house, the barn, the garden, the pasture and the orchards, reassuring himself that nothing was amiss and that the people he loved were safe.

One night, while Uncle Eb was on his rounds, a rider approached. It was Captain James Gordon, home for a brief stay at Lochinvar. A few days after he left, he was promoted to the rank of Colonel, returning to combat with the 2nd Mississippi Cavalry Regiment, Armstrong's Brigade.

Colonel Gordon and Uncle Eb would never meet again.

One rainy night, Uncle Eb was roused from his sleep by a strange sound. He took his lantern outside and crossed the grounds in the storm. He was soaked to the skin before he was sure that everything was secure. A day or so later, what seemed to be a cold developed into pneumonia. In less than a week, old Uncle Eb was dead.

It was a long time before Colonel Gordon received word of his friend's death. He was in England at the time on a mission for President Davis. On his way home, he landed in North Carolina and was captured and imprisoned. He soon escaped and made his way to Canada. There, he met and befriended an actor named John Wilkes Booth. This casual friendship with Booth later pointed suspicion to Gordon when President Abraham Lincoln was assassinated. Luckily, Gordon was able to prove his innocence.

After the war, Gordon finally learned that Uncle Eb had passed away while carrying out his duties to the plantation.

Many believe that since Uncle Eb died before the war ended and before his guardianship of the Gordon home came to an end.... he has not rested in peace in the years since the Civil War. As the years have passed, his oil lantern is still seen roaming the grounds of the Lochinvar estate. It has been seen for decades and locals believe that the light belongs to the spirit of Uncle Eb, watching over his beloved family throughout eternity.

MISSOURI

The Civil War conflicts in Missouri are nearly forgotten today by those more interested in the epic battles of the south and the east. There are many who do not even remember that the issues which first boiled over into violence became so heated in what was then known as the "west". As the issues of the middle 1800's began to simmer into war, the American continent was only half settled. Beyond the Mississippi was a large, untamed area that was only beginning to enjoy the social structures that were so common in the east. In some areas, the division between the north and the south was taken very seriously and small battles were waged on a personal basis... family against family, one from the northern states and one from the southern. In other areas, the west was simply the frontier, where simple survival took precedence over politics and war.

The western state of Missouri had been in the thick of things almost from the very beginning. The act that made Missouri a state, the Compromise of 1820, had been an effort to balance the pro-slavery and anti-slavery scale more than 40 years before the war actually began. After that, the partisans who "made Kansas bleed" in the 1850's, became the guerilla fighters who burned and murdered across Missouri during the years of the war.

But Missouri was always torn in two directions. The state's early settlers had come from the south, yet her economy was linked directly to the north. The state's elected officials were mainly secessionists and intended to link Missouri to the Confederacy. They nearly succeeded in 1861 when the battle at Wilson's Creek drove the Federal Army out of much of the state.

The Union forces soon returned under the command of Major General Samuel Curtis, who managed to drive the Confederates out of Springfield. He followed them into northern Arkansas, where Major General Earl Van Dorn was waiting with a Confederate force of his own. Curtis soundly defeated the southerners at Elk Horn Tavern, seemingly putting Missouri in Federal hands. The Union Army even managed to hold onto northern Arkansas, where they threatened Little Rock and parts of Louisiana and Texas.

Unfortunately for Curtis, he had not counted on the rough territory of the region, nor the fact that the borders of southern Missouri were nearly impossible to defend. He may have held Missouri on paper, but in reality, his grasp was tenuous at best. The Rebels regularly led expeditions into the state and fighting raged in small pockets throughout the war. In fact, a total of 1,162 battles and skirmishes were fought in Missouri during the official years of the war, a total exceeded only by Virginia and Tennessee.

More dangerous than the military expeditions and regular army campaigns were the bushwhacking raids of the guerillas. The fact that Missouri was still considered little more than a frontier state seemed to add a savage madness to the war here. The years of border wars with Kansas had created a hatred that led many Kansas militants to prepare for an all-out invasion of the neighboring state. It seemed that Missouri had gained a reputation for being populated with slavers, secessionists, and border ruffians.

The most outspoken and radical of the Kansas men was Senator James H. Lane of Lawrence. Lane demanded retribution against secessionists and slave-holders and his "Jayhawkers" robbed and murdered throughout Missouri. One of the most bloody raids was an action directed by Lane against the town of Osceola, Missouri. The entire town was plundered and burned and nine Osceola citizens were executed. Needless to say, this turned a number of pro-Union and otherwise neutral Missourians into rabid Confederate supporters.

Missouri was quick to retaliate, in just as savage of a fashion. The leading guerilla bands, under William Clarke Quantrill, "Bloody Bill" Anderson, George Todd and William Gregg, were mostly backwoods farm boys. All of them seemed to share on thing in common though... all came from families who had been harassed, intimidated, robbed, burned out, or murdered by Federal soldiers or Kansas volunteers. These men would become the prototype for the outlaws of the post-war west. They attacked, using only light weapons, but with an element of surprise that only small bands of riders can utilize. They were not above sneak attacks, guerilla warfare and shooting their enemies in the back. Thanks to the amount of local support they enjoyed, they found it easy to outmatch detachments of Union troops. Often, they would even dress in blue uniforms and hail the Federal columns as comrades before opening fire on them. It was a brutal and ruthless method of fighting, but dangerously effective.

The guerilla bands even had Union General Henry W. Halleck to thank for bringing new recruits to their ranks. Halleck passed a declaration of "no neutrality", which meant that those who were not for the Union, would be considered against it. Then, he decreed that all civilians caught with weapons would be tried and executed on the spot. Executions were soon extended to any Confederate soldiers captured in Missouri and sometimes even to townspeople who were chosen at random to serve as examples. This sort of sanctioned brutality, along with heavy taxation of towns in guerilla territory, only served to send more men to the ranks of the bushwhackers.

In 1863, the Federals began a new method of attacking the guerillas. They began imprisoning the friends and families of the guerillas, along with anyone who provided food, weapons, information or shelter to the men. In August, a group of women, including Bill Anderson's sisters and Cole Younger's cousin, were imprisoned in a condemned brick building in Kansas City. A few days later, the building collapsed, killing four women and injuring others. The tragedy sparked an uproar in the south and newspapers accused Federal authorities of destroying the building on purpose.

Quantrill used the heated anger toward the Union to bring several guerilla bands together for a massive raid on Senator Lane's home of Lawrence, Kansas. Within six days of the tragedy in Kansas City, Quantrill had almost 500 raiders on the outskirts of Lawrence. They struck the unsuspecting town at dawn, burning and shooting, dragging men from their beds, and killing them in their own homes. Stores and homes were looted and destroyed and the guerillas killed every man who looked big enough to be able to carry a gun. Senator Lane, who happened to be in Lawrence on vacation, hid behind a log in his back yard and managed to escape.

Brigadier General Thomas Ewing's response to the raid was swift and deadly. His Order No. 11 virtually stripped the population from a four-county area near the Kansas border, requiring everyone who lived there to move out. He made no distinction between the Union and Confederate sympathizers... all of them were forced to abandon their homes, possessions and work. The order drew harsh criticism from the press, both northern and southern, but Ewing would not be deterred.

In the end, the order was fairly useless, because it did nothing to defuse the guerilla war. Within a few months, Quantrill's raiders destroyed a large Federal garrison at Baxter Springs, Kansas, then captured and slaughtered the escort party of Major General James G. Blunt, the commander of the District of the Frontier.

The campaigns, raid and guerilla actions continued throughout the war and while they alone would not decide the question of the war, they would certainly manage to keep things bloody and violent for nearly four years. They would also serve as a training ground for future violence to come, providing valuable lessons for men like Union scout "Wild Bill" Hickok, a 7th Kansas recruit named William F. Cody and of course, for the James and Younger gangs.... who would leave the most lingering mark on the state of Missouri.

THE JAMES FAMILY FARM

One would almost be surprised if the James Farm, near Kearney, Missouri was NOT haunted! It was hear that Zerelda Cole James Sims Samuel was married to three different husbands and bore eight children. It was also here that she saw her son Archie murdered by Pinkerton detectives in an attack where she lost her right hand. She also saw one of her husbands tortured and driven insane here and she lived in this house while her two famous, outlaw sons eluded capture, sometimes with her devoted assistance. She also guarded over the property where her son Jesse, after his murder, was buried in a grave that she could see from her bedroom window. Zerelda spent her years of widowhood on the farm, as did her daughter-in-law, Annie Ralston James.

And mostly they remained here alone, bereft of companionship save for the company of their household servants, a family of slaves who remained at the farm long after they were set free.

The James Family Farm has always had a reputation for being haunted... with lights that move about in the house and on the property, sounds of pounding hooves, shots, gun fire and cries that seem to come from nowhere. It has had a long and bloody history, dating back to events of the Civil War.

Robert Sallee James was a farmer and Baptist preacher who graduated from Georgetown College in Kentucky in 1843, just two years after he met Zerelda Cole at a revival meeting and married her. They settled on a farm in Clay County, Missouri and there, Zerelda gave birth to four children named Alexander Franklin (Frank); Robert (who only lived 33 days); Jesse Woodson; and Susan Lavina.

Reverend James was a well-liked and respected man in the community and in 1850, he was asked to serve as chaplain to a wagon train of local men who were going west to California to search for gold. Little is known as to what became of the Reverend, save for the fact that he died in a Placerville mining camp on August 18, 1850 and was buried in an unmarked grave.

Zerelda, faced with raising her children alone, married a neighboring farmer in 1852. He was killed in a horse accident a short time later, and in 1855, she married Dr. Rueben Samuel, a kindly doctor and farmer. She would go on to raise four more children with Dr. Samuel and he became the only father the James children would ever know.

The area where the James family resided was near the turbulent Missouri-Kansas border and it was hard to ignore the violence around them. Zerelda, who is remembered as a formidable frontier woman, had been raised in Kentucky and was a slave owner, so there was no question that at the outbreak of the war, her sympathies were directed toward the south. It came as no surprise in May of 1861 that Frank James enlisted in the Confederate Army. He fought under General Sterling Price in the battle of Wilson's Creek in southwest Missouri, then after a brief period at home, joined up with Quantrill and his band of raiders. Frank, and his friend, Thomas Coleman "Cole" Younger, from Lee's Summit, Missouri, were with Quantrill during the 1863 raid on Lawrence, Kansas.

Just three months after the Lawrence raid, a party if Union soldiers invaded the Samuel farm looking for information about the location of Quantrill's camp. Jesse, who was just fifteen at the time, was questioned, then horse-whipped when he refused to answer the soldier's questions. Dr. Samuel, who also denied knowing where the raider's camp was located, was dragged from his house and was repeatedly hanged from a tree in the yard. Somehow, the doctor managed to survive the interrogation, but his mental state was so affected by the ordeal that he was placed in an asylum in St. Joseph. He remained there until his death in 1908.

Jesse, at the age of only 16, but with a hatred for the Union, joined up with the raiders in early 1864. He went to war under the command of "Bloody Bill" Anderson, a comrade of Quantrill with a reputation for being even more ruthless. Jesse would later take part in a battle at Centralia, Missouri where 25 Union prisoners were shot down. He was also credited with the murder of Major A.V.E. Johnson, the Federal officer who led 100 men in pursuit of Anderson's band.

Jesse's Civil War service also included fighting in support of Colonel Jo Shelby's brigade in Northwest Arkansas, at Cane Hill near the Indian Territory and at Big Cabin Creek. He was mustered out in the spring of 1865 when he rode into Lexington, Missouri carrying a white flag. He was shot in the chest when he attempted to surrender.

After the war, he went to Rulo, Nebraska to recuperate from his wound and then returned to Missouri. He was living in Kansas City, with his aunt, when he fell in love with his cousin, Zerelda (named for Jesse's mother) Mimms. He became known as a very likable young man, standing just five feet nine and weighing only 135 pounds. He always dressed well, enjoyed a good practical joke, read his bible and always went to church. It was said that he never swore or took the Lord's name in vain, preferring when he was angry to make up his own swear words. His favorite was "Dingus!", which became his brother Frank's favorite nickname for him.

In 1866, Jesse, Frank and their friends, Cole and Jim Younger, gained a new profession when they engaged in the country's first peacetime bank robbery. On February 13, they robbed the Clay County Savings Association Bank in Liberty, Missouri and made off with around $60,000 a considerable fortune at that time. Several innocent bystanders were caught in the gunfire and killed.

And a new legend was born.

Over the course of the next 16 years, the names of the James-Younger gang would achieve both fame and notoriety. But the outlaws did not continue with their new profession right away. In fact, Frank and Jesse actually went to California for a time and did not return back east until 1868. When they did, meeting up with the Youngers around the Kentucky-Tennessee border, they discovered that the newspapers were blaming them for a number of robberies that had taken place in their absence. To live up to their reputation, they then proceeded to rob a bank in Russellville and made off with about $14,000.

Jesse and Frank spent most of 1868-1869 in the Nashville area, living under assumed names and spending their robbery proceeds at racetracks in Tennessee, Kentucky and southern Illinois.

Then, for the next 12 years, they stayed on the move, sometimes working with the Youngers and sometimes in partnership with other stage, train and bank robbers.

On December 7, 1869, Jesse and Frank robbed a bank in Gallatin, Missouri which gained them only $700 in cash but ended in the death of a teller named John Sheets. It turned out that Jesse hated Sheets, who was a former Union officer who may have been involved in the death of Bill Anderson. Jesse shot him in the back of the head. The Gallatin robbery resulted in a $3000 reward being posted for the brothers.

Shortly after this, began a public relations campaign, started by Zerelda James, during which the brothers were blamed for pretty much.. none of their crimes. This began the folksy tales of the James gang and their roles as Robin Hood figures, stealing from the rich and giving to the poor.

In 1874, Jesse took a respite from robbery and settled down for a time to marry and live with Zee Mimms, who he took to Texas for a honeymoon. Frank would marry a young lady named Annie Ralston later that year and their lives settled down... at least for a brief time.

In 1871, several bankers and railroad owners had hired Alan Pinkerton's famous national detective agency to track down the James gang. By the early part of 1875, Pinkerton himself had become infuriated by the agency's failure to arrest even a single member of the gang. Desperate times called for desperate measures...

In January 1875, Pinkerton had an agent posing as a field hand at work on a farm across the road from the Samuel Place. One afternoon, the agent thought he spotted Jesse and Frank at the farm house.... although in reality, the brothers were many miles away. On January 26, a force of Pinkerton detectives, brought in by special train, surrounded the Samuel farm house and tossed an incendiary device through the window. The bomb exploded and struck and killed Jesse's young half-brother Archie. The blast also mangled Zerelda's right forearm so badly that it had to be amputated at the elbow.

The Pinkertons later said the device was a flare, but contemporary newspaper reports simply called it "a bomb". It would later be discovered that the device had been a grenade-type explosive which had been obtained at the Rock Island, Illinois arsenal.

In August of that same year, Zee James gave birth to a son named Jesse Edward on a farm that Jesse had leased near Waverly, Missouri. It would be at this farm where plans for the Northfield, Minnesota Raid would be devised.

Jesse and Frank traveled to Minnesota in the company of the three Younger brothers, two Quantrill veterans named Clell Miller and Charlie Pitts and a local outlaw named Bill Chadwell. The gang had been lured up north by Chadwell's tales of easy pickings in his home state and so they began a tour of the region, gambling and staying in whorehouses in St. Paul, then meeting up in a town called Mankato, which they planned to make their first target.

Before they could act, Jesse was recognized and they left town. Riding in pairs, they headed out for Northfield, located 50 miles to the northeast. They met on the outskirts of town on September 6, cased the First National Bank, then made plans to rob it the following morning.

At dawn, they rode quietly into Northfield, wearing long, linen dusters over their clothes and sidearms. Jesse, Bob Younger and Charlie Pitts rode into town, ate breakfast and then sauntered over to the bank, where they tied their horses out front. At that moment, the other five men suddenly rode into town, firing their six-guns into the air, shouting and hollering and scattering the people who were on the streets. While this was happening, Jesse, Bob and Charlie charged into the bank with their guns drawn. Jesse clobbered a bank teller and Bob Younger forced the other employees and customers to their knees while he cleaned out the drawers of cash. One clerk ran out the back door and was shot down by Charlie Pitts.

Meanwhile, the five outlaws outside of the bank were starting to draw gun fire from the local citizens. Clell Miller was hit by a shotgun blast and was knocked from his horse. He was the first to die.

Inside of the bank, Jesse shot the bank teller that he had clubbed and the men ran outside. A crossfire had erupted from the surrounding buildings and the seven outlaws were caught in the middle of it. Bill Chadwell was shot from his horse and killed. Cole Younger got a bullet in the shoulder. Frank was hit in the leg. A bullet struck Jim Younger in the face and his brother Bob's horse was shot out from under him. Bob was hit in the thigh and in the right arm before his brother Cole could pull him onto his own horse.

The Northfield Raid was over in 20 minutes and the outlaws arranged to meet between the town and Mankato. After that, they scattered to the wind. Jesse and Frank headed out for the Dakota Territory. The Youngers were captured one week later, just east of Mankato. In the shootout that followed, Charlie Pitts was killed and the Youngers, all of them wounded, surrendered. Each was sentenced to a life term in prison.

Jesse and Frank pulled off a few more jobs over the next five years including a train robbery at Glendale, Missouri, a stage hold-up near Mammoth Cave, Kentucky, and a few others... but the Northfield disaster really marked the beginning of the end for the James brothers.

In 1879, Jesse took his family to Nashville and they lived for a time with Frank and Annie. That year, Zee gave birth to a daughter, Mary Susan, and Jesse took her to visit the Mimms family in

Kansas City. Shortly after, on Christmas Eve 1881, they moved to St. Joseph, Missouri where he rented a house under the name of Thomas Howard.

Here, Jesse began planning his last great bank robbery. He had decided to call it quits and retire, with enough money to become a gentleman farmer. He planned to purchase some land in Nebraska with the proceeds from this last robbery.

At this point, the Youngers were all in prison and Frank was running from the law himself, so Jesse took on two new gang members, Bob and Charley Ford. They planned to rob the Platte City Bank in Kansas City and on April 3, 1882, Jesse called the Fords to his home in St. Joseph to discuss the job. Jesse was relaxing in the parlor, reading the newspaper and Zee was working in the kitchen. The three men sat down and talked for awhile and then Charley went out into the backyard while Bob made small talk with Jesse.

As he was reading, he glanced up and noticed that a framed needlepoint picture, done by his mother, was hanging crookedly on the wall. He moved a cane chair over to the wall and stepped up to straighten it, his back to the room.

When he turned, Bob Ford pulled out a revolver and shot Jesse just below the right ear.

The gun shot resounded throughout the house and Jesse's children were the first to reach him. In seconds, Zee followed and tried desperately to stop the blood that was pouring from her husband's head. Bob Ford ran from the house, jumped the back fence and vanished. Charley spent a few moments trying lamely to explain the shooting as an accident, then he ran off after his brother.

In a few minutes, the authorities arrived and Zee tried to continue the masquerade that Jesse was actually a businessman named Tom Howard. This was shattered when the Fords returned to the house and revealed Jesse's true identity. Zee soon grew to believe that the assassination had been arranged by Missouri Governor Thomas T. Crittenden, who had previously offered a reward of $10,000 for Jesse James, dead or alive. And Zee may have been right... as Crittenden quickly pardoned the Fords for previous crimes and awarded them the bounty.

A coroner's inquest was held on April 4 and Zee and others formally identified the body. Jesse was then packed in ice and taken by train to Kearney, where he was displayed and viewed by hundreds of friends and admirers, including many old Quantrill veterans. Jesse was later buried on the family farm with only close family and friends present. His seven-foot deep grave was placed near Zerelda's front door, so that she could keep an eye out for trespassers and souvenir hunters.

Later, when Zerelda could no longer live alone, her son's body was moved, on July 29, 1902, to the Mount Olivet Cemetery in town. Zee had died in 1900 and Jesse was placed next to her.

Frank James was present at the re-burial of his brother. He had surrendered to Governor Crittenden on October 5, 1882 but despite the efforts of the state's attorneys, all cases against Frank were thrown out of court for lack of evidence and dismissed. He worked at various honest jobs for the rest of his life and in 1903, joined with Cole Younger (who had been paroled in 1901) in the James-Younger Wild West Show. Frank died at the James Farm on February 18, 1915.

Bob Ford, who became known as "the dirty little coward who shot Mr. Howard" was forced to leave Missouri after being pardoned by Governor Crittenden. He traveled about the west, spending some time performing in a stage show about (ironically) the James gang. He was shot and killed in Creede, Colorado in 1892, by an ex-policeman named Ed O. Kelly.

Ten years before, Charley Ford had committed suicide in Richmond, Missouri.

Jesse may have been re-buried beside his wife in the Mount Olivet Cemetery in 1902... but the question remains as to whether or not he really rests in peace?

Strange disturbances at the family farm have been commonplace for many years.. as have the unusual stories. In 1982, the Kansas City *Star* newspaper arranged an overnight vigil in the house, which was held on the 100th anniversary of the death of Archie Samuel, the only person to ever die violently in the house. Unfortunately, the three men, two from Chicago and the third a writer for the newspaper, experienced nothing more than cold chills in the house. Milton F. Perry, a curator of the house museum explained that this was typical... of any old unheated house in January.

Despite this less than encouraging "ghost hunt", people who work in the house, who are mostly volunteers and staff members of the museum, claim to have had some interesting experiences. They have been present when doors have slammed closed on their own, when lights have been seen moving about in the locked house and when a presence has been so intense in the house that guides refuse to be there alone.

One staff member also admitted that she has, more than one time, heard the low voices of men in the woods near the house and has heard the sounds of restless horses, when no horses are present. On several occasions, she has even gone into the woods later and has found no sign or tracks that any (living) horses had been there.

Restless phantoms... or the sounds of the violent past simply replaying themselves, like a needle stuck in a record groove on an old Victrola? You be the judge...

STEPHENS COLLEGE

In 1862, the Civil War was raging throughout the land and it was during this time that one of the greatest ghost stories of Missouri was said to have begun. The place was the Columbia Baptist Female College (now Stephens College), near Columbia, and the events that took place here occurred shortly after the defeat of Sterling Price's Confederate forces at Pea Ridge, Arkansas. This defeat brought an end to organized Confederate resistance in Missouri, save for the bushwhackers, and paved the way for the Federal occupation.

A short time after, Union forces, under the command of General Henry Halleck, moved into Columbia, upsetting the populace and most especially Dr. Hubert Williams, the president of the local Female college and its dean, Miss Clara Armstrong. The presence of the soldiers was of great concern and they feared for the safety of the young female students, as soldiers are not often known for their gentlemanly behavior.

One evening after dinner, a student named Sarah June Wheeler, was hurrying up to her room. She had just stepped inside when a soldier climbed over her window sill and staggered across the floor. Needless to say, Sarah was quite surprised, although even more shocked to see that the man wore, not the uniform of the local soldiers, but the dirty and bedraggled gray of the Confederacy.

Before Sarah could call out for help, the young man had grabbed hold of her and clapped his hand over her mouth. She struggled to get free of him and the man suddenly just slumped to the floor, unconscious. Just then, the door to the room opened and Sarah's room mate, Margaret Baker, came inside. She was also surprised, although not as frightened to see a Rebel soldier as Sarah had been. Margaret was a resident of the south, having been born and raised in Arkansas. She was fiercely loyal to the Confederacy and instead of payment to the school, her father had sent two slaves to work at the college instead. They cooked, cleaned and worked in the school's laundry.

Sarah and Margaret knelt down beside the soldier and looked to see if he had any injuries. They found nothing, so using some smelling salts, were able to revive him. He explained that he had collapsed from hunger because he had not eaten in days. The girls helped him into a chair, then Margaret sent her servants to bring back a tray of food from the kitchen. They were given strict instructions to say nothing of the soldier.

The young man proceeded to introduce himself as Corporal Isaac Johnson from Mississippi. He said that he had fought at Pea Ridge and had recently escaped from a prison in Illinois, traveling by night and hiding during the day. His father had been killed in Grant's attack on Nashville and Johnson had vowed to avenge his death in some way. The plan that he had come up with was to sneak into Columbia and assassinate General Halleck.

There was something about the young man that appealed to the girls, especially to Sarah, and they agreed to try and keep him safe. Their room was located in Senior Hall, just beneath the school's bell tower, and over the coming days, Sarah hid Johnson away. She brought him food and talked with him into the early hours of the morning. It was not long before the young couple had fallen in love.

But their relationship was doomed from the start...

Someone, possibly one of Margaret's slaves, let the secret slip that a Rebel soldier was hidden in Columbia. Eventually, word reached General Halleck's staff and it was hinted that the soldier was being sheltered by one of the young women at the college. General Halleck paid a call on President Williams and warned him that the school would be closed unless the soldier was captured.

That evening, Dr. Williams addressed the young women and explained to them what Halleck had threatened. Quickly, Sarah returned to her room and urged Johnson to surrender... but he had a better idea. He had stolen a suit from Dr. William's closet, and in disguise, he would escape to Canada.

The plan seemed perfect, except for the fact that Sarah's secret had somehow become public knowledge to the other young women at the school. A crowd gathered near Sarah's room and in loud voices, they urged her to turn the soldier over the Federals. The clamor grew louder until Dr. Williams and Dean Armstrong appeared.... behind them was General Halleck himself.

The college, the General stated, was now officially closed! The young women were told to pack up their belonging and be on their way before first light!

Just then, Corporal Johnson appeared from Sarah's room and surrendered himself. He begged that Halleck let the students remain and explained that he had been hiding there without their knowledge. Halleck reluctantly agreed and proceeded to arrest Johnson as a spy. Ironically, as he was now wearing civilian clothing, he was no longer afforded the rights of a soldier. A spy who was captured behind enemy lines was sentenced to death.....

Three nights later, Corporal Isaac Johnson was executed in the street near the school. When the last shots rang out, the bell in the school's tower began to ring. A short time later, Sarah's body was discovered... the rope of the tower bell was wrapped around her neck. She had taken her own life, hoping to join her lover in death.

According to the stories, it is believed that the ghost of Sarah June Wheeler still walks in Senior Hall, which has been restored today to look much like it did when she lived there. The legends claim that her spirit is still searching for the ghost of Corporal Johnson, hoping to be reunited with him in the afterlife.... or so they say.

In recent years, other stories have surfaced, claiming that Sarah and her lover actually died as they were trying to escape from Columbia. They allegedly perished by drowning in a nearby flooded river. This version of the story might make even more sense, as Stephens College did not actually have a bell tower in 1862... it was not constructed for another ten years or so afterward.

One thing that we do know though, is that strange things are still said to occur in Senior Hall and that the place has an "unusualness" about it, according to residents who have lived there. Perhaps the story of Sarah and the Corporal is merely a legend to try and explain the oddities of an otherwise spooky building... a piece of ghostlore which was created to help the residents understand why ghostly events were taking place in the building with them.

Then again... perhaps not.

NORTH CAROLINA

The state of North Carolina had an interesting position during the Civil War. To start with, it had little to do with the drama of secession just before the war began. Union sentiment was very strong in the state and most decided to adopt a policy of "watch and wait", preferring to see how the tide turned before they made a decision to join the Confederacy.

This stand of neutrality could have worked well in the favor of the Union until North Carolina objected to President Lincoln's demand for troops in April of 1861. Governor John W. Ellis received a demand for "two regiments of militia for immediate service" from the U.S. Secretary of War, Simon Cameron, but Ellis refused. He stated that no troops from North Carolina were going to be used for the subjugation of the southern states. From that point on, the people of North Carolina went from being "Unionists and Conservatives" to "Secessionists and Radicals".

North Carolina would go on to furnish a large number of troops to the Confederacy during the war and would take the responsibility of feeding and clothing her own men. Strangely though, it would also have the highest number of deserters among any of the southern states, almost one-fifth of those who enlisted.

The state's greatest triumph however, came in the form of blockade running. No other Confederate state would be as successful at slipping through the northern ships off the coast. It was thought that the amount of supplies that were brought into Wilmington managed to keep General Lee in the field as long as he did.

The blockade of the southern ports began in April of 1861, shortly after the fall of Fort Sumter. President Lincoln issued a proclamation that if any vessels attempted to leave or arrive in a southern port, it would first be warned and then, if further attempts were made, captured and confiscated. Lincoln's plan drew ridicule, not only from the Confederacy, but from Europe and even from his own cabinet. The idea seemed almost laughable... the Union was talking of trying to seal off 3,549 miles of coast, a waterfront opened with more that 180 bays, channels, rivers, lagoons and swamps. It would be the largest blockade ever attempted by any nation.

At first, the blockade was as ludicrous as everyone suggested. The Federal Navy consisted of mostly old ships in dry dock or scattered about in ports around the world. When the blockade began, it only had three ships in Washington.... but efforts tightened quickly. By December, the Navy had purchased 136 vessels, 34 had been repaired and put into commission and another 52 were under construction. Within four months, a blockade of the coast had been organized with ships stretching from Virginia to Texas. The hardest passes to block became the Mississippi River, with five separate entrances, and the coast of North Carolina, where Fort Fisher provided protection for ships who managed to make it through with contraband.

The effectiveness of the blockade gradually cut off the Confederacy. Many believe that it was the blockade that really destroyed the south, by choking off its economy, rather than the might of the Union's military force.

Before the fall of the south though, the practice of blockade running became a highly profitable business. Many of the ship owners made millions of dollars, although prices for ordinary good soared. People were forced to pay outrageous prices for goods shipped from Europe and the West Indies simply because they could get them no other way.

The Confederate government itself was forced to go into the blockade running business too, mostly because the independent blockade runners only concentrated on buying and re-selling light cargoes that brought the best profit. The government used its ships to haul steel, copper and munitions for the war effort and not a single blockade runner commanded by an officer of the Confederate Navy was ever captured.

Perhaps the most active port for blockade runners in the south was Wilmington, North Carolina, which was located about 28 miles up the Cape Fear River. This was such an effective location thanks to several forts which guarded the entrances to the port. The New Inlet passage was guarded by Fort Fisher, while the lower passage was protected by shore batteries and by Forts Caswell, Campbell and Holmes. Forts Johnston and Anderson, on the west bank of the river, also protected Wilmington from attack by sea. The Federal blockade was further stymied by the fact that it had to patrol a 50 mile stretch of coast near Cape Fear, plus stay out of reach of the Confederate guns. Also, until late in the war, Wilmington had good railroad connections with Virginia and South Carolina.

After the war began, many of its citizens abandoned Wilmington, at the same time that others were drawn to the city by the prospect of quick wealth through smuggling. For several years, Wilmington thrived while other ports collapsed under the Federal blockade. These times brought riches to those connected with the blockade running and public auctions included luxury items from the finest stores in Europe. Some became rich, while the common people suffered from the incredible inflation that made it difficult for all but a few to purchase even basic items.

By late 1864, the Army of Northern Virginia was largely dependent on Wilmington for the major portion of its supplies. Lee regarded the defense of the city as critical to the survival of the Confederacy. The Federals also realized the importance of the city and began assaults on it as early as 1862. When Fort Fisher, and Wilmington, fell in 1865, it was a major blow to the south's ability to continue the war.

FORT FISHER

The first documented sighting of a ghost at the abandoned ruins of Fort Fisher occurred in the late 1880's, when a group of Confederate veterans visited the site for an evening of companionship and reminiscence. They were gathered around a fire that night when one of the men called the other's attention to a strange figure, who was standing on the third wall of the fort, looking out toward the sea.

The hazy figure wore the gray uniform of a Confederate general. The men were stunned to see the figure..... for they recognized him as a man who had died many years before. His name had been William Henry Chase Whiting, or "Little Billy" as he had been known to the men, and he had been the commander of the fort years before, at the same time that it had fallen into Federal hands.

Amazed, the gathered group of veterans approached the pale figure.... only to see him vanish before their eyes. This was the first time that Whiting's ghost was seen at Fort Fisher, but it would not the last.

Just south of Wilmington, a peninsula of land rests between the Cape Fear River and the Atlantic Ocean. The distance between these two bodies of water gradually narrows until it reaches the point and here lie the remains of Fort Fisher. It is a fairly desolate place and one of sadness and mystery.... where mounds of sand are twisted with live oak trees and the ruins of the fort mark the place where some would say the Confederacy finally fell.

From the beginning of the war in 1861, the Federal plan of blockading the southern ports gained in strength. By late in 1864, the blockade was almost totally effective, leaving Wilmington as the only major port that was still open. The city became the lifeline to the south, and to the southern troops, and the only thing that kept that supply line open was Fort Fisher.

Constructed at the end of the peninsula, the fort was a huge earthen work in the shape of an L. The shortest side was at the northern end and had a wooden barrier, a shallow ditch and a mine field to guard against land attacks. The longest side lay along the beach, facing out toward the sea. The walls were constructed to withstand attack and were 20 feet high and more than 25 feet thick. Inside of the fort, 15 traverses were built to separate the gun platforms. In this way, no direct hit on any platform would damage another. Thanks to its 48 guns for land and sea defense, the fort was able to almost guarantee safe conduct to blockade runners who managed to make it past the Federal vessels off the coast. From Fort Fisher, it was a short run upriver to Wilmington.

Needless to say, the destruction of Fort Fisher was essential to the Federal plan of shutting down all of the southern ports. Near the holiday season of 1864, the Union Navy devised a method of blowing up the fort.... they would float a huge barge, loaded with explosives, up close to the fort and then detonate it. The explosion was said to have been an awesome sight, but did little damage to the fort.

A few weeks later, in January 1865, The Union fleet returned to try again, this time bringing with them 8,000 land troops under the command of Major General Alfred Terry. Admiral David Porter began bombarding the fort mercilessly, firing over 50,000 shells over a span of two days. Still, the Confederates of Fort Fisher hung on.

While the fort was being shelled, General Terry landed his men two miles upriver from the fort. Here, he instructed them to dig in and wait for the Confederate move that would come from the north. On the 15th, they would move against the fort itself.

Confederate Major General Whiting, known as "Little Billy", had commanded the North Carolina troops since 1862 but had been replaced by Major General Braxton Bragg around the time of the first Union offensive against the fort at Christmas. When the January assault began, Bragg and Whiting were upriver in Wilmington and Colonel William Lamb was in command of the fort. Lamb and his 2,000 men were in high spirits when Whiting returned as he had long been a favorite officer among the troops.

Although happy to see his men, Whiting did not share in their revelry. He had been informed that Fort Fisher was to be sacrificed to the Federals. At that moment, Bragg was already making plans to evacuate Wilmington, having already written off the defense of the fort. Whiting constantly cursed Bragg as incompetent and with his dying words he would later blame the demise of the fort, and Wilmington, on the stupidity of his fellow officer.

Bragg believed that Fort Fisher could not be saved, however, the defenders of Fort Fisher were determined not to let the place fall without a fight....

General Terry began his land attack in the early afternoon. About 2,000 Federal troops moved against the northeast corner of the fort, while another 4,000 infantrymen headed toward the northwestern point. The smaller group attacked first, but were driven back. The larger group followed, taking advantage of the fact that the defenders were concentrating on the other force.

The Confederates were just beginning to cheer over the fact that the attackers had been driven back when a cry of alarm went up behind them. They were soon trying to push back the wave of Federals who poured over the walls.

Among the defenders was General Whiting himself. He led the counterattack against the Union troops, slashing savagely with his dress sword. The invaders had already reached the third of 15 traverses inside the fort before the Rebels could begin to push them back. Whiting was in the thick of things when he was surrounded by a group of Federal troops and ordered to surrender. Reportedly, he responded with "Go to hell, you Yankee bastard".... and they shot him.

A few minutes later, Colonel Lamb was also wounded. The Confederates held out as long as they could, putting up a powerful defense, but they were just too greatly outnumbered. By late that evening, the battle of Fort Fisher had ended. Major James Reilly approached the Union line with a flag of truce and surrendered.

With Fort Fisher now gone, Wilmington soon fell also, effectively cutting off the Confederacy's last remaining supply line. Within two months, the war would be over.

General Whiting, although wounded at the battle, managed to survive, but was taken to a prison camp called Fort Columbus, which was located on Governor's Island in New York Harbor. It was here that he finally died from a combination of his wounds and dysentery in March 1865. His body was returned to Wilmington and was buried in Oakdale Cemetery.

But many would say that he does not rest there peacefully....

His ghost has been seen many times over the years, always standing along the walls of the fort, looking out to sea. Is it guilt that keeps him here? Does he despair over the fact that Fort Fisher was taken under his command, thus hammering the final nail into the coffin of the Confederacy?

Or is the ghost of General Whiting still lingering behind because of this seething anger with Braxton Bragg, a man of whom he showed nothing but contempt, even on his death bed?

Perhaps... atlhough it's unlikely that we will ever really know for sure. While "Little Billy" has been sighted many times at his lonely post, the forlorn figure has never been known to speak.

THE PHANTOM RIDER OF THE CONFEDERACY

Located near the North Carolina town of Fletcher is the Calvary Episcopal Church. While the church itself does not boast a ghost, it has become a famous location over the years where the "Phantom Rider of the Confederacy" has been seen.

This phantom rider is said to be the ghost of a young woman who rides on a palomino horse and who appears for a few moments on the road near this church and then gallops away, as if she is being chased by someone. On the portions of her ride where the highway is paved, she always rides along the gravel shoulder, her long blond hair and her Confederate cape billowing out behind her. Beneath it, she wears a filmy gown, a remainder from the time when she was a young lady of the region.

Legend has it that the ghost is that of a young woman who died shortly after she learned that her husband had been killed during the Civil War. She began to appear on her horse a short time later, unable to rest in peace and seeking revenge for her lover's death.... and it is believed that she still rides today.

In the spring of 1865, the first encounter with the ghost took place. In fact, it was said that she was responsible for the deaths of 23 men who were under the command of a Union General named George Stoneman. They were patrolling an area near Fletcher when they followed a young woman on a horse into a deadly Rebel ambush. Those who survived reported that the girl suddenly vanished just before the Rebels opened fire on them.

Stoneman was enraged and organized a search party to find the woman and punish her. She was sighted several times, but they could never catch her. When the soldiers would get within firing range, they found that their bullets seemed to pass right through her.

Since then, she has been seen many times over the years by reliable witnesses and townsfolk, even a former minister at the church claimed to catch sight of her. One has to wonder why she still rides... perhaps, as they say, revenge really is a dish best served cold.

SOUTH CAROLINA

Perhaps the most "ironic" of all of the Confederate states during the war was South Carolina. It would be the first state to secede from the Union on December 20, 1860 and yet would not suffer from an enemy invasion until nearly the end of the war, in February 1865. The official start of the war would occur with the firing upon of Fort Sumter, in the Charleston, South Carolina harbor, on April 13, 1861... and although Charleston would spend most of the war blockaded by Union ships, it was not captured until the city surrendered in 1865.

Interesting, isn't it?

South Carolina's invasion would be commanded by Major General William T. Sherman during the "Carolinas Campaign" of early 1865. Having just completed his legendary March to the Sea, Sherman moved north from Savannah over the soggy roads and through the endless swamps to Columbia, South Carolina's state capital.

Sherman's campaign called for feints on both Augusta, Georgia and Charleston and a march directly on Columbia, then on to North Carolina. Sherman planned to cut himself off completely from his base in Savannah, so he could expect no government supplies until he reached the Cape Fear River. His wagons would also only be able to carry limited provisions so the army would again have to forage for provisions, just as they did during the march across Georgia.

To regulate the foraging parties, and prevent them from simply becoming looting parties, very strict orders were again issued. But, as was the case previously, there was a big difference between the orders that were given and the way the soldiers chose to obey them. The foraging parties often deteriorated into marauding bands of thieves and pillagers, who operated under no command but their own. Most of the wanton destruction of property in both Georgia and the Carolina's was carried out by "bummers" as these groups of out-of-control "foragers" were called.

Sherman crossed the Savannah River into South Carolina in the last days of January and within a week had penetrated well into the state, encamping along the South Carolina Railway. By this time in the war, there was simply no one left in the region to oppose him. The thin Confederate forces which remained were now scattered about in Virginia and Mississippi. By February 12, the city of Orangeburg was in Sherman's hands.

From there, the Union army moved north toward Columbia, destroying the rail lines as it progressed. By late afternoon on February 15, Sherman was with four miles of the state capital, which the Federal soldiers referred to as "the hell hole of secession." That evening, the Battle of Columbia began.... although to call it a battle would really be overstating its importance.

It began when Sherman's men camped within range of some Confederate artillery just east of the Congaree River and were rewarded with some light shelling. The next morning, Federal troops attacked the Confederate defenses around the Congaree River Bridge, but found only the charred timbers of the structures remaining.

Sherman began to move into Columbia and issued orders for the occupation of the city. General Howard was to "destroy public buildings, railroad property, manufacturing, and machine shops" but was ordered to spare "libraries, and asylums and private dwellings".

As the Federal army moved closer, Columbia became a scene of chaos and a city with no law and order. The establishment of martial law by the remaining Confederate defenders on February 17 did nothing to prevent acts of robbery or outright looting. Local blacks, soldiers and citizens of Columbia fought one another for government provisions or simply turned their attention to the pillaging of shops and stores.

Early that same morning, Columbia was awakened by a thundering explosion at the South Carolina Railroad depot. It was thought to have been caused by a looter who accidentally ignited the powder magazine stored there. By daylight, the looting grew worse. The state commissary was plundered and stores and shops were virtually destroyed.

As the city tore itself apart, General Wade Hampton's Confederate cavalry was withdrawing from Columbia along the Camden and Winnsboro roads. This was a fight they had no chance of winning.

Columbia was not only a city gone mad, but it was now completely at the mercy of the enemy. Shortly before noon, Sherman and a few members of his staff rode into the city. Less than 12 hours later, a large part of Columbia, including the state house, a number of public buildings, dozens of private homes, several churches, and even a convent, lay in smoldering ruins. The city was nearly leveled by a great fire that burned uncontrolled throughout the night. How exactly this blaze started remains a mystery to this day....

The most likely explanation is that the fire started from burning cotton. Hundreds of cotton bales lined the streets of Columbia, many of which had been ignited before Sherman arrived. The wind spread the burning pieces of fiber across the city and eventually, a building caught fire, soon igniting others. Others believe the fire was started by the poorly disciplined and drunken Federal troops, who started a number of fires in the city. Regardless of how it started, each side blamed the other and to this day, no explanation exists as to what really happened.

The burning of Columbia would come back to haunt Sherman after the war. "Though I never ordered it, and never wished it," Sherman said, "I have never shed any tears over the event, because I believe that it hastened what we all fought for... the end of the war."

THE LUCAS BAY LIGHT

By the time that Sherman began his "Carolinas Campaign", many residents of the port city of Georgetown feared that their city would be somewhere on the General's list of places to loot and burn. The harassment of Georgetown began in early 1862, when Federal gunboats began patrolling the harbor as part of the Union blockade of southern ports and when Union troops began cracking down on the local planters and businessmen. Many of these men moved their families and slaves to property further inland, hoping to wait out the war. Little did they know that Sherman's army would march straight through the inner portion of the state, avoiding the coastline altogether.

Prior to Sherman's campaign, Georgetown officials made plans to move the city's historical documents and records to a safer location as their own city was a key southern port and it was unlikely that it would be spared Sherman's torch. In April of 1862, the records were moved to the city of Chesterfield for safekeeping.... although ironically, Chesterfield was burned by the Union army and all of Georgetown's records were lost.

The removal of the city records was not the only sign of panic in the region. The problems first began when word reached the area that Atlanta was in ruins. The coast cities of South Carolina reasoned that they were next and chaos spread from Charleston to Georgetown and to the tiny community of Lucas Bay, which was nestled next to the booming town of Bucksport on the Great Pee Dee River. The shipping and milling facilities of Bucksport were sure to be a target for the Federal invaders, and when the city was destroyed, it was sure to take Lucas Bay with it.

Many of the homes in the area were occupied only by women as the men had gone to serve in the Confederate military. As news arrived that Sherman was marching into South Carolina, many of the women began hiding their precious items and valuables, sometimes sewing them into their corsets and into the hems of their skirts. They hid their family heirlooms inside of mattresses, behind walls and ever buried them in secret.

One of the women of Lucas Bay had an even more precious item to hide and one afternoon, she carried her infant child away from her home. She disappeared away from the town and hid the sleeping baby beneath a nearby bridge that led over a rice field canal. She wrapped the baby in a soft blanket and then returned home to wait for the arrival of Sherman and the Federal troops.

As darkness fell, a violent thunderstorm moved over the area and a torrential rain began to fall. The young mother panicked.... sure that the rain swollen canal would surely drown her baby. She ran from her house, intent on rescuing the child. As she arrived at the bridge, she saw that the baby was still safe, but the water was rising quickly. She had to get the child to safety.

Beaten and drenched by the soaking rain, the woman ran across the bridge, too worried about the baby to pay attention to what she was doing. As she made it over the opposite bank and started beneath the bridge to the baby's hiding place, she slipped on the muddy bank and struck her head against one of the bridge supports. Bloody and dazed, she fell unconscious and tumbled into the rushing water of the canal..... and her baby soon followed her to her death.

As the years passed, a mysterious light began to appear near where the mother and her baby met their untimely demise. According to witnesses, the light begins on the bridge along Lucas Bay Road , first as a small red orb and then it grows into a glowing light about the size of a ball. It travels along the road, getting closer to the witness, before it finally blinks out. The legends say that this is the light of the young mother's lantern as she searches for her baby.

Although it hasn't been seen in some time, older residents recall that the light was seen most frequently back in the days before automobiles and especially on rainy nights, just before dark.

Was it really the ghost of the young woman who so tragically lost her life along this old and unpaved road.... or some sort of natural phenomenon that defies explanation? You will have to be the judge of that yourself.

MORGAN HOUSE

Built around 1825 in the historic coastal city of Georgetown, Morgan House was originally constructed by a wealthy rice planter who also owned a Black River plantation. He had built the house for his niece, whom he and his wife had raised as their own child. When the time had come for her to marry, the planter built the elegant home and presented it to her husband-to-be as a part of her dowry.

The niece's new husband, Arthur Morgan, was also a prosperous businessman, although he had made his money as an enterprising local merchant. He and his beautiful wife's new home came to be known as Morgan House and they entertained there often. The house became one of the fixture's of Georgetown society and the Morgan's some of the most popular hosts.

The happy days at Morgan House ended with the coming of the war. Eventually, Federal forces occupied the town, blockading the port, and halting most of the business being conducted in the city. Soon after the Union soldiers arrived, the Morgans left their home, feeling that it was not safe to remain in the city.

Finding the structure abandoned, the Federals seized Morgan House and put it to use as a hospital for wounded troops. The large dining room in the front corner of the house was turned into a bloody operating room and the rooms were gutted and equipped with cots and pallets for dying and suffering men.

When the war was over, the Morgans returned to their home. Despite the damage inflicted by the Union troops, they were able to make repairs and try to go on with their lives. Of course, nothing would ever be the same again, although the family was determined to make the best of things.

A few years passed and life returned to normal in Georgetown. Like many other small towns in the south, the city decided to hold a reunion for Confederate soldiers at the Winyah Indigo Society Hall, located just across the street from Morgan House. The reunion, although both happy and sad, was a resounding success. It lasted far into the night with speeches, food, plenty of drink and hours of dancing, music and laughter.

The final guests left the hall in the small hours of the morning and a number of revelers from out of town crossed the street to Morgan House, whose doors had been opened for the weary. Not long after the party-goers retired to the beds, a horrible noise erupted in the downstairs area of the house. The sounds seem to come from the dining room and those who were awakened would later swear that they heard shattering glass, clanging silverware, and what sounded like heavy furniture being dragged and dropped on the hardwood floors. The physical noises were accompanied by a low-pitched moaning and groaning that seemed to come from the mouths of dying men.

Needless to say, there was not a soul in the house who was able to sleep through this and Morgan and most his male guests rushed downstairs. They were sure they would encounter a group of vandals... or at least a number of drunken practical jokers from the evening's festivities.

Instead, they found nothing.... only a dark and silent room with not a thing out of place.

Unable to find an explanation for the sounds, the men returned to bed. They were exhausted and believed that perhaps everything would seem logical in the morning.

The next day, following breakfast, the strange noises from the night before became the topic of conversation. No one in the homes nearby had noticed anything out of the ordinary so apparently the ruckus had been confined only to Morgan House. In the end, they decided that the sounds had been merely the noise of the house settling, a perfectly rational explanation for what they had heard.

But was it really?

Over the next century, the Morgans would not be the only owners of the house to hear strange noises in the dead of night. Stories began to be told as to what could be causing such an awful sound and some believe that the noises are the restless stampings of the Federal soldiers who died in the house during the period when it was a hospital.

But why did the sounds begin years after the war? Those same story-tellers believe that the Confederate reunion, held at the society hall across the street, was the event that awakened the Federal ghosts.... and once awakened, they have never rested again.

GHOSTS OF HAGLEY LANDING

One of the most eerie, and sadly believable, tales of war-era South Carolina involves a young couple who lived near Hagley Landing, on the sea coast of the state. The tale actually begins during the war, although its horrifying conclusion came a short time after.

The period following the war was a grim time in the region. Many of the homes and plantations in the area had been ravaged by Union troops in the last days of the war and the Reconstruction years which followed were a time of lawlessness and despair. Many of the local families had been devastated by the loss of loved ones during the fighting and thanks to the unreliable mail service, many others were unable to learn the fate of the men who had gone off to fight for the Confederacy. They often did not hear of a young man's death or injury until many months had gone by.... while still others would not learn of those tragedies until a wagon bearing the deceased arrived at their home.

Thankfully though, other families managed to be blessed with the unexpected homecoming of a lost soldier, sometimes months after the last shreds of hope for a safe return were gone.

But most were not that lucky....

One case in point was that of a young couple who had been separated by the war, just days before they were to be wed. The wedding was to have been held at the local Episcopal Church and would have been a grand and extravagant ceremony. Unfortunately, their plans had to be postponed when the prospective groom left to serve in the Confederate military. They vowed to have a large and wonderful wedding once the war was over.

Sadly, this was not to be.

The war lasted for years and as the Confederate death roll grew longer, the young bride-to-be longed for news of her lover's fate, yet dreaded that she might learn of his death... still no word came. Even after the war ended, and most of the local men had returned home, she still heard nothing. His letters had stopped coming long ago and now, she could only fear the worst.

The only consolation the young woman had was her lover's best friend, who was equally as worried about the missing man. He had also served with the Confederate forces and when he came home and no word had arrived from his friend, he wrote letters and contacted everyone he knew who might know the other man's fate.... but he received no news.

Each day, he rode to the home of the young woman and together, they talked about their happy childhood together and of the wonderful things the three of them had done in years gone by. The two of them remained devoted to the memory of their friend and companion, but after three years, they began to face the reality that he might be dead.

As time passed, the two friends slowly began to fall in love. Neither of them wished to betray their lost friend, but soon their mutual affection deepened and they decided to get married. They were convinced that their dead loved one would approve.

The small ceremony took place at St. Mary's, a former slave chapel at Hagley Plantation. Everyone who attended knew what the bride had suffered through and were pleased that she was able to finally find happiness.

After the wedding was over, the family and friends of the young couple gathered on the front steps of the church. A few moments later, their voices and laughter were cut short by the pounding hooves of an approaching horse and rider. The man atop the sweating animal was dressed in a ragged and torn Confederate uniform. His hair was long and unkempt, his face drawn and unshaven and his eyes were red-rimmed from lack of sleep. He quickly dismounted from his animal and approached the now silent group.

As he limped toward them, the bride gasped as she recognized the man to whom she had once been betrothed. She began to sob as he drew closer. She wept as she tried to explain to him what had happened... they had waited three years, no word had ever come and they believed him to be dead. If only she had known the truth.....

The man in the tattered uniform looked from the bride to his best friend, his eyes now downcast and tortured. His voice was a whisper.... pretend as though I never came back, he told them and turned to go.

In a shambling gait, the soldier ran away toward the pier at Hagley Landing. Never slowing, he threw himself from the end of it and into the rushing water of the Waccamaw River. In a few seconds, he had vanished beneath the stream.

Then, according to the legend, the bride ran after him and she too plunged from the pier and into the water. She was followed moments later by her new husband.

None of them were ever seen again.... not alive anyway.

In the years that have followed, the ghostly trio has often been spotted on the road leading to Hagley landing. The earliest report came in 1918, when a young man claimed to have to swerve his car and stop to avoid running down three strangely dressed figures in the roadway. To make matters worse, they vanished before his eyes.

He claimed the people he saw were a man and woman in bridal clothes and another man in an old Confederate uniform.

Since that day, the three spirits have been seen from time to time, strolling together beneath the trees and sometimes walking hand in hand.

Perhaps they have been able to find peace after all......

THE GRAY MAN

One of the most famous (dare I say, *the* most famous) ghosts of South Carolina has to be the spirit known as the "Gray Man" who haunts the beaches of Pawleys Island. There are many legends as to the origins of this elusive spirit, but at least one of them claims that the ghost was once that of a fiery Confederate commander, still intent on watching over the local residents.

For those not versed in the local lore of the Carolina coast, the Gray Man is a ghost who appears to warn residents of the impending dangers of hurricanes. In 1989, just before the arrival of Hurricane Hugo, two Pawleys Island residents were out walking when they encountered a man who suddenly appeared beside them. They turned to speak to him and he suddenly vanished, even though there was nowhere that he could have gone. They believed that they had seen the ghost of the Gray Man, and although he said nothing to them, they immediately packed and left the island. Two days later, the island was devastated by the hurricane.

A similar event occurred in 1954, when Hurricane Hazel struck the island. An automobile dealer named Bill Collins was honeymooning on the island when he and his wife were awakened in the early morning hours by someone knocking on the door of their cottage. Collins went to the door and when he opened it, he saw an old man standing on his porch. The man wore gray pants, a gray shirt and a rumpled gray cap that was pulled down low over his eyes. He explained that he had been sent to warn Collins about a storm blowing in. It would be best to evacuate the island.

Then, the man simply vanished.

In less than hour, Collins and his wife were packed and back on the mainland. A short time later the hurricane hit the island. When they returned later, they found that most of the cottages had been washed out to sea... although the house where they had been staying was untouched.

Bill Collins will always believe that he met the ghost of the Gray Man.

The story of the Gray Man has been around for many years, dating back to sightings which are more than a century old. There are several likely candidates for this helpful spirit, and while no one knows for sure about his actual identity, one of them may just be related to a Confederate commander during the Civil War.

His name was Plowden Charles Jeannerette Weston and he was the original owner of a house on Pawleys Island that is now known as the Pelican Inn, a place which boasts several Gray Man sightings. He was born in 1819 at Laurel Hill Plantation, where he was privately tutored and was raised as a privileged member of a family who had created a fortune growing rice. When Weston was 12, his family took him to England so that he could be properly educated. Although his family later returned to South Carolina, Weston stayed behind to study at Cambridge and here, fell in love with a young woman named Emily Frances Esdaile.

They were married in August of 1847 and established a home at Hagley Plantation, a wedding gift from Weston's father. The plantation included vast rice fields which extended from the Waccamaw River to the Atlantic Ocean. Just off shore from the estate was Pawleys Island, a beautiful spot where Emily and Weston planned to build a summer home. It was the custom at that time to build summer homes away from the humid inland and where the breezes from the ocean could keep away the heat and the disease-carrying mosquitoes.

The next decade passed in peace and happiness for the young couple. They divided their time between the plantation and the island home, constructed a beautiful chapel for their slaves called St. Mary's and led a productive, although secluded, life.

By the late 1850's, Weston began to feel that their perfect life could not last forever.... or at least would not endure without a fight. Weston had often published articles about South Carolina history and the questions of certain issues involving the south and the central government. Now, he began to turn his literary skills toward the deep division that was growing between the northern and southern states. He gave a number of passionate speeches which warned of a coming confrontation and which defended the rights of the southern cause.

At the beginning of the war, Weston made a stand which contained more than just words. He became the company commander of the Georgetown Rifle Guard and he personally armed and supplied gear and uniforms to 150 men. In the early years of the fighting, when the Confederates still believed that the war would end quickly, and in their favor, Weston and Emily entertained many of the regiment's men and their wives at their Pawleys Island home.

But Weston would pay a price for his involvement in the war..... In 1863, he contracted tuberculosis and it gradually worsened to the point that he became seriously ill. Weston's friends urged him to return home, but he refused to give up his command and abandon his men. Finally, several friends in the state legislature, knowing that he would not give in, elected Weston to the office of South Carolina's lieutenant governor. He finally agreed to give up command of the regiment for this office, but he would not serve for long.

In late January 1864, his tuberculosis worsened and it became clear that he was near death. His last moments were spent with Emily and he asked for her to bury him in the church yard at Hagley, the same place where the two of them had been married. He died that same day.

Because of Weston's devotion to his home, and to Pawleys Island, many believe that he has never left the place..... claiming that he has returned as the legendary Gray Man. They are sure that the man who warned his neighbors of the coming war is the same spirit who now warns them of the impending doom of the storms.

Most likely, we will never know who the Gray Man really is, but regardless of his identity, he does not appear to be leaving Pawleys Island any time soon. His faithful watch will continue long after the rest of us have long departed this world.....

TENNESSEE

Perhaps no state was as sharply divided during the war as Tennessee. While its neighboring state of Kentucky saw personal strife and division over the questions of secession and war, Tennessee was divided not so much by personal lines, but along regional ones. The eastern side of Tennessee remained loyal to the Union, while the central and western portions of the state leaned toward the Confederacy. Ironically, throughout the majority of the war, these two parts of the state would remain under the military command of the opposite side... the Federal Army inhabited the west, while the Confederates kept hold of the east.

When the question of secession first reared its head, Tennessee dismissed a legislative call for a vote on the subject. The state had just backed a conservative Unionist candidate named John Bell (a relative of the John Bell of "Bell Witch" fame) in the 1860 presidential campaign and had no interest in splitting away from the Federal government.

Things would soon change however... Shortly after the attack on Fort Sumter, the state governor, Isham G. Harris, pushed a vote through the legislature that allied the state with the Confederacy. A number of counties in Eastern Tennessee attempted to break off from the state and remain in the Union, but by June of 1861, it was too late. Confederate forces in the region managed to dampen enthusiasm for this maneuver.

The southern hold on the state capital would not last long however and Abraham Lincoln would quickly install Andrew Johnson as the military governor of the region. Although whether in southern or Union hands, Tennessee suffered more than any other state during the war, save for Virginia. The state was a major battleground, endured long campaigns, foraging by both armies and guerilla activity that nearly devastated portions of the state. Relatives, friends and neighbors also frequently found themselves on opposite sides of the battlefield, causing rifts that would last much longer than the war itself.

The collapse of Confederate control in Tennessee actually began in Kentucky. During the summer of 1861, in the earliest days of the war, strong Confederate and Federal forces waited on the borders of Kentucky, neither side daring to cross over into the state. It was tense time as both sides hesitated beginning the war in the west.

Finally, on September 3, Confederate General Leonidas Polk seized Columbus on the Mississippi River. Unfortunately for his cause, this move outraged the people of Kentucky, turning many neutral citizens into Unionists. At the same time, it also gave the Union an excuse to invade Kentucky also. On September 6, Brigadier General Ulysses S. Grant countered Polk's invasion by occupying the northern city of Paducah. Other Union forces soon took control of the northern parts of the state, leading the Confederate commander in the west, General Albert Sidney Johnston to send troops from Tennessee to block a further incursion by the Union of the south.

Armies were being moved about like chess pieces, but no real fighting was taking place. Each side, in the tradition of George McClellan, badly overestimated the other side's strength and held back from confrontation.

At last, it was Grant that struck first. On November 7, he loaded 3,000 troops onto boats at Cairo, Illinois and sent them down the Mississippi to attack an outpost that Polk had established at Belmont, Missouri, across the river from Columbus. The Confederates, who outnumbered Grant's men, drove off the attackers, but the battle did get their attention and they became convinced that the main Union assault would be in Mississippi.

The night after Grant's attack at Belmont, a band of Unionists burned five railroad bridges in Eastern Tennessee. This guerilla attack had been approved by Lincoln, hoping to set the stage for the liberation of the eastern part of the state. The Confederate authorities hurriedly placed more troops in the area, declared martial law and hung any man they suspected of aiding the Unionists. Hundreds of residents escaped to the north, while others remained behind, waging a ruthless guerilla war against the southerners.

The next step in the destruction of Confederate Tennessee again came in Kentucky as Union General George H. Thomas began marching his troops toward East Tennessee. Early in the morning of January 19, 1862, Thomas' men were attacked by 5,000 Confederates under the command of Major General George B. Crittenden at Logan's Crossroads. It was a surprise attack against a smaller force and the troops under Thomas were at first driven back, but quickly rallied and then routed the Confederates. The beaten southerners retreated back into East Tennessee, which was now open to Federal occupation. However, supply problems prevented the Federals from moving forward and the victory was never followed up.

What it did accomplish though was the destruction of the right wing of General Johnston's line across Kentucky. The following month, Grant smashed the left wing. On February 6, Union gunboats captured Fort Henry on the Tennessee River, then five days later, Grant marched his army to the Cumberland River, where he launched an attack on the Confederate garrison at Fort Donelson. Shortly after, the Confederates almost escaped to the south but Grant attacked again, driving the Rebels back to their fortifications.

On February 16, Brigadier General Simon Bolivar Bruckner asked Grant for terms of surrender, leading Grant to answer with his now famous reply... "No terms except unconditional and immediate surrender." Bruckner had no choice but to agree and nearly 12,000 Confederate soldiers became prisoners of war.

It was the biggest Union victory in the war and it forced Johnston to retreat all of the way to Corinth, Mississippi, where he began concentrating his scattered troops. By April, he had troops organized into four divisions commanded by generals Polk, Braxton Bragg, William J. Hardee and John C. Breckenridge. On April 3, he set out to attack Grant at Pittsburg Landing on the Tennessee River. If the attack was successful, the Confederacy would be able to hang onto Tennessee and the tide of war in the west would be reversed.

It was only a short distance from Corinth to Pittsburg Landing, or Shiloh, as the south would refer to the battle ahead, but bad roads and problems with the troops slowed Johnston to the point that it took him nearly three days to cross 20 miles. Finally, at dawn on April 6, the Confederates attacked.

Even though some of the Union patrols had seen and heard the approaching army, and some of them had even clashed with Johnston's advance units, most of the Federals were taken by surprise. Grant simply had not expected that Johnston would bring the fight to him. The Confederates attacked with their trademark ferocity and drove back Grant's men, causing many of them to flee in wide-eyed panic.

But not all of the Union troops were so easily frightened. Several thousand men, under Brigadier General Benjamin Prentiss, stationed in a sunken road that would gain infamy as "the Hornet's Nest", repelled wave after wave of attackers. Johnston urged his men to continue the attack and while nearby, was wounded in the leg by a stray bullet. He bled to death that same afternoon, just shortly before the Confederates forced Prentiss to surrender.

By this time, Grant had been able to form a defense line around Pittsburg Landing, which was bolstered by river gunboats and heavy artillery. Toward twilight, a wave of desperate Confederates made one last charge against Grant's position, but were driven back.

The night which followed was one of horror. Torrential rains fell upon the area and thousands of wounded and abandoned men screamed and moaned in agony, creating a horrible cacophony that could be heard even over the sound of the storm.

During the night, Union troops under Brigadier General Lew Wallace joined Grant's army, as did 20,000 soldiers under Major General Don Carlos Buell. The next morning, Grant counterattacked and by afternoon, the Confederate were in full retreat. The Federals, happy to see them go, did not follow them.

The Battle of Shiloh, or Pittsburg Landing, was the biggest and the bloodiest of the war to that point. Nearly 11,000 Confederate troops and 13,000 Union soldiers were killed, wounded or captured. For the Confederacy, the loss was damaging both to the morale of the army and to the strength of their military power in the west.... although to the Union, the strategic victory was essential to control of Tennessee.

THE HAUNTINGS OF FRANKLIN

There are few locations in Tennessee which have as much reason to be haunted as Franklin. It was here in 1864, that one of the most violent battles of the final days of the war took place. While this is not the section of the book reserved for "haunted battlefields", we were forced to make an exception with Franklin.... for it is not the battlefield here which is haunted, but three houses which still stand where the bloodiest of the fighting took place.

In November 1864, the middle region of Tennessee would again become a battleground. General John Bell Hood, on retreat from his defeat in Atlanta, devised a plan which would take his army deep into Tennessee. Hood crossed the Chattahoochee River and attacked the Western & Atlantic Railroad, which General Sherman had been using a supply line for his occupation of Atlanta. After the attack, Sherman started out in pursuit of Hood, who in turn, turned tail and fled into the hollows of northwest Georgia and into Alabama.

Sherman left one corps behind to hold Atlanta and spent the next little while vainly trying to catch up with Hood's army. Finally, on November 8, Grant called him back to Atlanta, where preparations were being made for Sherman's "March to the Sea".

When Hood did not turn and follow the Union army back to Atlanta, Sherman directed Major General John M. Schofield to join General George M. Thomas in Tennessee. Scholfield quickly reached Nashville by train and moved part of his corps to the west to strengthen the troops who had been run out of the supply depot in Johnsonville by Major General Nathan Bedford Forrest's calvary. Scholfield then took command of the troops assembled in Pulaski to oppose any advance by Hood.

On November 21, Hood put his army into motion again. Using Forrest's calvary to screen his advance, Hood sent his three infantry corps along different roads. Unfortunately, the weather was not very cooperative and the men spent three days traveling through snow, sleet and ice storms.

Word soon reached Scholfield of the Confederate advance and he evacuated Pulaski, sending his supplies to the rear. They reached Columbia on November 24 and managed to arrive in time to reinforce the Union calvary against Forrest's own riders. It took two full days for Hood's infantry to arrive and by then, Scholfield, who had been Hood's classmate at West Point, was able to prepare a strong defense of the Duck River crossings.

Hood realized that a frontal assault across the Duck River would be suicidal, so he devised a plan to slip his men over the river and to flank Scholfield... all the while, Forrest's calvary charged against Thomas' men, who retreated toward Franklin.

At daybreak, Hood began crossing the Duck River with a pontoon bridge, while Lieutenant General Stephen D. Lee was left to distract Scholfield in front of the Columbia bridge crossing. Several of Forrest's brigades led the Confederate charge toward Spring Hill, a village on the Columbia pike which was eight miles north of Columbia. If the Rebels could have blocked the road, Scholfield's troops would have been trapped into a disastrous position.... but the Confederates failed and Scholfield held Spring Hill just long enough to get the army pointed towards Franklin.

Scholfield's army retreated 14 miles to Franklin, undisturbed but for several skirmishes with Confederate calvary. A division under General Jacob D. Cox was the first to reach Franklin on the last day of November. Cox established his command post at a home belonging to Fountain Carter, which fronted on the west side of the Columbia pike south of town. Once Scholfield arrived, he deployed two divisions to hold a bridge south of Franklin and to shield the army as it crossed to the north of the Big Harpeth River.

By this time, Hood's men were angrily marching north after having let the Federals escape from Spring Hill. Hood himself was in a foul mood, convinced that his subordinates had failed and had been responsible for the Federal escape. He was determined to crush Schofield's army before they could reach the safety of Nashville.... and he chose to make a frontal assault.

Many would call this one of the greatest mistakes that Hood ever made.

It was late afternoon before the Confederate began their assault. Hood launched 15 brigades against the Federal position. Troops under Confederates Cleburne and Brown clashed with George D. Wagner's advance division and the Federals broke and ran for the rear. In moments, General Emerson Opdycke pushed his men into the opening and in terrible fighting that was centered around the Carter House, drove back the Confederates.

The Rebels continued to attack, taking horrifying losses. As darkness fell, the fighting continued with men firing at the muzzle flashes of the opposing army. Late that night, the Federal army, which was battered, yet emerged victorious, finally withdrew and escaped to Nashville, leaving the Confederate army in chaos behind them. They managed the leave the field with only 189 killed, 1,033 wounded and 1,104 missing. The Confederates took the worst of the fighting, reporting more than 6,300 casualties in the skirmish of only a few hours. It was also reported that five Confederate generals were killed, six were wounded and one captured.

It was a bloody and ultimately pointless fight... and one which left dire consequences in its wake.

The **Carter House** in Franklin was built in 1830 by Fountain Branch Carter, who, of course, never realized that it would someday be in the center of one of the most terrifying battles of the Civil War, a battle in which nearly the entire Army of Tennessee was destroyed.

And in the midst of all of the carnage of the battle stood the Carter house.

When the Union troops had arrived in Franklin, General Cox had commandeered the house as a command post. The Carter family had been roused from their beds in the middle of the night, only to watch helplessly as the Federal troops moved in.

During the fighting the next day, the Carter's took refuge in the basement. Fountain Branch Carter was the head of the family but he was elderly and a widower, so his oldest son, Lt. Colonel Moscow Branch Carter, took charge of the family. Carter, having been taken prisoner in an earlier battle, was home on parole. He rounded the family into the cellar beneath the house. Besides the two Carter men were three daughters, a daughter-in-law, children, a few neighbors, and servants, leaving twenty-two people to huddle in the darkness.

The Carters were cut off from the battle, except for what they could hear taking place. They heard gunfire, bullets striking the house, screams of dying men and even a cannonball crashing into the side of the building. Soldiers fought hand-to-hand on the porch and in the rooms. During the fighting, a Union soldier even managed to break open a door and crawl inside of the house for cover from the murderous rain of bullets outside.

The Confederates charged the Union position a dozen times near the house, but each time they were beaten back.

The Carter family somehow survived the battle. Late that night, after it was all over, they left the basement and got some terrible news. Another son, Tod Carter, had been with the Confederate troops in the assault. He was lying somewhere on the battlefield with the thousands of other soldiers who were wounded, dead or dying.

Moscow Carter immediately went in search of his brother with only a lantern to guide the way in the blackness. He wandered aimlessly for hours, searching everywhere. While he was gone, General Smith arrived at the Carter house. Tod had been on Smith's staff, serving under General

Hood, and Smith knew how close the boy had been to home. He rallied all efforts to find the lost soldier. Smith took another lantern and started his own search, finding Tod Carter some time later. The boy had only been about one hundred yards away from the house when he had been hit.

Smith and Moscow Carter carried Tod into the house and placed him in a first floor bedroom. Tod's sisters tended to him for two days before he died.

The Carter House was opened to the public in 1953 and in 1961 was listed as a Registered National Historic Landmark. It operates today as a historic museum and a monument to commemorate the Battle of Franklin.

Despite heavy tourist traffic, the staff members and visitors are not the only ones who walk in this house. Most agree, given the history of the place, that it is not surprising that it is haunted.

Poltergeist-like pranks often occur in the house and have been attributed to the ghost of Annie Carter, one of Tod's sisters. During a tour one afternoon, one of the staff members was interrupted during a talk by a visitor who pointed out that the statue behind her was jumping up and down.

Other events also point to a playful ghost like objects that appear and disappear and the sensation of a child tugging at staff member's sleeves when they believe they are the only ones in the house. One staff member even claimed to have seen the apparition of a little girl disappear along an upstairs hallway and down the steps. Others have spoken of hearing the friendly and welcoming voice of a woman in the house.

Not surprisingly, Tod Carter has also made an appearance in the house. The young man has been seen several times and recently, a visitor was looking into the bedroom where he died and saw his apparition sitting on the side of the bed. He was visible for only a few moments before he vanished.

And that is not the only time that Tod Carter has made an appearance at his former home.... although on this occasion, he didn't just simply sit on the side of the bed and vanish!

This story was passed on to me by Fiona Jackson, a friend of mine and a native of Franklin, whose grandmother, Bernice Seiberling, was once the director of the Carnton Mansion, another ghostly site in town. Prior to that, she was a tour guide at the Carter House. Mrs. Seiberling has since passed away... but this was one story that she never grew tired of telling.

"My granny worked as a tour guide at the Carter House before taking the director's position at Carnton," Fiona told me. " She was giving a tour to about 15 people one afternoon. Among the tourists was a young man. She noticed him right away because his clothing was out of season. It was the middle of summer, and yet this man was wearing winter clothing, not to mention clothes that were out of date. He was wearing brown pants she said looked like wool with suspenders. Also a heavy shirt that was a brown color. He was young, she said, probably in his early '20s with brown hair.

"All through the tour he would contradict what she was saying... but she didn't really pay much attention as she thought the guy was some nut case. At one time in particular, she mentioned where the family had parties. She said they were always held in the formal rooms and the rest of the house was closed off. He corrected her by saying 'No, we didn't always have parties and dances inside. During the warm months, they were always held on the back porch since it was much cooler to do so.'

" Well, my granny prided herself on being historically accurate, so this really annoyed her. And furthermore, the repeated use of the pronoun 'we' was also bothering her. She thought the man was off his rocker for sure.

" She was coming to the last part of the tour, which is the basement. All of the tourists made their way down the narrow stairs... except for the young man. She looked up at him and asked him to come down. He said, 'No, I can't go down there.' She tried to tell him there were some interesting artifacts on display but he said he couldn't and then turned around and walked off. Granny went back upstairs and followed the young man around the corner. As she rounded the house, she saw him walking toward the road. She started to call out to him... but he disappeared right before her eyes. She had no idea that she had been giving a tour to a ghost!

" Then, something dawned on her and she ran back into the house to look at a picture. She had guessed right... she had given a tour to none other than Tod Carter...."

Tod Carter had finally made it home that winter's night in 1864, only to die there... but after all that he went through to make it there, it doesn't appear that he will be leaving any time soon.

From the back porch of the **Carnton Mansion** in Franklin, which was very near the fighting, you can look out over the 1481 marked graves of Confederate soldiers who died in the fighting here.

Before the War, the Carnton Mansion had been a peaceful and quiet place. It had been built in 1826 and inherited by John and Caroline McGavok in 1844. It had played host to dignitaries like Andrew Jackson and Sam Houston. It was not until late November of 1864 that life was forever changed at Carnton.

Late in the afternoon of November 30, Caroline looked out of the house and noticed that the livestock seemed to be frightened. The cattle could apparently hear the charge that had been started by General Hood on the Union positions. Soon, the sounds of the cattle could not be heard over the sounds of gunfire, cannons and the screams of dying men. Evening came and the battle wore down. The night began to fall and wounded men began to gather near the Carnton Mansion. The battle wore on until midnight, when it started to rain and sleet.

Caroline ordered the servants to roll up the carpets and help the wounded men into the house. More than 200 soldiers were brought inside, where Caroline tore clothing for bandages and tried to feed all of those she could. Doctors operated in the parlor and the dead were carried out and laid on the back porch until there was no more room. Legends say that there were so many dead men stacked up behind the house that they stood erect in a column.

Two days later, the Confederate Army started to bury the hundreds of dead men outside of the nearby Carter House. But John McGavok was so troubled by the experience of the battle, that in 1866, he had the hastily buried men moved to a permanent resting ground at Carnton.

This ghastly task was given a purpose as Caroline recorded all of the information available about each man from names to initials to anything he carried. She hoped this would give the mourning families of these men some peace of mind. But not everyone who was laid to rest at Carnton Mansion has rested in peace....

The most famous ghost here is the restless soldier who has been seen walking through the house and across the back porch. Some visitors have reported that he has been spotted a few times marching around the perimeter of the yard. Everywhere that he goes, the sound of his heavy boots accompanies him in his wandering.

This ghost has been joined at the house by an eerie woman in white who is believed to be Caroline herself, the spirit of a girl killed here in the 1840's and a ghost who is fond of breaking glass. Although staff members don't mention the many ghosts on their tours, they are often asked about them by visitors.... some of whom claim to hear heavy walking or who have seen a phantom soldier in one of the bedrooms.

Another mysterious phantom here is the spirit of a former cook, of whom an anomalous photo was taken years ago showing her hovering head in the hallway. Legends say this young woman met her end at the house some time before the war. It is believed that she was a house slave who was married to a field hand. It was said that the two of them met in the smoke house one afternoon, where the man brutally murdered the cook with an ax. The stories say that he was in a jealous rage over some imagined slight.

This spirit has been seen in the house on many occasions, including one memorable sighting by my previously mentioned friend, Fiona Jackson.

" I was 12 years old at the time and it was in 1981. My grandmother had just been made director of Carnton, which had recently been purchased to restore as a historic home for the public.

" The house was in terrible shape. Apparently, it was used as nothing more than a hay barn in recent years. Animals had even been living in it. The plaster was cracked and peeling from the walls. The once-beautiful hardwood floors were warped from leaks in the roof. But even then, you could see what a beautiful home it could be... with a lot of work.

" My Grandmother, my Dad, and myself were standing in the large foyer. She was pointing out things that were going to be improved right away, starting with the lovely (well, it's lovely now) archway supported by columns on either side. I asked her if I could take a look around and she told me I could, as long as I didn't touch anything.

" I walked into the room which is now, and was at the time the McGavok's lived there, the formal dining room. At this time (in 1981) it was a modernized kitchen. As I walked in, I saw an African-American woman standing with her back to me. She was slender and wearing a dark, floor-length skirt and a light-colored blouse with a high neck. I was delighted thinking my grandmother had hired tour guides to dress 'the part'. She was even wearing a bandana (or some type of cloth) on her head. It was when she turned to face me that I noticed I could see right through her! Well, of course, I took off back into the foyer and told Granny and Dad what I had seen.

" My granny chuckled and said 'Oh, that's just the kitchen ghost. Don't be afraid of her, she won't hurt you."

Our Final Franklin haunt, the **Shy House**, actually had its genesis a short distance away, in Nashville, and occurred roughly two weeks after the Battle of Franklin took place. It was the early morning of December 16, 1864 and unseasonably warm for the winter, causing a thick layer of fog to hang in the air. It would later be said that the two armies, under John Bell Hood and George Thomas actually had trouble finding one another.

Two weeks had passed since the bloody events at Franklin and the Army of Tennessee was on its last legs, running short of ammunition, food and men. But Hood had never run away from a fight, as evidenced by his left arm, which hung useless as a reminder of Gettysburg, and the crutches that were strapped on his saddle to replace the leg that he had been forced to have amputated after Chickamauga. The Confederate survivors gamely prepared for the battle ahead.

Nearby, on Felix Compton's hill, the remains of several Tennessee regiments had been grouped together under the command of Lt. Colonel William M. Shy of the 20th Tennessee Infantry.

Shy had been originally from Kentucky and his family had moved to Williamson County, Tennessee when he was a small boy. They settled on a farm called "Two Rivers", which was a few miles west of Franklin. At the outbreak of the war, he had enlisted as a private, along with Moscow, Francis and Tod Carter, whose home would later be at the center of the fighting in Franklin.

After the Battle of Mill Springs in January 1862, Shy was promoted to lieutenant and after Shiloh, to the rank of major. Just before the campaign in Atlanta, he would advance to lieutenant colonel, serving on the staff of his friend General Thomas Benton Smith. He would go on to serve under Hood during the Tennessee Campaign... a series of brutal battles that would bring tragedy to the young men from Franklin.

Once the battle of December 16 began, the Confederate position on Compton's Hill came under fire from Union artillery and then was attacked on three sides by Federal troops. It would later be reported that the entire hill top was completely obscured by dark smoke.

In the aftermath, Colonel Shy's body was found among the other casualties. His face was found to be blackened by the point-blank blast of a rifle. The ball entered his skull on the forehead, high above his left eye, and exited the back of his head with a hole that was five times larger than the entry wound. He had died instantly.

The Colonel's body was taken to the Compton Home and then later transported back to Franklin, where he was buried in the backyard of the family home. And here he remained, until Christmas Eve of 1977...

The holidays season of 1977 was a festive one for the new owners of "Two Rivers". Having just taken over the property, the new lady of the house was showing some friends her new home, and the grounds around it, when they made a startling discovery. The grave of Colonel Shy had been opened up and a headless corpse was sticking out of the hole that had been broken into the Colonel's coffin.

Merry Christmas.

The sheriff was quickly called and after a quick examination of the area jumped to the conclusion that someone had probably been attempting to hide a recent murder victim in the old grave when they had been frightened away by the new home owners and their guests. The house having just changed hands seemed to support such a theory as the killer could have believed the place to be vacant. When the coroner arrived, he confirmed that the corpse seemed to be that of a person who had died within the last year. The torso was dressed in a black suit and, other than having no head attached to it, seemed to be in good shape.

Needless to say, rumors quickly spread that a killer was loose in the community.

Things soon got even weirder.... because an examination of the casket showed that Colonel Shy was not in it! However, a search of the grave did uncover the fragments of a skull and a shoe with bones inside of it. Did they belong to Colonel Shy?

A forensic anthropologist was called in and he set to work reconstructing the skull, which appeared to have a small hole in the forehead and a much larger hole in back. According to local historians and Civil War buffs, this matched the way that Shy had been killed.

Then, he examined the torso of the "recent" murder victim that had been found. He discovered that the body had been saturated with arsenic, a common embalming method... during the Civil War era. The corpse which had originally been thought to be recent was actually 113 years old and indeed was that of Colonel Shy.

What was thought to be an insane killer on the loose was actually now believed to be a relic hunter, looking for valuable items in Shy's grave. The relic hunter was never caught, although I would bet that he had a sleepless night or two, wondering if he would be caught and charged with murder instead of trespassing.

In January of 1978, Colonel Shy was reburied at "Two Rivers" with full military honors by the Sons of Confederate Veterans.... although many wondered, as the casket was lowered into the ground, if this time William Shy would stay where he belonged.

Not surprisingly, many say that he has not. Many believe that his sudden death, and possibly even the disturbance of his grave, has created a restless spirit who is doomed to walk the grounds of "Two Rivers".

Others claim that his ghost still walks on Shy's Hill... the hill, once owned by the Compton family, that was re-named in Shy's honor after his death. The hill is located near the intersection of

Harding Place and Granny White Pike and is marked with a historical plaque which points visitors to the location of the battle.

The woods here are so thick that it is impossible to get a view of the entire area, even from the summit of the hill. There are traces of the earthworks still remaining, where the Confederates fought to defend their position, but where Colonel Shy actually died is a mystery.

More than one person who has come here has claimed to leave with a strange and unsettling feeling, as if they were not alone. There are no sounds of guns or the screams of the dying here, as in so many haunted places of the war, but the eerie sound of total silence... a silence so thick and disquieting that many who come here vow to never return.

There have also been strange lights reported here, flickering in the trees, and stories of soldiers in gray who appear and then disappear out of the corner of the eye. Is this place haunted?

I would hazard a guess to say it is....

VIRGINIA

To attempt to write a brief military history (or even the military highlights) of Virginia during the Civil War would almost be like trying to write an entire history of the war itself. More battles, skirmishes and deaths took place in Virginia during the war than in any other state.... and because of this, ghosts here abound!

The state of Virginia seceded from the Union on April 17, 1861 and in doing so, became the most important state in the Confederacy.... and it also became the major battleground of the east. On the occasion of Virginia's formal allegiance with the Confederacy, the city of Richmond was named as the new capital of the south. The state also became known for contributing the Confederate military's greatest trio of leaders.. Robert E. Lee, Thomas J. "Stonewall" Jackson and J.E.B. "Jeb" Stuart.

In the years which followed the outbreak of war, the entire state would become a terrible battleground where huge battles and small skirmishes would nearly destroy the countryside.

And all of this would leave "Spirits of the Civil War" in its wake....

There are probably hundreds of ghost stories relating to the Civil War in Virginia, of fine old homes that were turned into field hospitals where phantom soldiers still linger behind or silent stretches of fields where the restless dead still wander... but we obviously could not include them all here. Instead, I offer you a sampling of some of the best, and some of the most blood-chilling tales of Virginia and her Civil War ghosts.

So, read on and enjoy... just be sure to keep the lights on!

THE GHOSTS OF HARPER'S FERRY

Despite Virginia assuming such a major role in the drama of the Confederacy, not all of the residents of the state were so eager to leave the Union. In fact, in no other Confederate state were opinions so sharply at odds as in Virginia.

When the state seceded in April 1861, residents of the western counties beyond the Allegheny Mountains immediately called mass Unionist meetings to oppose the action. Few of the residents of this region owned slaves and their lifestyles and philosophies gave them little in common with the wealthier Virginians of the east. The region's main rivers and roads generally connected them more to the north and their economies depended on resources from Pennsylvania and Ohio.

Virginia's decision to join the Confederacy and the region's strategic importance to the Union only strengthened the longstanding differences between the western and eastern parts of the state. Within a month of secession, the western counties had become a battleground.

On June 11, 1861, delegates from 26 counties met in Wheeling. After two months of debate, the delegation passed ordinances to reorganize the government of Virginia and to create a new state, the state of Kanawha, which would consist of 48 counties, plus two more which were added later.

These (highly illegal) proceedings ultimately created the state of West Virginia. The delegates authorized a reorganized legislature, who in turn called for a constitutional convention, which met in November. By the following April, the state of West Virginia was ratified by voters, who had taken an oath of allegiance to the Union. The new state legislature then requested admission into the Union.

Congress quickly passed the bill and President Lincoln reluctantly approved it. By June, West Virginia had formally entered the United States.

The Civil War had created West Virginia but the new state suffered from its own war during the four years of conflict. In addition to the regular troops, guerilla fighters waged their own war through the rugged forests and mountain regions... leaving behind a bitterness that would take decades to heal.

One place in West Virginia where the Civil War left its indelible mark is Harper's Ferry. Remembered by most as the place where the abolitionist John Brown created havoc, the town also played a part in the ongoing battles of the war. Although described as unimportant from a military standpoint and "impossible to defend" by General Joseph Johnston, Harper's Ferry still saw an amazing amount of activity during the war.

The town changed hands between the Union and Confederate armies a number of times, all in the midst of skirmishes, minor battles and artillery fire. Local citizens evacuated the town so many times that no record remains of the actual count. The town was burned twice and even a nearby railroad bridge was destroyed and rebuilt nine times between 1861 and 1865.

As most all of the readers know, this type of activity is bound to leave ghosts behind.

The involvement of Harper's Ferry in the war began in April 1861 when a hastily organized group of Virginia militia began marching north to capture the poorly guarded armory there. The mission was supposed to be a secret, yet word soon reached Harper's Ferry and the armory was burned on April 18 by concerned local citizens. By the time the Confederates arrived, nearly 20,000 weapons had been destroyed. What remained was only saved by southern sympathizers, who managed to wet down the gunpowder that had been strewn about the building.

The Confederates didn't stay for long and soon, Harper's Ferry was in Union hands. More than a year later, Stonewall Jackson, while invading Maryland, raided Harper's Ferry and took 12,000 prisoners and captured 13,000 weapons, 73 artillery pieces and several hundred supply wagons. Later, the Union controlled the town again, but were routed once more as Lee was marching toward Gettysburg. The Federals would again seize control of the town, to be driven out still another time in 1864 when Harper's Ferry was attacked by General Jubal Early.

After all of this, there are several sites in town which are haunted by ghosts of the Civil War. One of these is an old building called the Town House, which was used during the war as quarters for Union troops. The story goes that the men who lived there took a young Confederate drummer boy as a prisoner. Instead of sending him on to a prison camp, they decided to keep him at the house as a servant, making him wash clothes, clean up after them and prepare their food.

Soon after they brought him to the house, the boy began to cry and plead for his mother. He was obviously homesick, but the boy's constant weeping only angered the Union soldiers. One night, as the men were engaged in a bout of heavy drinking, the boy began crying again. Angry, one of the men grabbed the boy and tossed him out of an upper window. He fell to his death on the hard street below.

According to reports and stories, the spirit of the boy has never left. A number of people who have visited and who have worked at Town House over the years claim to have witnessed the sound of a young boy crying and moaning for his mother. When they go to investigate, they find that no such boy is present.

Another famous haunted place is St. Peters Catholic Church, which looms above the town at the top of a steep flight of stone steps. St. Peters was the only church in the area to actually make it through the war intact and is said to be haunted by two very different ghosts.

According to the legends surrounding the church, the building survived the war thanks to the quick thinking of its priest, Father Costello. The stories say that each time the town was shelled, by either army, the priest would raise the British flag from the steeple. It was said that the artillery gunners always diverted their fire so as not to cause an "international incident".

As time has passed, people who walk past the church in the evening are often surprised by the sight of an old priest, who wears a black friar's hat. He always leaves the rectory and walks toward the church, never answering the greetings of the passersby. Those who have seen these priest are always in for another surprise as he turns and walks directly through the wall of the church!

The other ghost who lingers at St. Peters is said to be that of a young soldier who lay wounded in churchyard during the fighting. For a brief period, the church served as a field hospital and many dying and injured men were brought here for treatment. This particular young man had wounds that were first diagnosed as "not serious" and he was left unattended through most of a day. All the while, he was slowly bleeding to death from a hidden wound.

When the hospital attendants finally reached him and as he was carried by stretcher through the doorway of the church, he was reported to whisper the words, "Thank God, I'm saved." These were his final words as he died immediately after uttering them.

Since then, it has been said that people who enter the church, on certain nights, and who have stood in the threshold of the building, have heard a chilling voice which whispers "Thank God, I'm saved."

SPIRITS OF THE SHENANDOAH VALLEY

A large part of the legendary status of Virginia during the Civil War centers around the area known as the Shenandoah Valley. It was here that a man named Colonel John Singleton Mosby, called the "Gray Ghost of the Confederacy" , became one of the south's many legends. He commanded a group of men known as the 43rd Battalion of Virginia Cavalry, or as they were generally known, Mosby's Rangers.

Mosby carried out a guerilla war against the Federal forces in Virginia, and a highly successful one at that. He used hit and run tactics to surprise the enemy, de-rail trains, cut supply lines and capture tons of Union supplies. His men never numbered more than 800, but that was enough, and the Rangers soon became one of the most famous legions of Confederate fighters.

While they operated without regard for standard military tactics, the Rangers nevertheless fought with honor.... which was something that could not always be said for other guerilla fighters in the Shenandoah. Many of these men were not much above common outlaws, attacking Federal forces and yet pillaging and plundering the local populace too. They also had a habit of indiscriminately killing any Union soldiers who were separated from their units as well.

These sorts of tactics did not sit well with General Lee and his staff, nor with Colonel Mosby, whose men were usually blamed for such atrocities. In addition, this type of "bushwhacking" infuriated the Federal officers as well. This was one of the reasons the Shenandoah was so devastated during the war. The Union officers believed that by burning the farms and homes of the Valley and destroying the crops, it would drive the guerillas out of the area.

Federal revenge against the guerillas grew so bad that by 1864, whenever a guerilla fighter was caught, he was punished on the spot. This generally meant a hangman's noose or the wrong end of a rifle, whichever was more convenient.

These random executions were overshadowed by two similar events which took place in 1864... events which have left a lingering tale behind.

On September 23, 1864, in Front Royal, a group of Federal cavalry executed seven of Mosby's Rangers for alleged atrocities against Federal forces. Three of the Rangers were hanged and the other four were shot.

When Mosby learned of the executions, he secured permission from General Lee to hang an equal number of Union prisoners in reprisal. On November 6, Mosby ordered 27 prisoners, mostly from George A. Custer's and William H. Powell's brigades, to draw slips of paper from a hat. When the lottery was finished, seven men who drew marked papers from the hat would be killed.

Mosby instructed Ranger Edward Thomson and a detail of men to escort the unlucky prisoners to the Valley Pike. They were then to execute the seven men as close to General Phil Sheridan's headquarters as possible... four of them to be shot, three of them hanged.

As the group rode through the wet darkness, one of the prisoners managed to loosen the ropes that bound him and was able to escape into the forest near Berryville. Knowing that he was already taking a chance with Federal patrols in the area, Thomson decided to go no further and he hanged the six remaining men at a place called Beemer's Woods, north of Berryville. Before he left, Thomson pinned a note to the clothing of one of the hanged men which explained that they had been executed in retaliation for the Rangers who had been killed. "Measure for measure," Thomson had written.

When it was all over, Mosby ordered one of his scouts, Lieutenant John Russell, to deliver a message to General Sheridan. Russell, carrying a flag of truce, crossed Federal lines and was taken to Sheridan's headquarters in Winchester. He carried a letter from Mosby stating that no more Federal prisoners would be harmed as long as captured Rangers were treated the same. Following that meeting, there were no more hangings by either side.

A number of years after the war, Mosby received a package in the mail from a former Ranger named Charlie Dear. When he opened it, he discovered a tree limb that had been cut from Beemer's Woods. Dear had expressed the wish that Mosby should make a walking stick from one of the branches from which a Federal soldier had been hanged. Mosby was angered by the gift and later wrote that he "would have preferred something that would make me forget rather than remember the dread affair."

As the years passed, local folk who lived near Beemer's Woods often spoke of the eerie sounds and creaking limbs of the place where the men had been hanged. Some even claimed to feel a strange presence near the entrance to the woods... as though something remained behind there... something which would never rest in peace.

And this was not the only instance where those executed in the Valley returned from the grave. As mentioned, the Federal forces were known for their random executions of men who they believed were guerilla fighters, or were a member of Mosby's Rangers. In some cases, even the innocent became victims of such revenge. This is exactly what occurred to a young man who lived in the Front Royal area. He was accused of being a member of the Rangers and then was beaten to death by a mob of Union soldiers. The story says that when they were finished with him, his body was thrown into a cattle pen, where it was further battered.

It would be the ghost of this same young men who reportedly returned to the Valley many times over a span of years from the 1870's until about 1925. It was said that accounts of his appearances spread fear through entire communities as he was seen every six or seven years.

One eye-witness, in 1912, was Judge Sanford Johnson, who lived near Riverton. He was outside feeding his dogs on one cold winter's day and happened to notice a thin, ragged figure near the creek which crossed his property. He saw the form of a young man in a Confederate uniform and with a cap pulled down low over his brow. The Judge said that the figure jerked and stumbled from the creek and then shambled along down the long road in front of the house. What was the Judge doing at the time? He had run headlong into the house... not sure why he was doing so, but only knowing that the figure filled him with fear.

He would later notice that although the figure crossed directly in front of the house.... he left not a single track in the freshly fallen snow!

The chilling apparition would appear several more times but strangely, there have been no reports of him since 1925. Did the wrongly executed young man finally find peace?

Perhaps the most famous tale of the Shenandoah Valley is the story of the Phantom Stage of Valley Pike. There is little doubt that this tale falls into the realm of ghostly legend... and yet there are some who stubbornly maintain that it is true.

The story begins on May 24, 1862, the eve of the Battle of Winchester. Stonewall Jackson had his army in New Market and was prepared to move against Union General Nathaniel P. Banks, who had moved his troops from Strasburg to Winchester, where he planned to meet Jackson.

The road which connected New Market to Winchester was a portion of the 80-mile long Valley Turnpike. The road had been opened in 1840 and was ahead of its time for 19th century road construction, being 18 feet wide and paved with crushed limestone. It was a technical marvel of its time as most other roads tended to be abysmal. Jackson would use the Valley Pike to its greatest advantage, moving his army quickly along its length, and it enabled him to fight battles at either end of it within days of each other.

The story of the spectral stagecoach actually begins in New Market. It was said that a Federal spy stole the coach and then escaped toward Winchester to warn General Banks of Jackson's impending attack. Shortly after the spy made off with the coach, his plans were discovered by two Confederate officers who quickly went in pursuit.

Although he had a good lead, the spy was hampered by the heavy coach and the Confederate pursuers quickly closed the distance. As they grew closer to him, lightning flickered across the sky and they could see the man hunched over, snapping the reins and urging the horses to go faster.

The Confederates were only yards behind when the spy turned and saw their drawn pistols. He reached into his coat and withdrew his own revolver, then desperately attempted to take aim at them while trying to steady his arm against the jostling of the stage.

Suddenly, a brilliant flash and a thundering roar swept over the stage and the driver. Somehow, a bolt of lightning from the dark clouds above had streaked down and blasted the stagecoach. The coach literally exploded into flame and the driver simply vanished from his seat.... utterly destroyed.

The pursuing Confederates were thrown from their horses and struck the surface of the roadway. Their animals mewled in terror and whipped around quickly, somehow avoiding the burning remains of the stage. The two men were stunned by what they had seen and after calming their horses, returned to New Market to spread the story.

The following day, Stonewall Jackson triumphed at Winchester, thanks to the fact that Banks had no warning of his attack. The Union defenses collapsed and the Confederates were given a warm welcome by the grateful residents of the city.

Time has now passed and the war has long since ended but they say that on certain nights, when lightning dances across the sky, travelers along the Valley Pike (now US Highway 11) still report seeing a ghostly stagecoach rattling silently along the road. The driver frantically cracks the reins across the back of the horses, urging them on toward Winchester... still trying to complete his final mission.

WAVERLY FARM'S GRAY MAN

By the Fall of 1864, the Shenandoah Valley had become the most hotly contested piece of ground in Virginia. It was vital to the Confederacy for its location and for the rich stores of food and crops that could be found there... and for this same reason, the Federals were intent on destroying the place. That season became known as the time of the Burning.

Major General Philip Sheridan had been ordered to the Valley by General Grant for the sole purpose of laying waste to it. He was to clear the Confederates out of the Valley and then destroy the place, burning every field and farm and making sure that nothing remained behind.

Sheridan carried out the mission without regret, much to the dismay of the local residents, who watched everything they owned going up in flames. It was said that smoke from burning farms and crops could be seen from more than one hundred miles away.

The Confederate army, led by General Jubal Early, could only watch the devastation, enraged but helpless against the Federal's superior numbers. When Sheridan had arrived in the Valley, the Confederates had run the Union troops ragged, marching and countermarching in an attempt to deceive the new Union commander. Early had been intent on reclaiming the Valley and with Sheridan concentrating his troops around Harper's Ferry, he was lulled into a false sense of security. He would soon learn that he had misjudged Sheridan and within months, the Valley would be lost.

As with many of the other battles of the war, lingering spirits have sometimes been left behind and the fighting over the Shenandoah Valley (as seen previously) is no exception. The story of the "Gray man" of Waverly Farm has its beginnings in this fighting and in fact, begins on September 19, 1864, with the death of North Carolina Colonel Charles C. Blacknall.

The North Carolina man was a hardened veteran of the early days of the war. He had been wounded and captured twice, one time at the Battle of Gettysburg. He had been shot in the face on that occasion, his jaw broken and several teeth lost. He had been imprisoned at Johnson's Island after his capture but was exchanged in February 1864, returning to his regiment as its colonel.

Blacknall was awakened on that September morning by the sounds of guns coming from his picket line along the Berryville Pike, about three miles east of the town of Winchester. He quickly mounted his horse and rode toward the sound. He arrived at the picket lines to find his men being driven back across the Opequon Creek by Federal cavalry. The troops along the picket lines were forced back into the camp of the 23rd North Carolina and they began to make a fighting retreat. In the midst of the fighting, Blacknall was wounded in the foot.

Blacknall was assisted into Winchester and painfully settled in the home of a woman named Smith. While he was in bed, the regiment, along with the rest of General Early's troops, was driven out of Winchester. Blacknall was left behind what were now Union lines.

He was later examined by a Federal surgeon, who recommended that Blacknall's foot be amputated. The Colonel refused, insisting that the foot would heal and that he would be able to walk again. The Confederate Colonel was soon moved out of Winchester and taken to Waverly. The farm was owned by the sister of one of Blacknall's nurses, a Mrs. Washington.

Despite fine care in a more tranquil setting, Blacknall's condition worsened. According to the stories, he only improved for a brief time on October 17, when he heard the sound of cannon fire in the distance. The guns came from the Battle of Cedar Creek, about twelve miles south of town but Blacknall believed that it was Early's army, returning to Winchester. He asked his servant to help him into his uniform and he hobbled over to the window, convinced that he would soon be reunited with his men. To his dismay however, the guns grew distant and Blacknall realized that Sheridan had beaten the Confederates again. Heartbroken, he returned to his bed.... and he never rose from it again.

Blacknall's health continued to worsen. The surgeons were fetched from town and the Colonel's leg was amputated at the knee in hopes that this might stop the spread of infection. Unfortunately, it did no good, and on November 6, Colonel Blacknall died.

He was buried in the Episcopal churchyard in Winchester, although his body was later moved to nearby Stonewall Cemetery, where he was laid to rest beside his fallen comrades from the 23rd North Carolina.

But as you may have already guessed, the legends say that he does not rest there in peace....

The sightings of the "Gray Man" at Waverly began a short time after the war. A woman named Mrs. Joliffe was visiting the Washington family when she was awakened by the opening of the guest room door. She was surprised to see a man in a gray Confederate uniform walk across the room and stop at the window. It seemed as though the man was watching for someone.

Obviously, Mrs. Joliffe was not accustomed to having strange men appear in her room at night and she demanded to know what the man was doing there. He gave her no answer and seemed oblivious to anyone else being in the room. Finally, after several minutes, he bowed his head as if disappointed and turned away from the window. For a moment, as he was leaving the room, Mrs. Joliffe caught a glimpse of the expression on his face and later remarked that he seemed utterly without hope. Then, the man was gone. The description that she would later provide to the Washington's matched Colonel Blacknall exactly.

And she has not been the last to see depressed soldier take up his post in the guest bedroom of the house... the same room in which Blacknall died. In fact, sightings have continued for many years and even continue to occur today. Those who have encountered the apparition, whether he be a conscious spirit or a lingering impression, report the same things... the sounds of footsteps entering the room, the ghostly figure and even sometimes, the image of a man who is framed in the window when he is seen from outside. All of them report seeing a man in a gray uniform who matches the description of Colonel Charles Blacknall.

Why does he remain here at Waverly, which is now a private residence and closed to the public? Or does he remain at all? Could the energy of Colonel Blacknall's dying days and his disappointment over Early's loss to Sheridan have left an impression on the place... one that keeps repeating itself over and over again?

Perhaps.... or maybe Blacknall's spirit has simply never found rest. Perhaps he is still waiting for the return of the Confederate army to Winchester... a day that will never come.

BLACK WALNUT PLANTATION

Black Walnut, in Halifax County, was built sometime between 1765 and 1776 and for decades, was a thriving plantation with more than 2,000 acres of land, a grand manor house and a dozen outbuildings. In 1850, the manor house was added onto again and it became known as one of the most attractive homes in the area. The house is still standing today and in fact, has been listed on both the Virginia and National Register of Historic Places.

Besides being a historic house, it is also regarded as a haunted one.

On June 25, 1864, Black Walnut plantation was the scene of the only Civil War battle of any consequence that was fought in Halifax County. On one portion of the property, the Battle of the Staunton River Bridge took place. While largely forgotten today, the battle was of some significance, for if the Federals had carried the day, they would have destroyed the railroad line beyond it and cut off a key Confederate supply line. As it turned out though, this would not be the only significance of the battle....

By 1864, the local area, and Virginia as a whole, was suffering badly from the damaging effects of the war. All of the young men of the area had left home to fight in the Confederate military and because of this, nearly every able-bodied man of the region had left his home or farm in the hands of their younger sons and elderly fathers. Unfortunately, they had been forced to leave the protection of the homes and farms in those hands too.

When word came that Union troops were going to cross the Staunton River Bridge, the Confederate forces only had about 250 reserve troops, so a call went out for volunteers. Most of the soldiers came from the Halifax County "Home Guard", which mostly consisted of young boys from farms and a local school, plus a collection of old men in their 60's and 70's. They formed what is now remembered as the "Old Men and Young Boy's Brigade", gathered what weapons they could find, and went off to defend the bridge.

Two companies of regular Confederate troops were positioned on the right side of the bridge and the volunteers were placed on the left. They dug in and waited for the Federals to arrive. Late in the afternoon of the following day, the battle began. The Union troops charged the bridge four times, but each time, the outnumbered and outgunned Home Guard pushed them back. By the end of the day, the Federals had lost 300 men and the Confederates only 35... and they had held onto the bridge.

The ghostly tale related to this battle is not connected to the fighting itself, but rather to Black Walnut plantation. The story recalls a young woman who lived there, the daughter of the owner, who fell in love with a local Confederate officer. He was one of the regular troops who fought at the Staunton River Bridge. Just before the battle, he came to see her, excited at the prospect of encountering the Federal soldiers. He waved goodbye to her as he rode away but that was the last time that she ever saw him... he was killed in the fighting the following day.

It was said that the young woman became deeply depressed and refused to eat or take care of herself. Within a year, she too had died, of the proverbial "broken heart".

According to the stories, the ghost of the young woman has never left the grounds of the plantation. Witnesses say that she roams the house at night and that they have heard the sound of her rustling skirts and tapping footsteps. She has also been said to look in on visitors who spend the night in the house, as though searching to see if one of them might be the soldier that she so tragically lost.

THE HAUNTINGS OF JEFFERSON DAVIS

There are two very different locations associated with hauntings and Confederate President Jefferson Davis and his family. Both of them are located in Virginia and both are connected to great tragedies suffered at the hands of the Davis' both during and after the Civil War.

Jefferson Davis had been born in Kentucky in 1808 and ironically had been raised just miles away from the early home of Abraham Lincoln. He attended and graduated from West Point in 1828 and was sent to the infantry. He soon fell in love with Sarah Taylor, the daughter of his commander and future president, Zachary Taylor. He left the military in 1835 with a career that was only distinguished by several blow-ups with superior officers. Davis never believed that he had the temperament to be a common soldier. He was a man suited to command and in later years, would have preferred a military command to the presidency of the Confederacy.

Davis left the army and moved to Mississippi, where he helped run the Davis plantation with his brother Joseph. The family had many slaves, but by the standards of those days, treated their slaves quite well. Their food was never rationed, they were allowed to choose their own names and the slave quarters were far above those found on most plantations of the time. However, they were still property and in Davis' eyes, rightfully his under the laws of the Constitution.

In 1835, Davis married Sarah Taylor without the blessing of her parents. Five weeks later, both of them fell ill from malaria, a disease, like yellow fever, not uncommon in the swampy regions of the south. A short time later, Sarah died at the age of 21 and became the first of many tragedies to come in Davis' life.

In 1845, Davis entered the political arena and was elected to Congress as a Democrat. That same year, he married Varina Howell, a beautiful young woman who was half his age. Davis served for one year in the House of Representatives before resigning to lead a group of Mississippi volunteers during the Mexican War. As fate would have it, he found himself with a command under Zachary Taylor, who now greeted him warmly, their differences forgotten in their shared grief over Sarah's death. Davis was wounded at the Battle of Buena Vista and gained a reputation for bravery, which he used to his advantage during the next Senate election. He handily won the seat and remained in office until 1853, when he was named war secretary by President Franklin Pierce.

In 1857, Davis reclaimed his Senate seat and became one of the most forceful advocates of southern rights, regularly threatening secession if those rights were challenged. A few years later, Davis would test the waters for a run at the White House as a Democratic candidate in 1860. At the Baltimore nomination convention, his name was placed under consideration, but Davis never pressed the issue, knowing that he would never gain enough northern support to win an election.

Later, when the Democrat vote was split between Stephen Douglas and John Breckinridge, they were defeated. Although cautious and still hoping to compromise, Davis pushed for Mississippi's secession. He made an emotional farewell speech to the Senate on January 21, 1861 and then withdrew from his seat with four other senators. He was soon named the commander of the militia in Mississippi and also a compromise candidate for the presidency of the six states that now made up the Confederacy. He was elected on February 9 and inaugurated nine days later in Montgomery. Despite his poor health, an ongoing illness related to the malaria he had contracted years before, he still would have preferred a military command.

The years that would follow Davis' election as the President of the Confederacy would be terrible ones and they weighed heavily on Davis, just as the concerns of the north brutally wore down Abraham Lincoln.

And this would not be the only sadness and despair the two men would share during the war....

The home that would serve as the "White House of the Confederacy" was located on Clay Street in Richmond and was built in 1818 by Dr. John Brockenbrough. The house was remodeled in the 1840's, again in 1857, and in 1861, was chosen to serve as the home of Jefferson Davis and his family. When the war had broken out that same year, the capital of the Confederacy was moved from Montgomery, Alabama to Richmond. The city purchased the Brockenbrough house and offered it to Davis as his residence. He declined to take the house for nothing and began renting it instead.

The family remained in the house until April 1865, when Richmond was evacuated. It then served as a Union Army headquarters until 1870 and then became a public school. In 1893, the house was purchased by the Confederate Memorial Literary Society and was made into a historical museum, as it remains today.

There is every indication that the Davis family was happy living in this house, despite the pressures of the war and the agonizing hours that President Davis spent working, often until the darkest hours of the night. As time wore on, his health declined to the point that friends and associates urged him to rest and exercise.

It was said that Davis' only remedy for the long hours of work was his family. He often said that they eased his mind for precious minutes every day, especially his children, whom he constantly indulged. It was said that many important meetings and consultations, with anyone from General Lee to the presidential staff, would be interrupted by the arrival of the children.

Davis' special favorite was little Joe, who turned five in April 1864. He often remarked that Joe was the hope and greatest joy in his life. Unfortunately, like President Lincoln's favorite son, Willie, that greatest joy was taken away all too soon....

On April 30, 1864, Varina Davis left the children playing while she made lunch for her husband. A short time later, Joe, and his older brother, Jeff, wandered outside and onto the balcony in back of the house. Apparently, Joe was climbing on the railing when he lost his balance and fell to the brick pavement below. The fall fractured his skull and he died a short time later.

Varina became hysterical and it was said that passersby could hear her screaming inside of the house throughout the afternoon and into the evening. President Davis was himself crushed. He sat beside his wife for more than three hours, turning away everyone who called, including a courier with an important message from General Lee. Then, he vanished into the upper floors of the house, where his footsteps could be heard, incessantly pacing back and forth.

Over the course of the next few days, cards and letters flooded the Davis home, including a heartfelt message from Abraham Lincoln, who was returning the gesture extended by Davis when his own son had died. The funeral took place a short time later and the Hollywood Cemetery in Richmond offered a free plot for the boy's burial. An immense crowd gathered at the cemetery on the day of the burial and it was reported that children from all over the city, many of them Joe's playmates, covered the grave with flowers and crosses. The children also collected $40 and bought a monument to place on the boy's burial site which read "erected by the little boys and girls of the southern capital."

The last year that Jefferson Davis spent in Richmond was one of extreme sadness and grief. The house had become a place haunted by the memories of Joe's smiling face, and his horrible death. Davis even had the balcony that the boy fell from removed from the house and destroyed. The only moment of joy the Davis' experienced in the house was the birth of Winnie Davis on June 27, 1864. She would be called the "Daughter of the Confederacy."

On Sunday, April 2, 1865, word reached Davis from General Lee.... the army was evacuating the Petersburg and Richmond lines and soon the city would fall. As the Federal forces neared the city, Davis assembled his cabinet and staff and directed the removal of public archives, the treasury, and all records to Danville. Later that afternoon, Davis himself left the city on a special train.

The next 24 hours in Richmond were chaos as the residents struggled to flee the city and the Union Army moved in. Disorder increased with every hour as the streets filled with people trying to make their way to the railroad depots. Two regiments of militia were supposed to be maintaining order in the city, but the panic was beyond their control. Terror ruled the streets and left destruction in its wake... plundering and looting was rampant; straggling soldiers seized and consumed massive amounts of liquor; the windows were shattered and shops destroyed; and four tobacco warehouses were set on fire. The flames from the blaze soon spread to nearby buildings, burning out of control through the night.

Richmond, the capital of the Confederacy, had fallen into Union hands.

But in all of the chaos, Davis and his family somehow escaped. After the fighting ended and after Lee had surrendered at Appomattox, Davis and Varina managed to avoid the soldiers who were looking for them and planned to start out for Texas. Here, Davis would gather his still-loyal soldiers, then would establish a new capital of the Confederacy and continue the war. It was during this time of flight when Abraham Lincoln was assassinated. Patrols were stepped up and the gauntlet was tightened around Davis for most believed that he had somehow been involved in Lincoln's death.

On May 10, 1865, a contingent of Federal cavalry surrounded a group of tents near the town of Irwinville, Georgia. It was here that Davis and his followers were hiding and forced to come out. The Confederate president was quickly arrested. When the commanding officer informed him that he had been implicated in the Lincoln assassination, Davis immediately denied it. "I would rather have dealt with President Lincoln than Andrew Johnson," he reportedly said.

Davis and Varina were taken into custody and transported by ship to the country's most escape-proof prison of the day, Fort Monroe. The location of the fort dated back almost to the first settlements on the American continent.

In 1608, Captain John Smith had discovered the area and deemed it a worthy place for a fort. A year later, Governor John Ratcliffe was dispatched from Jamestown to build an earthworks called Fort Algernourne, which by 1611, was well-stockaded and fortified by seven heavy guns and a garrison of 40 men.

The War of 1812 prompted the defense department of the United States to begin a series of forts for coastal defense that would stretch all of the way from Maine to Louisiana. This fort was selected to be a key post in the chain and construction and renovations extended over a period dating from 1819 to 1834. The name of the fort was finally changed too, in honor of President James Monroe, a Virginian.

When it was completed, the fort was fitted with nearly 200 guns which could control the channel into Hampton Roads and also dominated the approach to Washington using the Chesapeake Bay. It was called the "Gibraltar of Chesapeake Bay" and remains today the largest enclosed fortification in the United States and one of only two American forts surrounded by a moat.

Fort Monroe was known for being so impregnable that it was one of the few Federal forts in the South not captured by the Confederacy during the war. For this reason, President Lincoln did not hesitate to visit the fort in May 1862 to help plan the attack on Norfolk, nor did General Grant in April 1864 when he stayed at the fort while designing his battle plans to bring about the end of the war.

There have been a number of supernatural events reported at Fort Monroe, from apparitions of soldiers to the phantom clumping of boots; the rustling of phantom skirts; the sounds of laughter; and even the ghost of Abraham Lincoln himself. The former president has been spotted a number of times, clad in a dressing gown and standing deep in thought by a fireplace, in a room that has been appropriately called the "Lincoln Room".

But perhaps the most commonly reported ghosts here are those of Jefferson and Varina Davis. Mrs. Davis has been known to appear on late evenings and has been spotted in the second floor window of quarters directly across from where her husband was once imprisoned.... but it is Davis himself most commonly associated with the haunting at the fort.

President and Mrs. Davis arrived at Fort Monroe on May 19. Their ship docked at the fort's Engineer's Wharf and Davis was roughly taken ashore and hustled into a casemate cell which was about one step above a dungeon. He was imprisoned here for the next several days, until sunset of May 23. On this evening, the door to his cell opened and Davis was greeted with the sight of Captain Jerome Titlow, followed by a blacksmith and his assistant. To the Confederate president's dismay, the assistant was carrying a set of leg irons and chains.

These men were followed by two privates from the Third Pennsylvania Heavy Artillery who entered the cell with fixed bayonets. Two more soldiers were stationed outside, while another pair guarded the casemate door. More sentries were positioned on the ramparts overlooking the area and along with the armed guards on the other side of the moat, Davis had 70 captors in all. They were taking no chances that he might escape, either with or without assistance from still loyal Rebel troops.

As Captain Titlow entered the room, he explained to Davis that he had been given orders to put him in leg irons. Almost apologetically, he insisted that he was just following orders. The instructions to place Davis in chains came from Edwin Stanton, Lincoln's Secretary of War. At that point, most believed that Davis had somehow been involved in the assassination of the northern president. Davis paced about the small cell and then nervously rested his left foot on a chair. Thinking that Davis was submitting to this indignity, he instructed the blacksmith to go about his work.

The blacksmith knelt down to shackle the chains on the president's leg when suddenly Davis attacked the man holding the chains, sending him sprawling onto the floor of the cell. The blacksmith jumped to his feet and raised the hammer above his head to strike Davis, but Titlow pushed between them. It took four men to hold Davis down as the chains were shackled to his legs.

Captain Titlow was the last men to leave Davis' cell. As he walked out the door, he turned and looked back at the Confederate leader. He later remarked that Jefferson Davis was seated on the edge of his prison cot, his head in his hands and tears streaming down his face. Even though Captain Titlow held no sympathies for the Confederate cause, he believed that the utter destruction of Jefferson Davis was one of the saddest things he had ever seen.

The days which followed were filled with humiliation for Davis. The fort's chief medical officer, Lieutenant General John Craven, recommended that Davis' chains be removed. The Confederate president's health was fragile and being chained like an animal was simply cruel. Not surprisingly, his recommendation was ignored. Soon however, word of the shackling leaked out and reached the newspapers. Public disapproval of the punishment, in the south and the north, created so many problems that the War Department finally ordered Davis to be unchained.

After more than four months in solitary confinement, Davis was moved to better quarters, although he remained a prisoner. Soon, the public would also begin to clamor for Davis' release. There was no proof that he had, in any way, been involved in the Lincoln assassination. Even men like Horace Greeley and Senator Thaddeus Stevens got behind the effort and created a stir that was simply too big to ignore.

At last, on May 13, 1867, after two years of confinement, Jefferson Davis was released. He lived on for 24 years after the end of the Civil War, traveling extensively and writing about the "Lost Cause" and its consequences. When he died in 1889, he was buried in Metairie Cemetery in New Orleans, where he had been living.

A short time later, Varina Davis had her husband exhumed and moved to Beauvoir, their family home in Mississippi. This did not prove suitable either as the estate was located on a narrow peninsula on the Gulf of Mexico. It was feared that flooding might someday destroy the site and Varina pondered what to do.

At this time, large numbers of Confederate veterans wrote to her and asked that she choose Richmond for her husband's final resting place. Here, in the city's Hollywood Cemetery, he would rest among the honored dead of those who had fought and died for the South.

Varina agreed and moved Davis' body to Richmond, aboard a special train, in the Spring of 1893. The trip took several days, stopping frequently in towns across the south so that people could pay their last respects to the Confederacy's first and only president. They arrived in Richmond on May 30 and the coffin was taken to the rotunda of the capitol building, where it lay in state for a day.

On May 31, a black hearse, drawn by six white horses, took the coffin to Hollywood Cemetery. It was followed by a band which played "Dixie" and passed along streets which were draped in mourning for the deceased president.

But still the legends persist that Davis does not rest quietly in his honored grave....

Down through the years, numerous witnesses have reported sighting apparitions in and around the casemate where Jefferson Davis was confined. Most of the sightings have been of strange mists and energy masses of different shapes and forms... but most believe the ghost seen here is that of Davis, perhaps reliving the trying ordeal that he suffered through.

But this is not the final ghost story connected to the Davis family.

The legends say that there is one more... that of the ghost of little Joe Davis. It has been said that for more than 30 years after Jefferson Davis left Richmond, dozens of witnesses reported seeing the apparition of a little boy, who resembled Joe Davis, wandering aimlessly near the Confederate White House on Clay Street in Richmond. The boy was oblivious to passersby and was heard to walk back and forth, muttering "He's gone! He's gone!", just before vanishing in front of startled witnesses.

In 1893, when the body of Jefferson Davis was returned to Richmond, and placed in Hollywood Cemetery, the body of Joe Davis was moved and placed beside his father. Strangely enough, the apparition of the little boy who cried "He's gone!" was never seen again.....

SOURCES

Don't Know Much about the Civil War by Kenneth C. Davis (1996)
The Civil War: An Illustrated History by Geoffrey Ward with Ric Burns & Ken Burns (1990)
A Short History of the Civil War by James L. Stokesbury (1995)
Historical Times Illustrated Encyclopedia of the Civil War edited by Patricia Faust (1991)
Complete Idiot's Guide to the Civil War by Alan Axelrod (1998)
Civil War Times: The Civil War by William C. Davis and Bell I. Wiley (1998)
Sherman's March by Burke Davis (1980)
A House Divided edited by Edward L. Ayers (1997)
Historic Haunted America by Michael Norman and Beth Scott (1995)
13 Alabama Ghosts and Jeffrey by Kathryn Tucker Windham & Margaret Gillis Figh (1969)
Ghosts! Washington's Most Famous Ghost Stories by John Alexander (1975- Revised 1998)
Guide to Haunted Places of the Civil War from Blue and Gray Magazine (1996)
Blue and Gray Magazine (various issues)
Georgia Ghosts by Nancy Roberts (1997)

Banshees, Bugles and Belles: True Georgia Ghost Stories by Barbara Duffey (1995)
Haunted Illinois by Troy Taylor (1999)
Life Magazine (various issues)
New Orleans Ghosts by Victor C. Klein (1993)
Haunted Houses by Richard Winer and Nancy Osborn Ishmael (1979)
More Haunted Houses by Richard Winer and Nancy Osborn Ishmael (1981)
Houses of Horror by Richard Winer (1983)
Haunted America by Michael Norman and Beth Scott (1994)
Phantom Army of the Civil War edited by Frank Spaeth (1997)
Battlefield Ghosts by B. Keith Toney (1997)
Ghosts and Haunted Houses of Maryland by Trish Gallagher (1988)
Ghosts and Legends of Frederick County by Timothy Cannon and Nancy Whitmore (1979)
13 Mississippi Ghosts and Jeffrey by Kathryn Tucker Windham (1974)
Ghosts! Personal Accounts of Modern Mississippi Hauntings by Sylvia Booth Hubbard (1992)
Civil War Ghost Stories and Legends by Nancy Roberts (1992)
Haunted Heartland by Beth Scott and Michael Norman (1985)
Missouri Ghosts by Joan Gilbert (1997)
Legends and Lies of the American West by Dale L. Walker (1997)
The Haunted South by Nancy Roberts (1970)
North Carolina Ghosts and Legends by Nancy Roberts (1967)
Coastal Ghosts by Nancy Rhyne (1985)
Ghosts of Georgetown by Elizabeth Robertson Huntsinger (1995)
More Ghosts of Georgetown by Elizabeth Robertson Huntsinger (1998)
Ghosts of the Prairie Magazine (various issues)
Haunted Houses USA by Dolores Riccio and Joan Bingham (1989)
Civil War Ghosts of Virginia by LB Taylor (1995)
A Ghostly Tour of Harper's Ferry by Shirley Doughtery (1982)
Ghosts of McRaven by Janis S. Raley (Ghost Preservation League)
Haunted Places: The National Directory by Dennis William Hauck (1996)

Personal Interviews and Correspondence

(Left)
The historic streets of Harper's Ferry, where events took place that would later plunge the country into Civil War.
It is along the streets where the ghost of radical abolitionist John Brown is still said to walk.

(Right)
The Piper House on the Antietam Battlefield was once the headquarters of General James Longstreet. Some say the spirits of the past still linger here.
(Below)
The Burnside Bridge at Antietam played a role in the battle and today is reportedly haunted by soldiers slain here long ago.

(Left)
Antietam's famous "Bloody Lane" where many claim to have glimpsed and have heard the battle itself being replayed.

(Right)
Wilder Tower on the Chickamauga Battlefield was constructed as a tribute to one of the heroes of the conflict. In recent years, strange incidents have caused many to question whether or not it may be linked to the supernatural.
(Below)
The fields at Stone River, where witnesses claim to have encountered apparitions of Confederate soldiers.

(Above)
The Cashtown Inn, near Gettysburg, is one of the most haunted hotels in America. Incidents of strange happenings here date back to the early 1900's and continue today in the form of ghostly apparitions, unexplained sounds and incredible phenomena.

(Below)
Pennsylvania Hall at Gettysburg College was just one of many buildings used as a field hospital during the fighting here. In this case, it appears that the traumatic death and suffering which occurred inside has left an indelible mark on the structure.

(Left)
The daunting tangle of rocks at Gettysburg called the Devil's Den is believed to be the battlefield's most haunted location.

(Below)
The notorious photo of the Confederate sharpshooter which was taken at the Devil's Den. The photo, which came to be considered one of the most famous of the battle, was an outright lie, as was the story behind it.
(US Army Military Historical Institute)

CHAPTER FIVE
HAUNTED PRISONS OF THE CIVIL WAR

It's huge doors swung open and we were in the presence of.... I do not know what to call them. It was evident they were human beings but hunger, sickness, exposure and dirt had so transformed them that they more resembled walking skeletons, painted black.
Lucius Barber, Union sergeant under Sherman, on the Confederate
Prison at Andersonville

The supply of wood issued to the prisoners during the winter was not enough to keep the most modest fires for two hours out of every twenty-four, and the only way to avoid freezing, was by remitting devotion to the blankets... For my part, I never saw any one get enough of any thing to eat at Point Lookout, except the soup, and a tea spoonful of that was too much for ordinary digestion.
Anthony Keiley, a Confederate officer and a prisoner of war at
Point Lookout, Maryland in 1864

There are deeds, crimes, that may be forgiven, but this is not among them. It steeps its perpetrators in blackest, escapeless, endless damnation. Over fifty thousand have been compelled to die of starvation.... reader, did you ever try to realize what starvation actually is?... in those prisons... and in a land of plenty!
Walt Whitman, on the state of the southern prisons

Atrocity came in many forms during the Civil War, from the shedding of blood in battle to outright slaughter. In battle, the art of "killing" becomes part of the strategy of winning the battle but other kinds of cruelty and killing took place during the war... in both the north and the south.

When you refer to the prisons of the Civil War, the images of horror from places like Andersonville immediately springs to mind. However, not all of the prison commanders were sadists who enjoyed torturing their prisoners. Most of these men were diligent and honorable soldiers who were doing the best they could with a bad situation.

Prior to 1861, there was simply no precedent for the care of prisoners of war. In February of that year, the United States Army had less than 16,000 officers and men of all ranks and most of these were serving on the western frontier in scattered companies. One year later, after the surrender of the Confederate garrison at Fort Donelson, General Grant captured nearly that many men after one battle. It was the first large surrender of the war and at that point, how to house, feed and control such a massive number of prisoners was a complete mystery.

Possibly the best way to handle the situation with prisoners was to exchange them. This was how it was handled in Europe at the time. In these countries, prisoners were exchanged on a regular basis through formal treaties and gentleman's agreements between officers. However, in America, President Lincoln refused to agree to a formal exchange treaty. To agree to a treaty with the Confederacy, he maintained, would mean that the United States was recognizing the Confederacy as a nation, rather than as an illegal collection of rebels.

Regardless, the Union and Confederate generals made their own informal exchanges beneath the flag of truce. By 1862, a formal agreement was made between the opposing armies that prisoners would be exchanged within 10 days of capture.... but it wouldn't last. The system quickly broke down and prisons and prison camps on both sides began to fill with prisoners awaiting exchange. A new system would soon be needed to combat the terrible overcrowding in the camps.

Soon, another idea was attempted. From the beginning of the war, civilians suspected of disloyalty or spying for the opposite side were not imprisoned, but were "paroled". The military decided to try this also and some prisoners were not housed in the camps, but were returned to their own lines in exchange for a promise that they would not return to duty until they were "formally exchanged".

Any guesses as to how well this turned out?

The system was officially ended by General Grant. After his victory at Vicksburg, Grant found himself burdened with more than 31,000 Rebel prisoners. Rather than try to feed and guard these men, he decided to parole them instead.

Then, during the Chattanooga Campaign, Grant discovered that a very high number of the Confederate prisoners who were captured were the same men that he had paroled at Vicksburg. After Grant was given command of all of the Union armies, he called a halt to all prisoner exchanges in April 1864.

Not only was Grant irritated by the Confederate violations of the parole system, but he also knew that the Confederacy desperately needed their prisoners to be returned to them. They were already short on men and greatly outnumbered and by refusing to return their prisoners, the Union could hurt them even more. Secondly, Grant was also aware of the tremendous cost involved in keeping the Federal prisoners in the southern camps. This would put an additional burden on a government who was already having trouble feeding and clothing their own army, let alone their prisoners too.

Grant was forced to make a grim decision when he halted the prisoner exchanges... and one that he would be harshly criticized for. He knew that the conditions in the Confederate prisons were unspeakably filthy and dangerous. The Federal prisoners were given only starvation rations and disease was common. He knew that by not allowing these men to be exchanged would most likely kill them, but he felt that he had no choice. Grant believed that the needs of these few men were overshadowed by the needs of the entire nation.

And if things were bad in the prison camps before.... they were about to become worse.

In the early days of the war, the prison camps on both sides were fairly civilized places (at least as far as prison camps go). Both the Federal and the Confederate armies treated their prisoners well, as it was believed that they would be only short term detainees and soon exchanged. Local ladies, out of a sense of Christian decency, often would visit the prisons and bring the inmates bundles of food, socks, blankets and other small comforts.

However, the war continued on, and supplies grew shorter, men grew more bitter against the other side and the desire for revenge grew stronger. Soon, it was not uncommon to give the prisoners just a little less to eat, or a little less fire wood to keep warm with.... and in some cases, downright cruelty became the order of the day.

The Confederate military had been the first to have to deal with large numbers of prisoners. Even before Grant's mass capture at Fort Donelson (and even before the attack on Fort Sumter), the Confederates had forced the surrender of United States regulars stationed in Texas, who were then imprisoned in temporary camps. Then, after their victory at Manassas, the south had to provide for 1,000 prisoners who were captured in the fighting. These men were sent back to Richmond by train.

The officer placed in charge of these new prisoners was Brigadier General John H. Winder, a West Point graduate who was a friend of Jefferson Davis. To house the prisoners from Manassas, and the increasing number which followed, Winder used several warehouses. One of them became known as "Castle Thunder" and was mainly used for political prisoners and other Confederate criminals.

In 1862, Winder took over another warehouse, this one owned by ship chandlery and grocery company called Libby & Son. The building was unfurnished, but did have running water and primitive toilets. Libby Prison soon became a prison for Federal officers and became known as one of the most notorious places in the south. The floor plan of the three-story building measured only 100 x 150 feet, but into it was jammed nearly 1,200 men. In 1864, 109 men would escape from the prison through a makeshift tunnel.

In the fall of 1861, the north named Colonel William H. Hoffman as the commissary general of prisoners. Hoffman was a graduate of the United States Military Academy and while he was well-known for his economical regulating of the peace-time army, he was now faced with the prospect of controlling thousands of Confederate prisoners. There are many who remain convinced today that he was not up to the task.

Hoffman's first assignment was to find a central prison where captured men could easily be taken and stored until exchanged. One temporary location was the Old Capitol Prison in Washington City, which was used primarily for political prisoners and other civilians. He also commandeered several Atlantic forts like McHenry in Baltimore, Delaware near Philadelphia, Lafayette and Columbus at New York and Warren in Boston. The army in the west took over a former medical college in St. Louis, which became the Gratiot Street Prison, and later moved prisoners into the abandoned Illinois State Prison at Alton.

Hoffman continued his search for suitable locations and after inspecting several islands on Lake Erie, decided upon Johnson's Island as the location for a prison. The island was a small piece of land, near Sandusky, Ohio, which was not only free of inhabitants but prevented escape by being located far out into the icy waters of the lake.

In 1862, Hoffman realized that he was in over his head. With the fall of Fort Donelson, he suddenly had more prisoners that he knew what to do with. He then turned to camps that had once been used to train Federal volunteers and had these turned into prisons. Among them were Camp Butler near Springfield, Illinois, Camp Randall at Madison, Wisconsin and Camp Douglas in Chicago, which was perhaps the worst of the temporary prisons. The site was undrained, disease-ridden and filthy and had no sanitation to speak of. Hoffman's staff explained that the site needed a sewer, but Hoffman considered this an extravagance. It would not be until the death rate reached ten percent a month in 1863 that Hoffman allowed the camp to be drained.

The build up of prisoners on both sides came to an end in July 1862 when an agreement was reached between the opposing armies to permit prisoner exchanges. Under the agreement, prisoners were exchanged within days of capture and accordingly, the prison populations began to dwindle. Soon, the south was mainly using Libby Prison and a few other buildings in Richmond to temporarily house the prisoners. In the north, Hoffman was able to place most of the captured men at Johnson's Island, Camp Chase and at Alton.

The exchange program was very uneven throughout its short lifespan, but it did keep the prisons fairly orderly and uncrowded. Even when the program changed into the parole system, it managed to keep the prisoners from becoming a drain on the budgets of the two armies. It would not be until Grant's order in 1864 to cease the paroles that life in the camps would become completely unbearable.

Federal and Confederate reactions to Grant's order differed greatly. In the north, Hoffman immediately re-opened a number of prisons that had been previously closed and even opened two new ones at Rock Island, Illinois and at Point Lookout, Maryland. In the south, well, there was little reaction at all. It was almost as if the Confederates believed that the exchanges, or paroles, would start up again. There was no doubt about it... there were many more Confederate prisoners in the north than Union ones in the south and these were men that the southern army desperately needed to continue the war. They had no wish to continue holding the Federal prisoners and frankly, could not afford it.

Soon, however, they realized that the paroles were not going to begin again and they realized that measures had to be taken to provide for the long-term incarceration of the prisoners. At the time, most of the prisoners were housed in Richmond. As this was also the center for supplying the Confederate army, and a large civilian population, a food shortage quickly developed. The Union authorities soon got word that Federal prisoners were starving in the south and Secretary of War Edwin Stanton issued an order for northern prison rations to be cut to the same levels as those being given to Union men in Confederate camps. The secretary declared this to be equal, but many saw it as simply revenge.

Despite the lack of food on both sides, whether accidental or deliberate, hunger was not the only thing responsible for the deaths of prisoners. Many of the men received only meat and bread, and while this was certainly substance, they began to grow sick from a lack of fruit or vegetables. In the northern prisons, Hoffman only allowed the prisoners to have vegetables after an outbreak of scurvy and the Confederates provided vegetables even less frequently. Soon, dysentery and diarrhea were killing more men than hunger and were turning the survivors into living skeletons.

Meanwhile, the food shortage in Richmond grew worse and officials proposed a plan to remove the bulk of the prisoners from the city. In addition to the shortage, there was also a growing fear of a revolt at Libby Prison... a fear that convinced the army to plant a gunpowder mine under the prison in early 1864. It was hoped that this would deter the officer inmates from causing too much trouble.

General Winder sent two men to search out a location for a new prison in Georgia. After a location was discovered, Camp Sumter was constructed by erecting a stockade of timber. It was designed to hold 10,000 men and enclosed an area of 16 acres. In February 1864, even before the fence was completed, rail shipments of prisoners began arriving from Richmond. There was no shelter and the men were forced to improvise huts, tents and burrows that were impossible to keep clean. There was no medical care, little food and the only water came from Stockade Creek, which also served as the prison sewer. At the height of its operation, the prison saw arrivals of more than 400 men each day. Although originally designed to hold 10,000 men, by August 1864, it was packed with more than 30,000.

The camp became known as the "hell-hole of the south" and most will recognize it from the name of the town which was adjacent to it.... Andersonville.

But the south was not alone in its poor treatment of prisoners. At Elmira, New York, Colonel Hoffman had a large fence erected around a former camp for Union recruits and began moving prisoners into it. It quickly became known as the worst of the Federal prisons and even the guard's barracks were badly constructed and flimsy. The prisoners, of course, had it much worse and many of them quickly sickened and died from lack of warm clothing and fuel for fires. Like Camp Douglas, the Elmira prison also suffered from virtually no drainage of waste. A small pond within the confines of the camp provided the drinking water and was also used as the prison toilet.

In addition to disease, the prison also suffered from poor management and bad medical care. Records say that about one-fourth of the 12,000 prisoners incarcerated there are still buried on the property.

At other Union prisons, retaliation for suffering in the south caused conditions to become even worse. Hoffman ordered that all Confederate prisoners be treated in the same way that Federal prisoners were being treated, which resulted in fewer rations, malnutrition and scurvy. It was said that at several prisons, inmates actually organized to hunt rats.

The Confederate camps in Georgia were the first to release their prisoners, but not initially to freedom. In the late summer of 1864, there was a growing concern about Sherman's invading army. It was thought that if Sherman released the Union captives, then the south would have little chance of gaining of the release of their own men in the north. Soon, the Rebels began to move their enlisted men from Andersonville and the officers from a camp in Macon. After placing them first in Savannah, they were then moved to a stockade near Millen. Soon, after the immediate danger of Sherman's march had passed, most of the inmates were returned to Andersonville.

Other prisoners had been moved to Charleston and there were housed in an old hospital which was in immediate range of the Union siege guns. The Federals, believing that the Confederates had purposely placed the men under fire, moved 600 southern officers from Fort Delaware and housed them in a stockade on Morris Island near Charleston. Here, the Confederate prisoners were also in danger of being killed in the bombardment.

By 1865, it was over. Grant, believing that the war was nearly won, ordered a general exchange of prisoners. At City Point, Virginia and at Wilmington, North Carolina, thousands crossed the enemy lines while fighting continued nearby. After the collapse and surrender of the Confederacy, the remainder of the prisoners on both sides finally went home. Over the span of years, more than 56,000 men died in the horror of the camps.

After the war, United States authorities attempted to hold a number of camp commanders responsible for the deplorable conditions in the southern prisons. Several of them were tried in court and one of them, the commander of Andersonville, actually went to the gallows. In the end, there was blame to be found on both sides....

Why were such terrible conditions tolerated by commanders and citizens of the respective sides? Bitterness and revenge? Lack of food and a poor economy? Or simply the darker side of human nature? These questions will never be answered and even though the war has been over for well over a century... the devastating effects of the prison camps are still reverberating today....

With ghosts and hauntings.

THE OLD BRICK CAPITOL

Located in the area of First and East Capitol Streets in Washington is the imposing edifice of the United States Supreme Court.... but this was not the first structure to stand on the piece of ground. Until the early part of this century, the land was occupied by a building known as the Old Brick Capitol, which once served as one of the Union's first prisons during the Civil War. Although the old prison has been gone for some time now.... legends and stories say that some of the guards and captives of the place still remain here.

The Old Brick Capitol dates back many years and holds a number of illustrious (and not so illustrious) spots in our nation's history. After the British burned the Capitol building in 1814, Congress used the building as a temporary meeting place during the five years that it took to rebuild their original home. The people in the area, known as Jenkins Hill, continued to refer to the building as the "Old Brick Capitol" for many years after and the name managed to stick. In 1819, Congress moved to the new Capitol and the Old Brick Capitol was divided into townhouses. It served as a home to a number of well-known congressmen and lawmakers, including John C. Calhoun from South Carolina.

Shortly before his death, Calhoun claimed to be visited by the ghost of George Washington while at home in the building. The spirit was said to have warned Calhoun about the growing movement toward secession in the country. Strangely, just before his death in 1850, Calhoun did make a pronouncement which said that the Union would dissolve within the next ten years.

And Calhoun would not rest in peace either... It was reported that his spirit roamed the Old Brick Capitol for many years, becoming most restless when the Federal military turned the building into a warehouse for Confederate prisoners. The former southern congressmen was said to have been especially upset and active during this period.

It was said that the building was in an advanced state of decay when the Union took it over and turned it into a prison. According to John Alexander's book *Ghosts! Washington's Most Famous Ghost Stories*, the building was "a dingy, crumbling structure, with rambling passages, and with quaint rooms where one least expected to find them". Once the building was converted to a prison, iron bars were placed on the windows, adding another element to the austere countenance of the structure.

After the stories of John Calhoun's ghost had faded into memory, new tales came along to take their place. It was said that long after the physical forms of the Civil War prisoners left the old building, their spirits lingered behind.

Or so say the stories... including one of the most famous tales of the site, that of an eye-witness report from an unidentified congressman from the 1920's. It was said that this gentleman was on his way to the office one morning, in the early, pre-dawn hours, when he happened past the Old Brick Capitol. As he was walking along, he noticed another form in the dim light ahead of him. Something about the man struck him as odd and he noticed that the other fellow appeared to be pacing back and forth, as though marching or standing guard. As the congressman drew closer, he saw that the man wore a hat with an upturned bill and a saber at his waist.

Startled, the congressman started to speak when the faint light of the sun appeared over the horizon. As it did, the blurry form of the soldier winked out and was suddenly gone. This eerie apparition had appeared near the entrance to where the old prison had been.

And this was not the only tale to be told. There were other whispers of strange goings-on in the building, many of which came from members of the National Woman's Party, a suffrage group who had moved into the building in 1922. In addition to a headquarters for the group, the building also served as a dormitory for the women. They had converted the old prison cells into bedrooms.

During the time of the group's residence in the Old Brick Capitol, stories, and even newspaper articles, told of strange experiences the ladies had in the building. The stories told of the sounds of "moaning, weeping and sighing" which often kept them from sleeping at night. On certain nights, their peaceful sleep would be ended by the sounds of bone-chilling screams, heart-rending cries, phantom footsteps, strange laughter or cell doors slamming closed.... cell doors that had been removed years before.

Some have suggested that the sounds of crying may be traced to Mary Surratt, who had been incarcerated at the prison after being convicted as a conspirator in the Lincoln assassination (see our later chapter, **Spirits of the Assassination**). On several anniversaries of her execution, the image of a woman was reported in one of the building's windows. A witness reported that the apparition appeared to be weeping.

Others have traced the eerie laughter to the notorious Confederate spy, Belle Boyd, who was imprisoned at the Old Brick Capitol for many months during the war. The pacing footsteps were linked to the tortured spirit of Confederate prison camp commander Henry Wirz, who was judged responsible, and executed, for the deaths of more than 13,000 Federal soldiers at Andersonville. Wirz spent the last days of his life confined to Old Brick Capitol. He was hanged in the courtyard.

The building was finally torn down a short time later. Despite the strange events, the National Woman's Party worked hard to save the building. Unfortunately, the Supreme Court had grown too large for its old location and Chief Justice William Howard Taft was determined to have a new court house constructed where the Old Brick Capitol already stood. He finally got his wish.

And where do the ghosts of old buildings go when the wrecking ball finally claims their quarters? In this case, some people, like a certain unknown congressman, would say that they have not strayed very far at all.

ALTON CONFEDERATE PRISON
The picturesque city of Alton, Illinois lies just across the Mississippi River from the urban sprawl which becomes St. Louis. It is a mostly quiet town, filled with antique shops, small stores and decades of history... it is also a town which is known for its ghosts. If some of its residents are to be believed, there is a very good chance that Alton may be one of the most haunted cities on the Mississippi River.... and some of the our "Spirits of the Civil War" make up a few of the resident haunts.

Located at the corner of Broadway and Williams Streets in Alton, just as you are leaving town on the Great River Road, is a small stone building. It has been called the "Blaske" building over the years and it was constructed in 1916 by the Sparks Milling Company and has had many owners. It is owned today by a local grain processing company, which allows it to be used as a social service agency. Aside from the actual structure, the building site itself has a much stranger past.... a past which is filled with death, disease, torment and despair.

And it is a site where many say the dead do not rest in peace.

The first prison in the state of Illinois was located in Alton in 1833. The prison was cursed from the very beginning.... it would always be a grim place that became well-known due to the fact that it was plagued by rats and disease. In 1847, social reformer Dorothea Dix would visit the prison and declare the place unfit for habitation, even by criminals. In spite of this, it would later be used as housing for Confederate prisoners during the Civil War.

And conditions then would be no better.

The first building of the penitentiary was completed in 1833 and held 24 cells. Shortly before the prison opened, the legislature amended the criminal code to abolish the use of stocks and whippings as punishment for crimes and had suggested confinement and hard labor instead. The prison was run under the lease system. It would be leased from the state by an individual who was then supposed to feed, bed and guard the prisoners, also paying for their medical care. This person would receive about $5000 from the state and would take on the role of a warden. This man was then responsible for the conditions of the prison... as money allowed.

As more prisoners were incarcerated, additional cells and buildings were added to the prison, along with a warden's residence, which was located at the southwest corner of the site. In 1846, 96 new cells were added and by 1857 they numbered 257, with an average of 2 convicts per cell.

One has to wonder just how the leasing system worked and how much money the wardens managed to pocket in the years the prison was in operation as a state facility. Conditions deteriorated badly here, as mentioned earlier, and the prison would be replaced by a new penitentiary in Joliet by 1859. In May of that year, the prisoners were transferred to Joliet in batches of 40 or 50 and by June of 1860, the Alton prison was abandoned.

Early in the years of the Civil War, Alton was made a military post, thanks to its location on the Missouri border and its access to the river. The first garrison stationed here consisted of three or four companies of the Thirteenth US Regulars, under the command of General William T. Sherman. The local troops were commanded by Lieutenant Colonel Sydney Burbank.

It had become apparent by 1862 that the war was not going to come to a swift end and more space was needed for the growing numbers of prisoners of war. In February 1862, General Halleck obtained permission to use the old Alton penitentiary as a military prison. By this time, the buildings had been empty for several years but were perfect for what was needed as the site was an extensive one.

The first prisoners arrived on February 9 by way of a river steamer. They were marched from the river landing to the prison. Not all of the prisoners were soldiers. They included spies; bridge burners; train wreckers; guerilla fighters; and southern sympathizers. They would never settle into the prison compliantly either. In July, several prisoners would escape by tunneling under the west wall and among them would be Colonel Ebenezer Magoffin, the brother of the governor of Kentucky. Colonel Magoffin had been imprisoned with a death sentence for killing a Union soldier. The following November, a fire would break out in a wooden building at the northwest corner of the grounds. The blaze was put out by the Alton fire brigade, but several more prisoners escaped in the excitement.

But escapes were not all that common and life in the Alton Prison was brutal. While the prison was under the command of the US Army, it was still managed by the last of the prison wardens, Samuel Buckmaster. He was not a military man, but a businessman who had leased the prison from the state from 1846 to 1860, when it had closed down. He still held the lease when the military moved into it and the government paid Buckmaster a sum of $20,000 per year with which to maintain the prison and feed the prisoners. Any money left over was kept by Buckmaster... and it was said that he became a rich man during the war.

Some of the commanders of the prison may not have been much better. After the Thirteenth left to join Grant's army at Vicksburg, the garrison was taken over by the Seventy-Seventh of Ohio with Colonel Jesse Hildebrand in command. After a disastrous rout of his men at Shiloh, Hildebrand had been transferred to Alton. He was ridiculed by his own men, local townspeople and the prisoners alike. He had a habit of canceling all meals for prisoners if he detected any signs of trouble. Needless to say, he was not well-liked and was relieved of his command in March 1863. He returned home to Ohio and died soon after.

As the war continued on, new prisoners arrived in Alton on a regular basis. The prison sometimes contained as many as 2,000 inmates from all over the south. Plots to escape were constantly hatched and while most failed, there was an escape attempt worth noting in July of 1864. There were 46 prisoners at labor in a nearby stone quarry who made a desperate effort against their guards. Acting at a given signal, the prisoners nearly overpowered the soldiers and seized a number of rifles before the guards could act. The escape was not to be however and the guards quickly recovered and killed seven and wounded five of the prisoners. All but two of the Confederates were quickly recaptured.

Many of the escape attempts failed because of the health of the prisoners themselves. Living conditions in the prison were sometimes unbearable and most of the men were badly clothed; food was often withheld or not edible; bathing facilities were not available; gnats and lice were common, as were rats; and diseases like dysentery, scurvy and anemia felled many of the men.

Then, in 1863, several isolated cases of smallpox broke out among the prisoners and then spread, quickly turning into an epidemic. Smallpox is a disease which is spread by direct contact. The prisoners, at the time of the outbreak, probably numbered several thousand in quarters which were designed for 1,300 or less. They slept three in a bed, ate standing up and used a common latrine. Nothing was clean in the prison and the men were often unshaved and had long hair. As mentioned before, they could not bathe, their sleeping mattresses were never changed or washed and the prison yard was filled with pools of stagnant water and urine.

The prison death toll began to climb but Alton's mayor, Edward T. Drummond, refused to have any of the prisoners transferred to city hospitals. The patients were quartered in hallways, storage rooms and stables as the prison hospital was woefully inadequate with only five beds. Before the outbreak, there had been about a half dozen deaths per week in the prison but soon, they were counting more than five a day. Once the disease started to spread, there was no way to stop it. The men were weakened by poor diets and filthy living conditions and were helpless against the disease.

By the second week, prison guards also began to be inflicted with the disease. It was said that those soldiers who were not sick had to be threatened with court-martial to get them to continue with their duties.

Soon, there were other problems... namely, where to bury the bodies of the prisoners who died? Previously, any prisoners who perished were buried in a small meadow in north Alton but when news of the epidemic spread throughout the city, residents of Alton demanded the bodies be taken elsewhere. The bodies of the smallpox victims were then taken to a small island in the middle on the Mississippi River, called "Smallpox Island" in some chronicles and the "Towhead" in others. The island was located about 200 yards upstream of the prison and a temporary hospital was also set up there. The healthy prisoners were ordered to act as hospital attendants and stretcher bearers although few of them were well enough to work. By the end of the third week of the epidemic, about 70 prisoners had died and more than 600 were infected.

The epidemic lasted throughout the Winter of 1863 and into the Spring. Prison officials were said to have given up trying to keep an accurate account of the dead. Estimates made after the war ranged from 1,000 to over 5,000 deaths. Official numbers listed anywhere from 1,354 to 1,434.

Finally, by the Summer of 1864, a group of St. Louis nuns from the Sisters of Charity arrived at the prison. They demanded better medical supplies and permission to conduct burial services for the men. Later that Summer, the epidemic started to subside and by September, the hospital on the island was closed down. Those who were buried there remain unknown today and their graves, and the island itself, are now lost, thanks to the changing channels of the Mississippi River.

The burying ground in north Alton however, does remain today. Several years after the war, wooden markers were placed on the graves of the Confederates buried there, but soon, the burial ground was allowed to deteriorate badly. Since that time, a large monument has been placed in memory of the men who died at Alton prison.

The prison itself was closed down after the war and abandoned, despite a brief effort to once again have it used as a state facility. The walls were torn down and the prison vanished for all time.... unless you know where to look. Visitors and residents of Alton can still find the stones of the prison in the walls, steps and buildings of the city.

After the building was destroyed, the south wall was left standing as a monument and the stone was sold for building material. In 1894, a quarry was approaching the remaining wall so it was torn down and shipped to Crystal City, Missouri to be used for roads there. The area where the prison was located was turned into a public park and playground called "Uncle Remus Park" in honor of the character created by southern author Joel Chandler Harris.

Even then, the entire wall was not demolished and whenever Alton residents needed stone for any sort of construction, they would bring a wagon to the old prison wall and take what they wanted. Sadly, even a number of Confederate veterans, who once were incarcerated at the prison, returned to Alton after the war and took away stones to use for their own grave markers.

Today, only a small portion of the wall still remains on the site of the penitentiary, where visitors can find historical information and displays about the prison and the Civil War. Near the historical marker is the Blaske building, the only structure still standing on the prison site. Many have suggested that energy, and spirits, from the time when the prison existed still linger at this place. Could that be why, according to an article in *Fate* Magazine and local stories, there are so many reports of supernatural happenings in the Blaske building? Could the spirits of the dead soldiers still be lingering near the place of their torment and suffering?

No one knows for sure just who may be haunting the place, but there have certainly been some strange things reported here in the past. Staff members and visitors have reported everything from actual apparitions to doors slamming open and closed, to things moving about the building on their own. There seemed to be little doubt that something had taken up residence here... or perhaps it had never left.

The surrounding area, which had once been the prison buildings and yard, has also claimed it share of ghostly reports. On certain nights, residents and passersby claim to have seen apparitions of men and soldiers still lingering on the ground where the prison once stood. These ragged-looking men have been generally accepted to be either the ghosts of the former prisoners, or at least the residual impressions they have left behind.

And some of these encounters have been more than a little unsettling.

One Alton man I spoke with (who asked that his name not be used) was walking near the old prison site one evening. He was cutting across the parking lot, which is located next to the historical marker, and stopped for a moment to tie his shoe. He bent down quickly and when he looked up again, he saw a man standing not more than three feet away from him. The man appeared to be solid and was wearing a pair of heavy pants that ended near his shins. He was barefoot and was wearing a filthy shirt. He had cropped hair but a long, scraggly beard.

"To be honest, I thought he was like a homeless man or something," the witness would later recall. "He was absolutely filthy... but I never thought for a moment that he wasn't real."

At least until the man vanished! The sighting lasted for not more than 45 seconds or so before the man simply disappeared. Not surprisingly, the witness was shaken by the event and hurried home to tell his wife about it. It had been she who suggested that the ragged man may have been the ghost of a Confederate prisoner.

"I'm still not convinced about that," he told me. "But then I don't have any other explanation for it either."

POINT LOOKOUT

Located at the southern tip of St. Mary's County in Maryland is Point Lookout State Park, a popular recreation and historic area where thousands come every summer to enjoy the weather and the outdoors. It is hard to imagine that this place was once a camp where thousands of Confederate soldiers were imprisoned and where more than 4,000 of them died.

But those facts are true.... and just as true are the stories which say that many of those soldiers are still lingering here.

The area known as Point Lookout had its beginning in the mid-1800's as a pleasure resort. When the Civil War broke out, the owner sold the property to the government as a site that could be used as a military hospital. The Hammond General Hospital was soon built, but it was quickly decided, after the prison population increase in 1864, that the area would best be served as a prison camp.

Officially, the place was known as Camp Hoffman. There were never any barracks built and the prisoners had to sleep in tents. Later, when the place became overcrowded, they were not even afforded that luxury. The low, marshy land of the area bred disease among the prisoners and men soon started to die from smallpox, dysentery and scurvy. The place was a hellhole and instead of the 10,000 prisoners it was supposed to hold, more than 20,000 were crowded in at one time, making it one of the largest prison camps built during the war.

The Confederates tried several times to take the camp and free the prisoners. With the prison located in Maryland, a fairly pro-Confederate state, there were many opportunities and plans devised to arrange a mass escape. Every plan failed and because of this, a number of southern sympathizers joined the ranks of the prisoners incarcerated here. Finally, one plan was formulated which seemed to be foolproof but the Union troops got wind of it and Fort Lincoln was built nearby to stop any future plans of freeing the prisoners.

With the hospital being located in the camp, doctors were able to administer to the soldiers. It consisted of many buildings, arranged in a circle like spokes on a wheel. There were fifteen buildings used as wards. However, this did little to stop the spread of disease. As conditions worsened late in the war, literally thousands died from hunger and illness.

After the war, Camp Hoffman was dismantled, although many of the buildings still stand today as reminders of the past..... and some say that many of the soldiers imprisoned here stay also. It is not only the buildings here that are haunted, but the very land the camp stood on also.

There have been many people over the years who have had strange experiences in the park, from staff members to visitors. They claim to have seen apparitions of soldiers appear in front of their vehicles and have seen and heard things which they cannot explain.

Most frightening are the strange voices that have been heard and captured on audio tape in the park.... voices that seem to belong to prisoners from the past. Ghost investigations and even seances have turned up all sorts of odd phenomena and hundreds of reports are documented every year.

In the 1970's, a park manager saw the ghostly figure of a young man outside the window of his residence and then vanish, while another employee saw a ghostly woman standing at the top of a stairway. The sounds of phantom footsteps, slamming doors and windows and even ghostly snoring have been reported and recorded in a duplex dwelling in the park. It had served as a functioning lighthouse until 1965. It was also here that park employees managed to snap a photograph of a blurry young man in a military uniform.... although no such man appeared to be present when the photo was taken.

There have also been reports of ghostly sightings by fishermen and tourists on the roads and pathways in the park. Unlike many of our national parks, the rangers here keep track of strange sightings and reports and even conduct a ghost tour each October.

Point Lookout remains perhaps one of the most haunted places in the state of Maryland.

JOHNSON'S ISLAND

In the frigid waters of Lake Erie lies a piece of land called Johnson's Island. It was here in 1861, that Colonel Hoffman proposed the construction of a prison camp for captured Confederates. The site was located about three miles north of the city of Sandusky, Ohio and was determined to be close enough to the shore to be easily supplied by boat, yet far enough that escape by water was nearly impossible. The island consisted of 300 acres of land, half of which was timbered, so there would be plenty of wood for fuel. While it seemed the perfect place for an "escape-proof" camp, to the southern soldiers, who had never seen snow or frigid weather, it was a forbidding place in the winter months.

The land for the prison was cleared from fifteen acres of forest at the southeast corner of the island. The area was surrounded by a wooden stockade and within the confines were built 13 barracks to house the prisoners. The buildings were constructed of a single layer of knotty pine lumber, nailed to upright beams. No plastering was done and the cold and damp air soon caused the boards to warp and crack, creating wide gaps where the wind could blow directly through. Needless to say, they offered little protection from the cold, northern Ohio weather.

The first prisoners arrived at Johnson's Island in April 1862. They were a mixed bunch at first, comprised of officers, enlisted men and civilians, but by June, orders from the military commanders made Johnson's Island a prison for Confederate officers only. These men would grow to include as many as seven generals and they constantly worked to keep up morale and order among the men. They managed to organize their own government, hold debates and even teach dancing, music and French lessons.

There have been many estimates as to how many men the prison actually held and while it had been built for 1,000, even conservative estimates place the number around 12,000. Somehow, shelter managed to be adequate, although food and clothing were in short supply. In the early days of the war, the men ate, if not well, at least regularly. It would not be until 1864 when the changes implemented throughout the northern prison system would hit Johnson's Island. Rations were reduced sharply, care packages from home were stopped and even purchases made by the prisoners for food from outside sutlers were put to a halt. This would continue for the rest of the war.

The island prison was separated from the nearest land by a half mile of water in the warm weather and by that same distance of solid ice in the winter. Confronted by this, only the most daring of prisoners ever tried to escape. In total, there were a reported 12 men who actually managed to vanish from the prison, which was excellent compared to other Federal prisons.

The attempted escapes were more frequent during the winter months, when the ice was passable and the guards were less watchful as they tried to keep themselves warm. However, even a successful escape required scaling the 14 foot stockade wall and then crossing the open countryside in bitterly cold conditions. Several escapes were actually made when prisoners, dressed in blue uniforms, casually strolled out of the gates with guard details, who were leaving at the end of their watch. Their comrades would delay detection by answering roll call for the men who vanished.

But it was not the fear of individual escapes that bothered the Union commanders, but rather an organized revolt among the prisoners (who vastly outnumbered the guards) or a raid by Confederate sympathizers against the island. This kept the Federal authorities in a constant state of worry, for false alarms and threats of attacks by Confederates in Canada were constantly reported.

After several rumored attacks, which never materialized, the threat from Canada came in September 1864. On September 19, a party of 30 paroled or escaped Confederates, armed with revolvers and knives, took passage on a steamer named the *Philo Parsons* which traveled to Lake Erie islands. Near Kelley's Island, they seized the boat and proceeded to sink another boat, the *Island Queen*, after letting off the passengers. That night, they cautiously approached a gunboat called the *Michigan*, which according to a pre-arranged signal, they were supposed to board and capture.

The signal would be a rocket, fired into the air by a Confederate spy named Charles Cole. For weeks, he had been living in Sandusky, posing as a northern banker, although he was actually a paroled officer from Nathan Bedford Forrest's cavalry. He had become friends with several officers on board the *Michigan* and arranged to have dinner on the ship that night. He, and several compatriots, were going to drug the ship's officers and seize the vessel.

Meanwhile, that same evening, a group of southern sympathizers from Ohio were to arrive by train in Sandusky and seize the Federal arsenal there. They would arm themselves and the prisoners on the island, thus creating an attack by land, by water and from within the prison itself.

Nothing could go wrong... and soon a Confederate force would be free to raid cities and ports on the Union's Great Lakes. Or, that was what supposed to have happened....

In reality, there was no dinner on board the *Michigan* and so, of course, no rocket. The authorities had been tipped off to the plan and Cole had been arrested that afternoon in his hotel room. Seeing no signal, the Confederates on the *Philo Parsons* lost their nerve and returned to Canada. The trains that arrived in Sandusky were also thoroughly searched, although strangely, the fighting force of men were never discovered... if they existed at all.

The misery and suffering caused at Johnson's Island was more the result of poor planning and short-sightedness than cruelty. The poor quality of the buildings, with single walls and no foundations, had been created for a short term residency... not for the 12 to 16 months for which many of the men were incarcerated there. The buildings had not been made to withstand the cold and the gale force winds from the lake, nor had they been built to house the much greater than expected number of prisoners.

The camp was badly run and seldom were the facilities ever in complete working order. The supplies were constantly short, the food often rotten and the water pipes often frozen or broken. As mentioned previously, this usually bred disease and sickness among the men... leading to the deaths of many.

Today, Johnson's Island is a lonely place with little trace remaining from the time when it was a prison. The years and the elements have removed the remnants of the stockade and the prison buildings. There is nothing remaining of the Confederate soldiers who were held captive here, save for the cemetery, and if you believe the stories... the ghosts.

The cemetery is a grassy spot which is surrounded by an iron fence. Years ago, the graveyard was in a horrible state of decay. The area was overgrown and the wooden markers that had been used to locate the graves of the soldiers buried here were slowly rotting away. In 1889, a party of public officials from Georgia visited the site and, by private subscription, raised the money to mark the burial plots with marble stones. Each stone is carved with the name of the man buried beneath it, and his regiment, except for a few stones which bear the marking of "unknown".

Over the years, the stories have persisted that not all of the men who died on Johnson's Island rest in peace. It is said that on certain nights, the spectral forms of the Confederate prisoners still wander about the former grounds of the prison and they have also been reported within the confines of the cemetery.

Strangely, their voices have been heard also. Many years ago, Italian workers who were hired to dig at the stone quarry on the island, began singing a song that many of them had never heard before. In fact, according to the superintendent, many of the men did not even speak English.

It was not a song which reminded the Italian immigrants of anything they were familiar with, and they could not even explain where they had heard it before. However, it may have served as a reminder to previous occupants of the island of places and people who seemed far away....

The song the workers were heard to be singing was "Dixie".

ANDERSONVILLE

The camp at Andersonville had been originally intended to provide some relief for the city of Richmond. The city was already experiencing a food shortage in 1863 and after General Grant ended prisoner exchanges and paroles, the people of Richmond found themselves with many more Federal prisoners than they could possibly feed.

General John H. Winder sent his son, Captain W. Sidney Winder to scout out a location for a new prison in Georgia. He discovered what he believed was the perfect site around November 24. The parcel of land was located in Georgia, deep in the heart of the Confederacy, and was far removed from attack. It was also a site where food would be abundant. Confederate officials planned a new prison on the property called Camp Sumter and it would contain a number of barracks which were designed to hold 8,000 to 10,000 men.

Captain Winder's location was in southwestern Georgia, along Station Number 8 of the Georgia Southwestern Railroad. Because of this, it would be easily accessible by train. A local resident named Benjamin Dykes, who also owned the area's sawmill and gristmill, offered a parcel of land for the prison (which was extremely convenient since the army would be forced to buy his wood and grain for the prison construction and for food for the prisoners). The piece of land was heavily wooded with pine and oak and the ground sloped down on both sides of a wide stream.

Orders were given from Richmond to start construction, but the local people were violently opposed to the prison being located so close to them and labor was impossible to find. Work was delayed for some time before finally, soldiers commandeered slaves from nearby farms for the construction.

Just as the prison compound was being started, conditions in the south made it impossible to build barracks for the prisoners. Rail lines and distribution centers were greatly stressed by the war, so out of desperation, the government ordered that a simple stockade be erected around the compound as quickly as possible. This work began in January. Trees were felled and then stood on end to form a large fence around the camp, enclosing an area of just over 16 acres. Only two trees had been left standing inside of the compound itself.

On February 25, 1864 the first prisoners arrived at the camp, before the stockade was even completed. Just shortly before they arrived, the camp's first commander, Colonel Alexander W. Persons took over his duties. He continued to serve until June 17, when he was replaced by General Winder. In March, the camp's most infamous commandant arrived, Captain Henry Wirz, and although he is closely linked to Andersonville, he was never the camp's supreme commander.... although his influence left a definite mark on the prison. By the time that General Winder had arrived, more than 22,300 men would be confined to the pen that had been built for half that many... and more than 2,600 of them would have already died.

From the very first, there was no organized arrangement for the compound. The prisoners had simply been placed in the stockade and then left to themselves. Many of the prisoners who were transferred from other camps were in horrible condition when they arrived... infested with disease and vermin, which quickly spread to the other men.

The first arrivals at the camp had built huts within the compound, using pieces of wood that had been left within the stockade. Later arrivals lived in tents or in holes they dug in the ground and covered over with blankets or scraps of cloth. In July 1864, the stockade was enlarged to accommodate more men and within a week of the construction, the camp's population had risen to 29,000 prisoners. In less than a month later, it would rise again to it's highest point of more than 33,000. In his book Portals to Hell: Military Prisons of the Civil War, author Lonnie R. Speer points out that Andersonville actually became the fifth largest "city" in the Confederacy.

As time progressed and the stockade became more crowded, the food rations began to dwindle. The first staple to vanish was salt, followed by the sweet potato, which had once been plentiful in the region. In time, the authorities reduced the amount of corn meal handed out and later, meat was eliminated altogether. The rations continued to decrease and soon they were not even handed out every day. On one occasion, when the bread wagon entered the stockade to deliver food, it was mobbed by the inmates and all of the bread was stolen. Captain Wirz responded to this by canceling all further rations for the day. According to some prisoners, the more sadistic guards (usually those of the 55th Georgia) would toss chunks of cornbread into the pen, just to watch the men scramble after them.

Many of the prisoners began to devise ways to capture low flying birds, which swarmed about the stockade in the evenings. The swallows that were snared were often eaten raw, such was the hunger of the prisoners.

Security precautions at the prison camp became almost as legendary as the horrible conditions. The two regiments of Georgia and Alabama troops who guarded the camp were also assisted by a battalion of cavalry and a large pack of savage bloodhounds. These dogs had been used before the war to track down runaway slaves and now were being used to bring back any escaped Federal prisoners.

Although despite the ferocity of the bloodhounds, there will still 329 successful escapes from Andersonville during the 15 months when it was in use. Most of them took place during work details, although the very first attempt occurred within a week of the opening of the camp. A group of 15 men managed to scale the east wall, using ropes made from woven pieces of cloth. All of them were recaptured, thanks to the dogs, but the attempt caused the establishment of the "deadline" within the stockade itself. This deadline was a boundary that was erected inside of the stockade walls and was made by placing wooden stakes within about 20 feet of each other. Then, a four-inch wide strip was stretched between the stakes, creating a very visible barrier. An order was then issued which stated that if a prisoner crossed, or even touched, the line, the guards would fire upon them without warning.

Soon, word got into the northern press about the Andersonville deadline and it became infamous. The newspapers railed about the savagery of the southern prisons and the barbaric design of the deadline. At war's end, it would even be publicly condemned by the Union government. The problem was that, despite all of the public posturing, the Federal condemnation of the deadline was sheer hypocrisy. All stockade-type prisons had some sort of deadline for security, including the Federal ones. This fact was hidden from the American public until after the war, when Confederate prisoners returned home. It is ironic that while the American press was railing against the deadline at Andersonville, Confederate prisoners were being shot for crossing the same sort of lines in places like Rock Island, Camp Douglas, and other spots.

Once the deadline was established, the digging of tunnels became the preferred method of escape. With the digging came many problems. Every tunnel requires a huge amount of secrecy and in a situation where thousands of men are packed into a stockade, privacy is a hard thing to find.... and, like most prisons, Andersonville had its share of informants.

In one well-known situation, in May 1864, the commandant entered the camp with a squad of guards, searching for escape tunnels. One prisoner, thinking that he might get special treatment for informing on his comrades, told the commander about a tunnel that was under construction. The Confederates punished the prisoners involved and forced them to fill in the escape route. That night, the informant was nearly beaten to death by other prisoners. He was pursued through the night and into the next morning and finally, he crossed over the deadline and called for protection from the guards. He was sure that he had earned it because of the assistance that he had given them. Instead, they shot him for crossing the deadline.

Soon, escapes grew even more innovative. There were so many dead men being carried out of the camp that little attention was paid to them. When a prisoner died, he was placed in front of his tent and then carried away by a detail of other prisoners. Several quick-thinking men pretended to be dead and were carried outside of the gate, then placed in a pile to await burial. As soon as darkness fell, they would escape. This plan was successful a number of times before Captain Wirz got wind of it and changed the burial policy. After that, all of the bodies were left inside of the stockade until a surgeon could examine them.

There were certainly many opportunities for escape using this method as death was no stranger to the camp. The main causes of death were scurvy, dysentery, typhoid, smallpox, gangrene and diarrhea.... but outright murder became commonplace as well. In fact, the murder of prisoners by guards, and even by other prisoners, became a daily occurrence.

Among the prisoners were groups of men referred to as "raiders". These groups ruled the stockade using fear and retaliation against any who opposed them. They preyed on the other inmates, taking food and belongings and even beating and killing just about anyone they wished to. The largest and most vicious of the "raider" groups was led by William Collins of the 88th Pennsylvania Regiment. His men dominated not only the other prisoners, but the other "raiders" as well, looting and murdering as they saw fit.

Finally, a group of prisoners banded together and somehow obtained aid from the commandant. He allowed them to take matters into their own hands and they arrested the "raiders". A military trial was held and 24 of them "raiders" were punished, and even six of them were hanged. Three of the other 18 men later died of beatings.

In the years that have passed since the closing of Andersonville, and the end of the war itself, the ghosts of the "raiders" have been blamed for most of the strange encounters and happenings in the area. This is perhaps merely legend, or tradition, but many have claimed the "raiders" to be responsible for the weird events. The odd sights and sounds include apparitions of soldiers around the location of the former camp; the sounds of groans and echoing voices; and the marching footsteps of what appears to be a number of men tramping about, among other things.

By September 1864, the majority of the prisoners had been transferred out of Andersonville because of Union activity in the area and because of the northern occupation of Atlanta. In the weeks that followed, it was reported that as many as 6,000 prisoners were sent to other camps. Those who were too weak or sick to travel remained behind, leaving just over 8,000 men in the camp. A huge number of those prisoners died in October, so by November only 1,359 men were left.

In October, General Winder was transferred out and Colonel George C. Gibbs arrived to assume command of Andersonville. From that point, the camp took the role of a convalescent prison. As soon as the prisoners gained enough strength to travel, they were transferred to other facilities for a short time. The remaining Andersonville prisoners were paroled in May 1865.

This brought an end to the history of the Civil War's most notorious prison camp.

Or did it?

As mentioned already, many people believe that at least some of the former inmates of Andersonville still linger in this world... but what of the camp's commander?

According to legend, the ghost of Captain Henry Wirz was rumored to have haunted the Old Brick Capitol in Washington for a number of years, but this is not the only place this restless specter has been sighted. Some believe that it may be his ghost who has been seen walking along the road near the site of the old camp. They believe that his spirit does not rest because of the terrible blot on his reputation, which came about after the war. Was Captain Wirz unjustly hanged for crimes committed at Andersonville? Apparently, he believes so!

Heinrich Wirz was an immigrant to America from Switzerland who had served a prison sentence in the 1840's for some unknown offense before coming to America. He referred to himself as a doctor, although there is no record of him ever having medical training. In 1849, he was working in a factory in Lawrence, Massachusetts before moving to Kentucky, where he worked as a doctor's assistant. A short time later, he was living in Louisiana and was employed as a "doctor" on a plantation.

In 1861, he enlisted in the 4th Louisiana Infantry and served in Virginia. During the Battle of Seven Pines in May 1862, Wirz was wounded and lost the use of his right arm. He was soon promoted to captain and placed under the command of General Winder at a Richmond military prison.

Wirz was disliked by his nearly everyone, including his subordinates and his own staff. He was especially hated and ridiculed by the prisoners for his accent and overbearing personality.

In 1864, Wirz was sent to Andersonville as the commandant and continued in service here until after Lee's surrender. At that time, he turned over the camp to Union General J.H. Wilson and ended his career in the Confederate military. A short time later, he was placed under arrest by Captain Henry E. Noyes. He was charged with misconduct against Union prisoners at Andersonville. Wirz protested the arrest, stating that the conditions of the prison had been beyond his control and he begged his captors to allow him to leave and take his family to Europe. Instead, he was taken to Washington and officially charged with "impairing the health and destroying the lives of prisoners".

The arrest of Wirz was in further response to the American thirst for revenge against the Confederacy. It was believed that by arresting Wirz, the government might be able to placate the public. Whether Wirz was responsible for the horror of the camp though, was questionable. There was no question that terrible suffering took place at Andersonville and little doubt Wirz was a harsh and possibly sadistic commander. However, southern contemporaries insisted that he did the best job possible under extreme conditions... Andersonville was the south's most impoverished and overcrowded prison. It is believed today that Wirz was nothing more than a scapegoat for the Confederate prisons and a victim of the post-war backlash against the south.

The trial of Henry Wirz began in August of 1865, ending a three and a half month feeding frenzy by the press. While the former captain waited in jail, the northern newspapers had already tried and convicted him many times over. He had been portrayed as a monster who maliciously sent scores of Union soldiers to their deaths.

Attorneys for the federal government began their case against Wirz, presenting evidence in the form of records, documents and testimony from former prisoners and from Union officers who had inspected the camp after its surrender. The witnesses were not always convincing either, as several of them stated that they had seen Wirz "strike, kick and shoot prisoners" in August 1864... a time when the commandant was absent from the camp on sick leave.

Of all the testimony, perhaps the most damaging came from a man named Felix de la Baume, who claimed to be a nephew of the Revolutionary War hero, General Lafayette. He spent several hours on the stand describing the defendant's cruel treatment of prisoners and his total disregard for the nightmarish conditions of the camp. Baume's testimony appeared in newspapers across the country and in the end, sealed Wirz's fate.

Baume was rewarded with a position in the Interior Department for his testimony. After the trial, it was later learned that he had been a deserter from the Union Army and was not descended from General Lafayette.

On November 6, 1865, Wirz was condemned to death. Not long before his sentence was carried out, a secret emissary from the War Department offered Wirz a reprieve in exchange for a statement that would convict Jefferson Davis of conspiracy to murder prisoners. Wirz refused.

Henry Wirz was hanged in the yard of the Old Brick Capitol on November 10, 1865. He was the only Confederate officer to be convicted and executed for war crimes. He maintained his innocence and was defiant until the very end.

"I know what orders are, Major," he said to the officer who was in charge of directing his hanging. "I am being hung for obeying them."

The question remains... was Captain Wirz responsible for the conditions at Andersonville? Was he to blame for the deaths of thousands of Union soldiers?

The controversy continues to be examined today, but regardless, if Captain Wirz is one of the lingering ghosts of Andersonville.... there is little doubt as to why he may be so restless.

SOURCES

Portals to Hell: Military Prisons of the Civil War by Lonnie R. Speer
Historical Times Illustrated Encyclopedia of the Civil War edited by Patricia L. Faust (1986)
Civil War Times: The Civil War by William C. Davis and Bell I. Wiley (1998)
The Complete Idiots Guide to the Civil War by Alan Axelrod (1998)
A House Divided edited by Edward L Ayers (1997)
Civil War Prisons edited by William B. Hesseltine (1962)
Sherman's March by Burke Davis (1980)
Don't Know Much about the Civil War by Kenneth C. Davis (1996)
None Died in Vain: The Saga of the American Civil War by Robert Leckie (1990)
Civil War Prisons and Escapes by Robert E. Denney (1993)
Haunted Illinois by Troy Taylor (1999)
Haunted Houses USA by Joan Bingham and Dolores Riccio (1989)
More Haunted Houses by Joan Bingham and Dolores Riccio (1991)
Ghosts and Haunted Houses of Maryland by Trish Gallagher (1988)
Ghosts! Washington's Most Famous Ghost Stories by John Alexander (1975- revised 1998)
Haunted Houses by Richard Winer and Nancy Osborn Ishmael (1979)
Civil War Ghost Stories and Legends by Nancy Roberts (1992)
Georgia Ghosts by Nancy Roberts (1997)
Haunted Ohio III by Chris Woodyard (1994)
Guide to Haunted Places of the Civil War from Blue and Gray Magazine (1996)
13 Georgia Ghosts and Jeffrey by Kathryn Tucker Windham (1973)

CHAPTER SIX

THE HAUNTED PRESIDENT
The Spirit-Filled Life and Death of
ABRAHAM LINCOLN

*"Who is dead in the White House?", I asked one of the soldiers.
"The President", was the answer, "he was killed by an assassin."*

President Abraham Lincoln recalling a dream that
he had a few days before he was killed

No book about the ghosts and hauntings of the Civil War would be complete without some mention of Abraham Lincoln. To many, he is one of the greatest symbols of the war and whether loved or hated, Lincoln was almost always respected.

The president endured great hardships during his life but the perhaps the greatest of these was watching his country being torn apart by bitterness and strife. It is little wonder that many believe that Lincoln lingered behind after his death... unable to find peace after all that he had seen and experienced.

The connections between the late president and the supernatural were maintained throughout his life... and beyond. Much has been made of Lincoln's prophetic dreams and of his belief in the spirit world, but why did those beliefs become such a prominent part of his life and what event caused Lincoln to turn to contact with the dead?

If even some of the stories of Lincoln and the supernatural are true.... then he may be the most well-traveled ghost in America! There are legends which claim the president haunts the White House; the old Illinois state capitol in Vandalia; his home in Springfield; and even his tomb. While this may be beyond the bounds of belief, there are certainly many unanswered questions about Lincoln's life (and death) that need to be explored.

There are still many mysteries in the pages to follow. As with ghosts and the Civil War, I can never come close to saying that I know everything there is to know about Abraham Lincoln. I am certainly no Lincoln scholar, although I have long been fascinated with the subject. I simply hope to entertain with a little history... and quite a few haunts.

So, does Abraham Lincoln rest in peace?

I'll present the evidence of his troubled life, his turbulent term as war-time president, the hysteria and horror of his death, and his ghostly here-after... then I will let you decide for yourself.

THE EARLY LIFE OF ABRAHAM LINCOLN

Abraham Lincoln was always a melancholy person. The death of his mother when he was still a child; hard labor to make an existence for himself in the wilderness; and his struggle for an education, all combined to make him a serious man, even when he was making a joke.

The Civil War caused him great sorrow and the heavy losses on both sides filled him with sadness. Lincoln paid obsessive detail to everything about the war and by 1864, portraits of him show a face etched with lines. He slept very little in those years and during the five years he lived in the White House, he spent less than one month away from work. His only escape was afforded him by the theater, a late night buggy ride or from his books.

But what forces combined to make him the man that he was? Lincoln always stated that he longed for a life of peace and contentment, but seemed to also know that he would never live to find it. The question is, has he found it in death?

Abraham Lincoln was born in Kentucky in 1809. His father, Thomas Lincoln, had married Nancy Hanks, a tall, pretty, uneducated girl, three years before and they had built a log cabin at a place called Sinking Springs Farm. Thomas was known as a good man and a good storyteller and one who was adept at many things, although he rarely settled down to try any one thing in particular.

Abraham looked to follow in his footsteps. He was a thin and spindly-looking boy who showed remarkable curiosity about everything. He would toddle into the nearby village of Elizabethtown and watch the travelers of the Cumberland Gap pass by him. He was already much taller than the local children by the age of seven when he and his older sister, Sarah, began attending "blab" school, which meant all of the students read their lessons aloud at the same time. Years later, Abraham would be remembered as being the best reader in school.

The Lincoln family pulled up stakes and moved across the Ohio River to Indiana, where they settled on Little Pigeon Creek. Abraham soon learned the ways of the outdoors and hard work, helping to clear land around their new home. He became known as an honest and self-reliant boy, but lonely and withdrawn too, sometimes vanishing into the woods for hours at a time.

In 1818, Lincoln's life changed abruptly when the family was struck by a terrible frontier disease dubbed "milk sickness". Tom and Betsy Sparrow, close friends of the Lincoln family, died first, while Nancy Lincoln faithfully nursed them to their last hours. Then, Nancy too was struck down with the disease and followed her friends to their graves.

Abraham helped to fashion his mother's coffin with his own hands and then placed her in the ground. It was later said that he held his head in his hands and wept for hours. At that point, his father and sister forgotten, Lincoln later said that he felt completely alone in the world.

In 1819, Thomas Lincoln traveled back into Kentucky and returned with the widow of an old friend. Her name was Sarah Bush Johnston and she became his wife and a new mother for Abraham and Sarah. He also brought along him Sarah's three children and an orphaned cousin named Dennis Hanks. The cabin was now jammed to capacity with the expanded family and Lincoln recalled escaping into the woods with his books for some peace and quiet.

In school, Lincoln stood out among the other backwoods students. He composed poems and essays and often mounted a tree stump for speeches on whatever subject took his fancy. He was obviously a born politician, but on the other hand was also an expert log-splitter, a master with a farm plow and skilled as a hog butcher. He was also regarded as an insatiable reader. He started with the Bible and then read anything he could get his hands on. He was definitely a young man of many contrasts and not surprisingly, was considered a unique and rather odd fellow.

Lincoln's physical strength was also said to be extraordinary. At the age of ten, he was kicked in the head by a horse and feared dead, but somehow made a remarkable recovery. By the age of seventeen, he was nearly six feet tall and could outwrestle anyone in the surrounding counties. He could also best any of them with his mind too. Local teachers and ministers admitted that the young man was better read than they were and that a life of hard labor on a farm would never suit him. Lincoln agreed and dreamed of far-off places and adventure.

Thomas Lincoln pulled up stakes once more in the late 1820's and moved his family to a small farm outside of Decatur, Illinois. Abraham stayed with the family until the following Spring, helping his father build a cabin and clear land for a farm. When warm weather came, he started out on his own for the first time, working on a riverboat which hauled cargo to New Orleans. At the end of the job, he found a place that he liked in the village of New Salem, Illinois.

In those days, New Salem was barely listed on any map, providing a home for only about twelve families, but Lincoln loved the place. Here, he could be his own man and he got a job working in a small store. Soon, more stores opened, along with the saw mill, a tavern and the school. In addition, the inhabitants expected even more new arrivals when the steamboats began navigating the Sangamon River.

Lincoln became very popular in the small village and was liked for his sense of humor and his storytelling ability. He was also a hard worker and a powerful wrestler, which earned him many friends and admirers. He seemed a good and simple man and so many of the locals were perplexed to see that he joined the New Salem Debating Society and also persuaded the local school master to lend him books to further his education. Those questions were put to rest however when they heard the young man speak publicly for the first time. Soon, they persuaded him to take up politics. In March of 1832, he decided to run for the state legislature.

His first campaign got off to a good start when he was chosen to pilot the ill-fated *Talisman* when it attempted to make the trip upriver to Springfield. This steamboat was to be the first to navigate the Sangamon River and many believed that it would open the city of Springfield for a booming river economy. The plan turned out to be a disaster and marked the first and last trip that a riverboat would take on the river. Despite this outcome, Lincoln was never blamed for the fiasco. Then, a short time later, his campaign was interrupted by the Black Hawk War and he ended up serving two months in the Illinois militia. He was delighted when his fellow soldiers asked him to serve as captain, but often complained about there being more mosquitoes to fight than Indians. He was mustered out after the campaign and set out for home, only to have his horse stolen. Lincoln ended up walking most of the way back to New Salem from the Wisconsin border.

When Lincoln arrived home, he discovered that the store where he worked had closed down, so he took the position of New Salem's postmaster. He took the liberty of reading dozens of newspapers every week before delivering them and soaking up the information they contained. He also became a deputy surveyor and used both jobs as a way to campaign for the legislature again in 1834. He drummed up votes at dances, barbecues, cock-fights and wrestling matches, where he normally served as referee since everyone refused to fight him.

That following November, at the age of 25, he left for Vandalia to serve in the legislature. He was wearing the first suit that he ever owned. In 1836, he was elected again and this time headed for Springfield, where he would also practice law. He had read all of the books required and in March of 1837 passed the exam which made him an attorney. He borrowed a horse and bid goodbye to the dwindling town of New Salem. The citizens had lost all hope of the river bring prosperity to the town and three years after Lincoln departed, New Salem was a ghost town.

When Lincoln arrived in Springfield, he was already well-known and liked. The New Salem wrestler and speaker was also respected in the legislature and because of this, many people sought him out. While he was always friendly, Lincoln was still introverted and hard to know and made only a few close friends. His closest friend became Joshua Fry Speed, a local merchant.

At that time, Springfield was a growing city of about 1500 people but was still cursed with unpaved streets, no sewers to speak of, no sidewalks, and the bane of the city, a pack of wild hogs which had been roaming the streets for more than a decade. Still, the city did manage to have a social circle. One of the members of the city's elite was Ninian Edwards, the son of a prominent politician. His wife, Elizabeth Todd Edwards, was a born matchmaker and delighted in finding husbands for her sisters among Ninian's friends. Her sister, Mary Todd, came to visit in 1839. Mary was described as being "high strung" but was said to have an engaging personality and a quick wit. She became the center of attention among Springfield socialites and had plenty of potential suitors to choose from, including Stephen Douglas, who was the most insistent.

In December of 1839, during the grand Christmas cotillion, Mary met a young attorney and political hopeful named Abraham Lincoln. They were attracted to each other from the start. Mary's sister soon noted with disapproval that when Lincoln would call, he would sit in rapt attention to everything Mary said. But the following year found Mary still being courted by other men and Lincoln still pining away after her. At the close of the year, he made his decision, he would marry her.

Whether or not Lincoln formally proposed to her or not, Mary promised to become his wife. For some reason though, on New Year's Day of 1841, Lincoln decided to break off the engagement.

Some have speculated that Lincoln was intrigued by the idea of marriage, but afraid of it also. He feared his loss of freedom but was unsure that he wanted to live without Mary. His friend, Billy Herndon, noted that Lincoln was acting as "crazy as a loon". He didn't eat, he didn't sleep, he let his work slide and refused to meet and dine with friends. Another friend, Dr. Anson Henry, suggested that Lincoln take a trip out of town and try to ease his state of mind.

Some time before, Lincoln's friend Joshua Speed had moved to Louisville, Kentucky and so Lincoln decided to stay with him for awhile. Unfortunately, things were no better here. Speed was also in the midst of a turbulent relationship with a local woman named Fanny Henning. After a short visit, Speed returned to Springfield with Lincoln. He wrapped up his business affairs to move to Kentucky permanently. He would soon be marrying Fanny but he left his good friend with one piece of advice... either give up Mary for good or marry her and be done with it.

In the Summer of 1842, Lincoln again turned his attentions to Mary Todd. A friend cleverly arranged a surprise dinner so the two of them would meet and it worked. By November, marriage was on Lincoln's mind again. In fact, it was so much on his mind that on the morning of November 4, he and Mary announced they were going to be married.... that evening.

Their friends were in great haste to make the preparations, surprised by the announcement. There was no time for Joshua Speed to travel from Kentucky, so Lincoln asked another friend, James Matheny, to stand in as best man. Matheny would later write that during the ceremony, Lincoln "looked and acted like a lamb being led to the slaughter." While he was getting dressed, his landlord's son asked him where he was going and Lincoln answered, "To Hell, I suppose."

Despite the haste in making arrangements and Lincoln's obvious foreboding, the ceremony proceeded without a hitch and Lincoln was now a husband.

The Lincoln's had their honeymoon at the Globe Tavern, where they lived the first years of their marriage. There was every indication that their marriage was a happy one, despite Mary losing track of her socialite friends and her sister's warnings that her husband was unsuitable. It was not long before they were expecting their first child and Robert would be born just three days short of nine months after the wedding.

By 1844, Lincoln was able to afford to purchase a home in Springfield. It was a one-and-a-half story cottage at the corner of Eighth and Jackson Streets. They moved into the house in May of that year and in 1856, the cramped quarters were expanded into a full two stories.

Lincoln's love for travel and the law caused his marriage to suffer badly in those early years. At that point in his career, he was active in court cases all over Illinois and was constantly away from home. Mary, left alone with a toddler, was sure that something terrible was going to happen while he was away. Their second son, Eddie, was born in 1846 but only lived to the age of four. Willie followed in 1850, not long after the death of his brother, and Thomas "Tad" Lincoln was born in 1853. The children drew Lincoln closer to home but his marriage was still sometimes rocky. He was nine years older than Mary and almost a foot taller than she was. She often complained that he treated her more like a child than a wife.

Lincoln served a term in Congress in the late 1840's, but his law practice kept him too busy to consider much of a political career. He had always been opposed to the further spread of slavery in the country and was contented that the Missouri Compromise had outlawed slavery further west, where America's future would be built. But in 1854, a congressional act, provoked by Lincoln's long-time personal and political rival, Stephen Douglas, threatened to allow slavery in the territories. Lincoln's anger at this got the best of him and he made the decision to return to politics.

AN EERIE VISION IN SPRINGFIELD

In the Summer of 1854, Lincoln decided to campaign for a seat in the Illinois State Assembly. He easily won the position, but then quickly resigned. What he really wanted was a seat in the US Senate, where he believed he could really make a difference for his country. In February 1855, he sought but failed to get the coveted seat. Things started to change in early 1856 however, as a new political party was created called the Republican party. The first political move by the party was to try and keep Democrat James Buchanan out of office. They failed, but were gaining attention.

Buchanan's term in the White House pushed back the anti-slavery movement by years. During his time in office, the US Supreme Court ruled in the Dred Scott case, effectively deciding that blacks would never be considered as American citizens. Passions were beginning to ignite in the nation and dire predictions began to be made about the possibilities of secession and Civil War.

Also at this time, Stephen Douglas stepped forward with an abrupt turnabout and announced that he was now totally against allowing slavery into the western territories. Despite his new platform, Illinois Republicans were unconvinced and in June 1858, nominated Lincoln to run against Douglas for a seat in the Senate.

That night, in a speech before the excited nominating convention, Lincoln made his famous "House Divided" speech, declaring that the country could not endure as a divided nation. It was a speech that had been months in the planning.... and one that has endured for more than a century.

On July 24, Lincoln proposed that the two opponents meet in a series of debates before audiences all over the state. Douglas agreed and the two began a series of appearances that have become legend in Illinois for their volatile content. "The prairies are on fire," wrote one reporter, after witnessing a clash between Lincoln and Douglas.

The debates were bitter and powerful between the two long-time rivals. Lincoln argued that slavery must be abolished, while Douglas insisted that it could be contained and allowed to flourish in the South, as long as the states there wished it. The final debate was held in Alton and the story was reported all over the country in newspapers.

Finally, in November, word reached Lincoln that he had lost the race for the Senate seat. Surprisingly, this loss was the best thing that could have happened to him. Wise political analysts, on both sides, had watched this race very closely and had seen the way the debates had captured the attention of the entire country. Soon, word among the Republicans began to favor Lincoln as their choice for President in 1860.

Lincoln began to travel all over the country, backed by the Illinois Republican contingent, making his name known and becoming a recognizable entity. On May 16, 1860, the Republican National Convention opened in Chicago and decided among three real contenders for the nomination, William Seward, Edward Bates and Lincoln. In the end, after three ballots, Lincoln had won the nomination. Once again, he was to face his rival, Stephen Douglas.

When the news of Lincoln's nomination reached Springfield, it was immediately greeted by a 100 gun salute. That evening a huge crowd gathered at Lincoln's home and he spoke to them from the front steps, inviting as many into the house as could crowd inside.

Outside of Illinois, Lincoln was not greeted so warmly. Many saw him as nothing more than a "country lawyer" and a "huckster". Even the abolitionists saw Lincoln as a losing figure in the Presidential race and one even declared he was nothing but a "half-horse, half-alligator", bemoaning the fact that he was a backwoodsmen from Illinois and Kentucky.

By May of 1860, the nation's attention was focused on Springfield and politicians from all over the country were traveling to the city to size Lincoln up. He had become a very real threat to the southern politicians because should Lincoln carry the election, they saw the damage that he could do to their way of life and to the institution of slavery. Many of them came to Springfield to discuss issues because Lincoln's advisors suggested that he remain at home during the campaign. He had others traveling the country and speaking on his behalf. Lincoln was told that this way he could just focus on the issues, but in reality, it was to keep him hidden away. While the Republican leaders had great faith in Lincoln as a candidate, they hesitated to let the public see his lanky frame in his wrinkled suits, frumpy hat and sweat-stained shirts. He was not exactly the picture of a future president, they decided.

The city of Springfield had a carnival-like atmosphere about it that Summer, highlighted with a Republican rally at the fairgrounds. The parade took more than eight hours to pass the Lincoln home and ended with a picnic, where tubs of lemonade and whole cooked steers awaited the revelers.

Election day in the city dawned with rousing blasts from a cannon, with music and contagious excitement. Lincoln spent the day and evening with friends at a telegraph office. By midnight, it was clear that he had been elected President of the United States. A late night dinner was held in his honor and then he returned to the office for more news. Guns fired in celebration throughout the night.

Lincoln may have won the day, but he fared poorly in the popular vote. He had soundly defeated Douglas in the Electoral College, but had won just forty percent of the vote among the people. He had become a minority president with no support at all in the southern states. The current president's cabinet was filled with secessionists and their strong words were starting to be heard among more than just the politicians in the South. Lincoln was even hanged in effigy on election day in Pensacola, Florida.

The country truly seemed to be coming apart.

Lincoln finally managed to return home in the early morning hours although news of victory and telegrams of congratulations were still being wired to his office. He went into his bedroom for some much needed rest and collapsed onto a settee. Near the couch was a large bureau with a mirror on it and Lincoln started for a moment at his reflection in the glass. His face appeared angular, thin and tired. Several of his friends suggested that he grow a beard, which would hide the narrowness of his face and give him a more "presidential" appearance. Lincoln pondered this for a moment and then experienced what many would term a "vision"... and odd vision that Lincoln would later believe had prophetic meaning.

He saw that in the mirror, his face appeared to have two separate, yet distinct, images. The tip of one nose was about three inches away from the other one. The vision vanished but appeared again a few moments later. It was clearer this time and Lincoln realized that one of the faces was actually much paler than the other, almost with the coloring of death. The vision disappeared again and Lincoln dismissed the whole thing to the excitement of the hour and his lack of sleep.

Later on that evening, he told Mary of the strange vision and attempted to conjure it up again in the days that followed. The faces always returned to him and while Mary never saw it, she believed her husband when he said he did. She also believed she knew the significance of the vision. The healthy face was her husband's "real" face and indicated that he would serve his first term as president. The pale, ghostly image of the second face however was a sign that he would be elected to a second term.... but would not live to see its conclusion.

Lincoln apparently dismissed the whole thing as a hallucination, or an imperfection in the glass, or so he said publicly. Later, that strange vision would come back to haunt him during the turbulent days of the war. It was not Lincoln's only brush with prophecy either. One day, shortly before the election, he spoke to some friends as they were discussing the possibilities of Civil War. "Gentlemen," he said to them, "you may be surprised and think it strange, but when the doctor here was describing a war, I distinctly saw myself, in second sight, bearing an important part in that strife."

Lincoln spent the remainder of the year in Springfield, growing a beard and preparing for the move to Washington. His daily mail, which secretary John Nicolay carried into the office by the basket, was starting to be liberally sprinkled with hate letters. He was concerned, but never seemed to let it bother him. Lincoln appeared every afternoon in a room at the Capitol building and met with the people, talking and laughing and feeling as though he were still one of them. This went well for some time, but the crowds never seemed to stop coming, so Nicolay cut down the visiting time to only an hour or so each day. Lincoln was becoming exhausted and was starting to worry about the future.

Mary went east to New York in January and her delayed plans prevented her from being home until the night of the last open house in their Springfield home. By this time, their belongings had all been packed away and their steamer trunks had been moved to the Cherney House to await their departure. Two weeks earlier, Lincoln had traveled to Charleston to say goodbye to his elderly step-mother, and now his farewells were complete.

Lincoln bid goodbye to Springfield on a rainy morning in February 1861. He rode alone in his carriage to the train station. Mary and the boys would meet him in Indianapolis. Lincoln requested that there be no public demonstration over his departure, but several hundred friends and well-wishers lined the streets near the station anyway.

His voice was thick with emotion as he said farewell and then boarded the train. He never looked back.... never realizing that he would never see his beloved city again.

THE WAR AND THE SUPERNATURAL

Lincoln's life was already in danger when he departed Springfield. His mail had already started to contain hate letters and death threats. The threats were starting to be taken very seriously by the men who vowed to protect the new president. Lincoln's family joined him for the twelve-day journey to Washington, boarding the train in Indianapolis. Unfortunately, not even the presence of his wife and children prevented disaster from almost striking several times. One assassination attempt was averted when guards discovered a grenade in a satchel near the president's seat.

By the time the Lincoln family reached Pennsylvania, real trouble was brewing. Lincoln was forced to don a disguise and slip aboard a special train that would take him into Washington. He was spirited aboard a single-car train and even the telegraph wires were cut to insure secrecy and to keep anyone from leaking his true location. Railroad detective, and later Secret Service director, Allan Pinkerton, arranged the car to travel by night and arrive before the official presidential train, which still carried the Lincoln family. The car was reserved under a false name, supposedly for an invalid who was being accompanied by his sister. The "sister" was in reality a secret service agent named Kate Warne. It was an inauspicious arrival into Washington, but at least Lincoln was safe and alive.

Lincoln was soon sworn in as President and began one of the most troubled periods of American history. Lincoln would later go one to believe that perhaps the reason he was born was to guide America through the War Between the States. His leadership during this period, although often questioned, never faltered and the events of 1861-1865 both strengthened and destroyed the man that Lincoln was.

The great loss of life and the bitter turmoil of the war took their toll on him. His personality changed and he became more bitter and dark. Gone was the humorous man who was apt to take off his shoes during staff meetings to "let his feet breathe". In his place was a sad, gloomy leader who was prone to severe depression. It was as if the weight of the entire nation had fallen on his shoulders.

Lincoln's times of prayer and contemplation became much longer and he seemed to turn inward. He spoke more and more often of the "hand of God" in certain battles and it was almost as if an uncanny perception somehow strengthened as the war raged on. By this time, Lincoln had truly taken on the mantle of America's military commander. Few realize today just to what extent Lincoln actually orchestrated the Union Army during the bloodiest points of the war, enduring complaints and barbs by ineffectual generals about his "meddling".

Documents of the Union War Department contain one occasion when Lincoln burst into the telegraph office of the department late one night. He had visited earlier, looking for the latest news, but when he came back, he was in a panic. He ordered the operator to get a line through to the Union commanders. He was convinced that Confederate soldiers were just about to cut through the Federal lines.

The telegraph operator asked where he had obtained such information and Lincoln reportedly answered, "My god, man! I saw it".

THE DEATH OF WILLIE LINCOLN

" Do you ever find yourself talking with the dead? I do... ever since Willie's death. I catch myself involuntarily talking to him as if he were near me..... and I feel that he is!"
Abraham Lincoln, speaking to the
Secretary of the Treasury, Salmon P. Chase

The war took a terrible toll on President Lincoln but there is no doubt that the most crippling blow he suffered in the White House was the death of his son, Willie, in 1862. The boy had been born in Springfield in 1850, shortly after the funeral of the Lincoln's second son, Eddie. Willie was much like his father and probably because of this, was the special favorite among his much-loved sons. The two of them shared many interests, especially reading, humor and a love for animals. In Washington, Lincoln bought a pony for Willie and it became the pride of the small boy's life.

Lincoln and Mary grieved deeply over Willie's death. Eddie had passed away a number of years before and while they didn't know it at the time, Tad would only live to be age eighteen. This left Robert as the only Lincoln son to see adulthood. Lincoln was sick at heart over Willie's death and it was probably the most intense personal crisis in his life. Some historians have even called it the greatest blow he ever suffered. Even Confederate President Jefferson Davis expressed condolences over the boy's death.

William Wallace Lincoln, named for a family doctor in Springfield, was a quiet, thoughtful boy who excelled at reading and education. His brother Tad was just the opposite and could not read or write by age 12, while Willie was beyond the basics by 8. He had a wonderful memory and could recite long passages from the Bible with ease. He often told his parents that he was going to be a minister when he grew up.

The reports of what Willie actually died from vary from story to story. In the end, it remains a mystery. He was said to have been a delicate child, despite his rough play with his brother and his outdoor activities. Like his brother Eddie, he may have suffered from "consumption" or according to some accounts, he contracted either an acute malarial infection or typhoid. In either case, the lack of proper sanitation would have been a factor. During the 1860's, Washington had open sewers and a filthy canal for drinking water. The city's garbage was dumped into the water just a short distance from the White House.

The onset of Willie's sickness occurred during the last days of January 1862. He was out playing in the snow with Tad and both of them developed a fever and a cold. Tad's illness soon passed, but Willie seemed to get worse. He was kept inside for a week and finally put into bed. A doctor was summoned and he assured Mary that the boy would improve, despite the fact that Willie's lungs were congested and he was having trouble breathing.

Before the boy had taken sick, the Lincoln's had planned a large reception with over 800 people in attendance. The evening turned out to be a dismal affair for the worried parents as they continually took turns climbing the stairs to check on Willie. His condition did not improve.

The doctor was summoned back and by then, everyone in the household and the offices knew that Willie was seriously ill. More doctors were called in to consult and soon, Willie's illness made the newspapers. The reporters conjectured that he may have contracted bilious fever. One parent stayed with the frightened and sick boy at all times and a nurse came to spell them from one of the local hospitals. After a week of this, Mary was too weak and exhausted to rise from her own bed but Lincoln never left the boy's side, sleeping and eating in a chair next to his bed. The doctors had no hope for the child as he grew worse. Soon, his mind wandered and he failed to recognize anyone, including his beloved father.

Death came for Willie on the afternoon of February 20, 1862. Lincoln covered his face and wept in the same manner that he had for his mother years ago. He looked at Willie for a long time, refusing to leave his bed side. "My poor boy," the President is reported to have said. "He was too good for this earth. God called him home. I know that he is better off in heaven, but then we loved him so. It is hard.... hard to have him die."

The funeral was held in the East Room at the White House. It is said that Willie only appeared to be sleeping in his imitation rosewood coffin. His friends and family passed slowly by him, their faces twisted with grief. The day of the funeral was a stormy one, as if the forces of nature reflected the anguish in the Lincoln's hearts. The procession to the cemetery was several blocks long and it ended at Oak Hill Cemetery in Georgetown. Throughout the day, the rainstorms wreaked destruction upon the city. Steeples had fallen from churches, roofs had been torn form houses, trees and debris littered the roadways, and even the funeral procession cowered under the torrents of rain. But as soon as they reached the cemetery, the storm passed over and the air became silent... almost as in deference to Willie Lincoln.

The service was short. Willie had been embalmed to make the trip back to Springfield and be buried beside his brother, but Lincoln changed his mind about that at the last minute. He accepted an offer made to him by a friend, William Thomas Carroll, to place the body of Willie in one of the crypts in the Carroll family tomb. This would be until Lincoln retired from the presidency and returned to live in Springfield himself. He could not bear the idea of having Willie so far away from him just yet.

In fact, Lincoln returned to the cemetery the next day to watch the body as it was moved from the cemetery chapel to the crypt itself. The tomb was located in a remote area of the cemetery and was built into the side of a hill. It was a beautiful and peaceful spot but Lincoln wouldn't be able to leave his son unattended there for long.

Word got out that Lincoln returned to the tomb on two occasions and had Willie's coffin opened. The doctor had embalmed Willie so perfectly that he everyone said he just seemed to be sleeping. The President claimed that he was forced to look upon his boy's face just one last time.

Three years later, the undertakers would remove Willie's body from the vault one final time and transport it to a funeral train which stood ready for departure. The funeral car, draped in black, was divided into three section. One was for the honor guard, while the other compartment held the body of Willie's slain father. Together, they would make the long-delayed journey back to Springfield.

After the funeral, Lincoln tried to go on about his work, but his spirit had been crushed by Willie's death. One week after the funeral, he closed himself up in his office all day and wept. It has often been said that Lincoln was on the verge of suicide at this point, but none can say for sure. He did withdraw even further into himself though and he began to look more closely at the spiritual matters which had interested him for so long.

LINCOLN AND THE SPIRITUALISTS

Although many Lincoln scholars say otherwise, it is more than possible that Abraham Lincoln didn't just believe in the supernatural, but that he actually participated in it. Many have scoffed and said that Lincoln had no time for ghosts and spirits, but there are others who say that he actually attended seances which were held in the White House. Whether he accepted the movement or not, it is a fact that many Spiritualists were often guests there. Several of them were even said to have given him warnings about the dark shadows which hung over his life.

Of course, Lincoln himself was convinced that he was doomed and adopted a very fatalistic attitude during his presidency, especially after Willie's death. After the boy died, Lincoln treasured small items and drawings given to him by Willie, sometimes sitting them all over his desk while he worked, hoping to capture his essence. Small toys that had belonged to Willie were placed on his fireplace mantel, along with a framed picture of Illinois. Lincoln would tell visitors that it had been painted by "my boy, who died." His friends stated that Lincoln would often watch the door while he worked, as if expecting the boy to run through it and give his father a hug, as he often did in life.

Lincoln also began to speak of how Willie's spirit remained with him and how his presence was often felt in his home and office. Some mediums theorized that Lincoln's obsession with the boy's death may have caused Willie's spirit to linger behind, refusing, for his father's sake, to pass on to the other side.

Regardless of how he felt about Willie's spirit, Lincoln publicly avoided connections to the Washington spiritualists, so much of what is written about his contact with them comes through accounts and diaries written by friends and acquaintances. One such acquaintance would even claim that Lincoln's plans for the Emancipation Proclamation, which freed the southern slaves, came to him from the spirit of Daniel Webster and other abolitionists of the spirit world.

While Lincoln avoided the spiritualists in public, Mary embraced them openly. She had been quick to turn to contact with the other side for comfort after Willie's death. Once he was gone, Mary never again entered the White House guest room where he died or the room in which the funeral viewing was held. Some historians claim that this was the beginning of Mary's mental instability, but not because of the mediums, because of her fervent grief instead. The obsession over Spiritualism was just one of the symptoms, but none could ignore the fact that her headaches, mood swings and bursts of irrational temper were growing worse.

Mary began meeting with a number of different Spiritualists and invited many to the White House, as each claimed to be able to "lift the thin veil" and allow Mary to communicate with Willie. Mary's closest spiritualist companion, and one of whom there is some record that Lincoln also met with, was Nettie Colburn Maynard. Many are familiar with a tale told about a seance held by Nettie Maynard in 1863 where a grand piano levitated. The medium was playing the instrument when it began to rise off the floor. Lincoln and Colonel Simon Kase were both present and it is said that both men climbed onto the piano, only to have it jump and shake so hard that they climbed down. It is recorded that Lincoln would later refer to the levitation as proof of an "invisible power."

Rumors spread that Lincoln had an interest in the spirit world. In England, a piece of sheet music was published which portrayed him holding a candle while violins and tambourines flew about his head. The piece of music was called "The Dark Seance Polka" and the caption below the illustration of the president read "Abraham Lincoln and the Spiritualists".

It was also rumored that Lincoln consulted with these mediums and clairvoyants to obtain information about future events in the war. He found that sometimes they gave him information about matters as mundane as Confederate troop movements ..... information that sometimes matched his own precognitive visions.

Despite these somewhat apocryphal stories, there is little doubt that Lincoln believed a dark cloud hung over his head. The constant threats of death and violence that he received kept he and his bodyguards on edge at all times. It is also believed that some of his spiritualist friends felt the end was near. During a session that he was said to have had with Nettie Maynard, she allegedly told him that "the shadows others have told of still hang over you."

Lincoln told her that he received letters from spiritualists all over the country which warned him of impending doom. When she got ready to depart, the president insisted that she come and visit he and Mary the following Autumn.

"I shall come, of course," Nettie answered, "that is... if you are still among us."

DREAMS OF DEATH

Perhaps the most famous supernatural incident connected to Lincoln would be his last prophetic dream of the his assassination. And as mentioned, Lincoln was not the only person who experienced a foreshadowing of that dire event. Spiritualists all over the world were deluging the White House offices with letters warning the president of danger.

Of course, you could also say that these letters aren't really convincing evidence of paranormal predictions. As the war dragged on, threats of death and murder seemed to multiply. Lincoln's secret service men and bodyguards were constantly thwarted from their duty by Lincoln himself. He often slipped out of the White House at night for solitary strolls and refused to take precautions that were necessary to keep him protected. Many felt that it was only a matter of time before the assassin's bullet caught up with the president...

One of Lincoln's old friends from Illinois was a lawyer with whom he had ridden the legal circuit named Ward Hill Lamon. Lincoln had appointed him to a security position in the White House and he worried constantly over Lincoln's seeming indifference to threats and warnings of death. Lamon often resigned his position because his friend did not take the danger seriously. Lincoln always convinced him to stay on, promising to be more careful.... as he vanished out of the White House at night, or attended the theater without protection.

Lamon became obsessed with watching over Lincoln and many believe that the president would not have been killed at Ford's Theater had Lamon been on duty that night. As it turned out, the security chief happened to be in Richmond, Virginia, on an errand for the president, when disaster struck. He would never forgive himself for what happened... especially since he believed that he had a forewarning of the event, from Lincoln himself.

Years later, Lamon would remember that Lincoln had always been haunted by the strange vision that he experienced in the mirror in 1860. Several years after that, it was to Lamon and Mary Lincoln to whom the president would recount an eerie dream of death, just shortly before his assassination.

> "About ten days ago, I retired late. I soon began to dream. There seemed to be a death-like stillness about me. Then I heard subdued sobs, as if a number of people were weeping. I thought I left my bed and wandered downstairs. There the silence was broken by the same pitiful sobbing, but the mourners were invisible. I went from room to room; no living person was in sight, but the same mournful sounds of distress met me as I passed along.
>
> "It was light in all the rooms; every object was familiar to me, but where were all the people who were grieving as if their hearts would break? I was puzzled and alarmed. What could be the meaning of all this? Determined to find the cause of a state of things so mysterious and so shocking, I kept on until I arrived at the East Room, which I entered. Before me was a catafalque, on which rested a corpse wrapped in funeral vestments. Around it were stationed soldiers who were acting as guards; and there was a throng of people, some gazing mournfully upon the corpse, whose face was covered, others weeping pitifully.
>
> " 'Who is dead in the White House?', I demanded of one of the soldiers.
>
> " 'The President', was his answer, 'He was killed by an assassin.'
>
> "Then came a loud burst of grief from the crowd, which awoke me from my dream. I slept no more that night; and although it was only a dream, I have been strangely annoyed by it ever since."

Lincoln was murdered just a few days later and his body was displayed in the East Room of the White House. Mary would recall this dream of her husband's quite vividly in the days which followed. It was said that her first coherent word after the assassination was a muttered statement about his dream being prophetic.

On April 14, 1865, a few days after the horrifying dream and on the night he was to attend Ford's Theater, Lincoln called a meeting of his cabinet. Edwin Stanton, Lincoln's Secretary of War, arrived twenty minutes late and the meeting began without him. As Stanton and Attorney General James Speed were leaving the meeting, Stanton commented to him that he was pleased about how much work was accomplished.

"But you were not here at the beginning", Speed said. "When we entered the council chamber, we found the president seated at the top of the table, with his face buried in his hands. Presently, he raised it and we saw that he looked grave and worn".

" Gentlemen, before long, you will have important news", the President told them. The Cabinet members were anxious to hear what news Lincoln spoke of, but he refused to tell them anything further.

"I have heard nothing, but you will hear tomorrow, " he said, and then continued, "I have had a dream. I have dreamed three times before; once before the Battle of Bull Run; once on another occasion; and again last night. I am in a boat, alone on a boundless ocean. I have no oars, no rudder, I am helpless. I drift!"

That evening, while attending a performance of a play called "Our American Cousin" at Ford's Theater, Lincoln was killed by an assassin named John Wilkes Booth. He died the next morning, April 15, the anniversary of the southern assault on Fort Sumter, the event which officially started the Civil War.

Lincoln spoke of death and prophecies to other members of his staff also, like Colonel WH Crook, a member of the White House security team and one of Lincoln's personal bodyguards. Crook took his task seriously, often staying awake at night and sitting outside Lincoln's bedroom while the president slept. Crook even refused to read a newspaper while on duty so that he would be ready should an emergency arise.

Crook was on duty the evening of April 14 and that same afternoon, Lincoln spoke to him about the strange dreams that he had been having. Crook pleaded with the president not to go to the theater that night, but Lincoln dismissed his concerns, explaining that he had promised Mary they would go and that he needed a night away from the problems of the country. Crook then asked to accompany the president, but Lincoln again refused, insisting that Crook could not work around the clock.

Lincoln had a habit of bidding Crook a "good night" each evening as he left the office and went to his bedroom. On that fateful day, according to Crook, Lincoln paused as he left for the theater and turned to the bodyguard. "Good-bye, Crook," he said significantly.

"It was the first time that he neglected to say 'Good Night' to me", Crook would later recall. "And it was the only time that he ever said 'Good-bye'. I thought of it at that moment and, a few hours later, when the news flashed over Washington that he had been shot, his last words were so burned into my being that they can never be forgotten."

Lincoln's final premonition was not the last however. General Ulysses S. Grant and his wife Julia were also scheduled to attend the performance of "Our American Cousin" that night. But that morning, Julia awoke with a terrible sensation. She wanted to leave Washington immediately, despite the fact that the entire city was celebrating her husband's victory over Lee and the surrender of the southern armies.

She was sure that something terrible was about to happen.

General Grant, who according to the plans of the conspirators was also supposed to be assassinated, was not present at Ford's Theater because Julia simply refused to attend the play that night. She pressed Grant so hard about her premonition that he finally agreed not to go.

Would Grant have also been killed that night if he had attended the performance? Thanks to Julia Grant's strange premonition, we will thankfully never know.

President Abraham Lincoln was dead...killed by an assassin's bullet. In the following chapter, we will discuss the assassination of the president, the mysteries surrounding it... and of course, the ghosts who have lingered because of it.

For now, we will continue to explore the mysterious afterlife of Lincoln himself.

THE RETURN TO ILLINOIS

In the midst of the all of the clamor of Washington, the search for a killer, and the matter of getting a new president into office, there was another matter that needed to be attended to and that was Lincoln's funeral. The how and where of the service was decided by Edwin Stanton, as Mary had taken to her bed and Robert was still too stunned to be of much assistance.

The nation cried to see the fallen president and telegrams arrived from around the country asking to be the final resting place of President Lincoln. It was decided that Lincoln would be entombed beneath the dome of the Capitol building, a crypt which had originally been intended for George Washington, but he was later moved to Virginia. Originally, Mary agreed to this plan, but soon changed her mind after being visited by a delegation of friends and officials from Illinois. It was decided that Lincoln would be taken back to Springfield for burial. It was a place which he always planned to go back to after leaving office. Unfortunately, he was not returning to Illinois in the way that he had planned.

Because of the national demand to see Lincoln one last time, it was decided that he would be taken to Springfield aboard a special train. This funeral train would follow a route through the east's major cities, but first, they had to attend to the funeral service in Washington.

The funeral was planned for the following Wednesday and the public would be allowed to view the body the day before. The White House doors opened on Tuesday and people crushed inside, inching past the body, weeping and speaking to Lincoln. By the end of the day, an estimated 25,000 people had crowded past the mahogany coffin.

The following day was the service, which Mary Lincoln was still too distraught to attend. Robert was there in his Captain's uniform, holding the hand of Tad, whose face was swollen with tears. Near them stood General Ulysses S. Grant and other military officials along with 60 clergymen, the Presidential cabinet, President Andrew Johnson, mayors, congressmen, and government delegates from across the country.

After the service, the pallbearers carried the body from the White House as church bells all over the city began to toll. From the forts that still surrounded the city, cannons began to boom. Throngs of people lined Pennsylvania Avenue and thousand more peered from windows and roofs along the parade route. Many of these people had been in position for hours, waiting for Lincoln's casket to appear. Federal troops moved into formation to accompany the hearse, which now waited outside the White House. The coffin was placed on a high platform, surrounded by glass and elevated so that everyone could see. Soon, the hearse moved forward, pulled by six white horses, all festooned with black cloth and decoration.

Lincoln's body was then carried to the Capitol Building and placed in the rotunda. An honor guard took up position around it and remained in place until the next morning. Shortly after the sun appeared, wounded soldiers were allowed to file past the casket and pay their final respects. After this, the viewing was opened to the public once more. The crowds were so large that the soldiers outside had to remove wooden barricades around the building so that no one would be injured. It was said that over 3,000 people per hour filed past the coffin before the doors were finally closed at midnight.

On Friday, one week after the president had been killed, a procession accompanied the body to the Baltimore and Ohio Railroad depot, where the funeral train waited. Over the course of the next fourteen days, the train steamed north and then westward, passing through perhaps the greatest crowds ever assembled in America. Reporters followed its passage, telegraphing details to their newspapers back home of the strange, circus-like atmosphere surrounding the funeral train. It is believed that 7 million northerners looked upon Lincoln's hearse or coffin and that 1.5 million actually looked upon his silent face. Ninety different funeral songs were composed in his honor while thousands (or even millions) cried, fainted, took to their beds, and even committed suicide in the frenzy of Lincoln's passing.

The train arrived first in Baltimore, where buildings had been draped with black cloth; maudlin sayings had been painted on banners; and where photos of Lincoln decorated buttonholes, signs and wreathes. Over 10,000 people viewed the body in less than three hours.

As the train passed through Pennsylvania, people began to line the tracks and watch it pass. Little towns were filled in honor of the president and local bands played funeral dirges as the train went by. In Harrisburg, thousands waited all night in the rain for a glimpse of Lincoln the following morning. In Philadelphia, more than 500,000 were already waiting at Independence Hall when the train arrived. The crowd passed through the hall until midnight, when the doors were finally closed and thousands stood in line all night to hold their place in line. People already in line at dawn took more than five hours to reach Lincoln.

The train moved on to New York. In the hours before its arrival, the streets of the city became impassable. The police and military fought to keep them open, but it was no use. The body of Lincoln was taken to City Hall and more than 600,000 spectators accompanied it while more than 150,000 stood in line for a glimpse of the president. The honor guard had a full-time job on their hands trying to keep people from touching Lincoln and trying to keep women from kissing his face and hands.

That night, after the doors were closed, the embalmer brushed a heavy coating of dust from Lincoln's face, beard and clothing. They also rearranged his facial features, which had become twisted from exposure.

At some time on Monday, a New York photographer named Gurney took photos of Lincoln's cadaver and sent proofs to Mary in Washington. He planned to make the photo available for sale within a few days but Mary objected. It was said that she was shocked by the "unnatural" expression on her husband's face. When he heard that a photograph had been taken, an outraged Edwin Stanton ordered the plates be broken and the photo destroyed. A number of telegrams were sent begging Stanton to reconsider, but he refused. The plate was eventually destroyed but not before Stanton was sent a copy of the photo to show how unobjectionable it was. The photo ended up being lost in Stanton's papers for years and was later sent to the Illinois State Historical Library. It was found in 1952 by a student who was researching Stanton's files.

The train finally moved on to Albany, leaving thousands disappointed. Many who did not get a chance to see the president boarded trains and planned to try again in Chicago or in Springfield. The Illinois delegates, who were accompanying the train, realized in horror just how many people could be descending on the small city. One of the delegates hurried to Springfield to prepare for the worst.

The train continued on through New York and into Ohio. Vast crowds stood on the hills outside of Cleveland as the train passed beneath prepared arches that bore sad inscriptions. In the city park, a Chinese pagoda (I don't know why either) had been erected and the president's casket was placed there for more 100,000 spectators to view. In Columbus, a queer Oriental temple (I suppose to outdo Cleveland) was constructed as a hearse and in Urbana, more than 3,000 people surrounded a huge, floral cross as the train steamed on toward Indiana.

In Richmond, Indiana, the church bells of the town rang for an hour as the train arrived and over 15,000 people greeted the funeral with pantomimes, scenes and stage effects that must have looked both ghastly and somewhat horrifying to the party looking out from the railroad car windows. In Indianapolis, the casket was taken to the State House, where it lay under a black velvet canopy which was sprinkled with golden stars.

From here, the train passed into Illinois, bound first for Chicago. The casket was taken from the train and placed on a platform which had been fitted with an arch bearing a bust of Lincoln. Thirty-six young women walked beside the platform that carried the president and they showered flower petals in all directions. The streets were packed with over 100,000 people as excursion trains had been coming into the city for more than 24 hours, carrying curiosity-seekers from the east.

Thousands lined up at the court house in the rain and mud to see Lincoln. Exhausted soldiers and police officers recalled that the lines moved less than one foot per hour on Monday and Tuesday. More trains arrived, bringing more people to add to the chaos as at least 125,000 lined up to view the casket. Ambulances came and went, carrying injured onlookers and women who fainted from grief and exhaustion. At one point, a section of wooden sidewalk gave away and plunged hundreds into the mud and water below.

The train finally began the last leg of its journey on the night of May 2, leaving Chicago and passing under arches which were illuminated with bonfires and decorated with sentiments like "Coming Home". In Springfield, the casket was removed very late at night and taken to the House of Representatives, where Lincoln had spoken years before. Over the next 24 hours, thousands more streamed past the coffin but these were not the hysterical crowds of New York and Chicago, these were the folks that Lincoln had known and loved in life. They were the people he talked to in the street, laughed with, ate with and the people he had missed while living in Washington. They were now the people who wept at his open casket.

On the morning of May 4 , the last service was held in Springfield. Robert Lincoln had arrived and had left his mother in Washington with Tad. She had not yet risen from her bed and missed the country's frantic farewell to Lincoln completely. She was far too involved in trying to contact Lincoln's spirit to care about funeral services.

Shortly before the service, embalmer Charles Brown worked to make Lincoln presentable for one last occasion, dressing him in a clean collar and shirt applying powder to his face. He finished just before the procession formed outside. The procession included Robert Lincoln, who rode in a buggy with members of the Todd family; John Hanks, one of Lincoln's only remaining blood relatives; elderly Sarah Lincoln; Thomas Pendel, Lincoln's door man from the White House, and a representative of the household servants; and Billy, Lincoln's barber and friend. He was placed at the end of the procession, being a Negro.

The final parade was begun by General Joe Hooker, one of Lincoln's Generals, and he led "Old Bob", the tired and rider-less horse whom Lincoln had ridden the law circuit on. The parade, like the others before it, was long and marked with music, banners and signs. The journey ended two miles away at quiet Oak Ridge Cemetery.

When it was all over, "Old Bob" was taken back to the stable, but by the time he arrived there, his blanket and a banner with the words "Old Abe's Horse", had been stolen. The souvenir hunters had stripped him of everything.

The endless days of travel and the grand spectacles were finally over. Lincoln was laid to rest in Oak Ridge Cemetery in a holding crypt while his tomb was constructed. But he would not rest in peace for some years to come......

THE SECRETS OF THE GRAVE
When the body of President Lincoln arrived in Springfield, he actually had two different graves waiting for him. One grave was located in a remote, wooded cemetery called Oak Ridge.

The cemetery had been started around 1860 and it mostly consisted of woods and unbroken forest. In fact, not until after Lincoln was buried there was much done in the way of improvement, adding roads, iron gates and a caretaker's residence. In 1865, according to Springfield officials, it was no place to bury a fallen president!

The other grave site planned for Lincoln was a small hill located in the heart of Springfield. Construction was started here when it was learned that the president would be brought back to Illinois. The location was a spot called Mather Hill, which is now the site of the State Capital building.

The grave was ready by May 1, while the funeral train was still in Chicago. Suddenly, word was sent from Washington that Mary Lincoln had changed her mind. She had now decided that her husband would be buried at Oak Ridge Cemetery instead.

Springfield remembered the Mrs. Lincoln of old and recalled her erratic nerves and fits of temper, so they tried to be very diplomatic with the widow. They telegraphed Edwin Stanton and told him that her wishes would be respected. Nevertheless, they hoped to change her mind when the funeral train arrived in Springfield. They were still lobbying for the grave site on Mather Hill. It was reported that Robert was waiting for his mother's final decision on the matter less than an hour before the funeral was to begin. She chose Oak Ridge.

Lincoln was taken to the receiving vault of the cemetery and placed there with his sons, Willie and Eddie. Willie's body had accompanied his father's from Washington, while Eddie's had been exhumed and brought over from another cemetery.

Although Springfield officials had placed Lincoln at Oak Ridge, they still had no intention of leaving him there. In Washington, Mary's friends were urging her to return Lincoln to the Capitol dome, while in Springfield, plans marched ahead to place the president in a tomb on Mather Hill. In fact, plans had already been drawn up for a huge memorial.

Mary was furious when she read in the newspapers of Springfield's intentions. Immediately, she sent word and threatened to remove Lincoln's body from the city if the monument was not built at Oak Ridge. She claimed that she would further have him removed back to Washington if they did not cooperate. Oak Ridge, she declared, was where her husband would have wanted to sleep. After Willie's death, he had spoken of being buried in a quiet and secluded place and the remote cemetery was perfect.

In the Summer of 1865, Mary moved to Chicago and a delegation from Springfield went up to plead with her again. She refused to see them and at last, they surrendered. A temporary vault was built for Lincoln and in seven months, on December 21, he was placed inside. Six of Lincoln's friends wanted to be sure the body was safe, and a plumber's assistant named Leon P. Hopkins made an opening in the lead box for them to peer inside. All was well and Lincoln and his sons were allowed a temporary rest.

The new construction on a permanent tomb would last for more than five years and the catacomb would actually be completed first. It was during this time that strange things began to be reported in the vicinity of Lincoln's resting place.

A few days after the body was placed in the receiving vault, Springfield residents and curiosity seekers began to tell of sighting a spectral image of Lincoln himself wandering about near the crypt. The legends and reports say that he was taking walks to investigate the broken ground where he and his sons would be placed when the tomb was completed.

And the stories didn't end there either.... after the bodies were moved to the monument tomb, strange sobbing noises and sounds like footsteps were often heard at the site. Many of the locals believed that the ghost of President Lincoln was haunting Oak Ridge Cemetery and the new tomb.

Many believe that he still walks today.

On September 19, 1871, the caskets of Lincoln and his sons were removed from the hillside crypt and taken to the catacomb. The tomb was not quite finished yet, but the completed portion was a suitable place for them to be moved to. The plumber, Leon P. Hopkins, opened the coffin once more and the same six friends peered again at the president's face. There were several crypts waiting for Lincoln and his sons, although one of them had already been filled. Tad had died in Chicago a short time before and his body had already been placed in the nearly finished monument.

During the move, it was noticed that Lincoln's mahogany coffin was beginning to deteriorate, so his friends brought in a new iron coffin, to which the inner coffin of lead, containing Lincoln's body, was transferred. The dead president was laid to rest again, for another three years, while the workmen toiled away outside.

On October 9, 1874, Lincoln was moved again. This time, his body was placed inside of a marble sarcophagus, which had been placed in the center of the semi-circular catacomb. A few days later, the monument was finally dedicated. Money had been raised for the groups of statues which were situated outside and the citizens of Springfield seemed content with the final resting place of their beloved Abraham Lincoln.

But then a new threat arose from a direction that no one could have ever predicted...

The events which unfolded next began in Lincoln, Illinois, which is just a short distance from Springfield. Although most who lived there had no idea, the city had become a hide-out for a gang of counterfeiters run by a man named "Big Jim" Kneally. The place was an ideal refuge for Kneally's "shovers", pleasant-looking fellows who traveled around the country and passed, or "shoved", bogus money to merchants.

At some point, in the Spring of 1876, business turned bad for the Kneally gang. Their supply of counterfeit money had dwindled because their master printer was serving a ten year sentence in Joliet prison. Now, there was no one to print new money and things were starting to look a little grim.

That was when Kneally worked out a plan. He would have his men steal the body of Abraham Lincoln from Oak Ridge Cemetery and then he would use the body to negotiate for the release of Kneally's master printer from jail. The prisoner's freedom would be the price the Illinois officials would have to pay for the return of Lincoln's body.

In June, Kneally started on his plan. He sent five of his men into Springfield to open a saloon and make preparations for the grave robbery. One night, one of the men got very drunk and spilled the details of the plan to a prostitute. He told her to look for a little extra excitement in the city on the night of July 4. He and his companions planned to be stealing Lincoln's body while the rest of the city was celebrating the holiday. The plan was to stash the corpse under a bridge about two miles up the Sangamon River.

The story was too good to keep and the woman passed it along to several other people, including the city's chief of police (although one wonders how they knew each other?). The story spread rapidly and Kneally's men disappeared.

Kneally didn't give up on the plan however. He moved his base of operations to a tavern called the Hub at 294 West Madison in Chicago. Kneally's man there was named Terence Mullen and he operated a secret headquarters for the gang. One of Kneally's operatives, Jack Hughes, came into the Hub in August and learned that a big job was in the works. Kneally wanted to steal Lincoln's corpse as soon as possible. Hughes and Mullen had no desire to do this themselves, so they brought another man into the mix. His name was Lewis Swegles and he had a reputation for being one of the most skilled grave robbers in Chicago. They decided he would be perfect for the job.

In 1876, grave robbery was still a national horror and would remain that way for some years to come. Illinois, like most other states, had no laws against the stealing of bodies. It did however, have a statute which prevented selling any bodies. Needless to say, this put medical schools into dire need. They often had to depend on "ghouls", or grave robbers, to provide corpses for their anatomy classes. These "ghouls" had become the terror of communities and friends and relatives of bereaved families sometimes patrolled graveyards for several nights after a funeral, with shotguns in hand.

Swegles came in and discussed the ins and outs of grave robbery with the other two men and they quickly devised a plan. They would approach the Lincoln monument under the cover of night and pry open the marble sarcophagus. They would then place the casket in a wagon and drive northward to the Indiana sand dunes. This area was still remote enough to provide a suitable hiding place for however long was needed.

Swegles, being the most experienced of the group, agreed to everything about the plan except for the number of men needed. He believed the actual theft would be harder than they thought and wanted to bring in a famous criminal friend of his to help them. The man's name was Billy Brown and he could handle the wagon while the others pillaged the tomb. The other two men readily agreed.

On November 5, Mullens and Hughes met with Swegles in his Chicago home for a final conference. They agreed the perfect night for the robbery would be the night of the upcoming presidential election. The city would be packed with people and they would be in downtown Springfield very late, waiting near the telegraph and political offices for news. Oak Ridge Cemetery, over two miles away and out in the woods, would be deserted and the men could work for hours and not be disturbed. It would also be a perfect night to carry the body away, as the roads would be crowded with wagons and people returning home from election celebrations. One more wagon on the road would not be noticed.

The men agreed and decided to leave for Springfield on the next evening's train. Swegles promised to have Billy Brown meet them at the train, but felt it was best if he didn't sit with them. He thought that four men might attract too much attention.

Hughes and Mullen conceded that this was a good idea, but wanted to at least get a look at Brown. Swegles instructed them to stay in their seats and he would have Brown walk past them to the rear car. As the train was pulling away from the station, a man passed by the two of them and casually nodded his head at them. This was the mysterious fourth man. Brown, after examination, disappeared into the back coach. Hughes and Mullen agreed that he looked fit for the job.

While they were discussing his merits, Billy Brown was hanging onto the back steps of the train and waiting for it to slow down at a crossing on the outskirts of Chicago. At that point, he slipped off the train and headed back into the city. You see, "Billy Brown" was actually Agent Nealy of the United States Secret Service.

Lewis Swegles was actually a government informant who had been putting together other charges against Hughes and Mullen when he learned of the body-snatching plan. He began boasting of his grave robbing prowess to get more details about the plan and then brought the information to the district chief of the Secret Service, Agent Tyrell, who had already been using Swegles' information for a counterfeiting case against the two men. Tyrell had instructed Swegles to go along with the plan and included his own man as "Billy Brown".

As Nealy was slipping off the train, more men were his taking his place. At the same time the conspirators were steaming toward Springfield, Tyrell and a half-dozen operatives were riding in a coach just one car ahead of them. They were also joined on the train by a contingent of Pinkerton detectives, who had been hired by Robert Lincoln after he got word of the plot to steal his father's body. The detectives were led by Elmer Washburne, one of Robert's law partners.

A plan was formed between Washburne and Tyrell. Swegles would accompany the grave robbers to Springfield and while assisting in the robbery, would signal the detectives, who would be hiding in another part of the monument. They would then capture Mullen and Hughes in the act.

When they arrived in Springfield, Tyrell contacted John T. Stuart, a former law partner of Lincoln and the head of the Lincoln National Monument Association, who cared for the tomb. He advised Stuart of the plan and together, they contacted the custodian of the site. The detectives would hide in the museum side of the monument with the custodian. This area was called Memorial Hall and it was located on the opposite side of the structure from the catacomb. They would wait there for the signal from Swegles and then they would rush forward and capture the robbers.

The first Pinkerton arrived just after nightfall. He carried with him a note for John Power, the custodian, which instructed him to put out the lights and wait for the others to arrive. The two men crouched in the darkness until the other men came inside.

Tyrell and his men explored the place with their flashlights. Behind the Memorial Hall was a damp, dark labyrinth which wound through the foundations of the monument to a rear wall of the catacomb where Lincoln was entombed. Against this wall, in the blackness, Tyrell stationed a detective to wait and listen for sounds of the grave robbers. Tyrell then returned to the Museum Room to wait with the others. Shortly after complete darkness had fallen outside, their wait was over.

A lantern flashed outside the door and a file made short work of the small padlock. The thieves came inside and using an ax, broke open the top of the Lincoln sarcophagus. They moved the lid aside and looked into it. Swegles was given the lantern and was stationed nearby to illuminate the work area. They began lifting out the heavy casket and once this was completed, Mullen told Swegles to go and have the wagon moved around. He had assured Mullen and Hughes that Billy Brown had it waiting in a ravine below the hill.

Swegles raced around to the Memorial Hall, gave the signal to the detectives, and then ran outside. Tyrell whispered to his men and, with drawn revolvers, they rushed out and around the monument to the catacomb. When they got there, they found the lid to the sarcophagus was moved aside and Lincoln's casket on the floor... but the grave robbers were gone!

The detectives scattered outside to search the place. Tyrell ran outside and around the base of the monument, where he saw two men near one of the statues. He whipped up his pistol and fired at them. A shot answered and they fought it out in a hail of gunfire, dodging around the monument. Suddenly, one of the men at whom he was shooting called out Tyrell's name.... he was firing at his own detectives!

Mullen and Hughes had casually walked away from the tomb to await the return of Swegles, Brown and the wagon. They never suspected the whole thing had been a trap. They had only wanted to get some air and moved into the shadows where they wouldn't be seen in case someone wandered by. After a few minutes, they saw movement at the door to the tomb and had started back, thinking that Swegles had returned. They heard the pistol shots and saw a number of men around the monument. They took off running past the ravine and vanished into the night.

The story broke in the newspapers the next day... to stunned disbelief. Only the Chicago *Tribune* would print the story as they were the only ones who believed it. No other Illinois newspaper dared touch a story that was so blatantly false! The people on the street didn't believe the *Tribune* story either, maintaining that the whole story had been hoaxed for some bizarre political agenda. Most people wouldn't believe the Secret Service and Pinkerton agents would be stupid enough to have gathered all in one room where they could see and hear nothing, and then wait for the criminals to act. Fingers of suspicion pointed toward Swegles, thinking that someone had put him up to telling a false story.

The Democrats in Congress charged that the Republicans had hoaxed the whole thing so that it would look like the Democrats had violated the grave of a Republican hero and in this way, sway the results of the election.

To put it bluntly, no one believed that Lincoln's grave had been, or ever could be, robbed!

The doubters became believers on November 18, when Mullen and Hughes were captured. The two grave robbers, fleeing from their close call, had returned to Chicago. They soon caught up with Swegles, who assured them of his own miraculous getaway. He claimed to have no idea how detectives could have gotten wind of the plot and they believed him. In fact, Mullen and Hughes never suspected him, or the elusive "Billy Brown", until they, and not Swegles, were arrested on November 17.

The newspapers broadcast the story the following day and America realized the story which had appeared in the Chicago *Tribune* had been true. Disbelief turned into horror. Letters poured into the papers, laying the guilt at the feet of everyone from the Democrats, to southern sympathizers, to the mysterious John Wilkes Booth Fund.

The people of Illinois were especially outraged and punishment for the two men was bound to be severe... or it would have been had the law allowed it. Two days after their arrest, the conspirators were under heavy guard in the Springfield jail. A few days after, they were indicted by a grand jury... for the charge of conspiring to commit and unlawful act.

There was nothing else they could be charged with. Grave robbery was not yet a crime in Illinois and the prosecution, bolstered by Chicago lawyers dispatched by Robert Lincoln, could find no grounds to charge them with anything other than the minor charge of conspiracy. Ironically, the charge was not even for conspiring to steal President Lincoln's body. It was actually for planning to steal his coffin, which was the property of the Lincoln National Monument Association.

The public was aghast at the idea that these men would get off so lightly, even though the grand jury had returned a quick indictment. Continuances and changes of venue wore the case along to May of 1877, when it finally came to trial. The jury was asked by the prosecution to sentence the men to the maximum term allowed, which was five years in prison. On the first ballot, two jurors wanted the maximum, two of them wanted a two-year sentence, four others asked for varying sentences and four others even voted for acquittal. After a few more ballots, Mullen and Hughes were incarcerated for a one-year stay in Joliet.

It did not take long before the story of the Lincoln grave robbery became a hotly denied rumor, or at best, a fading legend. The custodians of the site simply decided that it was something they did not wish to talk about anymore. Of course, as the story began to be denied, the people who had some recollection of the tale, created their own truth in myths and conspiracies.

The problem in this case however, was that many of these "conspiracies" happened to be grounded in the truth.

Hundreds of people came to see the Lincoln burial site and many of them were not afraid to ask about the stories that were being spread about the tomb. From 1876 to 1878, custodian John C. Power gave rather evasive answers to anyone who prodded him for details about the grave robbery. He was terrified of one question in particular and it seemed to be the one most often asked... was he sure that Lincoln's body had been returned safely to the sarcophagus after the grave robbers took it out?

Power was terrified of that question for one reason.... because at that time, Lincoln's grave was completely empty!

On the morning of November 8, 1876, when John T. Stuart of the Lincoln National Monument Association, learned what had occurred in the tomb the night before, he rushed out to the site. He replaced the casket and then repaired the marble of the sarcophagus. He was not able to rest after the incident, fearing that the grave robbers, who had not been caught at that time, would return and finish their ghoulish handiwork.

So, he made a decision. He notified the custodian and told him that they must take the body from the crypt and hide it elsewhere in the building. Together, they decided the best place to store it would be in the cavern of passages which lay between the Memorial Hall and the catacomb.

That afternoon, Adam Johnson, a Springfield marble-worker, took some of his men and they lifted Lincoln's casket from the sarcophagus. They covered it over with a blanket and then cemented the lid back into place. Later that night, Johnson, Power and three members of the Memorial Association stole out to the monument and carried the 500-pound coffin around the base of the obelisk, through Memorial Hall and into the dark labyrinth. They placed the coffin near some boards that had been left behind in the construction.

The following day, Johnson built a new outer coffin while Power set to work digging a grave below the dirt floor. It was slow work, because it had to be done between visitors to the site and he also had a problem with water seeping into the hole. Finally, he gave up and simply covered the coffin with the leftover boards and wood.

For the next two years, Lincoln lay beneath a pile of wood in the labyrinth, while visitors from all over the world wept and mourned over the sarcophagus at the other end of the monument. More and more of these visitors asked questions about the theft... questions full of suspicion, as if they knew something they really had no way of knowing.

In the Summer and Fall of 1877, the legend took another turn. Workmen arrived at the monument to erect the naval and infantry groups of statuary on the corners of the upper deck. Their work would take them into the labyrinth, where Power feared they would discover the coffin. The scandal would be incredible, so Power made a quick decision. He called the workmen together and swearing them to secrecy, showed them the coffin. They promised to keep the secret, but within days everyone in Springfield seemed to know that Lincoln's body was not where it was supposed to be. Soon, the story was spreading all over the country.

Power was now in a panic. The body had to be more securely hidden and to do this, he needed more help. He contacted two of his friends, Major Gustavas Dana and General Jasper Reece and explained the situation. These men brought three others to meet with Power, Edward Johnson, Joseph Lindley and James McNeill, all of Springfield.

On the night of November 18, the six men began digging a grave for Lincoln at the far end of the labyrinth. Cramped and cold, and stifled by stale air, they gave up around midnight with the coffin just barely covered and traces of their activity very evident. Power promised to finish the work the next day.

These six men, sobered by the responsibility that faced them, decided to form a brotherhood to guard the secret of the tomb. They brought in three younger men, Noble Wiggins, Horace Chapin and Clinton Conkling, to help in the task. They called themselves the Lincoln Guard of Honor and had badges made for their lapels.

The city of Springfield got their first look at the Guard during the funeral of Mary Todd Lincoln in July 1882. At the ceremony, the men conducted themselves so mysteriously that people whispered questions about who they were. It was assumed that the men concealed some great secret about the Lincoln family and rumors flew.

After the funeral, John T. Stuart told the Guard that Robert Lincoln wanted to have his mother's body hidden away with his father's. So, late on the night of July 21, the men slipped into the monument and moved Mary's double-leaded casket, burying it in the labyrinth next to Lincoln's.

Visitors to the tomb increased as the years went by, all of them paying their respects to the two empty crypts. Years later, Power would complain that questions about Lincoln's empty grave were asked of him nearly everyday. Finally, in 1886, the Lincoln National Monument Association decided that it was time to provide a new tomb for Lincoln in the catacomb. A new and stronger crypt of brick and mortar was designed and made ready.

The press was kept outside as the Guard, and others who shared the secret of the tomb, brought the Lincoln caskets out of the labyrinth. Eighteen persons who had known Lincoln in life filed past the casket, looking into a square hole that had been cut into the lead coffin.

Strangely, Lincoln had changed very little. His face was darker after 22 years but they were still the same sad features these people had always known. The last man to identify the corpse was Leon P. Hopkins, the same man who had closed the casket years before. He soldered the square back over the hole, thinking that he would be the last person to ever look upon the face of Abraham Lincoln.

The Guard of Honor lifted the casket and placed it next to Mary's smaller one. The two of them were taken into the catacomb and lowered into the new brick and mortar vault. Here, they would sleep for all time.....

"All time" lasted for about 13 more years. In 1899, Illinois legislators decided the monument was to be torn down and a new one built from the foundations. It seemed that the present structure was settling unevenly, cracking around the "eternal" vault of the president.

There was once again the question of what to do with the bodies of the Lincoln family. The Guard of Honor (who was still around) came up with a clever plan. During the 15 months needed for construction, the Lincoln's would be secretly buried in a multiple grave a few feet away from the foundations of the tomb. As the old structure was torn down, tons of stone and dirt would be heaped onto the grave site both to disguise and protect it. When the new monument was finished, the grave would be uncovered again.

When the new building was completed, the bodies were exhumed once again. In the top section of the grave were the coffins belonging to the Lincoln sons and to a grandson, also named Abraham. The former president and Mary were buried on the bottom level and so safely hidden that one side of the temporary vault had to be battered away to reach them.

Lincoln's coffin was the last to be moved and it was close to sunset when a steam engine finally hoisted it up out of the ground. The protective outer box was removed and six construction workers lifted the coffin onto their shoulders and took it into the catacomb. The other members of the family had been placed in their crypts and Lincoln's was placed into a white, marble sarcophagus.

The group dispersed after switching on the new electric burglar alarm. This device connected the monument to the caretaker's house, which was a few hundred feet away. As up-to-date as this device was, it still did not satisfy the fears of Robert Lincoln, who was sure that his father's body would be snatched again if they were not careful. He stayed in constant contact with the Guard of Honor, who were still working to insure the safety of the Lincoln's remains, and made a trip to Springfield every month or so after the new monument was completed. Something just wasn't right.... even though the alarm worked perfectly, he could not give up the idea that the robbery might be repeated.

He journeyed to Springfield and brought with him his own set of security plans. He met with officials and gave them explicit directions on what he wanted done. The construction company was to break a hole in the tile floor of the monument and place his father's casket at a depth of 10 feet.

The coffin would then be encased in a cage of steel bars and the hole would be filled with concrete, making the president's final resting place into a solid block of stone.

On September 26, 1901, a group assembled to make the final arrangements for Lincoln's last burial. A discussion quickly turned into a heated debate. The question which concerned them was whether or not Lincoln's coffin should be opened and the body viewed one last time? Most felt this would be a wise precaution, especially in light of the continuing stories about Lincoln not being in the tomb. The men of the Honor Guard were all for laying the tales to rest at last, but Robert was decidedly against opening the casket again, feeling that there was no need to further invade his father's privacy.

In the end, practicality won out and Leon P. Hopkins was sent for to chisel out an opening in the lead coffin. The casket was placed on two sawhorses in the still unfinished Memorial Hall. The room was described as hot and poorly lighted, as newspapers had been pasted over the windows to keep out the stares of the curious.

What actually took place in that room is unknown except from the reports of the select few who were present. Most likely, they were the same people who had been present several years before when the body had been placed in the brick and mortar vault.

A piece of the coffin was cut out and lifted away. According to diaries, a "strong and reeking odor" filled the room, but the group pressed close to the opening anyway. The face of the president was covered with a fine powder made from white chalk. It had been applied in 1865 before the last burial service. It seemed that Lincoln's face had turned inexplicably black in Pennsylvania and after that, a constant covering of chalk was kept on his face.

Lincoln's features were said to be completely recognizable. The casket's headrest had fallen away and his head was thrown back slightly, revealing his still perfectly trimmed beard. His small black tie and dark hair were still as they were in life, although his eyebrows had vanished. The broadcloth suit that he had worn to his second inauguration was covered with small patches of yellow mold and the American flag that was clutched in his lifeless hands was now in tatters.

There was no question, according to those present, that this was Abraham Lincoln and that he was placed in the underground vault. The casket was sealed back up again by Leon Hopkins, making his claim of years ago to be true.... he really was the last person to look upon the face of Lincoln.

The casket was then lowered down into the cage of steel and two tons of cement were poured over it, forever encasing the president's body in stone.

You would think that would be the end of it, but as with all lingering mysteries, a few questions still remain. The strangest are perhaps these: does the body of Abraham Lincoln really lie beneath the concrete in the catacomb? Or was the last visit from Robert Lincoln part of some elaborate ruse to throw off any further attempts to steal the president's body? And did, as some rumors have suggested, Robert arrange with the Guard of Honor to have his father's body hidden in a different location entirely?

Most historians would agree that Lincoln's body is safely encased in the concrete of the crypt, but let's look at this with a conspiratorial eye for a moment. Whose word do we have for the fact that Lincoln's body is where it is said to be? We only have the statement of Lincoln's son, Robert, his friends and of course, the Guard of Honor.... but weren't these the same individuals who left visitors to the monument to grieve before an empty sarcophagus while the president was actually hidden in the labyrinth, beneath a few inches of dirt?

Sort of makes you wonder, doesn't it?

And what of the stories which claim that Lincoln's ghost still walks the tomb?

Many have reported that he, or some other spirit here, does not rest in peace. Many tourists, staff members and historians have had some unsettling impressions here that aren't easily laughed away. Usually these encounters have been reported as the sound of ceaseless pacing; tapping footsteps on the tile floors; whispers and quiet voices; and the sounds of someone crying or weeping in the corridors.

Of course, the tile floors and marble walls are rather conducive to echoes and sounds that carry from other parts of the tomb.... right? Well, I know a number of people who would definitely like to use these explanations to scoff at their own strange experiences.

Are you one of them?

THE LINCOLN HOME

The house in which the Lincoln family lived in Springfield was located on Eighth Street, not far from Lincoln's law office in the downtown district. The Lincoln's lived in the house from a period shortly after Robert was born until they moved to Washington in 1861. At least that is what the history books tell us.... although some people believe that at least part of the Lincoln family is still residing in the house today.

The house was originally built in 1839 by a Reverend Dresser and was designed in the Greek Revival Style. Lincoln purchased the home in 1844, while it was still a small cottage. It had been constructed with pine exterior boards; walnut interiors; oak flooring; and wooden pegs and hand-made nails held everything together. In 1850, Lincoln improved the exterior of the property by having a brick wall constructed and by adding a fence along Jackson Street but nothing major was done to the house until 1856. At this time, the house was enlarged to a full two stories, adding new rooms and much needed space.

Today, the house is presented in much the same way as it looked during the Lincoln years. It is now owned and operated by the National Park Service and they are not publicly thrilled that the house has gained notoriety as a "haunted" site. They have always maintained that no ghosts walk here.... although many of the witnesses to the strange events have been *former* employees and tour guides of the house.

For many years, stories have circulated about a tall, thin apparition who has been seen here, accompanied on occasion by a small boy. Many would pass this off to wishful thinking, but in more than one circumstance, the image of Mary Lincoln has been easily recognized. Most believe that if any Lincoln spirit resides here, then it is hers. They believe this house was the one place where Mary was truly happy while she was alive. Is it possible that her spirit may have returned here after her death?

A number of years ago, the Springfield *State Journal-Register* newspaper interviewed some (then) current and former staff members of the house, all of whom claimed to have had brushes with the supernatural here. At that time, a woman named Shirlee Laughlin was employed at the house as a custodian. She claimed that her superiors were very unhappy with what they termed her "vivid imagination".

But were the events she experienced really all in her mind?

Laughlin claimed in her interview to have experienced ghosts in the house on many occasions. "I don't see the images as such," she said, "I see things happening."

Among the things she witnessed were toys and furniture that could be found in different rooms of the house at different times, seemingly moving about on their own; unlit candles that would mysteriously burn down on their own; and Lincoln's favorite rocking chair rocking back and forth under its own power.

"At times, that rocking chair rocks," she stated, "and you can feel the wind rushing down the hall, even though the windows are shut tight."

Laughlin also recounted an occurrence which took place while she was rearranging furniture in Mary Lincoln's former bedroom. Besides being a custodian, she was also an expert on historic home restoration and would often attempt to recreate the lay-out of the household furniture when the Lincoln's lived in the house. She was in the bedroom alone one afternoon when someone tapped her on the shoulder. She looked around the room, but there was no one there. She decided to leave the furniture the way she had found it.

And that was not the only weird experience linked to Mary Lincoln. Another anecdote concerned a key which turned up missing from a wooden chest in Mary's room. "We looked everywhere for it," Laughlin reported, "then one morning it just showed up in the lock with a piece of pink ribbon tied to it." No explanation was ever discovered for where the key had been or for who had tied the piece of ribbon around it.

But can we really claim this house might be haunted on just the word of a single, former employee? Perhaps not.... if she were the only one to have strange experiences here.

Staff members are not the only ones to have odd encounters. A number of tourists have also noticed things that are a bit out of the ordinary, like hearing voices in otherwise empty rooms; hearing the rustle of what sounds like a period dress passing by them in the hallway; experiencing unexplainable cold spots; and most common, seeing that rocking chair as it gently moves back and forth.

One tourist, an attorney from Virginia, even wrote the staff after he returned home to tell them of his own strange sighting. He claimed to see a woman standing in the parlor of the house... who abruptly vanished. He had enough time to recognize her as Mary Lincoln.

As mentioned earlier, the stories of ghosts in the Lincoln house are not only denied, but are laughed at by many of the staff members. They claim that the "ghostly" rocking chair is the product of park rangers having a little fun with the tourists using a piece of string to make the chair move. Pretty convenient, isn't it?

If this is true, well, then the house must not be haunted.... but what about the past and present rangers who have had their own experiences, even excluding Shirlee Laughlin?

One former guide said that she was on duty at the front door one afternoon when she heard the sound of music being played on the piano that used to be in the parlor. She turned to stop whoever had touched it and found that no one was in the room.

Another ranger who worked in the house recalled several occasions when strange feelings, and the touch of invisible hands, caused her to close up the house quickly on some evenings.

And again, she wasn't alone either. One ranger, who spoke to me anonymously, told me of one late afternoon when she was in the front parlor by herself. There is a display here of some of the items that could commonly be found in households of the period, including some children's toys. As she was standing in the room, she caught a movement out of the corner of her eye. When she looked, she saw a small toy as it rolled across the floor on its own.

She didn't stay in the room very long.

There are no ghost stories or legends associated with this house at all, the park rangers and officials will tell you if you are brave enough to endure their ridicule and ask. Really, this isn't much of a surprise, and as you have read in this book already and will most likely read again, there are a number of historical landmarks for which the "no ghosts" rule applies.

The Lincoln Home is no different. It is simply another house that, while not haunted, certainly seems to have a lot of ghosts!

THE HAUNTED WHITE HOUSE

There are a number of ghosts said to be haunting the White House, but perhaps the most famous of these is Abraham Lincoln. And those who have encountered the spirit of the late president have occasionally been quite famous themselves....

There is no doubt that few presidents left the sort of mark on the executive mansion that Lincoln did. Perhaps this is the reason that he still reportedly walks the halls... perhaps it is not Lincoln's ghost who haunts the place at all. Maybe it was simply the "spirit" of the man which seeped into the walls and corridors of the building. Possibly it is only Lincoln's image that has been seen standing at the center window of the Oval Room... the same spot where Lincoln stood during the war, looking out over Virginia and pondering the outcome of the battles ahead.

Or perhaps it really is the president himself, unable to remain in the grave.

One of the earliest reliable reports of Lincoln's ghost in the White House came from President Theodore Roosevelt, who took up residence in the house nearly forty years after Lincoln's death. "I see him in different rooms and in the halls," he admitted. In truth, it comes as no surprise that Roosevelt may have "attracted" the ethereal presence of Lincoln as he greatly admired the former leader and quoted his speeches and writings often.

Grace Coolidge is also reported to have encountered Lincoln. In a newspaper account, she was quoted as saying that he was dressed in black, with a stole draped across his shoulders to ward off the drafts and chills of Washington's night air.

On a television news broadcast, President Dwight D. Eisenhower's press secretary, James Haggerty, stated that the President often told him that he felt Lincoln's presence in his office and in the corridors of the White House.

Of all of the presidents who encountered Lincoln's ghost, the best known was President Harry S. Truman, who made no bones about the fact that he believed the White House to be haunted. He once recalled an incident that took place in the early morning hours, about one year after he took office. He was awakened that night by two very distinct knocks on his bedroom door. He got out of bed, went to the door and opened it, but found that no one was in the hallway. Suddenly, the air around him felt icy cold but the chill quickly faded as President Truman heard the sound of footsteps moving away from him down the corridor.

The late President Ronald Reagan even mentioned Lincoln's ghost in a 1987 press conference. He told the reporters who were gathered that he was never frightened by the spirit. "I haven't seen him myself," Reagan said, "but every once in awhile our little dog Rex will start down that long hall, just glaring as though he's seeing something." He also added that the dog would bark repeatedly as he stopped in front of the Lincoln bedroom. Reagan said that if he opened the door to the bedroom and tried to get the dog to come inside, Rex would growl fiercely.... but refused to step over the threshold.

Eleanor Roosevelt told reporters that she had never seen Lincoln, but she admitted that she had felt his presence. She also told of an incident that occurred with one of her staff members. Her secretary had passed the famed Lincoln bedroom one day and noticed a tall, thin man who was sitting on the edge of the bed, pulling on a pair of boots. She then realized that the figure was Abraham Lincoln! As the late president had been dead for about 75 years at the time, she was understandably frightened.... and she ran screaming back to her office.

In addition to the residents and staff members of the White House, a number of notable visitors have also encountered Lincoln. One story relates to Queen Wilhelmina of the Netherlands, who spent the night in the White House a number of years ago. It was said that she was sleeping in the Rose Room when she heard a tapping on the door. As the hour was quite late, she assumed the summons must be important and she quickly opened the door. There, standing in the doorway, was Abraham Lincoln!

According to a White House staff member, the Queen surprised President Franklin D. Roosevelt, and a number of cocktail party guests, the next evening when she recalled her encounter. She told them after seeing the apparition, everything went black and she later woke up on the floor. By this time, the ghost had vanished.

The late British Prime Minister Winston Churchill never discussed Lincoln's ghost, but many believe that he may have encountered him while visiting the White House. Churchill was always quartered in the Lincoln Bedroom during his stays, as were all visiting male heads of state, but the next morning, he would normally be found sleeping in a room across the hall. He confessed that he never felt comfortable in that particular room.

So does the ghost of Abraham Lincoln really walk in the White House?

Some of our country's most influential leaders have certainly believed so. But why does he still walk here? Is the apparition merely a faded memory of another time... or an actual presence? Does the ghost appear, as has been suggested, during times of crisis, when perhaps the assistance of the president who faced America's greatest crisis is most needed?

President Harry Truman had no idea why Lincoln's ghost, or any of the other reported phantoms, was still present in the White House. In her biography about the president, Margaret Truman stated that her father certainly had no ambitions to haunt the White House himself.

"No man in his right mind would want to come here of his own accord," he said.

SOURCES

Haunted Illinois by Troy Taylor (1999)
Ghosts of Springfield by Troy Taylor (1997)
Here I have Lived: A History of Lincoln's Springfield by Paul Angle (1935)
Springfield State Journal-Register Newspaper
Life Magazine
Lincoln by David Herbert Donald (1995)
The Great Abraham Lincoln Hijack by Bonnie Stahlman Speer (1990)
Myths After Lincoln by Lloyd Lewis (1929)
With Malice Toward None by Stephen B. Oates (1977)
Ghosts: Washington's Greatest Ghost Stories by John Alexander (1975- Revised 1998)

CHAPTER SEVEN

SPIRITS OF THE ASSASSINATION
The Events Surrounding the Murder of Abraham Lincoln and the Ghostly Tales Which Followed

Now he belongs to the ages.....

Edwin M. Stanton, U.S. Secretary of War, at President
Lincoln's deathbed on April 15, 1865

When the Civil War ended in April 1865, it did not end for everyone. There were many in the South who simply refused to believe that the Confederacy had fallen.

One of these men was John Wilkes Booth, an actor who professed and undying devotion to the South. Booth was the son of Junius Brutus Booth, a professional actor. The elder Booth was considered by many to be so eccentric that he was nearly insane, a trait which father and son apparently shared. John Wilkes Booth was also the brother of Edwin Booth, perhaps the most famous stage actor of the period. Edwin often spoke of his brother's strangeness and he would have had an even greater cause for concern had he known the dark secrets that his sibling hid in his heart.

While the war was still raging, Booth had been attempting to organize a paramilitary operation with a small group of conspirators. Their plan was to kidnap the president and take him to Richmond. After a number of failed attempts, it was clear that the plan would not work. Booth's hatred of Lincoln forced him to change his plans from kidnapping to murder. Booth did not explain to his confederates about this change until two hours before the event took place.

Booth had been a southern sympathizer throughout the war. He was revered for his acting in the South and during the war had been a spy and a smuggler, working with southern agents in Maryland and Canada. He was also rabid in his pro-slavery views, believing that slavery was a "gift from God". He was convinced that Lincoln was a tyrant and Booth hoped the murder of the president would plunge the North into chaos and allow the Confederacy to rally and seize control of Washington.

On the night of April 14, Booth stepped into Lincoln's box at Ford's Theater and shot the president in the back of the head. At the same time, another assassin tried to kill Secretary of State Seward. He was horribly scarred by a knife wound to the face, but survived. Secretary of War Edwin Stanton and General Grant were also slated to be killed and presidential successor Andrew Johnson was only spared because of an assassin's cold feet. The shadow of a greater conspiracy hung over Washington and many questions have not been answered to this day, including whether Edwin Stanton was really involved in the assassination.

Some historians believe that Stanton was one of the few to really gain by Lincoln's death in that he was a radical Republican who was opposed to Lincoln's gentle plans for the South. It seems that Stanton would have been able to gain power if the North imposed a military occupation upon the southern states instead. Regardless, Stanton's behavior both before and after Lincoln's assassination has raised some questions. For example:

- Stanton refused a request for Major Thomas Eckert to accompany Lincoln to Ford's Theater. The implication, according to some historians, was that Stanton knew something Lincoln didn't.
- Despite Lincoln's many death threats, Stanton only sent one bodyguard to the theater that night and this man abandoned his post to have a drink. He was never reprimanded for this.
- On the night of the assassination, telegraph lines in Washington, controlled by the War Department, mysteriously went dead, delaying the news of Booth's escape. Many believe this points to some sort of government conspiracy behind the murder.
- Booth's diary was given to Stanton after the assassination and it vanished for several years. When it was returned, eighteen pages were missing. A security chief would later testify that it had been intact when given to Stanton.
And there were other problems too, although none of this would be brought to light until more than seventy years later! Far too late by that time....

The Lincoln party arrived at the theater that night and took a reserved box to the cheers of the crowd and to the musical strains of "Hail to the Chief". The Lincoln's were accompanied by a young couple, Major Henry Rathbone and his fiancée, Clara Harris. The play was a production called "Our American Cousin", presented by actress Laura Keene. The play was a comedy, the sort of show that Lincoln liked best.

Booth lurked about the theater all evening and at thirteen minutes after ten, approached Lincoln's box. He showed a card to an attendant and gained access to the outer door. As mentioned before, he found the box to be unguarded and while this was out of the ordinary, Booth apparently expected it to be that way. As he slipped into the door of the box, Booth jammed the door closed behind him.

During the evening, the Lincoln party had been discussing the Holy Land. The President made a comment about wanting to visit Jerusalem someday as he leaned forward and noticed General Ambrose Burnside in the audience of the theater. At that moment, Booth stepped forward. Major

Rathbone stood from his seat to confront the intruder but before he could act, Booth raised a small pistol and fired it into the back of President Lincoln's head.

Rathbone seized the actor but Booth slashed him with a knife. Lincoln fell forward, striking his head on the rail of the box and slumping over. Mary took hold of him, believing him to have simply fallen while Booth jumped from the edge of the balcony. His boot snagged on the bunting across the front of the box and he landed badly, fracturing his leg. As he struggled to his feet, he cried out "Sic Semper tyrannis!" (Thus it shall ever be for tyrants) and he stumbled out of the theater.

A scream went up from the back of the theater, crying "Booth!", and the stunned audience was snapped out of its stupor. Soon, more voices began shouting the actor's name and yet somehow, he managed to easily escape from the close and crowded auditorium. Then, there were more screams, groans and the crashing of seats and above all of it came Mary Lincoln's shrill cry for her dying husband.

In the theater's audience was a young doctor named Charles Leale, who rushed upstairs to the president's aid. He found Lincoln bleeding badly, his heart barely beating. Even this inexperienced young doctor could see that Booth's shot had been a fatal one. A few moments later, Leale was joined by Dr. Charles Sabin Taft and the two men, with some help from bystanders, managed to get the president out of Ford's Theater. Soldiers cleared a path through the crowd outside, where people rushed madly back and forth and milled about in confusion. A man named Henry Safford beckoned to the doctors and they carried the president across the street into the Petersen home. Lincoln's unconscious form was laid in a small, shabby bedroom at the back of the house. His lanky frame was too long for the bed and they were forced to lay him down at an angle.

Help was summoned and soon Lincoln's aides and security men were attempting to try and calm the frenzy around them. Soon, witnesses were being questioned and when Booth's identity was learned, a search party was organized to look for him. Meanwhile, the Surgeon General, Joseph K. Barnes, and Lincoln's own doctor, Robert Stone King, set to work on the president. They soon realized that it was no use, there was nothing that could be done for him.

Lincoln's many friends, Mary and Robert Lincoln came and went throughout the night. By the next morning, the president's condition had worsened. His breathing was very shallow and then suddenly, he took one great breath, his face relaxed and then he faded into oblivion. The calm and collected Robert Lincoln finally broke down into tears.

The Surgeon General carefully crossed the lifeless hands of Abraham Lincoln at twenty-two minutes after seven on the morning of April 15, 1865.

Edwin Stanton, who was either innocent of the allegations of conspiracy or was the most consummate actor of his time, stood by the bedside of the slain president. He raised his head and with tears streaming down his face, uttered the most unforgettable words that a man not known for his poetic soul could ever manage... "Now, he belongs to the ages."

THE MYSTERY OF JOHN WILKES BOOTH

John Wilkes Booth escaped from Washington on horseback across the Anacostia Bridge, passing a sentry who had not yet learned of the assassination. He made it to a farm in Virginia with the help of his fellow conspirators, only stopping to rest because of his broken leg.

Soon, the hunt for Lincoln's assassin was on and by morning, more than 2000 soldiers were looking for Booth. On April 26, a detachment of 25 men finally tracked down Booth, and a comrade named David Herold, at a tobacco farm near Port Royal, Virginia. The barn where they were hiding was surrounded and Herold decided to surrender. He was manacled and tied to a tree. Booth decided to die rather than be taken alive... or so we are told to believe.

In the darkness outside, a decision was made to try and smoke Booth out. The barn was set on fire and in a few moments, the interior was engulfed in flames. Booth came to the door and raised his weapon, apparently looking for a target among the soldiers outside. One of the soldiers, a Sergeant Boston Corbett, saw Booth through the slats of the barn and, ignoring Edwin Stanton's specific orders to bring Booth back alive, shot him in the back of the head. Booth fell to the floor and the soldiers rushed to subdue him. He died two hours later, whispering instructions to tell his mother that he "died for his country and did what he thought best."

A search of the dead man's pockets turned up a few items, including a compass; a diary; and photographs of several women, along with one portait of Booth's fiancée, Lucy Hale.

Booth died on the porch of the farm house as light was beginning to show in the sky. The dead man was sewn into a burlap bag and was taken to Alexandria on a steamer. Booth's body was then placed on a carpenter's bench and identified from a crude tattoo of the actor's initials; by dental fillings; and by a scar on the back of his neck. Others claimed that the body only resembled Booth, but that it actually wasn't him at all. Regardless, the corpse was taken to the Old Penitentiary in Washington and, using a gun case for a coffin, was buried under the floor of the old dining room. The door to the room was locked and the body stayed there for another four years. Finally, pleas from Edwin Booth convinced President Andrew Johnson to allow the body to be exhumed and buried in an unmarked grave in the family plot in Baltimore.

But was it really the body of John Wilkes Booth in the grave?

The man who shot Booth, Sergeant Boston Corbett, had been assigned to Lieutenant Edward Doherty and had been given the task of helping to track down the assassin. The soldiers found several witnesses who recognized Booth and eventually discovered sympathizer Willie Jett, who had arranged lodging for Booth at the tobacco farm where he was later discovered.

It was Corbett who fired the fatal bullet which killed Booth. It was at this point where many of the conspiracy theories begin. Among the theories is the idea that Corbett was under different orders from Edwin Stanton than the other soldiers. Some believe he was actually told to silence Booth so that Stanton could not be implicated in the plot. It is unlikely that this was the case, however, as Corbett is not believed to have had contact with Stanton before leaving Washington. He did act on orders to kill Booth however, if not orders from Stanton, then from a higher authority.

He shot Booth on direct orders from God.

Corbett was a religious fanatic who believed that he was directed by voices from heaven. This is ironic considering that Booth also claimed to be acting on orders from God when he killed President Lincoln.

Corbett had been in the hat-making industry prior to the war and had been exposed to large quantities of mercury, which often caused insanity in this trade (thus, the expression "mad as a hatter"). Although he fought bravely in the Federal Army, his odd and erratic behavior often made his superiors wary about using him in some assignments.

As a radical fundamentalist Christian, Corbett also reportedly castrated himself in 1858 after being solicited by a prostitute. Needless to say, this ended his temptation for fleshly sins. He also refused any alcohol and often condemned his fellow soldiers who drank.

Could Stanton, or some other conspirator in the government, have used this unbalanced man as a pawn in the assassination plot? Perhaps... he certainly would have followed any orders presented in a way that made him believe he was involved in some holy crusade.

After the war, Corbett moved to Kansas, where he became the security chief for the state legislature. He stayed in this position until one day when he pulled a gun on two boys who were mocking a minister's sermon. After that, he was committed to the Topeka Asylum for the Insane. However, in 1888, Corbett escaped and seemingly vanished from the pages of history.

But the man who Corbett allegedly killed, while surely the murderer of Abraham Lincoln.... didn't fade away quite so easily.

The newspapers quickly spread the word that President Lincoln's assassin, gunned down in a Virginia barn, was an actor named John Wilkes Booth. There is no doubt in anyone's mind that the killer had been Booth, but the question remains as to whether or not Booth himself was ever brought to justice. That question still remains unanswered today.

Shortly after the assassin was gunned down, the word began to spread that it might not have been Booth in that barn after all. The government's handling of the body in question and of the witnesses who were present, did not add much credence to the official version of the story. The Union soldiers had certainly killed a man. The War Department and the newspapers told a breathless nation that the man had been John Wilkes Booth... but had it really?

From the day the body was brought back to Washington, there were already people on the streets denying the body was that of Booth. They believed the assassin had long since escaped and that the government was offering a secret substitution for the real killer.

The Secret Service and the War Department took a firm position on the matter and would not argue it further. They maintained that the corpse was Booth. In their possession were items which belonged to him and other evidence that proved they had the right man, including the left boot which Booth had abandoned to put his broken leg in splints; the revolver he had been carrying when killed; and affidavits from the soldiers who brought the body back, claiming that the face of the corpse matched the photos of Booth they had been given. The investigators studied these, but they were never shown to the public. The government refused to even consider the idea that the body might not be that of Booth.

In the official silence from Washington, people began to see something dark and mysterious, just like they would a century later when another beloved American president would be gunned down. In both cases, they may have had reason to doubt!

In the Lincoln assassination, there was something strange about the attitude of the government towards Lincoln's murder and towards the killer. Perhaps those who believed in Booth's escape were right in their questioning. They were certainly correct in the knowledge that no one but government employees ever identified the body. It had been quickly hidden away with only certain people allowed to see it. There was a not a single witness who was completely impartial, or free from suspicion, who could swear that he had looked at the face of the corpse and that the man had been John Wilkes Booth.

The mystery continued for many years. More than 20 men would later claim to be Booth with books, anecdotes and sworn testimony. The newspapers got hold of each story and fanned the flames of doubt. By June 1865, stories spread that witnesses had seen Booth on a steamer to Mexico, or to South America. It was said that several people saw him in the west and others recognized him in the Orient. In Ohio, a man claimed that Booth had stopped in his tavern on the way to Canada. In the Southwest, several people who claimed to know Booth, said that he owed his escape to Union troopers because of his membership in a fraternal order. They had spirited him away rather than see him hanged.

It was no wonder that before long, dark-haired, pallid men who walked with a limp began to be pointed out all across the country as John Wilkes Booth.

The story became so popular that in July 1867, Dr. John Frederick May, who had identified the body as Booth, felt that it was now necessary to make an emphatic denial of his once positive identification. He now stated that he could have been *wrong* when he said the dead man had been John Wilkes Booth. It seems that two years before the assassination, May had removed a tumor from the back of Booth's neck. The surgery had left a jagged scar behind and this scar was how the doctor had identified the remains. His said that the body he saw did not resemble Booth, but since he found a scar on the back of the neck, he assumed it must be.

His new testimony continued, bringing to light a more damning bit of evidence. He explained in detail his examination of the corpse in question and its broken right leg. Now, the word of the government, and the witnesses at Ford Theater, said that Booth had broken his *left* leg when he jumped from the theater box. The fact that the doctor noted the mysterious body had a broken *right* leg meant one of two things... either the body was not Booth's or that Dr. May was too careless of an observer to be credited with any authority in the matter of an accurate identification.

Suspicion thrived across the country, and by 1869, President Johnson decided to dispel of all the rumors and allow the assassin's brother to bury the disputed corpse in his family's cemetery plot. On February 15, 1869, government workers exhumed the body that had been buried beneath the floor of the old prison dining hall.

Many believed the mystery of the body would be settled once and for all by Edwin Booth, but he simply added to the confusion by bungling the whole thing. First, he attempted to keep the exhumation a secret and then decided that he couldn't bear to look upon the face of his dead brother. He remained outside of the undertaker's room while friends went inside to examine the corpse. Not surprisingly, they decided the body belonged to John Wilkes Booth.

Needless to say, the public had a good mystery and they weren't about to let it go. A reporter for the Baltimore *Gazette* was soon claiming that he had been present at the exhumation and that the body had a broken right leg and no bullet holes in it. Modern historians believe this reporter had either a vivid imagination or lied about being at the exhumation at all, still in those days, the story looked like new evidence that Booth was still alive.

The mystery continued into the 20th century and while Booth's skull was supposedly on display in a number of different traveling carnivals, there remained a question as to his eventual fate. Historians looked for answers in the early 1900's as many of the people involved in the case were still living. Statements were taken from surviving soldiers who aided in Booth's capture and all information was thoroughly researched. They even checked out the claims of men still posing as Booth and found all of them transparently fraudulent.

Could Booth have survived the days after the assassination? The question nagged at historians, although logic would say that he had been killed. Still though, it is interesting that after all of the conflicting evidence, there was not a single eye-witness, sufficiently impartial to be above suspicion, who had seen the corpse in 1865 and could say, with certainty, that it was John Wilkes Booth.

While the question of Booth's capture remains unsolved... there is suggestion that he does still walk the earth, along with many of the others spirits of the Lincoln assassination. One of the places where Booth's spirit is alleged to walk is Ford's Theater, where the assassin carried out his dark deed.

Shortly after the Lincoln assassination, Ford's Theater was closed down, but it was far from empty. The famous photographer, Matthew Brady, took a photograph of the interior of the building. It revealed a nearly transparent figure standing in Lincoln's box. Although not clear, some have suggested that it might be that of John Wilkes Booth.

After the theater shut down, Ford hoped to open it again once the memory of Lincoln's death faded with the public. The citizens of Washington refused to return however and Ford eventually sold the place. It soon became a clearing house for processing Army records. In June 1893, the third floor of the building collapsed and killed a number of staff members.

Finally, in 1933, the theater was given to the National Park Service but its restoration was not begun until 1964. Four years later, it had been turned into a showplace and theatrical museum in the daytime hours and a playhouse at night.

It has been reported that a number of actors, including Hal Holbrook who performed there in his Mark Twain one-man show, have experienced an icy cold presence which can be felt at left center stage. Many forget their lines and tremble involuntarily in the same spot. Many believe the effect is caused by impressions left behind by Booth on the night of the assassination. It has also been reported that mysterious footsteps, weird voices, laughing sounds and the sound of someone weeping can be heard in the darkened theater. Lights have often been known to turn on and off by themselves.

In recent years, a well-known singer was performing at Ford's Theater and complained of being distracted by a light which kept flashing off and on in the restored Lincoln box. The strange thing is that this box is permanently closed to the public, so there could not have been anyone in there.

One has to wonder just what she was seeing?

The tragic events of that Good Friday evening in 1865 sparked another chain of events involving people closely embroiled in the assassination. Because when Booth jumped from the theater box that night, he left behind not only a dead president, but several shattered lives as well... all of them destined to meet tragic ends.

THE CURSE OF MARY LINCOLN

Mary Lincoln, whose mental state had already been declining since the death of Willie in 1862, never recovered from the loss of her husband. She struggled with family problems and more heartbreak and eventually was committed to a mental institution for a time.

Her curse would be that she managed to live 17 years after the death of her husband. For months after his murder, Mary spoke of nothing but the assassination until her friends began to drift away, their sympathy at a breaking point. She began to accuse her husband's friends and his Cabinet members of complicity in the murder, from his bodyguards to even Andrew Johnson.

Mary lay in her bed for 40 days after the assassination and in the seventeen years that followed she deteriorated mentally and physically into a bitter old woman who wore nothing but black, mourning clothing for the rest of her life. Her attachment to Spiritualism turned into a dangerous obsession, reaching a point where she could not function without aid from her "spirit guides".

Mary also had a great fear of poverty. She often begged her friends to help her with money. Unlike the widows of generals and governors, for whom money was easily raised, Mary's handful of supporters found it impossible to raise funds on her behalf because she was just too unpopular. In fact, she was despised all across America. Newspapers wrote unflattering stories about her and she was ridiculed by members of Washington society.

In 1868, she abandoned America and took Tad to live in Germany. They lived there in hiding for three years before coming home. A government pension awaited her, as did an inheritance from Lincoln's estate, so she was finally a wealthy woman. The ocean crossing had dire circumstances for Tad however. He developed tuberculosis and although he lingered for six weeks, he eventually passed away.

Mary embraced Spiritualism once again and moved into a commune where she began to develop her psychic "gifts" which enabled her to see "spirit faces" and "communicate beyond the veil". She claimed to have daily conversations with her late husband.

In the Spring of 1875, Robert Lincoln decided to have his mother institutionalized. He was concerned not only for her sanity, but for her estate as well, which he claimed her medium "friends" had designs on. By this time, Robert was wealthy in his own right and had no plans for his mother's money, which Mary refused to understand. He did however hire detectives to follow his mother and gather information about her drug use, which included opium, and he paid doctors to testify about her sanity in court.

Mary was sent to a mental hospital but was later released. She severed all ties with Robert, calling him a "wicked monster". She would hate him for the rest of her days and before she died, she wrote him letters which cursed him and which claimed that his father had never loved him.

Mary went into exile again and moved into a small hotel in France. Her eyes were weakened and her body was wracked with pain from severe arthritis. She refused to travel until several bad falls left her nearly unable to walk. Her sister pleaded with her to come home and finally she returned to Springfield, moving into the same house where she and Lincoln had been married years before.

Mary lived the last years of her life in single room, wearing a money belt to protect her fortune. She kept all of the shades in her room drawn and spent her days packing and unpacking her 64 crates of clothing. She died on July 12, 1882.

THE "LINCOLN CURSE"

The President's oldest son, Robert, was also no stranger to death and foreboding. He was the only Lincoln son to survive into adulthood and by the time he died in 1926, he was a very haunted man. He believed wholeheartedly that a curse hung over his life.

His strange belief began in 1865 when he was with his father at the time of his death. Needless to say, it was an event that he would never forget.

Sixteen years later, in 1881, Robert was in the company of another American president whose life was ended by an assassin. President James Garfield, who had only been in office about four months, was walking through the railroad station in Washington, accompanied by Robert. Suddenly, a crazed killer named Charles Guiteau appeared from nowhere and gunned down the President.

In 1901, President William McKinley invited Robert Lincoln to tour the Pan-American Exposition with him in Buffalo, New York. While the two men were together, an anarchist named Leon Czolgosg managed to approach them with a pistol. In seconds, President McKinley was dead.

For the third time, Robert had been present at the death of an American president.

Not surprisingly, he became convinced that he was "cursed" and that somehow he had contributed to the deaths of these men, including to the death of his father. From that time on, he refused to ever meet, or even be near, another American president. Although invitations arrived from the White House and from other Washington social gatherings, he declined them all.

Was there truly a curse over Robert Lincoln's head? He certainly believed there was.

THE TRAGEDY OF MAJOR RATHBONE

Major Rathbone, who was stabbed by Booth, recovered physically from the attack but would forever be haunted by the terrible night of the assassination. He and Clara soon married and moved to Germany, but the marriage was anything but blissful. Clara soon found that her husband was prone to bouts of depression and moodiness, none of which he had been inclined toward before the night in Ford's Theater. Then one morning, on Christmas Day of 1883, he went over the edge and killed Clara in a fit of insanity. Their children were spared, thanks to the bravery of their nanny, and Rathbone failed in his attempt to take his own life. He managed to stab himself four times, but lived long enough to die in a German mental institution in 1911.

The news of the tragedy soon reached Washington and rumors quickly spread. It was not long before the neighbors were crossing to the other side of the street, rather than walk directly in front of the former Rathbone house in Lafayette Square. A few people expressed concern that the troubled spirits of the family might return to their old home, while others insisted they already had. It was said that the sounds of a man's weeping, accompanying by the heartbreaking sobs of a woman and children, could be heard coming from the grounds. The stories would continue for many years and eventually, would fade away.

THE HAUNTINGS OF MARY SURRATT

As mentioned in a previous chapter, Washington's Old Brick Capitol was said to be one of the haunts of Mary Surratt, the only woman convicted and executed as a Lincoln assassination conspirator. But it was certainly not the only place where her ghost was alleged to be seen and perhaps the destruction of the building many years ago freed the spirit to travel to other places. I suggest this because she is perhaps the most well-traveled spirit of the Lincoln assassination and reportedly haunts almost as many places as the slain president himself!

Mary Surratt's trial was possibly one of the great travesties of American justice. She had been the proprietor of a Washington boarding house where John Wilkes Booth has stayed while plotting the kidnapping, and then murder, of Abraham Lincoln. At midnight, on the same night that Lincoln had been shot, Mary was rousted from her bed by police officers and Federal troops. She was accused of being a conspirator in Lincoln's death and was taken to the prison at the Old Brick Capitol. From that point on, Mary never stopped insisting that she was innocent and that she barely knew Booth... but no one listened.

The testimonies of two people were instrumental in Mary's conviction. One of them was a notorious drunk and the other was a known liar, a former policeman to whom Mary had leased her tavern in Maryland. At the trial's conclusion, she and three other defendants were found guilty and sentenced to death by hanging. Mary Surratt was the last of the four to die on July 7, 1865.

It is true that Mary may not have been as blameless as she claimed to be. Besides Booth, the other residents of the boarding house included her son, John, who was a Confederate courier, and several southern sympathizers. It is possible that she knew more than she claimed to, but it is still doubtful that she was in any way involved in the murder plot. To say that the evidence against her was circumstantial is a gross understatement and in light of that, and other factors, the punishment certainly was much harsher than what was believed to be her crime.

Even though Mary Surratt was sentenced to die, the board which convicted her sent a petition to President Andrew Johnson to ask that her sentence be commuted to life in prison. Whether this is because she was a woman or because they had doubts about her guilt is unknown. The commander of the Federal troops in Washington was so sure that a last minute reprieve would arrive that he stationed messengers on horseback along the shortest route from the White House to the Washington Arsenal Prison, where the execution was to take place.

Until the time the hood was placed over her head, officials in charge of the execution were sure that Mary would be spared. While four of the defendants died that day, three others received long prison sentences, including the famous Dr. Samuel Mudd. John Surratt, who had fled to Canada, was later returned for trial but was acquitted. What actually forced the hand of the judge to sentence Mary to death, and what stopped President Johnson from issuing the reprieve is unknown... because many historians today believe that Mary Surratt was innocent.

And it is possibly just this injustice which keeps her spirit lingering behind...

In time, the Washington Arsenal Prison was converted into Fort Leslie McNair. In the courtyard on the north end of the fort is where the execution took place and is the spot where Mary and the other conspirators were cut down from the gallows and buried. They were later moved to permanent graves in other locations. There is an old story which maintains that Mary's spirit caused the sudden appearance of a boxwood tree on the spot where the scaffold once stood. It is claimed that the growth of the tree was her way of continuing to attract attention to her innocence.

The courthouse in which Mary was tried, and found guilty, was turned into an officer's quarters for the army base, while the courtroom itself became a five-room apartment. For years, it was reported that occupants of the apartment would hear the sounds of chains rattling throughout the rooms. According to records, the seven male defendants in the conspiracy trial were shackled together with chains and sat on a bench where the apartment is now located. Tradition holds that the reported sounds are these same chains, still echoing over the decades.

And sounds are not the only things reported....

A number of residents of this apartment, and others which are located close to it, have claimed to see the apparition of a stout, middle-aged woman, dressed in black walking down the hallways of the officer's quarters. They have also heard the unexplainable sound of a woman's voice and have reported the sensation of being touched by an unseen hand.

Could this be the ghost of Mary Surratt?

Within a few years of Mary's death, rumors began that something strange was taking place at her former boarding house on H Street in Washington. Her daughter, Annie, had sold the house for less than half its value not long after her mother was executed, which is not really surprising considering the notoriety of the case.

But that may not have been the entire story....

In the years which followed, the house was plagued with a rapid succession of new owners. People would move in and out very quickly, sometimes in a matter of months. Someone who worked for a newspaper got wind of the story and soon the local journalists began to interview the former owners.... after they got rid of the property, that is. Most of the accounts reported "strange sounds" and "whispers" in the building.... voices which seemed to come from nowhere and which would be heard inside of rooms where no living person was present.

It was also said that the phantom footsteps and creaking boards of the second floor were caused by the spirit of Mary Surratt, doomed to wander Washington until her name was cleared.

A real haunting? Or merely a good story?

We may never know for sure. In the years that followed, the Surratt house was renovated many times both inside and out and recent owners claim that nothing of a "spirited" nature has taken place there in quite some time.

Mary's ghost is also said to frequent her home in Clinton, Maryland, located off of Brandywine Road. She is believed to be just one of the ghosts who haunt the place. John Wilkes Booth was said to have stopped at the tavern after making his escape from Washington, leading the tenant (and former policeman) to inform the authorities of Mary's part in the assassination. Many believe that he had other motives for wanting to see Mary convicted, leading most historians to question the accuracy of his statements to the authorities.

Stories of odd events at the tavern began in the 1940's when a widow lived in one half of the house and rented out the other. People spoke of seeing the ghost of Mary Surratt on the stairway between the first and second floors while others spoke of hearing men's voices, engaged in conversation, in the back of the house when no one was there.

In 1965, the site was taken over by the state and turned into a historical landmark. People who have worked and have visited there claim to have seen apparitions of people in period clothing, have heard the phantom cries of children and have heard footsteps pacing through the upper floor of the house when no one else was present.

Who are the ghosts in the Surratt House? If one of them is Mary, why has she returned? Is she perhaps recalling happier times when she lived in the house with her husband... longing to forget the terrible events that took place in Washington? Perhaps....

But who are the others? Could one of them be Mary's former tenant, whose testimony convicted her in the conspiracy? If so, what has caused him to return.... perhaps his own guilty conscience?

THE GHOST OF DR. MUDD

On April 15, 1865, a loud pounding at the front door awakened Dr. Samuel Mudd from a deep sleep. He had been resting in one of the upstairs bedrooms of his farmhouse in Charles County, Maryland, about three miles from Beantown. No stranger to urgent calls in the middle of the night, the doctor hurried downstairs and opened his home to two men. One of them was badly in need of medical attention, so Dr. Mudd decided to allow them in.

Little did he know that this decision would not only entangle him in the Lincoln assassination conspiracy, but it would also make him a part of one of the greatest mysteries of the time. Was Dr. Mudd simply an innocent doctor, assisting an injured man, or did he aid John Wilkes Booth in his escape from Washington?

Dr. Mudd would later admit to the fact that he had met one of the late night callers, John Wilkes Booth, on an earlier occasion, but he claimed that on that April morning, he did not recognize him, nor his companion, David Herold. The two men were wearing makeshift disguises at the time and it is possible that Mudd truly did not recognize Booth. He would always maintain that he was simply administering to an injured man and that he was more interested in Booth's broken leg than in his identity.

Dr. Mudd proceeded to set Booth's leg and two men were given food and rest until the afternoon of the same day. They left the house toward evening and headed toward Zekiah Swamp, reportedly never revealing their identities or how Booth came to be injured.

Several days later, Dr. Mudd was arrested for his alleged role in the Lincoln assassination. He was tried and convicted by the military court and was sentenced to life in prison at Fort Jefferson, located on Dry Tortugas Island in Florida. He remained there for four years, until he was pardoned by President Andrew Johnson. The pardon was not because of new evidence which proved Mudd to be innocent, but because of a request that had been signed by the warden, the officials and all of the inmates at the Florida prison. They believed they owed the doctor their lives after his aid during a yellow fever epidemic which swept through the prison.

There is still disagreement today over Mudd's role in the assassination. It is known that he was a southern sympathizer, as were most of the residents of southern Maryland, but it is also known that Federal officials "rushed to judgement" in the aftermath of Lincoln's death. They were anxious to catch anyone who might have been in any way involved in the murder and innocent people like Dr. Mudd, and Mary Surratt, may have been caught in the frenzy.

In any case, Dr. Mudd's strongest supporters have been his descendants, who have fought to clear his name for many years. They have also made an effort to restore the Mudd farm house in Maryland and present it as a site of historical significance.

Strangely enough, this effort was prompted by the ghost of Dr. Mudd himself.

According to Louise Mudd Arehart, the doctor's granddaughter, she had always been interested in the family history and in preserving the house but that interest was piqued when she began experiencing some rather strange events in the place. She began to hear knocking on the front door, but when she went to answer it, she found no one there. She also began to hear footsteps going up and down the stairs and in the hallways... but again, she would find the areas to be empty when she would go to check.

Soon, she began to catch glimpses of a man on the grounds of the house. This odd figure was always dressed in black trousers, a vest and a white shirt with the sleeves rolled up to his elbows. After seeing him a few times, he also began appearing inside of the house, where she finally got a good look at him. She was convinced that the apparition was that of her grandfather, Dr. Samuel Mudd.

She became convinced that Dr. Mudd had returned to prompt her and her family to restore the old farm house, which had fallen into a state of disrepair. Thanks to her efforts, the house was listed on the National Register of Historic Places in 1974 and was opened to the public in 1983.

Since then, the spirit of Dr. Mudd has only returned when restoration of the house slows down, or when it seems as though it is not proceeding to his expectations.

So, was Dr. Mudd guilty of conspiring in Lincoln's assassination? That question remains a mystery but perhaps it would provide the answers to his ghostly return. Perhaps he lingers here, not only to prompt the restoration of his home, but as reminder of his innocence. Regardless, this is one of the only cases ever recorded where the intervention of a ghost was instrumental in the preservation of American history.

THE JUDGE'S GHOST
The aftermath of the Lincoln assassination conspiracy not only touched, and destroyed, the lives of the accused conspirators... but the life of one of their accusers as well.

Judge Advocate General Joseph Holt was the presiding judge at the conspiracy trial and he was said to have been the only one of the panel who insisted on the death penalty for Mary Surratt. In the years which followed, we have to wonder if perhaps the judge grew to regret what many felt was a heartless decision.... because according to those who knew him, he changed dramatically after the trial.

Holt had apparently never been a popular man in Washington, even before the assassination. It was said that he was "taciturn, vindictive and ill-mannered"... in other words, a very charming fellow. Attitudes toward Holt didn't change much after the trial either and he began to lead the life of a recluse. Newspaper articles from the period reported that he withdrew into his home and rarely saw, or spoke with, anyone. To further establish the fact that he was withdrawing from society, they also described his home as "decaying" with bars on the windows and heavy shades which did not permit outside light, nor the gaze of passersby, to venture inside.

It was also said that the gardens of the house became tangled and overgrown and that people who walked along the street would often cross to the other side to avoid passing directly in front of the dilapidated mansion. Holt spent his remaining years in almost total isolation, coming out only on occasion to buy food... or to wander the few blocks to the Old Brick Capitol prison, where he would stare at the barred windows for some time before returning to his house. Rumors began to spread that Holt lived in deep regret over his harsh punishment of Mary Surratt. It was also somehow learned, at least according to the local stories, that he spent hours reading and re-reading the transcripts of the conspiracy trial.

After Holt died, the new owners attempted to renovate the house and to remove some of the austere atmosphere of the place... but to no avail. Soon after they took up residence, people in the neighborhood began to speak of the strange chill that pervaded various rooms of the house and the phantom sounds of someone pacing in the upstairs library. The stories maintained that the ghost of Judge Holt had remained within the house, still wracked with guilt over the terrible decision that he had been forced to make.

Years later, after the house had been torn down, another tale began making the rounds. In this version, people reported seeing the ghost of the Judge himself. It was said that he would appear on 1st Street, very near his former home, and walk along it to the Old Brick Capitol.. then suddenly vanish.

What could the spirit have been seeking... was it the truth of Mary Surratt's role in the conspiracy? Or merely absolution for the events that had taken place?

SOURCES
Haunted Illinois by Troy Taylor (1999)
Ghosts of Springfield by Troy Taylor (1997)
Lincoln by David Herbert Donald (1995)
Myths After Lincoln by Lloyd Lewis (1929)
The Day Lincoln was Shot by Richard Bak (1998)
Twenty Days by Dorothy Meserve Kunhardt and Philip Kunhardt Jr. (1965)
Haunted History by Richard Rainey (1989)
Guide to Haunted Places of the Civil War from Blue and Gray Magazine (1996)
70 Greatest Conspiracies of All Time by Jonathan Vankin and John Whalen (1998)
Legends and Lies: Great Mysteries of the American West by Dale L. Walker (1997)
Haunted Places: The National Directory by Dennis William Hauck (1996)
Ghosts! Washington's Most Famous Ghost Stories by John Alexander (1975- Revised 1998)
Ghosts and Haunted Houses of Maryland by Trish Gallagher (1988)
More Haunted Houses by Richard Winer and Nancy Osborn Ishmael (1981)

CHAPTER EIGHT
HAUNTED BATTLEFIELDS OF THE CIVIL WAR

The Whole Region seems literally filled with soldiery. One of the finest
armies ever marshalled on the globe now takes up these long stagnant
fields and woods.
Reverend A.M. Stewart, 102nd Pennsylvania

We have had the dark hour. The dawn has broken, and the collapsed
Confederacy has no place where it can hide its head.
Captain William Thompson Lusk

I have seen the dreadful carnage in front of Marye's Hill at Fredericksburg....
But I had seen nothing to exceed this. It was not war; it was murder.
Confederate General Evander Law after Cold Harbor

In the glades they meet skull after skull
Where pine cones lay... the rusted gun, green shoes full of bones,
the mouldering coat and cuddled-up skeleton;
And scores of such. Some start in dreams; and comrades lost bemoan;
By the edge of those wilds Stonewall had charged...
But the year and the man were gone.
Herman Melville

Of all of the places of the Civil War where the dead are still said to walk... there are no locations quite as haunted as the battlefields. It was on these fields where men fought, lived, died, suffered, screamed and bled.... and where, most likely, they left a little piece of themselves behind.

On the battlefields, the spirits of the past still walk.

Are these strange visions, sounds and thundering guns, which are reported on the battlefields almost daily, merely images of the past? Are they simply the imprints of a brutal time gone by... imprints which replay themselves again and again?

Perhaps they are merely visible, or heard, because of atmospheric conditions... Perhaps the imprints of the past are nothing more than weather or temperature phenomena, now sometimes seen because of the energy expended there years ago?

Or perhaps the answer is something else altogether.

Many believe that the ghost of the soldiers who are reported on the battlefields are actually the spirits of the dead, still trapped in the locations where they died. Could these phantoms have died so suddenly they don't realize they are dead? Are they doomed to repeat their actions during the war over and over again... throughout eternity?

Perhaps the answer is actually each one of these..... but we may never really know for sure. But whatever you choose to believe, consider for a moment the amount of death, bloodshed and tragedy that could be found on these battlefields during the Civil War.

If ghosts actually exist... it is here where you will find them!

SPIRITS OF ANTIETAM

Located on the far western edge of Maryland is the Antietam Battlefield, which can be found just outside of the small town of Sharpsburg. This former battlefield is perhaps the best preserved of all of the areas that have been turned into National Park Battlefields, looking much as it did at the time of the battle in 1862.

On a clear day, when the crisp wind is blowing across the grass, you can almost imagine yourself in another time. You feel that if you looked up, you might actually catch a glimpse of a weary soldier, trudging on toward either death or victory.

Of course, some people claim to have done more than just imagined this....

The Battle of Antietam took place in September 1862, during some of the most brutal days of the war. The Union Army had been badly beaten at Manassas and was in the midst of turmoil as President Lincoln fired ineffectual general after general. At this point, it still looked as though the Confederacy might actually win the war.

The battle was fought on September 17 and marked the first of two attempts by Robert E. Lee to take the war onto northern soil. It would become known as the bloodiest single day of the entire war with combined casualties of 23,100 wounded, missing and dead. The battle itself was considered a draw but the effect on both sides was staggering.

By early September, Lee was on the move to the north. He had trounced the Union Army at Manassas in August, but his men were exhausted, low on ammunition and out of supplies. He marched them north into Maryland under the watchful eye of Union Commander George McClellan. As luck would have it for Lee, McClellan (as usual) believed that he was greatly outnumbered by the Confederate forces and he was slow to act in heading off Lee's march.

Then, a strange occurrence took place.... one that has never been fully explained, which changed the course of the battle to come. Copies of Special Order No. 191, which was Lee's plan for the invasion of the north, were sent out to all of Lee's generals. Stonewall Jackson received his copy of the order, copied it and then sent it out to his brother-in-law, Harvey Hill. Unfortunately, Hill received his own copy and the copy sent to him by Jackson was apparently lost.

On September 13, Union troops moved into an area that had been recently vacated by Hill and they found a copy of Lee's orders wrapped around some cigars.

The orders were presented to McClellan and he realized that he was now privy to Lee's secret plans. "If I cannot whip Bobby Lee," he stated when he received the orders, "then I will be willing to go home."

Needless to say however, McClellan was never known for moving with great speed. His failure to act had previously cost the Union Army dearly and he was frequently criticized by President Lincoln for being overly cautious. And this time was no exception....

Instead of starting in immediate pursuit of the Confederate forces, McClellan waited overnight and then started west to South Mountain, still believing that Lee's dirty, hungry and tired army still outnumbered him. Ironically, the Union Army outnumbered Lee by more than 35,000 men.

On September 14, Lee tried to block McClellan's pursuit at South Mountain but he was forced to split his army and send troops to aid Stonewall Jackson in his capture of Harper's Ferry. He was able to delay McClellan for one day and by September 15, battle lines had been drawn west and east of Antietam Creek near the town of Sharpsburg.

Harper's Ferry surrendered the same day and Jackson soon moved north and joined Lee at Sharpsburg. They moved into position along a low ridge that runs north and south of town.

The battle opened at dawn on September 17 when Union General Joseph Hooker's artillery began firing on Jackson's men in the cornfield north of town. They advanced, driving the Confederates before them. It was reported in eyewitness accounts that the corn in the field was "cut as closely as could have been done with a knife". This early harvest claimed not only the corn crop, but the lives of hundreds of Confederate soldiers as well.

The fighting raged on through the day, moving back and forth on the grassy ridges, each side taking and then losing ground.

Meanwhile, Union troops encountered Confederates under General D.H. Hill posted along an old sunken road which separated the Roulette and Piper farms. For nearly four hours, fierce fighting occurred along this road and it would later become known as "Bloody Lane". Finally, confusion and exhaustion ended the battle here.

On the southeast side of town, Union troops under General Ambrose Burnside spent hours attempting to cross a stone bridge over Antietam Creek. Southern troops made up of only 400 Georgians held them back for nearly four hours and when Burnside's men finally crossed, it took them almost two additional hours to reform their lines. They succeeded in driving the Georgians into Sharpsburg, threatening to cut off a line of retreat for the now weary and decimated Confederates.

Finally, late in the afternoon, Confederate reinforcements arrived under A.P. Hill. They had been left behind in Harper's Ferry and now joined the fight, driving Burnside back to the bridge that his men had just taken.

The Battle of Antietam was over.

The following day, Lee began withdrawing his army across the Potomac River. The wounded were left behind in places like the Lutheran Church in Sharpsburg and at a house west of town called Mt. Airy, or the Grove Farm, where President Lincoln visited after the battle. It has been said that the floorboards in this house are still stained with the blood of those who fell during the battle. Now, more than 135 years later, these stains refuse to be removed... no matter how much sanding or scrubbing is done.

More men were killed at Antietam than on any other single day of the war. The loss of life here was tremendous, as were the stories of heroism and valor. There are many tales still lingering on this battlefield.... and some believe the soldiers, and the deeds committed here, may linger too.

The morning battle at Antietam shifted directions several times and eventually became centered in the middle of Lee's line, at a country road which divided the fields of two local farmers. On the day of the battle, it served as a sunken rifle pit for two Confederate brigades.

Lee ordered the center of the line to be held at all costs. This task fell to Colonel John B. Gordon, the commander of the 6th Alabama. Gordon allowed the Union troops to approach to within yards of the road before he gave the order to fire. The Union commander fell at once, his men wavered and then retreated, only to charge the Confederate line five more times.

The Federals continued to try and overrun the sunken road, unit after unit falling back under the rain of fire from the Confederate position. Finally, a vantage point was reached where the Union troops could fire down upon the road's defenders. Now, the once seemingly impregnable position had become a deathtrap. It was described like "shooting animals in a pen" and the road, soon to be known as **Bloody Lane**, rapidly filled with bodies, two and three feet deep.

The Union troops continued to fire and they poured into the sunken lane, kneeling on the bodies of the slain Confederates to fire at the retreating survivors. "A frenzy seized each man," one soldier recalled. He remembered tossing aside his own empty rifle to pull loaded ones from the hands of the dead to continue firing.

The slaughter at the Bloody Lane became one of the most memorable and tragic events of the battle, and perhaps even of the entire war. Perhaps the most heroic participants were the 69th of New York, recalled today by their nickname, "The Irish Brigade".

The Brigade had been reformed in New York after the fighting at Manassas cost the lives of many of the men and many others were captured. They formed again under the command of Thomas Meagher, an Irish immigrant and a campaigner for Irish freedom. The Brigade were among the most colorful of the Union troops and brawling was common, as was heavy drinking. They brought along their own priest to war and he conducted mass for them on the Sabbath and on the eve of battles.

In 1862, the 69th came to Virginia and were designated the Second Brigade of Israel B. Richardson's First Division, Edwin V. Sumner's II Corps. They saw action at Fair Oaks, Gaine's Mill, Salvage Station and a number of other places before meeting their destiny at Antietam.

The Union troops attacking the road were in serious trouble when they saw the emerald banner of the Irish Brigade appear on the horizon. The Irish announced their arrival with the sounds of drums and volleys of fire as they attacked the Confederate position. They launched their assault, cheering loudly, while their priest, Father Corby, rode among the men offering prayers and absolution. As they charged, the Brigade screamed loudly and shouted a battle cry that sounded like "Fah-ah-bah-lah", which is Gaelic for "Clear the Way!" and is spelled Faugh-a-Balaugh.

The thunderous sound of weaponry filled the air and men fell on both sides. Father Corby, who seemed to be oblivious to the gunfire, dodged across the field, administering last rites to fallen Irishmen. Colonel Meagher fought alongside his men and when he saw the emerald banner fall, he ordered it to be raised again. The 69th lost eight color bearers at Antietam and once, the firing was so intense that the flagstaff was shattered in a man's hands.

Meagher's horse was shot out from under him as the fighting intensified. The Brigade fought fiercely and fell in huge numbers. They fired all of the ammunition they had and then collected what they could from the dead and wounded and fired that too. Eventually their cries of "Faugh-a-Balaugh" became fainter and the Irish Brigade lost more than 60 percent of their men that day.... and wrote their name in the bloody pages of American history.

Over the years, the sunken road called Bloody Lane has become known as one of the most eerie places on the battlefield. Strange things have taken place here which lead many to believe that events of the past are still being replayed today. Reports over the years tell of the sounds of phantom gunfire echoing along the sunken road and the smell of smoke and gunpowder which seems to come from nowhere. I recently spoke to a man who visited the battlefield a few years ago and he told me of seeing several men in Confederate uniforms walking down the old road. He assumed they were re-enactors, present at the park for some upcoming event... until they abruptly vanished.

And ghostly apparitions are not the only things experienced here.

One witness to "strangeness" was Lynn Scoville, who visited the park back in September of 1983. Lynn had grown up in southern Virginia and was very familiar with Civil War sites, so when she and her husband, Robert, visited Antietam one afternoon, she expected it to be much like the other Civil War battlefields she had seen.... but she couldn't have been more wrong.

"After picking up a touring map of the battlefield," Lynn told me, "we drove slowly through the park, stopping at such places as the "Dunker Church" and "Burnside Bridge". While I was interested in the tour and was enjoying the incredibly beautiful Fall day, I had visited so many Civil War sites in my life that I found my interest waning as the afternoon progressed. Frankly, I was becoming a bit more interested in the Washington Redskins game on the car radio."

Lynn and Robert continued on with their tour and Robert, being a big Civil War buff, insisted on spending a lot of time at each stop. When they reached the Bloody Lane, Lynn admitted to being "Civil Warred out" and was ready to head for home. Robert, however, wanted to listen to a description of the battle on an audio station in front of the battle site.

"As we approached Bloody Lane, there were a lot of people milling about and taking pictures," Lynn remembered. "I remember filling a little bit annoyed because I was getting bored with it all and I wanted to hear the rest of the football game.

" I looked down at Bloody Lane, a rather unassuming sunken road, and then out at the fields beyond. What happened next is as clear in my mind as if it had happened yesterday. I don't know how to describe it except that it suddenly felt to me as if a filter had been put over the sun. The air temperature felt as though it dropped at least 20 degrees in a matter of seconds. The sun was still shining brightly, the wind hadn't changed or increased, and yet I suddenly felt enveloped in a bone-chilling cold.

"At that same moment, I was overcome with such a powerful sense of death and abject terror my heart literally leaped into my throat. I dropped my eyes away from the battle site and stared directly at my feet, unable to look up. I knew, without a doubt in my mind, that if I were to look at the Bloody Lane at that moment I would see a sight so horrific that it would change my life forever!"

As Lynn stood there shaking at the edge of the battle site, she realized that no one else around her was experiencing the same thing she was. They were laughing and talking and completely oblivious to what Lynn was feeling. "I broke out in a cold sweat," she said, "and while still keeping my eyes averted, managed to grab Rob's arm and I shouted at him to take me back to the car. I was absolutely terrified and anxious to get away from there. Thinking I was sick, Rob took my arm and led me back to the car."

As the two of them started towards their car, Lynn began to hear a strange noise. It was a metallic, clanging sound, almost like someone repeatedly striking a large cowbell. The clanging continued as they walked and while Lynn wanted to see where it was coming from, she was too terrified to look.

When they got back to the car, Robert asked Lynn what was wrong, but she simply demanded that she wanted to leave. Seeing the state she was in, he didn't argue. "It wasn't until we were outside the park that I told him what I had felt," she continued. "He gave me a strange look but could tell by my shaken appearance it was not a good time to question my belief. I calmed down as we drove away and I was finally able to ask him if he had felt anything unusual. He said that he hadn't and that everything had seemed perfectly normal to him.

" I asked him incredulously about the metal clanging sound... surely he had heard that? He gave me another strange look and swore he had no idea what I was talking about."

I asked Lynn what she thought she might have encountered that day, but she didn't know. "I do not consider myself to be psychic or even "in tune" with the psychic world. I had never had an experience such as that before and have never had such an overwhelmingly terrifying experience since. I don't know what happened that day or why I felt such an incredible sense of death or heard that strange clanging sound. As weird as it sounds, sometimes in the back of my mind I wonder if what I actually heard was the sound of clashing bayonets from the battle... but I'll never really know for sure."

There is no question in Lynn's mind, nor in the minds of many other people, about the strangeness of the Bloody Lane.

Perhaps the most famous story of the sunken road involves a group of boys from the McDonna school in Baltimore. They toured the battlefield and ended the day at Bloody Lane. The boys were allowed to wander about and think about what they had learned that day. They were asked to record their impressions for a history assignment and some wrote brief remarks and poems. But the comments that got the most attention from the teacher were written by several boys who walked down the road to the observation tower, which is located where the Irish Brigade charged the Confederate line.

The boys described hearing strange noises that became shouts, coming from the field near the tower. Some of them said that it sounded like a chant and others described the voices as though someone were singing a Christmas song in a foreign language... a song like "Deck the Halls".

Most specifically, they described the words as sounding like the part of the song that goes "Fa-la-la-la-la". The singing came strongly and then faded away. But what if the singing had not been a Christmas song at all.... but the sounds of the Irish Brigade "clearing the way"?

Faugh-a-Balaugh.......

Located overlooking the battlefield is the **Phillip Pry House**, a brick farmhouse that was commandeered by General George McClellan to use as his headquarters during the battle. Shortly after the battle began, General Joseph Hooker was brought to the house with wounds that he received during the fighting. He was followed by General Israel B. Richardson, who died of painful abdominal wounds at the Pry House, more than 6 months after the battle ended.

The house today is owned by the National Park Service and is not open to visitors..... although this has not stopped strange stories from being told about the place. For many years, the house was simply used for storage, then in 1976, the Pry house caught fire and about one-third of it was gutted. It was during the restoration of the house that many strange events were recorded.

One day, during a meeting of park personnel, the wife of one of the men in the meeting met a woman in old-fashioned clothing coming down the staircase. She asked her husband who the lady in the long dress was but he had no idea who she was taking about.

A short time later, workers arrived at the house to see a woman standing in an upper window... the same room where General Richardson had died. They searched the house and after going upstairs, they realized the room where the woman had been standing had no floor! Could the apparition have been that of Richardson's wife, Frances, who cared from him on his deathbed?

It would not be the last time the ghost was seen, and on one occasion, a new contracting crew had to hired when the one working in the house caught a glimpse of the spectral figure and abandoned the project.

Another piece of reported phenomena is that of phantom footsteps that have been heard going up and down the staircase. Could they have belonged to worried generals, pacing up and down in anticipation of battle? Or perhaps to Fannie Richardson as she climbed the stairs to check on her dying husband?

No one knows for sure.... but those who have heard them are convinced they are not just the sounds of the old house settling.

Those who have spent time at the area known as **Burnside Bridge** on the battlefield, especially those park rangers and Civil War re-enactors who have been at the location after dark, say that there are strange things going on there as well.

Historians and experts report that the fighting which took place here in 1862 left a number of fallen soldiers behind and many of them were hastily buried in unknown locations near the bridge. Could these restless souls be haunting the area?

Visitors to the bridge at night have reported visions of blue balls of light moving about in the darkness and the sound of a phantom drum that beats out a cadence and then fades away.

Near the center of Sharpsburg is another site connected to the battle, the **St. Paul Episcopal Church**. It was used as a Confederate field hospital following the battle, although it was heavily damaged during the fighting and was later rebuilt.

Those who have lived close to the building claim they have heard the screams of the dying and injured coming from inside of the structure. They have also seen unexplained lights flickering from the church's tower.

The Piper House, located on the battlefield itself, is now a bed and breakfast owned by Lou and Regina Clark, but during the battle, it served as a headquarters to Confederate General Longstreet and the barn was used as a field hospital. The house was directly in the heat of the battle and after the fighting ended, three dead soldiers were removed from under the piano in the parlor. The old house remains in a prime location today, offering guests the chance to spend the night in a genuine historic landmark.

I visited the Piper house in March of 1998 and was told by Lou Clark that the house was not haunted.... although there was spirit energy there. The Clarks are not believers in the paranormal, but neither are they willing to completely discount the stories told to them over breakfast by visitors to the house.

Strangely, the area of the house with the most stories is a section that was added on long after the battle, around 1900. It is in the upper bedroom of this section where guests tell of hearing muffled voices and odd sounds and even report a misty apparition which appears in the doorway to the bathroom.

The Clarks have heard these stories too many times to dismiss them and yet have no explanation for them either. Some have suggested that perhaps the new section of the house was built over the top of graves that were dug at the time of the battle. Could these soldiers still be seeking peace?

Regardless of why the strange things happen, they do seem to be continuing. Lou Clark can provide no answers. "I've slept in every room in the house," he told me, "and I've never seen anything."

But on the other hand, he has no way to explain why people from various parts of the country, with no connection whatsoever, continue to report the strange, and strikingly similar, encounters with something from beyond the known.

Do ghosts still walk at Antietam Battlefield? You have to be the judge of that for yourself, but nevertheless, there are many questions here which will probably always remain unanswered.

THE HELL-HOLE OF GEORGIA
There is a place near New Hope, Georgia which has earned the unenviable nickname of the "Hell-Hole". It was here in 1864 where hundreds of soldiers were slaughtered, leading the place to become so haunted that generations of landowners have avoided the spot, relic hunters have had bizarre experiences here and even disaster struck in 1976.

What happened here to make the place so "tainted"?

In May 1864, General William T. Sherman was relentlessly pushing his army toward Atlanta. The only thing which stood in his way were the troops under Joe Johnston, who vainly attacked the Federals every step of the way, engaging them in running battles and bloody skirmishes. As Sherman would push ahead, Johnston would counter and the two armies clashed again and again across the expanse of northwest Georgia. But still Sherman marched on, claiming terrible mile after mile as Johnston attempted to slow him down.

In early May, Johnston made a stand near Resaca and the two armies battled for some time. Unable to break through the Confederate center, Sherman flanked Johnston's position and threatened his lines of communication. Wisely, the Confederates retreated once more and set up a new defense line, first at Cassville and then at Allatoona Pass. Here, Johnston was in a strong position and rather than attack directly, Sherman flanked him again, marching his army to the south and west around Johnston's left side. The Confederates countered the move and arranged a new defense line at Dallas, where a number of engagements were fought, including the one at New Hope Church.

On the morning of May 25, General Joseph Hooker's XX Corps encountered a Confederate corps under John Bell Hood, specifically A.P. Stewart's division, near New Hope Church. The Federals began their attack, squaring off against the massed fire of 16 canister-filled cannons and Confederate troops that were over 5,000 strong.

Just at the attack began, the overcast sky opened up and a blinding downpour of rain began to fall. The severe storm rumbled in and settled over the region and it was said that "the booming thunder kept pace with the roar of the artillery and the lightning vied with the flashes of the guns as the rain pelted down on the men struggling in the thick underbrush." Hooker's men, who were exposed to the devastating fire of Stewart's artillery quickly dubbed the area, the "Hell-Hole".

Reports from the battle, even Stewart's own, spoke of the fierce efforts made by the Federal soldiers as they hurled themselves against the Confederate position, only to be driven back. It was said that the wounded men crawled into a nearby ravine to escape the fire and even over the sounds of the fighting and the thunderstorm, their eerie moans could be heard along the Rebel line.

Is it any wonder that this battle was said to have left an indelible mark on the area?

In the early 1960's, two distinguished Civil War collectors from Atlanta named Beverly M. Dubose, Jr. and Sidney C. Kerksis drove out to the battlefield near New Hope Church. The two men were well-known in the field and had published a number of articles on war relics, along with having made generous donations to the Atlanta Historic Society. They had worked with a number of renowned historians and had excellent credentials.

In other words, neither man had any reason to lie about what they experienced that afternoon. Coincidentally (or not), the afternoon of their visit happened to be May 25, the anniversary of the battle.

When they arrived at the "Hell-Hole" they asked permission of the local farmer who owned the land if they could look for relics in his field. His family had owned that piece of property since before the Civil War but had no objections to the men digging up artifacts there. He left the two men to their own devices and went about his business. Dubose and Kerksis started walking out into the fields and soon were turning up belt plates, bayonets, bullets and even leather pieces that could still be salvaged. Some of the pieces were so near to the top of the soil they did not even have to dig for them.

Suddenly, they noticed something odd. It had not been there before, but the two were quickly overwhelmed by the powerful reek of death and decaying flesh. They looked about for some dead animal or another source for the smell, but found nothing. Just then, the sky turned overcast and in what seemed like seconds, it began to rain. Soon, lightning began to flicker across the sky and they realized they should look for some shelter.

They turned toward the farm house, and the welcome overhang of the barn, when they heard an unfamiliar sound. Just above the rumble of the storm, both men could hear the sounds of men screaming and moaning, as if in terrible pain. Needless to say, they picked up their pace to the barn and when they arrived, they convinced themselves the sound had belonged to an injured animal. They realized they should tell the farmer when he came back from his errands.

As quickly as the storm began, it moved off and the sun returned to the sky. The moaning sounds, which could even be heard from inside of the building, had stopped. A few minutes later, the farmer returned in his truck and invited Dubose and Kerksis into the house, where they could dry their clothes and get a bite of lunch. The two men were reluctant to mention the strange sounds they had heard but finally one of them suggested to the farmer that he look around the ravine for one of his cows as the animal may have been hurt.

He told them that this was impossible because he never pastured his cows back there. In fact, he seldom went near the place. When he was a boy, his father had forbid he and his brothers and sisters from even playing near the ravine. His father had insisted that there was something "evil" about the place. They had never planted crops nearby and had made it a point to pasture their animals somewhere else.

Was the battle at the "Hell-Hole" still being fought? If the traumatic events of the day had been somehow "impressed" upon the place, could the atmospheric conditions of the thunderstorm have caused the battle to seemingly "replay" itself? Or could the thunderstorm have even been part of the event itself?

Both Dubose and Kerksis, two well-respected and non-superstitious men, both insisted that something strange was going on at the "Hell-Hole" and while they delighted in telling their ghostly tale over the years, neither of them ever went looking for relics at the place again.

Then, in April 1976, a DC-9 aircraft with about 80 passengers on board crashed at New Hope. There were a number of casualties, including 73 people on the plane, seven people in cars, one lady in her yard and a man in a store by the highway. When the plane hit the gas pumps at the store, it veered down an embankment and came to a rest in the dead center of the "Hell-Hole"... just at the spot where the greatest number of Federal soldiers were killed.

Merely a coincidence? Perhaps.... but do you know why the plane crashed on that fateful night? A sudden, violent thunderstorm caused its engines to stall out.

STONES RIVER BATTLEFIELD

The Battle of Stones River, which was fought near Murfreesboro, Tennessee, occurred in late December of 1862 and lasted through January 2, 1863. The Confederate forces took the Union Army by such surprise here that only one division in the Army of the Cumberland, the third division under General Phil Sheridan, was alert and prepared to fight.

Today, the battlefield stands as a monument to the bitter fighting that took place. Nearby the battlefield is the Stones River National Cemetery, one of the oldest national cemeteries in the country. Visitors to the modern battlefield can take a walking, or driving, tour of the area and various stops on the tour are marked with numbers. These designate the sites where major events took place during the battle.

The location known as Stop No. 4 is also known by the more colorful, and graphic, name of the "Slaughter Pen". It was at this point on the battlefield where Sheridan's division was able to hold the Confederates back long enough for General Rosecrans to organize a proper defense. Sheridan fought a confusing battle in the heavy forest and the Federals soon found themselves in a tightening pocket which was collapsing on three sides.

The Confederates, headed by troops from Alabama and South Carolina, rushed out of the woods towards Sheridan's position, only to be met with artillery fire and small arms volleys from the Yankees. However, the defense did not hold and soon, the borders of Sheridan's defense began to collapse. Only his brigade of men from Illinois and Missouri stood strong.

Sheridan's three brigade commanders were killed in the "Slaughter Pen" and a third of his division was destroyed. Finally, the Federals ran out of ammunition and turned to fighting hand-to-hand with bayonets, scrambling through the forest and the underbrush.

Sheridan also lost 14 pieces of artillery, but not without a fight. The cannon crews defended their guns with everything they had, turning from guns to knives and even their bare knuckles. Captain Charles Houghtaling had been ordered to hold his artillery at all costs... a command he took literally. Only at the very last moment were his guns abandoned and even then, Houghtaling had to be carried from the field.

In the end, the battle at Stones River was declared a Confederate victory, although casualties were so high there was little cause to celebrate.

One memorable event of the battle took place one night after fighting had ended for the day. It was the holiday season and on both sides of the line, soldiers wished for home and were saddened by a Christmas without their families. In order to keep up morale, a military band played for the soldier's entertainment. The battle lines were so close together that the sounds of the opposing army's music carried through the forest. As the night wore on, the troops battled each other in another way.... as one side played a rousing rendition of "Dixie", the other band would try to drown it out with the equally loud strains of "Yankee Doodle". Finally, one of the bands struck up the chords to the song "Home, Sweet, Home" and the rival band joined in. Soldiers on both sides began to sing the familiar words and for one brief moment, the war was forgotten and the soldiers shared their mutual longings for the comforts of home.

When dawn came, the battle began once again.

There is no question that Stop No. 4, the Slaughter Pen, was the scene of the bloodiest fighting at Stones River. Today, the area is a wooded section with a number of rocks and sinkholes... and it is regarded as a haunted place.

Civil War re-enactors and living history groups often camp near the Slaughter Pen when they come to Stones River. There is something about the bravery displayed here by Sheridan's men which seems to appeal to them and to draw them to the place. Visitors often report a strange stillness to the area that should not be found in a wooded area, where birds and wildlife should be active, but are not. Many of them also speak of eerie feelings here... feelings that let them know they are not always among the living in this place.

The legends of the Slaughter Pen tell of a mysterious soldier who often appears here. Re-enactors claim they have seen him around the camp fire, or on the edge of the darkened camp. He is also seen leaning against a tree, or lingering in the shadows, aware of, and yet separate from, the activity around him. His uniform allows him to often blend in with the re-enactors, yet he is known to simply disappear if anyone tries to speak to him.

My wife and I visited Stones River in May of 1997. When we arrived at the battlefield, it was a gloomy and overcast day. Rain had started to fall and we couldn't help but feel a little depressed to be in a place where such terrible fighting took place.

When we reached the site of the Slaughter Pen on our driving tour, we stopped the car in a small parking area to take a look around. In the woods beyond the open field, I noticed a small light appear and bob along at the edge of the trees. I could see nothing behind it in the gloom and only saw it for a few seconds before it disappeared and did not return. Could it have been a car reflection or another natural explanation.... or does some lone sentry from Sheridan's brigade still walk near the scene of the battle?

Park rangers, and visitors that I have talked to, often report the Slaughter Pen to be about 10 or 20 degrees colder than the park around it. They also claim that you can sometimes hear the sound of someone following you if you walk there after dark.

We left the Slaughter Pen and drove on to Site No. 6, which is another place on the battlefield where strange incidents have been reported. In 1978, according to an interview given to author Richard Winer, a park ranger named Jeffrey Leathers was involved in a Civil War re-enactment on the battlefield and was encamped near Tour Stop No. 6.

He woke up in the middle of the night and needed a drink. Finding his canteen empty, he walked back to the administration building and along the way, noticed a man lurking in the bushes near the path. Thinking that it was one of his friends waiting to play a prank on him, he yelled for the man to come out of hiding.

The soldier, who like Leathers was dressed in a period uniform, raised a hand and walked out. He appeared to be very serious, but many re-enactors stay in their roles during the mock battles and apparently the mysterious man was pretending to be captured by the enemy. The soldier continued walking toward Leathers, who then ordered him to stop. Still playing his part in the "engagement", Leathers raised his rifle and just as he did, the man fell to the ground..... and vanished.

Still thinking this was all part of the re-enactment, Leathers looked around in the shadows, but quickly became convinced that the man had actually disappeared. The next morning, he returned to the spot in the company of several friends, but they found no footprints or any other trace of the soldier. In fact, there was nothing to say that he had ever existed at all!

CHICKAMAUGA... THE RIVER OF DEATH

The year of 1863 was a triumphant one for General Ulysses S. Grant. After the fall of Vicksburg, many believed that Grant could do no wrong. By the following season, he would be the commander of all of the Union forces and would achieve another great victory at Chattanooga, Tennessee in the autumn of that same year.

Chattanooga stood above the bend of the Tennessee river in the southeastern corner of the state. It was here where two important railroad lines met and was a place that many considered to be the gateway to the Confederacy. Just a short distance beyond were the Rebel war industries in Georgia and from Chattanooga, the Confederates launched expeditions into Tennessee and Kentucky. If the Union could capture the region, they could drive south into Georgia and divide the eastern Confederacy.

Throughout 1862, the Union had been trying to push the Confederates from Tennessee. The northerner who had been placed in charge of this task was William Rosecrans, a well-liked General from Ohio. His Confederate rival was Braxton Bragg, a Louisiana sugar planter who was a graduate of West Point and a friend to Jefferson Davis. Many say that this was the only reason he was able to hang onto his command... he was hated by the soldiers, disliked by his own officers and despised by the other southern commanders.

The two armies had previously met at Stones River and while the battle was considered a Confederate victory, Rosecrans never believed it to be anything but a draw. The Confederates had been beating them badly until Rosecrans rallied his men by riding up and down the lines. He seemed unaware of the heavy shelling that was going on all around him, even when the aide who was riding next to him had his head blown off. Each army had lost about one-third of its men and Bragg had retreated to Tullahoma.

For almost six months after Stones River, the two armies clashed and feinted at one another. Confederate cavalry commander John Hunt Morgan led a raid into Ohio, where he was captured, while the Union cavalry headed into Alabama, where they attempted to cut the Chattanooga-Atlanta Railroad. The Federals were captured by Nathan Bedford Forrest.

President Lincoln pushed Rosecrans for more action but the commander refused, demanding more troops and a little more time. Finally, threatened with dismissal, Rosecrans executed a series of flanking maneuvers that pushed Bragg back more than 80 miles, first past Tullahoma and then to Chattanooga.

Rosecrans again pushed him back but then ran into trouble when Confederate reinforcements under General Longstreet arrived by train. The Rebels succeeded in luring the army out of Chattanooga and then attacked them along Chickamauga Creek.

The furious battle here claimed more than 35,000 casualties in all and lasted two days. Bragg hit the Union troops with brutal force and on the second day, Rosecrans accidentally ordered his men to close a gap in the Union line that did not exist. In doing this, he managed to open another hole and Longstreet plunged through it, routing two Federal corps and sending the entire Union army staggering back to Chattanooga.

The only thing, or rather person, which kept the battle from becoming an even greater disaster for the Federals was a man named George Henry Thomas, a Unionist from Virginia who was known to his men as "Pap". He somehow managed to arrange his troops into a defensive withdrawal which protected the army's rear flank. This feat earned him the nickname of the "Rock of Chickamauga".

The Confederates had won the day, but Bragg refused to follow-up on their advantage, infuriating the other officers. Longstreet was so angry that he demanded Bragg's removal. A short time later, Jefferson Davis would actually travel to Bragg's headquarters to settle a dispute among the officers. Bragg has dismissed three members of this staff for failing to obey orders and was blaming everyone for his decision not to follow through against the Federals. Nathan Bedford Forrest was so enraged by Bragg that he refused to serve under him. He departed the battlefield and left for Mississippi to set up an independent command. He warned Bragg that if he interfered with him, it would be "at the peril of your life."

Davis finally asked each corps commander whether or not Bragg should be replaced. All said yes, but Davis disliked both of Bragg's possible replacements, Gustave Beauregard and Joe Johnston, so he paid no attention to his commanders and left Bragg in charge.

Meanwhile, the Federal troops were holed up in Chattanooga. They were hungry and cut off from all but a thin line of supplies. They had demolished houses and had hacked down every tree and fence line they could find for fuel, and to make matters worse, the fall rains were beginning. They were in miserable shape and were badly in need of a morale boost.

In October, President Lincoln placed Grant in charge of all of the Federal troops between the Appalachians and the Mississippi. He quickly headed for Chattanooga and replaced Rosecrans with Thomas as head of the Army of the Cumberland. Suddenly, things began to come together as Grant opened a hole in the southern lines and laid a pontoon bridge across the Tennessee River. Soon, food and supplies began arriving by way of the new line.

The Confederate troop placement was still strong however. Bragg's army occupied the six mile crest of Missionary Ridge, east of the city. They also had heavy guns on the 2,000 foot summit of Lookout Mountain which commanded a field of fire to the south and west.

Grant's plan was to drive them off and the Battle of Chattanooga began on November 24. Sherman attacked Bragg on his left flank in a rather ineffectual thrust that merely opened the way for Hooker to storm Lookout Mountain. They succeeded in planting the Union flag atop the mountain in such dense fog that the fight was nicknamed the "Battle Above the Clouds".

The following day, the troops under Thomas made an attack on the first line of Confederate trenches below Missionary Ridge, while Hooker attacked on the right. Despite the nearly impregnable Confederate placements (artillery on the crest of the hill; rifle pits on the slopes; and trenches at the base) Thomas' men quickly swarmed over the trenches and then waited for orders.

Attacking with Thomas was General Phil Sheridan, who recklessly pulled a flask from his pocket and toasted the Confederate gunners on the ridge. "Here's to you," he shouted and rifles opened fire at him, showering he and his officers with dirt. Sheridan was furious. "That was ungenerous!" he shouted at them. "I'll take your guns for that!"

Sheridan's boast was all of the incentive the men needed and they began charging up the hill toward the Confederate artillery. Worried, Grant was said to have asked an officer just who had ordered the men up the hill. "No one," his aide was said to have answered. "They started up without orders. When those fellows get started, all hell can't stop them!"

And apparently he was right. The Federals were determined to avenge themselves for their recent defeat and as they scrambled up the ridge, they shouted "Chickamauga!" at the top of their lungs. They soon overran the rifle pits and kept going, whopping and hollering as they went. Sections of the slope were so steep that the men had to sometimes crawl, using tree branches and bayonets to haul themselves up.

The Confederates on the top began to break and run and those who remained became more desperate as the Federals grew closer, screaming the word "Chickamauga" as they came. The Rebels fired and fired again and began rolling shells with lighted fuses down the slope, but nothing slowed the force of the charge. In moments, the Confederate gunners and defenders began to run. Bragg tried to rally them, but it was no use. Not surprisingly, he would blame everyone but himself for the defeat, saying that their position "was one which ought to have been held by a line of skirmishers."

True or not, 4,000 Confederate prisoners were taken on Missionary Ridge and sent north to the prison camps. The Federals had won the day and gained their revenge for the defeat at nearby Chickamauga.

While these two battles will be forever connected, it is actually the field where the Battle of Chickamauga was fought that is said to be haunted.

Many years before the Civil War, before the white man brought his armies to die here, the Native Americans of the region had already done their share of dying in this place. The Cherokee Indians had christened the stream "Chickamauga" or the "River of Death". The white armies who came here would cause this river to run red with blood.

In September 1863, the terrible battle raged in which Bragg's Army of Tennessee, reinforced by Longstreet, dealt a stunning blow to Rosecran's Army of the Cumberland. This battle would turn out to be one of the last major Confederate victories of the war.

The fighting was especially dangerous here because of the rough terrain and the heavily wooded areas. Men became lost in the forest and separated from their units. Messages sent by commanders to their troops vanished without a trace and much of the fighting was chaotic and deteriorated into hand-to-hand combat.

When the battle was over, the casualties numbered over 35,000. Bragg's army had pushed Rosecrans back into Chattanooga although strangely enough, both of the generals left the battlefield before the fighting was over. It was Longstreet instead of Bragg and Thomas instead of Rosecrans who saw the battle to the last volley of fire. Bragg was angry because the battle plan that he had devised had not been followed and he removed himself from the command of the battle and went to sulk at Reed's Bridge. His staff had to convince Bragg that the Confederates had been victorious, even bringing in Confederate soldiers to swear that the Federals had retreated in such haste that they had left wounded behind.

Rosecrans had retreated with the fleeing Federal troops. Charles Dana, an observer at the battle, and a military liaison with Washington, would later remark that he never believed Rosecrans forgot the tragedy of Chickamauga.

After darkness fell on the last day of the battle, within hours of the last shots being fired, women were seen searching the battlefield by lantern light. It has been reported that this eerie lights, along with the voices and cries of the women, are still present on the field today.

Thirty years after the war, a camp was established on the old battlefield to train men for the Spanish-American War. The camp was named after Thomas, the "Rock of Chickamauga". During the brief time the camp was in operation, disease ran rampant here and men died by the score.... ending with more deaths than the American forces suffered during all of the fighting in Cuba.

And the long record of death did not end there either. The sprawling park has been the continuing scene of death by murder and suicide. It has been reported that at least one death each year occurs in the huge park, which is accessible at night by many public roads. Thanks to this fact, the park is also used a dumping ground for victims who are murdered elsewhere.

One notable murder attempt in the recent past involved a woman and her boyfriend who plotted the death of the woman's husband. The murder did not go as planned and the husband escaped, badly injured. He was chased screaming through the park and was discovered by rangers with the killers still in pursuit, both of them carrying knives.

But is is not these strange and bizarre happenings, nor even the hauntings, which bring thousands of tourists to Chickamauga each year, it is the history. Of course, there are those tourists (like myself for instance) who are always in search of both.... history and ghosts.

Those who come to Chickamauga are not disappointed.

The park is one of the oldest and the largest of the battlefield parks. It is peaceful and tranquil in the daylight hours, but after the sun goes down, strange things are reported to happen...

The battlefield has long been associated with the macabre. Many of the corpses of the Union soldiers lay where they fell in battle for more than two months before they were buried... and they were buried everywhere in the park. One report claimed they were often buried in rows, from head to foot, and one grave would hold up to three or four bodies. There are no stones to mark these graves and it is said that even today, a park maintenance crew will occasionally uncover bodies were none were previously thought to be located.

There are said to be many ghosts and spirits roaming the woods and fields of Chickamauga. Rangers and visitors report many odd noises on the grounds, including sounds of men moaning and crying; shouts and screams when no one is present; and the sounds of horses galloping... where no horses ever appear. Some visitors, and even crew members, tell of feeling as though they are being watched in the woods at night. Others report seeing the underbrush move inexplicably, as though a squad of invisible soldiers are passing by. One of the rangers was even told by a "well-known minister" that he had witnessed a man on horseback ride past him at Chickamauga.... although the rider had no head.

One popular legend of the battlefield is that of the ghostly lady in white. She has been seen many times, by a wide variety of different people, roaming about the park. The legends say that she was the wife or lover of a soldier who was slain in the battle and that she is now searching for his spirit. Even after all of these years, she has reportedly never found him.

But despite all of the tales and stories of strange activity, there is one legend of Chickamauga who remains the most famous of all, "Old Green Eyes". This mysterious entity was given this colorful nickname by park visitors and rangers who have encountered him over the years. Who is he? Well, that's a good question, because there happens to be two very different legends to explain his presence in the park.

The first story (which frankly doesn't seem to match the creature's appearance or behavior) claims that "Old Green Eyes" was a Confederate soldier who had his head blown off his body during the battle. When he was buried, all that could be found of him was his head as his body had been destroyed. The stories say that his spirit now roams the battlefield at night, moaning and searching for his missing body.

Visitors and staff members claim to have seen green, glowing eyes coming toward them in the darkness and have heard the sounds of a soldier moaning in despair. In the early 1970's, two different and unrelated people had accidents near the same place in the park, wrecking their cars after reportedly seeing these glowing eyes.

The other legend of "Old Green Eyes" is apparently a much older one... and much more unnerving too. In this case, reliable witnesses have reported the creature to be, not a slain soldier, but a beast which barely even resembles a person. The story also states that "Old Green Eyes" was present at Chickamauga long before the Civil War. Some accounts also claim that the monster was seen moving among the dead at a place called Snodgrass Hill, after the battle was over.

The reports say that the creature is human-like, although he has glowing green eyes, waist-length, light-colored hair and huge, misshapen jaws from which fangs protrude. Obviously, he is not a pretty sight, nor a creature that you would want to meet in a secluded location in the dark.

Which is exactly where some people claim to have encountered him!

One of the most notable encounters occurred to a park ranger named Edward Tinney, who described his brush with the creature to author Richard Winer in a 1981 interview. He was walking through the park one night when he was struck by a strange chill, one unlike anything he had ever felt before. A moment later, he saw the creature appear out of the darkness. "When it passed me," he said, "I could see his hair was long like a woman's. The eyes -I'll never forget those eyes- they were glaring, almost greenish-orange in color, flashing like some sort of wild animal. The teeth were long and pointed like fangs. It was wearing a dark cape that seemed to be flapping in the wind, but there was no wind. I didn't know whether to run or scream or what. Then the headlights of an approaching car came blazing through the fog, and the thing disappeared right in front of me."

He assured the writer that the creature was real. "I've seen Green Eyes," Tinney said. "You know he's watching. We all know he's watching us. It's enough to make the hair stand up on the back of your neck.... and I'm not a superstitious man."

Finally, we should take a brief look at one of the strangest incidents to take place in the park, although it is unknown whether it is linked to the supernatural or not. The incident occurred at Wilder Tower. This monument marks the center of the Union lines where the Confederates finally broke through and routed the Federal forces.

The tower is a stone structure that stands 85 feet high. It was built in 1903 by men who served under Colonel John T. Wilder at Chickamauga. The colonel's mounted infantry, armed with Spencer repeating rifles, managed to hold off the attacking Confederate troops long enough for the Union men to make a somewhat orderly retreat.

When Wilder had been commissioned, the Union army was so poorly equipped that his men were given mules to ride and hatchets for weapons. He used every political favor that he could to get horses for his troops and he used his own money to purchase rifles. Wilder bought each of his men a Spencer Rifle that was equipped to hold seven shots. He purchased 2100 of them for $13 each. Thanks to these weapons, Wilder's men were able to hold off more than 14,000 Confederates during the retreat.

The tower was erected in Wilder's memory by survivors of the mounted infantry. Souvenirs of the war were sealed into the cornerstone of the structure, which was scheduled to be opened again in 1976. The stone would then be opened to celebrate the Bicentennial. Strangely, although the stone showed no signs of being disturbed in any way.... the contents placed inside in 1903 had vanished.

The strange incident at the tower took place in 1970 when a young man decided to climb the tower after dark. Since the park is open at night, the tower is kept locked in order to keep people from going out onto the observation deck at the top. But this didn't stop the man, as he instead climbed the lightning rod which was fixed the back of the tower. He then slipped into a gun slot which was placed about 14 feet off the ground. He went inside and ran up the steps to the top, where he called to his friends, who were about 50 feet away drinking beer.

Suddenly, the young people outside heard a scream from inside of the tower. Panicked the boy ran down the winding staircase and quickly jumped out of the small window from which he had entered the tower.... or so he thought. Instead, he fell about 25 feet onto solid concrete and although he survived, was paralyzed for the rest of his life.

He was never able to explain what had happened at Wilder Tower.

A COLLECTION OF BATTLEFIELD GHOSTS

Throughout the book, we have explored a number of places which could have possibly been included in this chapter... places where the battles of the war left spirits behind. What I attempted to do was to separate these places because their ghosts and hauntings seemed to be centered more around one particular location, like a house or a fort, rather than just the battlefield itself.

Also, in the time that I spent searching for battlefield haunts, I found a number of locations that while interesting, did not really qualify for a section of the chapter by themselves. Instead, I have decided to present some of these shorter stories in a collected section of tales.

Shiloh Battlefield

The Shiloh Battlefield in Tennessee was the scene of at least one unexplained occurrence several years ago. According to a park ranger, there was a man who often visited the battlefield who was illegally digging up relics and selling them. The rangers at the park had been wanting to catch him for a long time but he somehow managed to elude them. He was often spotted with a metal detector and they knew he was digging up the unmarked graves and stealing artifacts from the bodies. The problem was that they could never catch him in the act.

One night, some rangers were patrolling the woods and they found a broken metal detector. Then, sitting in a car at the edge of the woods, they found the man they had been looking for. They said that he seemed to be in shock and was incapable of talking or moving at all. They ended up taking him to a hospital and while he recovered, he refused to talk about what had happened to him and later was put under psychiatric care.

The story went that the man had encountered something in the woods that had scared him out of his mind. Rumor had it that he had been digging up a grave and stealing buttons from the corpse when a bony hand had reached out of the ground and snatched away his ill-gotten treasure.

Sounds unlikely? Perhaps... but something certainly scared him!

Petersburg

The terrible ten-month siege of Petersburg in 1865 has apparently left spirits behind at Fort Stedman, a Union stronghold during the fighting. The siege was a grueling affair that trapped the Confederate army to starve inside of the city. The burning of the Shenandoah Valley and the fall of Wilmington had led to a winter of misery for the Confederate troops.

But Lee refused to give in and in March 1865 desperately sought a way to break the Union's hold on the city. He assigned the duty of finding a spot to open the Federal lines to Major General John B. Gordon. Three weeks later, Gordon reported to Lee that he had found the location at Fort Stedman, near the center of the Union lines. He then outlined a confusing plan of attack that Lee had little faith in. However, at this point, they were desperate and the Confederates had little choice.

The attack began in the early morning hours of March 25 and at first, went remarkably well. Under the cover of darkness, they managed to take Fort Stedman quite easily. Their surprise was so complete that in the confusion which followed, the fort's commander, Brigadier General Napoleon McLaughlen, found himself commanding a group of men who he thought were Union soldiers. Shortly, he realized they were actually a detachment of Confederates and they soon realized they were taking orders from a Yankee commander. The southerners fixed the situation by taking McLaughlen prisoner.

Once Fort Stedman was secure, the attackers turned their attention to Fort Haskell, which lay about 600 yards to the south. As the sun came up however, the attack began to fall apart. This can mostly be blamed on the hunger of the Confederate troops. Starved through the winter, they began gorging themselves on the captured Federal supplies. Four hours after the fighting began, Lee sent word to Gordon to break off the attack. The battle was over and now only a few short weeks remained until Lee's final surrender at Appomattox Court House.

Despite the fact that the Union actually carried the day at Petersburg, it is said to be the ghosts of Federal troops who remain behind here. According to a reliable witness, who was at Fort Stedman early one summer morning, he noticed a group of Union soldiers on a ridge. They were formed up in a battle line facing the fort. The witness was more than a little surprised to see them as he knew of no re-enactments that had been scheduled to take place there.

He stood watching them for several minutes.... before they abruptly disappeared.

A former park supervisor has also reported hearing the sounds of music coming from a ridge where a Union corps was encamped during the siege. He swore the music was popular patriotic songs from the Civil War period like the "Battle Hymn of the Republic" and "The Star Spangled Banner". Although he tried, he was never able to find an explanation for the eerie, and possibly spectral, music.

Fredericksburg

There is a house located in Fredericksburg, Virginia that was built in the 1740's by a Scottish merchant named John Allan. Referred to as the Willis House in author L.B. Taylor's book, *Ghosts of Fredericksburg*, the house was then owned by Judge Jere Willis and his wife, Barbara. Besides being one of the few houses to withstand the Union bombardment in the winter of 1862... the house also reportedly harbored a ghost for many years.

The house was located in the midst of the shelling and fighting that took place here as 181 guns, lining Stafford Heights, opened up at dawn on December 11. All of the guns were brought to bear on the town of Fredericksburg itself. The shelling of the town was one of the most outrageous examples of overkill during the war.

Just prior to it, on the north side of the Rappahannock River, Union General Ambrose Burnside arrived with a force of more than 110,000 men. Meanwhile, on the other side of the river, 75,000 Confederate troops under Lee sat patiently and waited for the Federals to cross the river. They did not wait for long. Soon, the Union engineers began constructing a pontoon bridge across the Rappahannock. They were constantly hampered by a single brigade of Confederates, who fired away at the approaching Federals, killing a number of engineers. For some time, this handful of sharpshooters was able to hide within the homes and buildings of Fredericksburg and hold off the might of the Union force.

Burnside became so infuriated at this that he ordered his men to begin shelling the city. Because of this, nearly the entire town was destroyed, although it didn't stop the Confederate snipers. However, they were slowed down enough that the Federals were able to land an invasion force by boat. The skirmish which followed was a fierce, running battle through the streets and alleys of the town, turning Fredericksburg into one big battleground. Eventually, the outnumbered Confederates retreated to the outskirts of the city.

During the fighting, the Willis House stood directly in the line of fire. The ghost of the young Federal soldier who was seen here was believed to be a casualty of the battle. Apparently, the soldier took shelter in the house, or was perhaps using it is a cover during the fighting. He was standing behind one of the double doors in the back hall of the house when a bullet ripped through the door and killed him. The soldier was later buried in the back garden and a plug was placed in the door, which remains to this day.

In the years which followed, the soldier was often reported to enter the house by the side porch door. The many witnesses who saw him described him as wearing a Union army uniform from the war. Eventually, an old cook, who worked at the house during the 1920's, said a prayer by the soldier's grave and the sightings stopped. He has not been seen at the Willis House since.

Bentonville

The last major battle of the Civil War did not involve any of the places or people that one might expect. It had nothing to do with Appomattox Court House, nor were Grant or Lee in any way involved. This final battle occurred near Bentonville, North Carolina and it was here that General Joe Johnston and his ragged army made a last-ditch effort to stop Sherman as he stormed across the Carolinas.

Near the center of the battlefield was the home of John Harper. It was here that the farmer and his wife and children hid during the battle and then stood back and watched as their home was turned into a field hospital. It is commonly believed that the trauma experienced by the wounded and dying soldiers left a strong impression on the house... for it has been allegedly haunted for many years. There are dozens of reports of visitors who have come to the house, only to go away shaken and upset by what they have experienced here, including apparitions and the sounds of moans which may belong to the soldiers of long ago.

By February of 1865, the hopes of a victory for the South were nearly gone. Lee called on Johnston and gave him a dangerous assignment... to stop Sherman as he marched through the Carolinas. Johnston was ordered to gather up the scattered Confederate armies from Florida, Georgia and South Carolina and try to prevent Sherman from linking up with Meade's Army of the Potomac, which was in Petersburg, Virginia.

Somehow, Johnston was able to pull together about 21,000 men and given the state of the Confederate Army, this was nothing short of a miracle. He then began devising a plan. As Sherman crossed North Carolina, he had been forced to divide his army into two wings. Johnston realized that if he could somehow isolate one of the wings from the other, he might be able to crush it and bring Sherman's march to a halt.

On the morning of March 18, Lieutenant General Wade Hampton brought a plan to Johnston which would cut off Major General Henry Slocum's wing of Sherman's army near the small town of Bentonville. The Confederates would still be outnumbered, but it was the best they could hope for.

Johnston's army was a ragged bunch and ranged from old veterans to a brigade of the North Carolina Junior Reserves. But despite the questionable quality of the men, the army was not short on seasoned commanders. By this time, having few battles left to fight, Johnston had gathered around him the best generals the South still had to offer including A.P. Stewart, D.H. Hill, Wade Hampton, Joe Wheeler and Braxton Bragg (although whether or not Bragg was among the Confederacy's best is debatable).

On the 18th, Wade Hampton's cavalry spent the day harassing the approaching Union troops, trying to give Johnston enough time to get into position. The Confederate line was arranged in a sickle shape. On the right (handle) end, Robert Hoke's division formed a line across Goldsboro Road and into the woods to the south. North of the road was the farm of Willis Cole and through his woods lay the curved part of the sickle's blade, guarding the opening to the farmer's fields.

The Yankees soon learned they were facing more than a scattered cavalry unit and by mid-afternoon, Slocum had deployed troops which created a line farther south from the Goldsboro Road. Three Federal brigades had been formed into battle lines and they moved forward.

Along the Confederate lines, Bragg had placed himself in command of Robert Hoke's troops and when the Federals on the right began advancing, Bragg sent an urgent message to Johnston that he needed more men. Johnston sent a division commanded by Lafayette McLaws from William Hardee's troops. By the time that McLaws got to Hoke's position, the Confederates had the upper hand but instead of sending the men back to Hardee, Bragg sent them into the woods and swamps to the left of Hoke. They wandered about aimlessly here for hours and by the time that Bragg called them back, it was too late for them to offer assistance. Many would say this was a typical command decision for Bragg.

On the right side of the Confederate line, Stewart, Hill and Hardee led their men forward into the Union advancement and managed to smash the Federal line. The fighting continued on throughout the day with the Confederates trying gamely to break the Federal resolve, yet with each Rebel thrust, the Union forces countered and held them back. Late in the day, Hoke noticed a break in the Union line and he begged Bragg to let him lead a charge against it. He was sure that the attack, if successful, could turn the battle for the Confederates. But Bragg decided it was too risky and ordered Hoke to lead a pointless frontal assault instead.

The Confederates stayed on the field until the night of March 21, although more for the chance to allow Johnston to get the wounded safely away than for anything else. By this time, they knew the battle had been lost.

After both armies moved on, the village of Bentonville was left in ruins. The Harper family had been left with as many as 50 badly wounded soldiers, many of whom, despite excellent care, died shortly after. These men were then buried on the Harper farm.... but one has to wonder if their sleep of death is a restful one.

One ghostly story of the house was recounted in author B. Keith Toney's book, *Battlefield Ghosts*, and it was told by two hunters who claimed to witness a vivid re-enactment of the battle more than 45 years after it actually took place.

Many reports have come from the Harper House and the land surrounding it and apparitions spotted here range from phantom soldiers to the ghosts of the Harper family themselves. Workers and visitors have also claimed to hear voices when no one else is around and the sounds of crying and groaning in the vicinity.

According to Toney, a Virginia family visited the house in 1990 and were treated to a living history display of wagons and wounded soldiers at the back of the house. They even commented on the realistic portrayal that one actor gave to the role of John Harper. They would later find out that no such "living history" re-enactment ever took place!

THE SPIRITS OF GETTYSBURG

The next morning was the fourth of July, but it seemed at the time
to those who were at Gettysburg a somber and terrible national anniversary,
with the indescribable horrors of the field, as yet hardly mitigated by the
work of mercy, before the eye in every direction.
The army did not know the extent of the victory.... the nation did not
realize as yet what had been done.
Lieutenant Jesse Bowman Young

I am often asked to consider naming the most haunted places in America. Somewhere near the top of each list I compile is Gettysburg. Most Civil War enthusiasts would say the battle which was fought near the small Pennsylvania town in 1863 was the greatest battle of the war.... or at the very least, a turning point which led to the fall of the Confederacy. For ghost hunters, the mere mention of Gettysburg conjures up images of haunted buildings, strange battlefield encounters and restless ghosts.

To attempt to document every ghost or supernatural experience linked to Gettysburg would be foolhardy. Besides that, there are others who have previously made valiant attempts, like the fine *Ghosts of Gettysburg* series by Mark Nesbitt or the *Haunted Gettysburg* books by Jack Bochar and Bob Wasel. My goal here is to provide the reader with an overview of Gettysburg.... from the battle to its aftermath, and to give you a look at the events which created these ghosts and hauntings in the first place. Then, we'll take a look at the most famous of Gettysburg's haunted locations and find out where the dead still walk in the small town and on the adjoining battlefield.

So, let's take that next step... and meet the Spirits of Gettysburg.

THE GUNS OF GETTYSBURG

By early summer of 1863, the war in the east was going well for the Confederacy. Lee, confident after his victories at Fredericksburg and Chancellorsville, urged President Davis to once again take the war to the north. By doing so, this would take the fighting out of Virginia and relieve the pressure being felt by the government in Richmond. It would also ease the load on the Confederate supply lines because if the invasion could be pushed far enough to the north, it would allow the soldiers to live off the land. In addition, Lee's invasion would also draw attention away from Grant's siege of Vicksburg, plus, if any northern towns could be captured by the Confederates, it just might push the war-weary citizens of the north to the discussion of a settlement between the two nations.

It seemed as though the outlook for a northern invasion was completely positive and if a downside existed, Lee couldn't find it. So, moving in secret, Lee began his northern thrust on June 3, 1863. He marched his troops into the Shenandoah Valley and pushed them on, using the mountains as a shield. After the death of Stonewall Jackson a short time before, the Army of Northern Virginia had been re-organized into three corps, each commanded by A.P. Hill, Richard S. Ewell and James Longstreet. The cavalry was commanded by the magnificent J.E.B. Stuart.

Although unaware of Lee's plans, the Army of the Potomac, under the command of Joseph Hooker, realized that a major enemy troop movement was underway, following a cavalry engagement at Brandy Station on June 9. Hooker then cautiously followed Lee's march to the north, keeping his army east of the mountains and between Washington and the Confederates. On June 15, Lee overwhelmed a Union force at Winchester and then continued northward. By June 28, all of the Confederate troops had crossed over into Union territory. They were still widely scattered out, but all were converging on the Pennsylvania capital of Harrisburg.

Meanwhile, tension between Washington and General Hooker was increasing. Once again, Lincoln was disappointed by the inaction of one of his generals and on June 28, he appointed George Meade to replace Hooker as the head of the Army of the Potomac.

Coincidentally, on this same day, General Lee received a message that the Union Army was on the move, heading toward his new location. This came as a shock to Lee, as he had been depending on Stuart to keep him aware of all enemy activity. Although no one knew it at the time, Stuart had seemingly vanished. He was involved in a daring raid east of the Federal army and all communications with the main Confederate force had been cut off.

Lee's information came from a shadowy figure who has been remembered throughout history only as "the spy Harrison", a man who worked for Longstreet but who disappeared after the battle. He informed Lee that Meade was now in charge of the Union Army and was marching north to meet the Confederates.

With the news that the Federal Army was aware of his plans, Lee sent out an order to concentrate the Confederate forces at Cashtown, a small village between Chambersburg and Gettysburg. Here, Lee would prepare to confront the Federal advance troops. The Confederate Army was now in place to the north and west of Gettysburg, while Meade pushed the Federal Army from the south, moving northward from the area around Frederick and Emmitsburg, Maryland.

Both armies were in the dark as to the whereabouts of the other on June 30, the day that cavalry units under command of General John Buford rode into Gettysburg.

Before this time, there was nothing to set Gettysburg apart from hundreds of other small communities in America. The population of the small town was of about 2,400 people and aside from a thriving carriage industry, its only claims to fame were its two colleges, the Lutheran Theological Seminary and Pennsylvania College (Gettysburg College). It was nothing more than a sleepy little Pennsylvania town in 1863.... but all that was about to change.

Buford's cavalry rode into town on June 30 and established a picket line on the other side of the Lutheran Seminary to guard approaches to the town from the west. By coincidence, a brigade of Confederate Infantry under General John Pettigrew, of A.P. Hill's Corps, had been sent to Gettysburg from Cashtown to scout out the area that same day. Legend has it that the Confederates were actually looking for shoes, but they were actually on a reconnaissance mission. For whatever reason the two groups bumped into each other, it seems likely, with two large armies in such close proximity of each other, they were bound to run into each other at some point. However, once the Confederates spotted the Union pickets, they rode to the west to report the enemy's presence.

Gettysburg: Day One

Early in the morning of July 1, two Confederate brigades were sent to investigate the Federal presence in Gettysburg. It was possible that the cavalry troops had been nothing more than a local militia, but Lee needed to know for sure. Within a short time of the Confederate arrival, a skirmish had broken out between the Rebels and Buford's men. Although Buford knew that he was greatly outnumbered, and in a bad position, he chose to stand his ground and send for help from two Union corps which were a short distance to the south. The Confederates also sent for reinforcements and soon, both armies were headed toward Gettysburg.

Prior to this chance encounter, neither Lee nor Meade had planned to fight at Gettysburg.

For the next two hours, Buford's men, fighting dismounted, managed to hold off a number of Confederate attacks from the area known as McPherson's farm. Buford was later relieved by the arrival of General John Reynold's corps. One division crossed an unfinished railroad cut to the north of the Chambersburg Pike and formed a battle line. Another Confederate brigade was at the same time attacking McPherson's Woods, which lay to the south of the Pike. General Reynold's himself led the Federal's Iron Brigade into the woods, where he was killed instantly by enemy fire. Reynolds was the second in command to the Army of the Potomac and would be the highest ranking officer to perish during the three days of fighting at Gettysburg.

When Reynolds died, command of the Corps fell to Abner Doubleday, whose men continued to withstand the Confederate assaults. Later that morning, they managed to capture a number of Mississippi men in an attack on the railroad cut.

Around the middle of the day, the fighting broke off and the field was fairly quiet until the middle of the afternoon. During this time, a Confederate division under Robert Rodes arrived at Oak Ridge, north of the Union line, and began to press against the right flank of Doubleday's corps. This threat was reduced however by the arrival of a Federal corps under O.O. Howard, which marched through the streets of Gettysburg and formed a line just north of Pennsylvania College. Howard's battle line extended the Union right flank to a small hill known as Barlow's Knoll.

By that afternoon, the fighting had begun again with Hill's and Ewell's corps advancing against the Federals along a two-mile stretch that ran between the western and northern approaches to Gettysburg. Confederate reinforcements continued to arrive throughout the afternoon and around four, General Jubal Early's division struck the right flank of the Union's XI Corps, which was under command of General Francis Barlow. The attack caused Howard's entire line to begin to crumble.

The corps began retreating into Gettysburg, where they almost collided with Doubleday's retreating troops, who at the same moment had collapsed to Confederate pressure near the McPherson farm. Falling back from two different directions, the Union troops became confused and disoriented in the small town and stumbled along to the shelter of Cemetery Hill, a reserve position located on the southern outskirts of Gettysburg. Here, Union General Winfield Scott Hancock rallied the men into defensive positions on the hill, and along nearby Culp's Hill as well.

Needless to say, the elated Confederates followed and not only captured the entire town, but over 2,500 Unions soldiers as well.

And here they halted.... strangely, Lee's forces made no attempt to storm Cemetery Hill that night. One has to wonder what may have been the outcome of the battle if they had. Instead, Lee had given orders to Ewell to renew the attack before nightfall "if practicable". Unfortunately, Ewell took Lee's courteous order as having a choice of whether to fight or to retire from the field. He chose wrong.... Ewell decided his men needed rest instead and the first day's fighting came to an end.

Later, Lee was said to have groaned over Ewell's decision and was reported to say that "if I had Stonewall Jackson at Gettysburg, I would have won that fight."

Lee arrived in Gettysburg that afternoon and established his headquarters in a house along the Chambersburg Pike. Here, he began to make plans for the following day. General Longstreet advised Lee to swing the Confederate lines around the Union's left and take a stand somewhere between Meade's army and Washington, then wait for the Union to attack. Although Lee had no idea of Meade's strength, thanks to the fact that he still had not heard from Stuart, he chose to ignore Longstreet. "I am going to whip them here... or they are going to whip me," he reportedly said.

Although in poor health and suffering from diarrhea, Lee remained confident about the Confederate chances in the battle ahead. He felt the Union Army was weakened by its recent defeats at Fredericksburg and Chancellorsville and by yet another change in command. If he pressed hard enough, the Federals would break.

Gettysburg: Day Two

Throughout the night, the two armies continued to gather and by morning about 65,000 Confederate troops faced a Union force of around 85,000. The northern lines had assumed what has become known as the "Fishhook" formation. Cemetery Hill, became the curve of the fishhook, while Culp's Hill, located just to the east, became the hook, and right flank, of the Union line. The shank of the formation was occupied by Hancock's corps and they stretched south through the open fields to Cemetery Ridge. The Union left was be defended by troops under General Daniel Sickles, a former politician who was best known for killing his wife's lover before the war. Secretary of War Edwin Stanton had been his attorney and had gotten him off by using the first plea of "temporary insanity".

I have to wonder if the officer's serving under Sickles were aware of his legally insane state of mind. Of course, this mattered little as Sickles spent the entire morning of July 2 disobeying orders. He had shifted his corps position on lower Cemetery Ridge out into the Peach Orchard, which stood on a flat-topped ridge about a half mile in front of the Union line. This managed to leave the hills known as Little Round Top and Big Round Top, and the Union's left flank, completely undefended. When Meade got wind of this, he angrily ordered him back into position, but before the corps could be moved, Longstreet had begun his attack.

As Lee studied the Union formation on the field that morning, he noted that the Federal fishhook was overlooked by hills on both ends. Culp's Hill and Cemetery Hill stood above the right and the Big and Little Round Tops loomed over the left. Lee's plan called for the Confederates to take the hills, sending Ewell to attack Culp's Hill and Longstreet the Round Tops.

Little fighting took place during the morning and afternoon, aside from scattered fire from skirmishes. Lee's plan called for attack on both Union flanks at the same time, but the assault was delayed for several hours as Longstreet shifted his two corps into position on the southern edge of Seminary Ridge.

At the same time, Sickles was shifting his own line to the more forward position. By the time Longstreet was ready to attack, Sickle's new line extended northwestward from the tangle of boulders at Devil's Den, through Rose Woods and the Wheat Field, and then sharply to the northeast where it crossed the Peach Orchard and continued along the Emmitsburg Road. The new position was nearly impossible to defend and not only did it not connect its right flank to the left flank of II Corps, but it also left Little Round Top completely unoccupied.

The Confederate attack against the left Union flank began just after four in the afternoon. One of the first points to be struck was the Devil's Den, which fell to Hood's men after a bitter struggle that lasted for several hours. In waves, Longstreet's brigades swept over the Rose Woods and the Wheat Field and then advanced on the Federal positions at the Peach Orchard and along the Emmitsburg Road.

The fighting continued on through the afternoon and while Sickle's beaten line was reinforced by troops under George Sykes, Sickles himself was severely wounded near his headquarters at the Trostle Farm. The Confederates were relentless and after four hours of battle, all of the Union positions along Sickle's line were overrun.

Meanwhile, during the initial attack, the 15th Alabama managed to make it to the summit of Big Round Top. From here, Colonel William C. Oates realized that the summit of Little Round Top was virtually undefended. If he could haul guns to the top of the hill, he would be directly above the Federal lines and could destroy them.

As luck would have it, Little Round Top had also come under the scrutiny of the Union command. Meade had dispatched the army's chief engineer, General Gouverner Warren, and a lieutenant of engineers named Washington Roebling to the summit of Little Round Top to bring back a report of the state of the battle. They found only a handful of Union signalmen on the hill and one look around sent them into shock.... Warren quickly realized what was going to happen as he saw Sickles corps pinned down below and Confederate troops coming up the ravine which separated the Little and Big Round Tops.

He sent for reinforcements at once and the last of the four regiments ordered to the hill was the 20th Maine, under the command of Colonel Joshua Lawrence Chamberlain, a professor of rhetoric and languages at Maine's Bowdoin College. The colonel's orders were to hold Little Round Top "at all hazards" and with 350 men, he started up the south slope and they took shelter behind rocks and trees. Fortunately, at the last moment, Chamberlain sent a company of men across the hollow between the hills to bolster the left flank of the defense. Less than ten minutes later, Oates and his Confederates had arrived, attacking before the company could take shelter on the left. The Rebels opened fire and Chamberlain later stated that he assumed his men had been wiped out with the first volley of fire.

The Maine men attacked but the Confederates regrouped and charged again and again, slowly gaining ground and swinging around to Chamberlain's left. He ordered that portion of his line to drop back, forming again at right angles to the rest of the regiment. The men dropped back, continuing to fire as they regrouped.

In less than an hour, over 40,000 rounds had been fired on Little Round Top and still the Federals held firm. The Rebels had driven them from their position five times and yet each time, Chamberlain's men fought their way back again. He would lose 130 of his 386 men, a loss of nearly one-third of his force. He would describe the conflict by saying that "at times I saw around me more of the enemy than my own men; gaps opening, swallowing; closing again.. and all around, a strange, mingled roar."

The sounds of battle behind Chamberlain grew louder and he assumed they had been surrounded. His men had finally run out of ammunition and the only choices that remained were to surrender.... or die. Instead, Chamberlain ordered his men to fix bayonets. Then, while the right corner of the regiment stood firm, the men were told to wheel around like a great hinge toward the right.

The attacking Confederates were so stunned by the maniacal charge of the Federals that many of them actually dropped their weapons and surrendered. Others began to run, only to get another, more gruesome surprise.... the company of men that Chamberlain had sent over to guard the left flank had not been killed by the initial Confederate attack. They suddenly appeared from behind a stone wall and opened fire on the retreating Rebels.

The remaining Confederates broke and ran. Colonel Oates would later admit that "we ran like a herd of wild cattle". The Confederate dead literally covered the ground and while fighting continued on other parts of the slope, the summit of Little Round Top was secure.

Joshua Lawrence Chamberlain would go on to receive the Congressional Medal of Honor for his actions that day.

While the heroics of the men from Maine had saved Little Round Top, things were not going as well on other parts of the Union front. Sickle's corps was in desperate straits as the Confederates continued to attack. A Confederate artillery blast removed the lower portion of General Sickle's leg and he was carried from the field, still calmly smoking a cigar.

Union reinforcements began to arrive and fighting raged through the Devil's Den and the Valley of Death. The Federal troops, as they crossed the Wheat Field, opened a gap on Cemetery Ridge and a Confederate brigade began a drive toward it. Hancock spotted the opening and ordered a single, small regiment, the 1st Minnesota, to countercharge and hold the gap. The Minnesota regiment, made up of only 262 men, raced toward the opening with fixed bayonets... and came face-to-face with 1,600 Confederates. The stunned Rebels fell back and the gap in the lines was closed, although only 47 members of the 1st Minnesota came through the skirmish unhurt. They had lost 82 percent of their men in less than five minutes.

By the end of the day, the lack of coordination in Lee's attacks cost them the fight. Despite Longstreet's limited success against Sickles, the Confederate offensive had only worked in some locations and the plan of attacking both flanks at the same time had not worked at all. In fact, it was almost sundown before two divisions of Ewell's corps even began their assault on the hook and curve of the Union's right flank.

The Confederates had clashed with Union troops on the eastern slopes of the hill, which had previously been fortified with earthernworks, strengthened by felled trees and rocks. The Federals, although badly outnumbered, used the works to their advantage and the Rebels failed to dislodge them from the hill.

Meanwhile, two brigades under Jubal Early met with even less luck in their attempt to capture Cemetery Hill. The Confederates initially managed to break through the Federal lines at the northern base of the hill in the early evening but soon suffered a devastating blow from Union artillery on Steven's Knoll. The fighting on the hill became hand-to-hand combat but with no reinforcements from the Confederate infantry units on the south edge of Gettysburg, the Rebels soon retreated.

At the end of the second day of battle, Meade's fishhook remained intact.

Gettysburg: Day Three
The third day of battle began badly for the Confederates, further adding to the belief that Lee had created during the night that he must attack the Federal forces at the center. The failure of his attempts to crush the Union flanks suggested that Meade had fortified these areas at the expense of the center. By midday of July 3, Lee decided that the Confederates would take one last shot... a direct frontal assault against Cemetery Ridge. Lee's plan called for an artillery bombardment to weaken the Union line on the ridge, followed by an infantry attack.

During the morning hours, even Jeb Stuart had suffered at the hands of the Yankees. The cavalry commander had arrived in Gettysburg the afternoon before to be greeted by Lee's anger. One officer recalled later that Lee had even raised a hand as if to strike Stuart, as one would discipline an errant child, which perhaps was how Lee saw his relationship with the younger man. "I have not heard from you in days, and you the eyes and ears of my army", he was said to have chastised the cavalryman.

But Lee's anger quickly passed and on the morning of the third day, he put Stuart's men to work, launching an attack on the Federal rear. But the once weak Union cavalry stopped him, thanks to a series of reckless charges led by a 23 year old general named George Armstrong Custer.

Now, everything depended on the success of Longstreet's assault on the Union center. Longstreet opposed attacking in this manner, knowing what his own rebel gunners had accomplished at Fredericksburg when Union troops had advanced across an open expanse.

But Lee disagreed and ordered Longstreet to prepare the advance. "The enemy is there," he reportedly told the General," and I am going to strike him."

The man that Lee chose to lead the advance was a friend and compatriot of Longstreet, General George Pickett, a rather peculiar, but well-liked officer with a beard and long, curly hair. Pickett's men waited in the wood on the opposite side of a long field from the Union center. They passed the time by throwing green apples at each other. They laughed and joked, knowing that what faced them was a nearly impossible task.

At just after one in the afternoon, the Confederate artillery assault on Cemetery Ridge began. The earth shook as the cannons pounded the ridge, trying to weaken the Union line. General Meade had just left his commanders at the lunch table when the barrage started. As an orderly was serving butter, a shell literally tore him in two.

The top of the hill seemed to be tearing apart. Great mounds of earth were catapulted into the air and shells furrowed into the hillside, destroying grave markers and upending stones. Soon, the Union guns began to return fire and the casualty rate began to climb for the Confederate infantry, who were waiting in the woods for the signal to advance. But after about an hour, Meade ordered the Federal guns to silence, hoping to conserve ammunition for the fight that he was sure was coming.

And also to lure the Confederates out into the open field.

If you have ever visited Gettysburg, and have stood on the edge of the field which spreads out between where the Confederate forces and the Union troops were once positioned.... then you have an idea just what Pickett's men faced as they marched toward the Federal center. If you have not, then I can only tell you that it must have taken some very brave men to participate in that march. The vast, open field which lay before them was completely devoid of shelter. Any man who walked across it had little chance of reaching the other side....

I can only hope that the Confederate commanders truly believed that the silence of Meade's guns meant that the Federal battery had been destroyed.... to begin such a march under any other conditions would have been suicidal.

Pickett came to Longstreet and asked if his men should go forward. The Federal guns had been destroyed and nothing lay between the Confederates and the destruction of the Federal center but Union infantry. The time was now ripe for an attack.

Longstreet was unable to speak and he merely nodded his head, convinced that he was sending his friend to his death. Pickett hurriedly scribbled a note to his teen-aged fiancée and handed it to Longstreet to mail, then, with his usual flair for dramatics, gave the order to attack.

Three divisions, numbering about 13,000 men, started out of the woods and towards the stone wall at the edge of Cemetery Ridge. Although history remembers this advance as "Pickett's Charge", it was hardly a quick attack. The men walked at a brisk pace, covering only about 100 yards of the open field by the minute.

"It was", one northern officer recalled, "the most beautiful thing I ever saw."

Union cannons on Cemetery Ridge and Little Round Top began to sound, opening fire on the right side of the advancing line. Men were killed with every shot but the Confederates still kept coming. Behind the stone wall, Union troops waited, holding their fire until the Rebels came closer.

Finally, the order was given by General Alexander Hays and 11 cannon and 1,700 muskets went off at once.

Hundreds died in the first volley but the rest continued to come. The Confederates reached the line at just one place, a crook in the wall that has become known as the "Angle". They were led by General Lewis A. Armistead, who jumped the wall and managed to capture a Union battery before he was shot down. All of the other Confederates who breached the wall were either captured, killed or wounded. Soon, those Confederates remaining on the field broke and ran or gave themselves up as prisoners.

The assault was over... a complete and utter failure.

As the Confederates staggered back to Seminary Ridge, Lee rode out among them, urging them to regroup. "It was all my fault," he was said to have told them, "Get together and let us do the best we can towards saving what is left of us."

Pickett had watched the advance with disbelief. Half of his men, over 6,500, had been killed or captured; 16 of his 17 field officers were gone, along with three brigadier generals and eight colonels. When Lee ordered him to rally his division for possible counterattack by the Federals, Pickett replied, "General Lee, I have no division now."

In the years to come, Pickett would never forgive Lee for the what happened that day, always believing that his commander had sent his men into the field to be needlessly slaughtered.

By the end of the third day, the Battle of Gettysburg was over. It would be remembered as the bloodiest day of the war as almost one-third of the men engaged in it were lost.

The next day, July 4, both armies remained on the battlefield, with Meade and Lee each waiting for the other to move. When nothing of significance occurred that day, Lee realized that his invasion of the north had come to an end. He was now far from his supply line and was running low on ammunition, not to mention the fact that the Confederacy could not afford the over 28,000 casualties they had sustained. It was time to return home.

That afternoon, Lee began his long retreat back to Virginia while Meade, despite urgings from Washington, declined to attack the retreating force.

Behind them, the streets and fields of Gettysburg were littered with the bodies of the dead, slowly decaying in the heat of the Pennsylvania summer. The people of the town were also left with thousands of the wounded to attend to and homes and businesses were quickly turned into field hospitals. "Wounded men were brought into our houses and laid side-by-side in our halls and rooms," one local woman recalled. "Carpets were so saturated with blood as to be unfit for further use. Wall were bloodstained, as well as books that were used as pillows".

The dead also lined the streets and walkways, rotting in the summer sun. "Corpses, swollen to twice their original size," wrote a Federal soldier, "actually burst asunder.... several human, or inhuman, corpses sat upright against a fence, with arms extended in the air and faces hideous with something very like a fixed leer..."

In terms of significance, Gettysburg will always be remembered as one of the greatest battles in American history. It was the turning point in the war and it was probably not a coincidence(in the greater scheme of things, at least) that the day after the battle ended also marked the fall of Vicksburg to General Grant. The war had just taken a darker turn for the Confederacy.

The battle would have a lingering effect on the country, not only for the armies of the Civil War, but for the America itself.... an effect that still lingers today.

It goes without saying that the Battle of Gettysburg left a tremendous mark on the small town and on the fields where the fighting actually took place. Few are surprised to learn that many of the buildings in Gettysburg and many locations on the battlefield are now believed to be haunted. In places where so much death and destruction took place, the stories of ghosts and spirits often follow.

And in Gettysburg, such spirits make themselves known more strongly than just about anywhere else.....

THE CASHTOWN INN

Located about eight miles west of Gettysburg is the tiny village of Cashtown. It was through this town that much of the Confederate Army passed in the days prior to the battle in Gettysburg. Oddly, this was not Cashtown's first brush with the southern forces during the war. In October 1862, Jeb Stuart had made an appearance in the area, staying just long enough to plunder stores and farms and to commandeer enough horses to carry his men along the last portion of a raid around McClellan's Union Army.

This may have been the reason, when Lee and his Confederate Army appeared in late June 1863, that the innkeeper of the small hotel in Cashtown demanded cash, and not credit, for drinks and lodging. The Cashtown Inn, as it is called today, became the meeting place for all of the officers and staff members on the afternoon and evening before the Battle of Gettysburg. General A.P. Hill made the small inn his headquarters and all of the senior officers under Lee passed through the doors of the building.

It was also here that the decision to attack the Federals in Gettysburg took place. General Pettigrew had accompanied men to the outskirts of Gettysburg on the afternoon of June 30, and there had spotted Buford's picket lines. He had returned to Cashtown and reported the encounter with the cavalrymen to his superior, General Henry Heth. It was during the subsequent meeting with General Lee and the corps commanders that a decision was reached to fight in Gettysburg.

Despite the caliber of the guests at the Cashtown Inn that night, they were actually not the first Confederate occupants. The first was actually a mortally wounded soldier who had been hit by a sniper during a march through the Cashtown Gap just a day or two before. The young man was carried to the second floor of the inn, where he died. Many believe that it may be this soldier who is responsible for much of the strange activity that is reported at the inn.

Because the inn is certainly believed to be a haunted place.....

One of the local tales told about the inn was said to have taken place in the early part of this century. A local doctor was walking home one night after making a house call when he encountered a man wearing some sort of military clothing. The doctor quickly realized the man was wearing a Confederate uniform, just before the soldier grabbed hold of him and roughly pulled him over to an empty woodlot behind the inn. Here, he discovered a small campsite and another Confederate soldier, although this one had a bullet wound. He treated the fellow and then was sent on his way.

The frightened doctor hurried home and returned to the inn early the next day to inquire as to who the men were and why they were wearing Confederate uniforms. When he arrived back at the empty lot, he found it just that.... empty! All trace of the soldiers and their camp had vanished.

According to local tradition, the same occurrence happened once more to another doctor some years later, and with the same result. The soldiers, their camp and all sign of them had simply disappeared.

The unusual sightings and occurrences inside of the inn have also been reported for many years. The current owners of the inn, Dennis and Eileen Hoover, along with past owners Bud and

Carolyn Buckley, have heard more than their share of strange tales from guests.... and have had their own odd encounters too. Several years ago, the Buckley's reported often hearing footsteps in the attic and the sounds of things being moved about. When they would go upstairs to investigate, they would find that nothing had been touched.

A number of years ago, restoration started by the Buckley's seemed to "stir up" activity in building. They told a story of a well-known writer who was staying at the inn and who went to bed one night, only to be awakened by the sound of someone knocking on his door. When he went to see who it was, he found no one there. He had just fallen back to sleep when he heard the knocking again and once more, he found no one in the hallway.

On another occasion, visitors to the inn reported to Bud Buckley that they had passed through some unusually cold spots in the upstairs hallway, even though it was the middle of a very warm summer. They also told him that they had been awakened in the middle of the night by the sounds of horses outside. When they went to the window to see who might be riding in the dead of night, they found no one there.

Buckley told author Mark Nesbitt in 1991 that he could count at least eight times when guests had approached him about a Confederate soldier they had seen in the hallway or in a doorway that now leads into an area behind the bar.

Even the current owners have not been immune to strange events. According to a small book about the inn compiled by Suzanne Gruber and Bob Wasel, a late night menu planning session between Eileen Hoover and the chef was interrupted by the sounds of footsteps coming down the stairs from the second floor. Mrs. Hoover called out to her husband, as there were no guests at the inn that night, but he did not answer. After calling again, the footsteps continued and she went into the parlor to investigate.

She found there was no one on the stairs.....

Of all of the rooms where strange activity takes place at the inn, the most haunted room is said to be Room No. 4. It is here where the largest number of sightings of the Confederate soldier are said to take place and where odd events are most frequently reported.

A visitor from Illinois named Stacy McArdle stayed in Room No. 4 in the Spring of 1998 and hoped to possibly encounter one of the ghosts the inn was said to be famous for. She later reported that she was not disappointed....

Shortly after checking in, she went upstairs to change clothes and after undressing, hung her slacks by the belt loop on one of the pegs of the coat rack. She turned around and started walking toward the bathroom when she felt a chilling breeze across her back. She looked to make sure the door to the room was closed and caught sight of something else entirely. "Right before my eyes," Stacy reported, " I saw my slacks lifted off of the coat peg.. they were suspended in mid-air for a couple of seconds and then fell to the floor.... but not to the floor just below where they were hanging. It was almost as if they were tossed toward the middle of the room."

Later that day, after lunch and a nap, Stacy left for Gettysburg to meet some friends. On her way out, she was informed that the inn would be locked after eleven and she was given a combination to the lock on the door.

When she got back to the inn that night, she found that the door was indeed locked. "I tried the door twice, just out of habit," Stacy remembered, "then I put my backpack on the ground and began to dig for my flashlight and the note with the combination. At the same moment I found my flashlight, the door opened wide in front of me. Startled, but thankful, I went inside, but found no one in the area.

"In another room, I found the owner of the inn and two guests at the bar. Although I was thinking they could not have returned to the bar that fast, I thanked them for giving me a hand. They told me that hadn't moved, so I told them what had happened.

"The owner didn't seem very interested... that kind of thing happens all the time."

And perhaps it does. In addition to the strange experiences of guests and staff members, the inn also has a photograph that was taken of the place in the 1890's. In the photo, a man is posing on the front porch of the hotel... but he is not alone in the photo. Off to the left appears another man, standing stiffly in what appears to be the uniform of a soldier. Could this be the ghost who is said to haunt the inn, accidentally captured by the camera?

I suggest, should you ever get to Gettysburg, that you make a sidetrip to the Cashtown Inn.... and perhaps you'll find out for yourself.

GETTYSBURG HAUNTS

There's an interesting thing about visiting the Gettysburg Battlefield. You can go into just about any business in town and ask where to find the battlefield and they will tell you that you are standing in it! Of course, the "official" battlefield, which lies just outside of town, is operated today by the National park Service but during the fighting of July 1863, virtually the entire village was a battleground.

Skirmishes took place throughout the town and when the Federals retreated on that first day of the battle, they poured into Gettysburg, fleeing to the relative safety of Cemetery Hill. Many were killed here, their bodies left to await burial on the streets of the town. The fact that these bodies were left here in the July heat has given rise to one of the many ghostly tales of Gettysburg. As mentioned in the first chapter to this book, I had my own experience with one of the "phantom smells" of Baltimore Street, the lingering odor of peppermint. According to the tales, the ladies of the town were only able to walk the streets after the battle with scented handkerchiefs pressed to their faces to combat the horrible smell of death. The stories say these odors of peppermint and vanilla are still present today.... and as I mentioned earlier, I certainly believe they are, and I am not an easy person to convince of these things.

The Farnsworth House

The Farnsworth House Inn on Baltimore Street has a long, and some say haunted, history in Gettysburg. The original part of this structure, which today boasts an excellent restaurant and inn, was built in 1810 and a brick portion was added later in 1833, constructed by John McFarland. During the battle, the house was occupied by the Sweney family and was eventually opened as an inn by the George Black family in the early 1900's.

Today, the house is a showcase of history and it retains the original walls, flooring and rafters... and some believe it also retains a few of the occupants who passed through the house years ago.

During the battle, the house was occupied by Confederate sharpshooters, who used the garret (attic) of the house as a vantage point to fire at the Union troops on Cemetery Hill, just a few hundred yards away. According to the legends, a sharpshooter was taking aim at a door on a house a short distance away, between the Sweney House and the Federal lines. He was using the doorknob as a target to see just how hard the wind was blowing. He fired and when he did, the bullet pierced the wooden door and struck and killed a woman named Jennie Wade, who was in the kitchen kneading dough. She became the only civilian who was killed during the battle.

It has been said that the deeds and the presence of these sharpshooters has left an indelible mark on the Farnsworth House. According to the ghostly traditions of the place, the sound of a jew's-harp has been heard drifting down from the attic when no one is present there... a musical instrument commonly played by soldiers during the Civil War.

And if these soldiers still linger here... they do not do so alone.

After the battle, the house was used as a Federal headquarters, further adding to the history. The battle itself also left a mark on the place in the form of more than 100 bullet holes which can be seen on the south side of the house. Most of these marks still remain, even after all of these years, and many of the bullets removed from the wall are on display inside.

In 1972, the house was purchased by the Loring Shultz family, who began restoring the place to the way it looked in 1863. The inn and restaurant are operated today by the Shultz family who run the place and operate not only a theater for ghost stories but also organize the inn's popular "ghost tours".

The owners and staff members are a veritable treasure chest of stories relating to hauntings at the Farnsworth House, from the spectral sharpshooters to tales of guests who have heard phantom footsteps on the stairs; have detected unexplained noises; have felt invisible intruders sitting on the ends of their bed; and many more. If this is not one of the most haunted buildings in Gettysburg, then it most be near the top of the list.

A year prior to this writing, my wife and I were lucky enough to visit the Farnsworth House and be treated to not only a wonderful dinner, but to some of the numerous ghost tales as well. I have since spoken to staff members at the house, who while they choose to remain anonymous, gladly shared some of the strange happenings of the place.

While many of the stories here are the types of things that one might expect from a haunted place... the sincerity of the tellers sets them apart from what you might expect in a "typical" situation. In addition to the incidents already mentioned, staff members have reported seeing movement out of the corner of the eye, only to turn and find nothing there. Some have also reported seeing shadows moving through the dining room at night, after everyone else has gone home, only to find the place is deserted. There are also a number of reports of footsteps pacing through the main floor at night, and of employees hearing these footsteps following behind them, only to turn and see no one is there. On other occasions, staff members have been tapped on the shoulder, or touched, by unseen hands.

On one occasion, two different waitresses reported a similar experience. One summer evening, a waitress in period costume rushed into the kitchen and claimed that her long apron had been roughly yanked by something she could not see. The force of the pull had literally spun her completely around. This occurred in an outdoor dining area, adjacent to the Farnsworth courtyard. It had also taken place in front of a table of understandably surprised patrons, who also witnessed the apron being forcibly yanked.

A few days later, the same thing happened to another waitress, although this time it happened in the back hallway. The second waitress was not aware of what had happened to the first woman, although both of them were visibly shaken by their experiences.

On another occasion, two staff members were standing and talking in the inn's tavern. As they chatted, they were facing the back hallway which ran between the kitchen and the tavern. Suddenly, one of the women realized they were no longer standing there alone. Down the hallway, she spotted an older women in what looked like a period costume. The strange woman seemed to be looking at items stored on the shelves there. The staff member glanced away for a moment and when she looked back, the older lady was gone.

Concerned now that a customer may have wandered into a staff area, because she knew that she was certainly not an employee, she went into the kitchen to see if the woman had returned in that direction. No one had seen her come inside... even though the kitchen was the only place the old lady could have gone.

Not surprisingly, the "vanishing lady" fit the description of a ghostly visitor who has been reported many times at the Farnsworth House over the years, even though the woman who described her, while aware of this ongoing tale, was not aware of the lady's description. The apparition has been reported many times, by a wide variety of people, although who she actually is remains a mystery.

One Valentine's Day, which is a busy night during a normally slow winter season, the restaurant was packed with people and all of the extra work made it so that several staff members had to stay until the early hours of the morning to get things cleaned up. Just before they were ready to go home, an employee went to put away the last tray of clean silverware in the pantry off the dining room. Moments later, there was a loud crash in the pantry and a groan from the staff member who had just walked in there.

According to her story, she had just placed the tray where it was supposed to go, and was walking away, when the tray suddenly raised up under its own power, flew several feet and then dumped into the middle of the floor, showering the pantry with pieces of silverware.

Needless to say, the normally welcome spirits were very unwelcome that night as the staff angrily had to re-wash the tray of silverware.

Pennsylvania Hall

Located within the boundaries of the town is Gettysburg College, or as it was known in 1863, Pennsylvania College. This small, attractive campus seems a quiet place today and anyone who visits here would probably be surprised to learn that during the battle, the college was in the midst of the fighting. At the time, the college consisted of only three brick buildings, which provided lodging and classrooms for little more than 100 students. When the battle erupted, the campus was thrown into the midst of the fight, providing shelter for the wounded and dying as a field hospital.

Not surprisingly, the college is said to still bear the marks of not only the physical effects of the battle , but the spiritual effects as well...

One of the most haunted buildings on campus is said to be Pennsylvania Hall, a large building with stately white columns. It once served as a dormitory for students and now houses the campus administrative offices. The hall was constructed in 1837 and is often referred to as Old Dorm. The large structure was taken over by the Confederates during the battle, not only for use as a field hospital, but as a look-out post as well. A number of officers, including General Lee, used the cupola of the Old Dorm to keep an eye on the progress of the battle.

It has been said that on certain nights, students and staff members of the college have reported seeing the figures of soldiers pacing back and forth in the cupola of the building. The descriptions of the men vary but it is believed they may be sentries who were placed on duty there to guard the safety of Lee, or to deliver messages to the battlefield.

One student reported that he and his roommate, who lived in a dorm about 50 yards away from Pennsylvania Hall, saw a shadowy figure in the tower over a period of several nights. On another occasion, a figure was seen to be gesturing wildly, apparently to a student below. When the student called out to him, believing that perhaps someone was trapped in the tower, the figure vanished. An investigation by campus security found the building to be empty.

It is believed to be the terrible conditions of the field hospital however, which have left the strongest impressions on the building. According to the records of the time, blood sprayed the walls and floors of the rooms as doctors operated without anesthetic, dealing with bullet wounds by the preferred treatment of the time... amputation. Outside of the operating rooms was an area where those who could not be saved were left to die. There is no way that we can even imagine the horrible wails, groans and cries that echoed in this area.

Perhaps the most famous story connected to the time of the battle was related by author Mark Nesbitt. He told of two college administrators who were working on the fourth floor of the building one night. As they were leaving, they stepped into the elevator and punched the button for the first floor. Instead of taking them to their destination, the elevator mysteriously passed it and came to a stop on the basement level. The elevator doors then opened to a terrifying scene....

The basement storage room had vanished and in its place was the blood-splattered operating room of 1863. Wounded men were lying prone on the floor and administering to them were doctors and orderlies in bloody clothing. The entire scene was completely silent, although it was obvious that it was one of chaos.

Stunned and horrified, the administrators repeatedly pushed at the elevator button, desperately trying to close the doors and escape the scene which lay before them. Just before the doors closed though, one of the spectral orderlies was said to have looked up, directly at the two administrators, as though asking them for help.

Whatever happened that evening, the two administrators were shaken and frightened by it and needless to say, never forgot their strange experience. However, you couldn't fault them for their bravery. In the same circumstances, I am not sure what I would have done... but both of these men continued to work in the building. In small concession to the weird experience though, whenever they had to work at night, they always departed the building by way of the stairs.

The Thompson Barn... or Buried Alive

I cannot, in all of my imagination, mentally conjure up a worse fate than being buried alive. For many, in years gone by, the idea of such a fate became an obsession. An entire industry was based around methods and devices to contact the living... just in case a loved one awoke on the wrong side of the grave.

For some, such devices did not exist. For some, to awake inside of a coffin, buried far beneath the ground, became a horrifying reality. The only method they had to alert those among the living of their continued existence was to scream, to claw and to beg the heavens that their lives be spared. But unfortunately, those pleas were rarely heard and they ended up perishing in the graves that had already been dug for them... albeit prematurely.

Can you imagine such a fate? I don't imagine one young Confederate soldier could imagine that fate either when he came to serve his country at Gettysburg. Of course, his premature burial was perhaps even more gruesome than most, and while no one heard his pleas while he was still among the living... some folks took notice long after he had died.

The home of the widow Mary Thompson was located on Seminary Ridge, on the north side of the Chambersburg Pike. It is best remembered today as the headquarters of General Robert E. Lee during the battle, although Lee actually slept in a tent that was pitched in an apple orchard on the south side of the pike.

Not far from Lee's encampment was the Thompson barn. During the battle, both the barn and house were used as field hospitals. The house was only used for a short time, but the barn was used even after the fighting had ended. Local lore recalls that Mrs. Thompson tending the dying as best she could and was even seen "wrapping the dead up in her carpets".

Across the road in the barn however, the dead were not treated so kindly. The records say that they were piled like "cord wood" in what was called the "stone room" of the cellar beneath the building. During this, and other Civil War battles, ice houses and cool corners of cellars were often used as temporary storage places for the dead. In this way, they could be placed out of the way, in cold storage, until they could be properly buried.

The bodies of the dead soldiers were carried down into the cellar and stacked there, literally in piles. During the first day of the battle, the body count began to increase and soon stretcher carriers were placing more men there by the hour. The corpses were unceremoniously tossed one atop the other in a grisly pyramid of death. While this may seem horrifying to us, the carriers of the dead had little choice... and besides, what did it matter to those who had already died?

But to one of those men, lying beneath dozens of his fellow soldiers, it did matter.... for one of the soldiers had awakened, badly hurt but still breathing. Only now, he discovered that he was buried alive under a decomposing pile of his comrades!

A few days later, the battle was over and the Confederates had begun their retreat back to Virginia. Slowly, the Union troops moved into the area that was once behind the Rebel lines. It was not long before someone discovered the horrible pile of bodies rotting beneath the Thompson barn.

As the burial crews came along, they began removing the bloated cadavers one by one, carrying them out to the wagons to be taken away for burial. As they eventually reached the bottom of the pile, they tugged on the legs of one of the bloody corpses... only to see the man's eyes fly open and his limbs began to twitch and shake. Maniacal screams emerged from the corpse's lips and the Union crew hurriedly dropped him and scrambled away. The man had been alive... buried beneath the festering bodies for four days, imprisoned there to go slowly and terribly insane.

They fetched a doctor, but by this time, the man was raving mad. He never recovered his senses and died a few days later. He was buried properly this time... and you can bet the surgeons were very careful to be sure he was really dead before they allowed him to be placed in the ground.

Regardless of the fact the man was taken from the cellar alive, something of him remained there in the Thompson barn. Perhaps it was imprinted into the stone walls, or even onto the atmosphere itself, we'll never know.... but something stayed behind, be it his spirit or merely the impression of the terror he must have felt during those four days.

Some time in the late 1800's, the old barn burned down and later a house was built on the site, which incorporated the stone cellar room into the basement of the new dwelling. The room had been closed off from the rest of the basement by a door, leaving behind an earthen floor and plain walls... literally a room of no use for the occupants of the house.

Not long after taking up residence in the new dwelling, occupants of the house began to report odd sounds coming from the basement. These were not the usual creaks and groans associated with a house either.... these were sounds for which no one could provide an easy explanation. And they were coming from the stone cellar room!

At first they were disturbed by the sounds, but soon, they grew used to them.... that is until one summer night when a sound like the furnace exploding roared from the basement. The family had been sound asleep at the time and they ran from their beds to see what was going on. As one family member entered the kitchen, she realized that everything there was shaking. "The appliances, the cutlery and glasses were shaking violently and falling off the shelves," she recalled. "The furniture in the hallway... was moving from one side of the hall to the other. It felt like an earthquake."

The family member, now joined by others, descended into the basement and soon discovered the source of the sounds was behind the door to the stone cellar room. It was as if someone were on the other side of the door with a sledge hammer, pounding away at it. They could actually see the door bend outward with each blow, the wood seemingly straining against the pressure being applied to it. It seemed as if the heavy oak door was literally going to fly off its hinges and hurtle across the room.

Needless to say, they fled the basement, and most likely the house, that night. They refused to return to what had become a terrifying place without some sort of assistance. Despite what they may have initially believed, the family could find no explanation for what had occurred that night other than a supernatural one. The strange sounds in the house had progressed far beyond the unusual creaks and groans and so the family turned to a church official for help.

A few days later, an older priest arrived to bless the house. He explained that he had many years of experience with sending spirits on their way from homes and other locations and most considered him to be somewhat sensitive to the supernatural. One visit downstairs to the stone room convinced him that the house was indeed haunted... although not by a spirit the family should fear, but one they should pity. The ghost who was trapped in the house was not evil, but terrified. The priest explained that he believed the spirit to be that of a young Confederate soldier who was still desperately trying to free himself from a horrible place that he was in just before his death.

A short time later, the old priest performed his ceremony and when he was finished, he used a white paste to place the sign of the cross on the oak door and around it, he drew a circle. From that time on, no further sounds were heard coming from the basement.

But the family who lived in the house, regardless of the priest's assurances, sold the place in 1987 and moved out. It is now owned by the Lutheran Seminary in Gettysburg and it is believed that no further disturbances have ever taken place there.

BATTLEFIELD HAUNTINGS

There are scores of ghostly stories and supernatural incidents which have been recorded and experienced by everyday people across the official confines of the Gettysburg Battlefield. Factor into this number the encounters of those ghost seekers who have purposely traveled to the battlefield in search of spirits, and the number of strange tales becomes an amazing one.

It is not, however, my intention to try and present all of those experiences here. As I wrote when I opened this section, such stories have been prolifically chronicled by others. My goal is to present you with an overview of the haunts connected to the official battleground... and a closer look at the most haunted places.

Do the spirits of the past still walk at Gettysburg?

This is one place where I feel safe in telling you that they most assuredly do!

There are a number of once private residences scattered across the battlefield which have reportedly played host to the spirits in the years that have passed since the battle. Most of these homes are now the property of the National Park Service and often they serve as residences to park rangers and personnel who stay in the houses to keep them occupied and in good repair.

Nearly all of the nearby homes were used during the battle as makeshift field hospitals and as shelters for the wounded during the fighting. Many believe that such incidents may be what has caused them to gain reputations for being haunted over the years. Perhaps these traumatic events served as catalysts for the ghostly events which have allegedly followed.

Not surprisingly, as employees of the United States Government, the rangers are usually very reluctant to discuss their supernatural encounters on the battlefield. Those who do speak, usually do so off the record, which nevertheless, creates a fairly impressive documentation of events beyond our understanding.

The **George Weikert House** is one such odd location on the battlefield. This small house has had a surprising number of different occupants over the years, many of whom have had stories to tell. One of the previous residents of the house spoke of a door on the second floor which refused to stay closed, no matter what they did to it. One ranger even nailed the door shut with a small wire nail, and yet it refused to stay closed.

Possibly connected to this, other tenants reported the sounds of footsteps pacing back and forth in the attic. They would hear the heavy tread cross the area above their heads, and then cross back, as if someone up there were worried or deep in thought. Needless to say, when they would go up to the attic to check for an intruder, they would find the area to be deserted.

Another residence is the **Hummelbaugh House**, where the stories say the cries of Confederate Brigadier General William Barksdale can still be heard on certain nights. Barksdale was wounded while leading a charge on Seminary Ridge and was brought to the Hummelbaugh House. According to an officer from the 148th Pennsylvania Volunteers, Barksdale was last seen lying in front of the house and a young boy was giving him water with a spoon. The General continued to call for water, as though the boy did not exist.... calling over and over again. In the years since, the legends say the sound of Barksdale's voice can still be heard.

And that is not the only story connected to the house, or to Brigadier General Barksdale either. The other story is connected to the days after the battle, when Barksdale's wife journeyed to Gettysburg to have her husband's remains exhumed and returned to their home in Mississippi. She was accompanied on her trip by the General's favorite hunting dog. As the old dog was led to his master's grave, he fell down onto the ground and began to howl. No matter what Mrs. Barksdale did, she was unable to pull the animal away.

All through the night, the faithful dog watched over the grave. The next day, Mrs. Barksdale again tried to lure the dog away, but he refused to budge, even though the General's remains had already been loaded onto a wagon to begin the journey back to Mississippi. Finally, saddened by the dog's pitiful loyalty, she left for home.

For those who lived nearby, the dog became a familiar fixture during the days that followed. He would occasionally let out a heart-breaking howl that could be heard for some distance. Many locals came and tried to lead the dog away, offering him food, water and a good home. The dog refused all of their gestures and eventually, died from hunger and thirst, still stretched out over his master's burial place.

Within a few years, a tale began to circulate that the animal's spirit still lingered at the Hummelbaugh Farm. It has been said that on the night of July 2, the anniversary of Barksdale's death, an unearthly howl echoes into the night.... as the faithful hunting dog still grieves from a place beyond this world.

The **Rose Farm** is another such location. During the battle, the house was used as a field hospital and burial ground. Hundreds of Confederate and Federal soldiers were buried in rows all around the house and property. They would later be exhumed in November 1863, although the claiming of the bodies and the re-burials would continue on for years afterward.

According to a local doctor named Dr. J.W.C. O'Neil, and reported by author Mark Nesbitt, one of the daughters on the Rose Farm actually went insane during the exhumations, having lived through both the battle and its aftermath. Allegedly, she was to have seen blood actually flowing from the walls of the house.... perhaps a grisly reminder from the days when the house served as a bloody field hospital?

Was the house actually haunted though? Or were the strange visions simply the workings of a fevered mind?

An account recorded by the Civilian Conservation Corps in the 1930's came from a man who reportedly worked at the Rose Farm just a few weeks after the battle. He was returning home one evening, shortly after darkness had fallen, and claimed to see an strange glowing shape appear near the graves of the slain soldiers. Could it have been a ghost?

In addition to these former private residences, spirits on the battlefield itself abound. There are numerous reports of apparitions of phantom soldiers.... seen marching in formation, riding horses, and still seemingly fighting the battle.... from various parts of the park. These ghosts haunt the fields where Pickett's Charge took place, the slopes of Little Round Top, the Peach Orchard, the Wheatfield, and many other places.

However, the highest concentration of ghostly sightings and strange experiences seems to be in the area called the Devil's Den, and also in the areas around it. It is in the nearby Triangular Field where electronic equipment and cameras are said to seldom work. It is in the aptly named Valley of Death where the apparitions of soldiers are frequently reported.

And it is in the Devil's Den itself where not only are the ghosts of the slain soldiers seen, but heard also.

If there is a place on the Gettysburg Battlefield which is more haunted than any other... there is little doubt that such a place would be the Devil's Den.

The Devil's Den... Gettysburg's Most Haunted

The event which created the lore and legend of the Devil's Den is undoubtedly the fighting which took place here on July 2, 1863, the second day of the Battle of Gettysburg. However, stories surrounded the place long before the battle was ever fought.

According to early accounts from the area, the tangled, outcropping of rocks was a Native American hunting ground for centuries and some say that a huge battle was once fought here, called the "Battle of the Crows" during which many perished. A Gettysburg writer named Emmanuel Bushman wrote in an 1880 article of the "many unnatural and supernatural sights and sounds" that were reported in the area of the Round Tops and what he called the Indian Fields. He wrote that the early settlers had told stories of ghosts that had been seen there and that Indian "war-whoops" could still be heard on certain nights. In addition, he reported that strange Indian ceremonies also took place here.

In 1884, Bushman also wrote, with the idea that an ancient tribe had once lived near the site of Devil's Den, that he believed the scattering of boulders to have once been part of a tall pyramid. He stated the crevices in the rocks bore evidence of this and that the pyramid had undoubtedly been destroyed by some forceful blast. While this is (extremely) doubtful, it does give the reader an idea of the lore that surrounded the area, even before the battle.

Also according to local legend, the name "Devil's Den" was actually in use before the battle took place. Most everyone, in their letters home and in the explorations of the battlefield after the fighting, referred to the rocks as a "desolate and ghostly place" or mentioned the "ominous" character of the rocks. Many others felt that the rocky outcropping actually marked the entrance to a cavern and while no cave exists here, those who visit the location can understand the mistake. The rocks are piled so high that the crevices between them seem to plunge down into total darkness.

But how the area got its name remains a mystery. Many believe that the strange atmosphere of the area itself may have contributed to the designation. Another legend persists that the Devil's Den was always known for being infested with snakes. The legends say that one gigantic snake in particular eluded the local hunters for many years and they were never able to capture or kill him. He was allegedly nicknamed "the Devil" and thus, the area of rocks was called his "den".

No matter how the area got its name, it was apparently already considered a strange and "haunted" spot before the battle, at least according to Emmanuel Bushman. In the years which would follow, the Devil's Den would gain an even more fearsome reputation.

On the morning of the second day of battle, General Lee was of the opinion that by simultaneously attacking the Union flanks, he could drive the enemy from the field. His plan was to send Longstreet's corps against the Round Tops, with his main thrust of attack being made by divisions under John Bell Hood and Lafayette McLaws against the Federal left flank. Lee ordered Longstreet to move his men southward, without being detected, and form lines against the Union flank.

Unfortunately, the southern troops had no guide to the battlefield and huge delays were caused by marching and countermarching. These delays then led to exhaustion and frustration on the part of the troops. By the time they were in position, some of the officers raised doubts about being able to mount much of an attack before dark.

To make matters worse, they also soon discovered that their battle lines did not envelop the Union flank, thanks to the fact that General Sickles had decided that he didn't like the area where he had originally been posted. The Union lines now stretched into the Peach Orchard and appeared to extend all of the way to Big Round Top. This relocation had placed Sickles in front of the rest of the army, opening up his flanks to attack. The Peach Orchard had become the center of Sickles' line with his second division, under Brigadier General Andrew A. Humphreys, curving back to fill the space between the Peach Orchard and the Devil's Den. He had all but abandoned Little Round Top.

The position of the Devil's Den was commanded by Brigadier General John Henry Hobart Ward and it was located at the far end of the Union line.

The men of Ward's Brigade moved into position about two hours before the Confederate attack. They set up an encampment around the rocky outcropping and spent the time eating and resting. As they relaxed, the gunners from Captain James E. Smith's 4th New York Light Artillery worked to get their guns in position atop the Devil's Den. It took them more than an hour to wrestle the guns over the rocks, but when finished, they had an excellent position with a sweeping field of fire and plenty of cover behind the huge boulders. The only problem was that the high position was unprotected from snipers in the nearby woods.... as the gunners would quickly learn.

Following their frustrating march, the Confederates arrived on the Union flank, only to wait. Hood spent the next short while with his commanders, forming lines for the battle ahead. Like Longstreet, Hood was reluctant to carry out a full frontal assault on what appeared to be an impregnable Union position. He sent out several of his Texas scouts to study the Federal line and they came back with news that the land east of the Round Tops was empty of northern troops and that their supply trains could be easily taken. Hood, encouraged by this report, requested three times to be allowed to go around Big Round Top and attack the Federals from the flank and rear. His request was turned down.

Despite reluctance on the part of Hood and Longstreet, the attack on the Union line was a powerful one and Longstreet later called the assault "the best three hours of fighting ever done by any troops on any battlefield."

The fight for the Devil's Den soon began and as the battle progressed, the terrifying terrain and the sharp piles of boulders created a maze for the troops on both sides. The lines were broken, first into regiments, and then it was man against man. The boulders provided dozens of hiding places and ambush spots and men ran from boulder to boulder, ducking and shooting as they ran, never knowing if enemy or friend lay around the next corner.

Before the Confederates could even reach the Devil's Den, they had to cross an area known today as the Triangular Field. Waves of Confederate troops from Texas, Arkansas, Alabama and Georgia crossed the field, clashing with the Union soldiers who hailed from places like New York, Maine and Pennsylvania. As the southerners came, they were cut down by the cannons posted atop the ridge ahead, and yet still they came, pushing hard against the Union lines.

As the Texas troops mounted the slopes toward the Federal position, they were attacked by the 124th New York, who soon withdrew from the ferocity of the Confederate charge. As the Union men fell back, Alabama troops swept into the Triangular Field and charged into the boulders beyond it. Deadly fire was poured down upon them and yet they managed to get through, but not without giving the area a gruesomely appropriate nickname, the "Slaughter Pen".

The Confederate men overwhelmed the enemy position and took control of the ridge.. but they would not hold it for long. The Federal forces counter-charged and the Maine and Pennsylvania troops pushed the Confederates back. The rocks of the Devil's Den had become a slaughterhouse. Bodies were strewn across the boulders and they had tumbled down into the wedges between them.

The Federals were attacked again, this time by troops from Georgia, who had been given the grim task of advancing across the Triangular Field against the Union position. As they reached the Slaughter Pen, they were charged by the 40th New York, who were soon driven back and forced to retreat as the Federals pulled back their lines. One last surge of men from Texas and Georgia finished the skirmish and the Confederates claimed the Devil's Den as their own.

The Texans swarmed over the ridge and once again reached the Union's abandoned guns. They turned them to point the muzzles toward the fleeing enemy, but there was no ammunition to be found. The Federal troops continued to fire upon their deserted position and many of the Texans continued to fall. George Branard, a color bearer, planted the flag of Texas on the highest rock above the Devil's Den, only to be hit by a Union shell.

After the withdrawal of the Federals, the Georgians reported the overwhelming sound of the Rebel Yell from the Devil's Den and they pushed hard against the Union troops still to the front of them. The Federals were moved back and began to suffer from heavy fire from the Devil's Den. Finally, it was more than they could take and they began to retreat.

After hours of bloody fighting the Confederates finally controlled the area. The fight for the Devil's Den may have been the most confusing and intense skirmish on the battlefield that day. The heat of the afternoon and the collapse of the battle lines, thanks to the difficult terrain, had caused the entire chain of events to happen so fast that many of the men were almost stunned to find the battle was over.

Stranger yet were the reports from the men who were ordered to stand guard in the tangle of boulders that night. Many of them later spoke of the macabre and unnerving surroundings... sharing the space in the looming boulders with the bodies of the dead.

Once the fighting had ended for the day, the Federals realized they could not recover most of their dead and wounded comrades from the Devil's Den.

Sergeant Ransom W. Wood of the 20th Georgia happened upon the body of a dead Federal captain wedged in between two rocks. In the man's pocket, he found a small bible, which he took for himself. A few days later, he found some words scrawled inside... "In case I am killed and my body left upon the field, the finder of this Testament will please send it to my father, John Nicoll,

Blooming Grove, Orange County, N. York, and confer and great favor on me.... Isaac Nicoll, Capt. Co. G 124th Regt. N.Y. State".

Sergeant Wood promptly mailed the bible to Mr. Nicoll.

Days later, the Federals would return to the Devil's Den, this time triumphant as the battle had come to an end with a Confederate defeat. As men approached, they were stunned by the scene which greeted them. The hills and boulders were covered in blood and carnage and the dead lay scattered about in every direction. One of the first soldiers to enter the area recalled that some of the dead men "had torn and twisted leaves and grass in their agonies and their mouths filled with soil... they had literally bitten the dust."

Another Federal soldier, A.P. Chase of the 146th New York described a scene of horror that July 4 afternoon. As he climbed the stones, he found "those rocky crevices full of dead Rebel sharpshooters, most of them still grasping their rifles."

That afternoon, the rain began to fall in a heavy downpour that lasted for several hours. The dead men, who were already bloated beyond recognition, were now drenched and beginning to decay. No one knows just how long the Confederate dead remained unburied around the Devil's Den but it could have been days or even a few weeks. And many of the bodies were said to not have been buried at all, but merely tossed into the deep crevices between the rocks.

On the afternoon of July 6, Wyman S. White of the 2nd United States Sharpshooters walked over the field and came to the Devil's Den. He noticed that a Confederate soldier had fallen into a cleft in the rocks and had swollen to the point that the body was now impossible to get out.

On July 7, a man named Jacob Hoke, along with several other men from Chambersburg, rode over the battlefield to view the aftermath of the fighting. As they reached the Devil's Den, Hoke described a number of unburied Confederates who were now "black and bloated, eyes open and glaring, and corruption running from their mouths". Hoke wrote that he had seen similar sights a year earlier at South Mountain, but those in his party who had not were "shocked and horrified."

This was the condition of the field when the first cameramen arrived to photograph the area. It would be at Gettysburg where Alexander Gardner and his associates James Gibson and Timothy O'Sullivan would record some of the most stunning scenes ever photographed. In those days, the camera was of little use, thanks to the slow shutter speeds, during the battles, so photographers had to content themselves with showing the gruesome aftermath of the fighting instead. And so they did.... as Gardner wrote in 1866, calling Gettysburg a "harvest of death."

Some of Gardner's most famous shots were taken around the Devil's Den, where the burial crews had not yet completed their work. It was also where he recorded the photo that has become his most notorious....

After taking a number of photos in the nearby woods and among the scattered rocks, the photographers came upon a scene which seemed to capture the essence of what the Devil's Den had become famous for. This ill-gotten fame seemed to center around the stories of Confederate sharpshooters, who hid among the boulders and fired at any Yankee who dared raise his head on Little Round Top. What they found was a stone wall that had been constructed by the Confederates on the night of July 2. It was from here that a sharpshooter could have plied his deadly trade. The scene was perfect with a roughly built barrier, huge boulders on either side and even Little Round Top looming in the distance. There was only one thing missing.... no dead body.

So, to alleviate this problem, the cameramen returned to an area they had just photographed. Here, they found the body of a young Confederate who seemed perfect for the shot. They bundled him into a blanket and carried him about 40 yards up the slope to the wall. They laid him a few feet away from the wall, propped a rifle against a nearby boulder wall placed a knapsack under the dead man's head.

In his portfolio of Gettysburg photographs, Gardner took credit for the shot, even though it was most likely taken by Timothy O'Sullivan. He also provided a description of the scene, explaining how the sharpshooter had been killed by a shell fragment and had then laid down against the wall to die. He also went on to say that he had returned to the spot four months later and had found the body (by then a skeleton) and the rusted rifle, both undisturbed. This added piece of fiction made the entire photograph a complete fabrication.... however it went on to become one of the most famous photos ever taken at Gettysburg.

Of course, one has to wonder, after reading this, if so famous a scene from the Devil's Den could turn out to be an utter lie.... then what are we to think of the numerous tales of ghosts and spirits which are said to be haunting this area of the battlefield? These tales, as with all other ghost stories, are only as credible as the tellers. However, the sheer number of supernatural incidents said to have taken place here do lend some credence to the belief that the Devil's Den may be haunted.

If Emmanuel Bushman was correct, then the forbidding jumble of rocks was already long haunted before the battle was even fought. If this was the case, then what sort of impact did the hundreds who suffered and died here have on the place?

A ghostly impact? I'll cite the evidence... you be the judge.

The stories about the Devil's Den being haunted began not long after the battle itself. Local legend had it that two hunters had wandered onto the battlefield one day and had gotten lost in the woods near the rocky ridge. They had completely lost their way when one of them looked up and saw the dim figure of a man standing atop the boulders. He gestured with one hand as if pointing the way and the hunter realized it was in that direction they needed to travel. He looked back to thank the man.... but the apparition had vanished.

Even those who are skeptical about the hauntings at Gettysburg, and who claim that the stories of ghosts here are a recent addition to the battlefield, admit that there have always been tales recalled about supernatural doings at the Devil's Den. While admittedly, most of these stories are of a rather recent vintage, Emmanuel Bushman wrote of "many unnatural and supernatural sights and sounds" back in 1880 and local lore has always included odd happenings in the area.

One afternoon in the early 1970's, a woman was said to have gone into the National Park Service information center to inquire about the possibility of ghosts on the battlefield. One can imagine just how many times this question must come up and, although the official position of the park is to neither confirm nor deny the ghostly tales, the ranger on duty was reported to have asked why the woman wanted to know.

The visitor quickly explained that she had been out on the battlefield that morning, photographing the scenery. She had stopped her car at the Devil's Den and had gotten out to take some photos in the early morning light. The woman stated that she had walked into the field of smaller boulders, which are scattered in front of the Den itself and had paused to take a photo. Just as she raised the camera to her eye, she sensed the uncomfortable feeling of someone standing beside her. When she turned to look, she saw that a man had approached her.

She described this man as looking like a "hippie", with long, dirty hair, ragged clothing, a big floppy hat and noticeably, no shoes. The man looked at her and then simply said, "What you are looking for is over there," he said and pointed over behind her.

The woman turned her head to see just what the unkempt fellow was pointing at and when she turned around again, he had vanished. There was no trace of him anywhere.

A month or so later, the same ranger was on duty at the information desk when another photographer had come in and asked almost the same question. He too had been taking photos at the Devil's Den, only this time, he had taken a photo about a month before in which the image of a man had appeared on the exposed frame... a man who had not been there when the photo was taken!

When asked what the man had looked like, he also described the man as looking like a "hippie" (remember, this was the early 1970's) and also mentioned his long hair, old clothing and the fact that he was barefoot.

Could this have been the same man? And if so, who was he?

During the war, many of the Confederate soldiers, and especially those connected with the fighting at the Devil's Den, were from Texas. At that time, this was America's most remote frontier and most of these men did not receive packages from home containing shoes and clothing as many of the men from states in the immediate vicinity did. Because of this, the "wild" Texas boys were often unkempt and dirty, lacking shoes and new clothing.

Could this reported specter be one of the soldiers from Texas, still haunting the rocks of the Devil's Den? Since those reports from the 1970's, this same soldier (or at least one fitting his description) has been reported several times in and around the rocks of the Devil's Den. According to some of the stories, a number of visitors have mistaken the man for a Civil War re-enactor and have even had their photographs taken with him. The accounts go on to say that when they return home and have their film rolls developed, the man is always missing from the photo.

In addition to this apparition at the Devil's Den, there are also reports of a ghostly rider who has been seen and who in turn vanishes; the sounds of gunfire and men shouting which cannot be unexplained (not unlike Bushman's phantom "Indian whoops" from long ago); and literally dozens of photographs which allege to be evidence of supernatural activity.

And speaking of photographs... another paranormal happening in the immediate area is the reported failure of cameras in the nearby Triangular Field. According to the stories, it has been said that video and still cameras do not work properly, if at all, while the photographer is standing in the field. How much truth there is to this allegation is unknown, as I have seen many photos (including my own) which have been taken there without incident. However, there are also dozens of anecdotal reports, from reliable people, who claimed unnatural failures of their equipment in the area.

Could this be the result of an energy still lingering behind?

So, after all of that.... what's your final verdict?

Do the Spirits of Gettysburg still walk the lonely battlefield?

As much as I would like to tell you that they do, the answer to that questions remains in the hearts and minds of the reader, and with the other ghosts and hauntings of the Civil War.... you'll have to be the judge of that one for yourself.

SOURCES

The Civil War: An Illustrated History by Geoffrey C. Ward and Ric and Ken Burns (1990)
The Civil War by William C. Davis and Bell I. Wiley (1998)
Don't Know Much About the Civil War by Kenneth C. Davis (1996)
They Met at Gettysburg by General Edward J. Stackpole (1956)
Witness to Gettysburg by Richard Wheeler (1987)
Antietam by William A. Frassanito (1978)
Ghosts of Antietam by Wilmer McKendree Mumma (1997)
Battlefield Ghosts by B. Keith Toney (1997)

Blue and Gray Magazine (various issues)
Ghosts of the Prairie Magazine
Guide to Haunted Places of the Civil War (Blue and Gray Magazine) (1996)
Civil War Ghost Stories and Legends by Nancy Roberts (1992)

More Haunted Houses by Richard Winer and Nancy Osborn Ishmael (1981)
More Haunted Houses by Joan Bingham and Dolores Riccio (1991)
Civil War Ghosts of Virginia by L.B. Taylor Jr. (1995)
The Ghosts of Fredericksburg by L.B. Taylor Jr. (1991)
Gettysburg: A Journey in Time by William Frassanito (1975)
Devil's Den: A History and Guide by Garry E. Adelman and Timothy H. Smith (1997)
School Spirits by Mark Marimen (1998)
Haunted Gettysburg by Jack Bochar and Bob Wasel (1996)
More Haunted Gettysburg by Jack Bochar and Bob Wasel (1997)
Haunts of the Cashtown Inn compiled by Suzanne Gruber and Bob Wasel (1998)

Ghosts of Gettysburg by Mark Nesbitt (1991)
More Ghosts of Gettysburg by Mark Nesbitt (1992)
Ghosts of Gettysburg III by Mark Nesbitt (1995)
Ghosts of Gettysburg IV by Mark Nesbitt (1998)

The Farnsworth House: Candlelight Walking Tours
Personal Interviews and Correspondence

AFTERWORD

One of the first supernatural tales to be told about the Civil War concerned a sighting that was said to have taken place in June 1863, as Joshua Chamberlain and his men from Maine were on the road to their destiny at Gettysburg.

They marched along in silence, trudging along the dark, winding, rutted roads until they reached a crossroads. As the officers were debating about which direction to take, the clouds suddenly parted and the moon appeared overhead. From nowhere, a horseman appeared and rode toward them. The man was mounted on a magnificent pale horse and he was dressed in a bright blue coat and wore a tri-cornered hat. He rode ahead of them down one of the roads in question and waved at the Union troops to follow.

At the turn of the road, an officer told Chamberlain that the man ahead was General McClellan, who was in command again and that he was leading them toward Gettysburg. At that, the men of the 20th Maine began to cheer for the well-liked McClellan, throwing their hats in the air and calling out to him. Although tired from the hours of marching, a renewed enthusiasm swept through the troops and they picked up the pace.

Then, one of the officers got another look at the mysterious rider. It was not McClellan at all. "It's Washington," he exclaimed. "General Washington himself has come to lead us". Soon, the name swept over the ranks invigorating the men and, according to Chamberlain, renewing their confidence for the battle ahead.

Since that first ghostly tale, many more have followed. There have been a number of books prior to this one which have collected supernatural tales related to the Civil War and I hope that you have found this book to be one which can proudly join the ranks of those which have come before.

I know that I have only managed to scratch the surface for stories connected to America's greatest conflict, but hopefully, my efforts might encourage you to go out and explore on your own. I have always been of the mind that if we do not embrace our history, we are doomed to repeat it. Although I have often been criticized by historians for my promotion of ghost stories and the unexplained in regards to our history, I have yet to find a better way to pique the interest of the reader. If a single story in this book encourages you to go out an explore even a single location connected to the war... then my duty here has been fulfilled.

Happy Haunting!

ABOUT THE AUTHOR
- TROY TAYLOR -

Troy Taylor is the author of ten books about ghosts and hauntings in America, including his latest releases, Haunted Illinois and Spirits of the Civil War.

He is also the editor of "Ghosts of the Prairie" Magazine, a travel guide to haunted places in America. A number of his articles have been published here and in other ghost-related publications. He is also the president of the "American Ghost Society", a network of ghost hunters which boasts more than 400 active members in the United States and Canada. The group collects stories of ghost sightings and haunted houses and uses investigative techniques to track down evidence of the supernatural. In addition, he also hosts a National Conference each year in conjunction with the group which usually attracts several hundred ghost enthusiasts from around the country.

Along with writing about ghosts, Taylor is also a public speaker on the subject and has spoken to more than 100 private and public groups on a variety of paranormal-related subjects. He has appeared in literally dozens of newspaper and magazine articles about ghosts and hauntings and has been fortunate enough to be interviewed over 300 times for radio and television broadcasts about the supernatural, including a number of documentaries.

Born and raised in Illinois, Taylor has long had an affinity for "things that go bump in the night" and published his first book "Haunted Decatur" in 1995. For six years, he was also the host of the popular "Haunted Decatur" ghost tours of the city. His final "Haunted Decatur" Tour was for Halloween of 1998, after re-locating to Alton.

Taylor married Amy Van Lear, the Managing Director of Whitechapel Productions Press, on New Year's Eve of 1996. They currently reside in Alton.

ABOUT THE PUBLISHER
- WHITECHAPEL PRODUCTIONS PRESS -

Whitechapel Productions Press was founded in 1993 is a small publisher of books about ghosts and hauntings, located in Alton, Illinois. They also produce the "Ghosts of the Prairie" magazine and the "Ghosts of the Prairie" internet web page.

In addition to publishing ghost books, they also distribute the "Haunted America Ghost Book Catalog", which features over 300 different books about ghosts and hauntings from authors all over the United States. To get a copy of the catalog, write to the address below, or visit their Internet web page.

WHITECHAPEL PRODUCTIONS PRESS
515 East Third Street
Alton, Illinois 62002
(618) 465-1086

GHOSTS OF THE PRAIRIE ON-LINE!
www.prairieghosts.com

Visit Whitechapel Productions Press on the Internet and browse through our selection of over 300 ghostly titles, plus information on ghosts and hauntings; haunted history; spirit photographs; information on ghost hunting and much more!!

CURRENT AND UPCOMING TITLES BY TROY TAYLOR & WHITECHAPEL PRODUCTIONS PRESS

In addition to **Spirits of the Civil War**... watch for these titles by author Troy Taylor!

NOW AVAILABLE!

HAUNTED ILLINOIS: A chilling trip through the haunted history of Illinois.... Discover the dark side of the Prairie State with tales both familiar and unknown. Join the author on a trip like no other you have ever taken before with tales spanning the entire history of the state and various regions of Illinois! Stories and places include: The Old Slave House; Allerton Mansion; Voorhies Castle; Ghosts of Springfield; Haunted Alton; the Watseka Wonder; Haunted Chicago; Resurrection Mary and much more! More than 80 locations in all!

AND COMING SOON!

GHOSTS OF THE PRAIRIE: HEARTLAND HAUNTINGS --- A collection of haunted places from America's Midwest, including the Bell Witch Cave; Bachelor's Grove Cemetery; the Lemp Mansion... and more!

THE GHOST HUNTER'S GUIDEBOOK --- A complete guide to investigating ghosts and hauntings and an essential handbook to conducting paranormal investigations. Don't just read about ghosts... this book will help you find your own!

GHOSTS ALONG THE RIVER ROAD --- A collection of ghostly tales and haunted locations along America's Great River Road, including haunts of New Orleans, Vicksburg, St. Louis and more!

BEYOND THE GRAVE: AMERICA'S HAUNTED BURIAL GROUNDS --- Travel along with the author as he takes you to the most haunted cemeteries in America.... places where the dead still walk!

Printed in the United States
1559